COURAGE TO CHANGE

O GOD, GIVE US

SERENITY TO ACCEPT WHAT CANNOT BE CHANGED,
COURAGE TO CHANGE WHAT SHOULD BE CHANGED,
AND WISDOM TO DISTINGUISH THE ONE FROM THE
OTHER.*

* This prayer was composed by Reinhold Niebuhr in 1934 when he preached occasionally in the small church near his summer home in Heath, Massachusetts. After the service, Howard Chandler Robbins, a summer neighbor, asked for a copy. He is reported to have been handed the original, with words to the following effect:

"Here, take the prayer. I have no further use for it."

Other people, it is clear, have felt differently. Robbins published it as part of a pamphlet the following year. Since then it has been adopted as the motto of Alcoholics Anonymous; the U.S.O. distributed millions of copies to servicemen during World War II; the National Council of Churches has reprinted it; and even today it is used commercially on Christmas cards.

Courage to Change

AN INTRODUCTION TO THE LIFE AND THOUGHT OF

REINHOLD NIEBUHR

BY *JUNE BINGHAM*

Charles Scribner's Sons, New York

Thanks are due to the following publishers to quote from the titles indicated.
Meridian Books, Inc., from *Leaves From the Notebook of a Tamed Cynic* by Reinhold Niebuhr, copyright 1929 Reinhold Niebuhr. (Living Age Books)
The Macmillan Company, from *Reinhold Niebuhr: His Religious, Social and Political Thought*, edited by Charles W. Kegley and Robert W. Bretall. © The Macmillan Company 1956.
Oxford Press, from Christopher Fry's *The Dark is Light Enough* (1954) and from Lord Byron's *Don Juan*.

A-12.71 (V)

Printed in the United States of America
Library of Congress Catalog Card Number 72-37467
SBN 684-12789-X

To the two M. R.'s

Special Acknowledgments

WHILE the dedication of this book is to my parents, the two people without whom there would be no I, the chief acknowledgment is to the two people without whom there would be no book. They are John Coleman Bennett, Dean of the Faculty of Union Theological Seminary in New York City and The Right Reverend William Scarlett, retired Episcopal Bishop of Missouri. In person and by mail for a biblical seven years, these stalwart accomplices provided a generous source of encouragement, information, correction and assistance. They are in no way to be blamed for the flaws of the book, but they are to be credited that there are not more flaws than there are.

Others toward whom gratitude exceeds the power to express it include: Union Theological Seminary's late ex-president, Henry Sloane Coffin; its current president, Henry Pitney Van Dusen; its professors, former and current: Paul Tillich, and Robert McAfee Brown; its former chief of the stenographic pool, Mrs. Nola Meade, who was also Dr. Niebuhr's secretary for a quarter century; and its graduates, D. B. Robertson, Brewster Bingham and his wife, Frances, John Dillenberger, Robert F. Montgomery and Carl Hermann Voss.

In Chicago: Mrs. Gustav Niebuhr, Reinhold's late mother, and Professor Hulda Niebuhr, his late sister.

In New Haven: Professor H. Richard Niebuhr, his brother, and Professor William Lee Miller.

In St. Louis: Professor and Mrs. Samuel Press, and the three ministers who served as Niebuhr's assistants during his pastorate in Detroit, Dr. Ralph C. Abele, Theodore C. Braun, and Harold A. Pflug.

In Cambridge: Professor Arthur Schlesinger, Jr. and his wife, Marian.

In Washington: Justice Felix Frankfurter, and the late Herbert B. Elliston.

In Saranac Lake: James Loeb, Jr., and his wife Ellen, and Horst Mendershausen who became acquainted with Niebuhr's ideas in pre-Hitler Germany.

In London: the Late Lord Stansgate, and Lady Stansgate.

In Salem, Connecticut: Alfred M. Bingham.

In Groton, Massachusetts: The Reverend John Crocker.

In Albany, New York: The Reverend Laman Bruner.

In New York City and environs: Professor Will Herberg; Norman Thomas; Professor Sidney Hook; Councilman Stanley Isaacs; James Wechsler; Robert Bendiner; Joseph Lash; Dean John Palfrey of Columbia University and his wife, Clochette; George Keller and his wife, Gail; Dr. Lawrence Kubie; Joseph Kaskell and his wife, Lilo; the Reverend Robert Searle, and five persons who asked that their names not be recorded. My thanks also to the following disciplined thinkers who were willing to explain some of the more difficult economic or ecclesiastical concepts used by Niebuhr: William Phillips, August Heckscher, Douglas Auchincloss, Brendan Gill, Harold Mager, James Grossman and his wife, Elsa, the Reverend Forrest Johnson of Edgehill Church, Spuyten Duyvil, and Professor Dudley Shapere of the University of Chicago.

Additional thanks go to the following people who so generously either wrote letters about Reinhold Niebuhr or loaned letters from him, or both: From Great Britain—Bertrand Russell, and Arthur Koestler; from Princeton, New Jersey—Jacques Maritain; from Arizona—Joseph Wood Krutch; from Mexico City—Eric Fromm; from Detroit—Walter Reuther, Otto and Grace Pokorny; from California—Professor Robert Fitch and Dr. Jeremy Bernstein; from Washington—Bishop Angus Dun, Dean Acheson, Walter Lippmann, Professor Arnold Wolfers, Professor Robert C. Good, and Charles Burton Marshall; from Jacksonville, Illinois—Sherwood Eddy; from South India—Reverend Paul Schroeder; from Webster's Grove, Missouri—Paul R. Zwilling; from St. Louis, Missouri—Theophil H. Twente; from North Bennington, Vermont—the late Miss Ethel Van Benthuysen; from Boston—Marshall D. Shulman; from Brooklyn, New York—Maurice J. Goldbloom; from Stonington, Connecticut—Anthony West; from New York City—Senator Herbert Lehman, Freda Kirchwey, Charles C. West, Robert LeKachman, and the patient librarians of the following institutions: Union Seminary Library, The New York State Education Building Library, and the Oral History Research Section of Columbia University.

Finally, to the following family members: Jonathan Bingham, my husband, who never tired of hearing about Niebuhr, thereby providing needed reinforcement; our children, Sherry, Micky, Tim and Claudia, who did tire of hearing about Niebuhr, thereby providing needed perspective: "We can always tell when you've been to Union Seminary," one of them said, "because you're so boring afterward." And last but by no means least, my aunt, Mrs. Carrie R. Carns, for her advice as an experienced librarian.

Table of Contents

PROLOGUE

The Camera's Angle

"He was at all events no pedant nurtured in libraries, but an enemy to solemn dullness. As a philosopher he must surely be classed as one of that breed we tend to call 'intoxicated'—because they seem always drunk with the wine of life."

MATTHEW JOSEPHSON

I

The Speaker

THE final speaker was introduced.

No one in the crowded dining room seemed to pay much attention.

It was a Saturday night in the Spring of 1949, and several hundred politically minded people had been in that Chicago hotel for thirty-six hours trying to hammer out recommendations for improving the nation's foreign and domestic policy.

By ten o'clock the air was stale and the people were stale. The stimulating effect of the cocktail hour had worn away, leaving a glaze in the eye, a weight in the limbs, and an irresistible desire to yawn. A young couple from New York noted with relief that the final speaker carried no prepared text.

The speaker straightened his tie, ran a big-knuckled hand over his shiny pate, pulled his long nose further downward, and spoke out rapidly in a deep voice. By the end of one sentence, he had every person's full attention; by the end of one hour, he had several hundred people on their feet, clapping, stamping, shouting their approval.

Few speeches can have rivaled this one for profundity, for range, for electromagnetism. Listeners sat bolt upright, their fists clenched, as the speaker bombarded them with startling new ideas, startling interpretations of old ideas, dramatic challenges to their long-accepted presuppositions, and sudden explosive humor.

One minute the deep voice would boom out; the next it would drop to a whisper—and then boom again. The blue eyes would fly open as he presented a nugget of thought; then squint in diabolic conspiracy as he demolished it. Yet wait—a long index finger would rise—there may be a phoenix stirring in those ashes. With both arms in motion, like an orchestra conductor, he swept his listeners into the soaring of that phoenix, and the "unpredictable," "incongruous," and "ironic" results, which in turn could lead to . . .

The suspense he built by these verbal, facial, and gestural dynamics became close to unbearable. And the depth of his own caring was so profound that the listener's racing intellect was finally accompanied by a racing pulse: the whole of the self was involved as well as the mind.

As the applause thundered, and finally slackened, the young wife turned to her husband. "Who *is* this man?"

"Famous," he answered, "but I'm not sure what for."

"What do you suppose his job is?"

"Minister."

"A *min*ister?"

The completeness of her incredulity made him smile. "Why not?" he said. "They've got to have *some* good ones."

By the next morning, the unity which Reinhold Niebuhr's speech had temporarily created among several hundred public servants, labor leaders, professors, economists, lawyers, writers, journalists, small businessmen, students, and wives, had evaporated. Such fragmentation is not unknown within political groups, especially when there are microphones available.

Having convened promptly at nine A.M., the group, by one o'clock, was only half-way through its agenda: the foreign policy platform.

Chairman of the meeting was Niebuhr. In place of the moderately well-fitting dark suit of the previous evening, he wore a moderately well-fitting grey double-breasted suit and a slate-blue tie. If the ringing of Sunday church bells had aroused in him a nostalgia for a more godly atmosphere, he gave no indication of it. The staccato of his gavel and his rapped-out rulings continued, as person after person spoke—and spoke.

To the relief of those who were both nonspeaking and hungry, someone suggested that a ten-minute limit be placed on the current motion which concerned the rehabilitation of post-war Germany.

Bang, came the Chairman's gavel. "All in favor please say aye."

There was a fair roar of ayes.

"All opposed?"

There was a fair roar of noes.

Bang, came the gavel. "The ayes have it."

There was a gasp from the crowd. Since there had been no clear mandate for cloture, the benefit of the doubt would ordinarily go to those who wished to continue, rather than to limit, the debate. Slowly, from the rear of the room, swelling as it moved forward, came a sound never before heard in that gathering. The delegates were booing, booing a decision whose end result almost half of them would have preferred, yet booing because they knew—and Niebuhr had been one of those to remind them—that means are as important as ends, and that shortcuts to democratic procedure are to be avoided whenever possible. Not for nothing had the group been named Americans for Democratic Action: their action would be democratic or it would not be approved.

Niebuhr stood for a moment, gavel in mid-air. His face, with the normal high coloring of a blond, was turning ruddier.

The booing died down: there was a charged silence.

Bang, came the gavel. The voice was deep and clear, unmuddied by either anger or defensiveness. "The Chair was evidently mistaken. The debate will continue."

And it did.

The clock on the coffeeshop wall said quarter to three when my husband, several friends, and I seated ourselves at a circular table and summoned the waitress.

Arthur Schlesinger, Jr., appeared in the doorway, caught sight of us, and waved. "May Reinie and I join you?"

Slumped forms straightened, chairs were pushed back, and there followed one of those interruption- and laughter-filled conversations that can long be treasured but never recapitulated. Chief interrupter and laugher, of course, was Niebuhr, challenging the others to argument, delivering himself of some enormous generalization and then watching them react, first with doubt and then with denial, cocking his head as the points against him were marshalled, and then, like a kingfisher, plummeting down and trying to gobble them up.

More surprising even than Niebuhr's gay informality was the gay informality with which he was being treated by the others who had known him before: James Wechsler, pithy and embattled editor of the *New*

York Post, Joseph Rauh, Jr., the benevolent legal dragon who ferociously guards the civil liberties of people whose opinions he deplores, and Arthur Schlesinger, Jr., vivid and Pulitzer-Prized historian whose enthusiasm for politics, like Hemingway's for bullfighting, is both knowledgeable and artistically expressed. Niebuhr, after all, was a man of the cloth, a renowned theologian a full generation older than they, yet these young men were treating him as if he were no more and no less than a bright, secular, beloved contemporary. And this was clearly what he enjoyed having them do.

"Damn foolishness," Niebuhr said, "that blueprint this morning for World Government . . ."

"World Government, Reinie," said Schlesinger with deceptive calm, "may wait, but I wonder if your train will."

The waitress was hurriedly summoned, the bill paid (Dutch, with a liberal tip), and all fled in different directions. My husband and I hailed a taxi and dashed through Chicago to the railroad station. No sooner had we clambered aboard the five-thirty to New York than it pulled out.

Breathless, we found our section, deposited impedimenta, and proceeded to the club car. A number of other people had evidently had the same idea. All the seats around the outside of the car were taken; only two were left on one of the sofas placed back to back in the middle.

Gratefully, we sank down and rang for the attendant. "A couple of scotch and sodas, please."

Before the attendant could answer, a bald head from the sofa backing on our own turned and a face full of amusement peered into ours. "Tough luck, Binghams," said Niebuhr. "It's Sunday and you're in a dry state. But will you join me for a ginger ale?"

Some five hours later, we were drunk—on that incomparable elixir: Niebuhr and ginger ale; or, if one considers the New York Central roadbed at the time, Niebuhr On The Rocks. For five uninterrupted hours—ending with a belated supper à trois in the dining car—we asked, and he answered, the kind of question, impolite but not insincere, that one dreams of being able to ask an open-minded minister, and then almost never does: "What's so special about Christ?" and "Isn't it just wishful thinking to believe in God?" and "How come so many lemons go into the ministry?"

No question we could think to ask surprised him, but some of his answers surprised us, not only because they seemed unbelievable, but because it was he who believed them. This towering intellect actually considered the Garden of Eden story not just a fairy tale.

Of course, he did not think, either, that it was the exact and literal truth. But it did, he said, embody a truth that was both invaluable and also had been forgotten by the modern world—at its peril. The Fall of Man applied not to one couple, in one place, at one time, but to all men, in all places, at all times—including right now.

He answered our questions and he questioned our answers, and as he talked, often with provocative quotation from a novel or a play, a philosopher, biographer, or the Bible, the sediment at the bottom of our minds became all roiled up. Here we were, as we assumed, well-educated, broadminded, and prepared to look facts in the face. Yet, this man was so clearly better educated, more broadminded, and more prepared to look facts in the face. Much of what we said he was able to take to a deeper dimension. Yet, when we approached his own preconceptions, the foundations upon which his wisdom rested, lo, we were in a strange and wondrous land where the shadows were darker and the light more brilliant, the people more complex, and the events both more meaningful and more mysterious than any we had known before. He spoke words that echoed back through the millenia, words like sin and grace, creation and revelation, redemption and Messiah. What, in God's name, we asked, could such things have to do with us, here on a streamliner, rocketing through the mid-twentieth century night? Had not our world, the modern world of science and enlightenment, long since left that primitive baggage behind?

"Honestly, Dr. Niebuhr, I don't see what's so good about religion."

"Nothing's good about religion—as such."

"What?"

"Bad religion can be worse than no religion."

"You mean it?"

He smiled. "Of course I mean it. The worst fanaticisms in history have been religious fanaticisms. In fact, even good religion can become a source of hidden pride, of what we call original sin . . ."

"You mean that original sin is pride?"

A smile. "Did you think it was something else?"

"Well . . ."

"That is a frequent misconception, based on some exaggerated forms of Christian asceticism." And back we went into the cloistered world of monks and matins, against whose closed-mindedness and corrupt leaders Luther and Calvin had rebelled, only to have some fruits of their rebellion transplanted to the shores of the new world by Puritan leaders who became so intent on destroying the sins of the flesh that they burned the living flesh of old women, and quite forgot about the sin of pride.

Ancient history no longer relevant? Niebuhr pointed to our ginger ale, a pale dry reflection of the puritanism of these leaders' descendants.

"Most of the evil in this world," Niebuhr continued, "does not come from evil people. It comes from people who consider themselves good."

"How do you mean?"

"The worst evil," he said, "is a corruption of the good. You might even say that evil is a parasite on the good." But before he could explain, the headwaiter had swooped down upon us and we discovered that we were alone in the dining car. In the process of defining the Christian virtues, we had done unto our poor waiter's bedtime what we would not have wished anyone to do unto ours.

We walked back through the train.

"Goodnight, Dr. Niebuhr. Thank you for the most wonderful . . ."

Embarrassed, he shook his head. "Say, I wanted to ask you both something."

"Yes?"

"That was a bit autocratic, that ruling of mine this morning . . .?"

One of us said, "Well . . ."

The other said, "Oh, but . . ."

He raised his hand in a gesture of farewell. His smile was wry but filled with understanding.

Although that morning's half-hearted "boo" was now burning like acid on the lips, it was impossible not to smile back.

2

The Words

THE experience on the train that was unique for us was not—it turned out—unique for Dr. Niebuhr.

For more than a quarter-century he had been devoting his weekends to explaining the basic concepts of Christianity to young people who knew little, and cared less, about them. As he himself wrote, in the introductory chapter of The Library of Living Theology volume devoted to his thought:[1]

> My avocational interest as a kind of circuit rider in the colleges and universities has prompted an interest in the defense and justification of the Christian faith in a secular age, particularly among what Schleiermacher called Christianity's "intellectual despisers."

As a circuit rider who used the train and plane rather than the horse, he made an unforgettable impact on many of these "intellectual despisers," or to use the more colorful translation, "intellectual contemnors." To them he appeared like a visible planet whose magnetized orbit around some invisible star makes it possible to postulate the incredible size and brilliance of the invisible one. Although many could not in all honesty see Niebuhr's God, and although some did not particularly wish to, they could still marvel at Niebuhr, in all his warmth and light, circling. It is, to use his own phrase in regard to another matter, "one hell of a sight."

The fact that there is mystery involved, both the mystery of human personality and the mystery of the creator of human personality, does

[1] This excellent collection of scholarly articles, hereinafter referred to simply as the Living Library Volume, was edited by Charles W. Kegley and Robert W. Bretall under the title *Reinhold Niebuhr: His Religious, Social and Political Thought*, and published in 1956 by The Macmillan Company.

not make the whole problem any the less fascinating or any the more accessible. Niebuhr believes that these two mysteries are connected with one another and that both are shot through with meaning. Some of this meaning comes to us through our faculty of reason, some through our own and mankind's general experience, and some through commitment on our part, the kind of commitment called faith. There are meanings in life and in history that can be wrested; others that can only be received. We can no more successfully demand of God than we can of another person that his deepest purpose be wholly shared with us. Yet, in both cases, a voluntary receptiveness on our part has been known to bring results that were as creative as they were unexpected. "Both the human and the divine person possess a freedom over and above the processes and structures . . . of existence," Niebuhr wrote to a student. "That is why we . . . know each other partly by making a 'scientific' analysis of the processes which bear us; but it is also why we do not know each other as persons . . . except by faith and love, and why we cannot know God except in the same terms."

After the train ride, I started reading Niebuhr's published works. He has written seventeen books and some fifteen hundred magazine articles.

Every month he used to dash off editorials for *The Messenger, The Lutheran,* and *The Episcopal Churchnews,* and he still writes regularly for *The New Leader* and *Christianity and Crisis.* He has been a frequent contributor to *The New York Times* and *The New York Herald Tribune* book review sections, to the Catholic magazine *Commonweal,* the Jewish magazine *Commentary,* the Protestant magazine *The Christian Century,* and to secular magazines such as *The Atlantic, The Nation,* and *The New Republic*; in their heyday he also wrote regularly for *Christianity and Society* (formerly called *Radical Religion*), and occasionally for *Common Sense.*

He also has written for *Life, Fortune, Harper's, The Reporter, The Virginia Quarterly Review, The Yale Review, The Saturday Review, Partisan Review, Foreign Affairs, World Politics, The American Scholar, The Bulletin of Atomic Scientists, The Harvard Business Review, Mademoiselle, The Saturday Evening Post,* and *The Kiwanis Magazine.* In Great Britain he is published mostly by *New Statesman and Nation* and

Spectator. If you go to look him up in any library file, you might as well take along a picnic lunch.

His books vary enormously as to difficulty but even in regard to the simpler ones, such as *Leaves from the Notebook of a Tamed Cynic, Beyond Tragedy*, and *The Irony of American History*, the one thing he can never be accused of is writing down.

Every book, moreover, contains ideas that are like Geiger counters in today's world, providing clues as to whether what lies beneath the surface of persons, events, and ideas is of value or dross. Niebuhr's own ideas can be received, of course, with a grain of salt, but there is more to be gained if they are received with a grain of faith, or at least with that "willing suspension of disbelief" with which one approaches the theatre. Some people who thus receive Niebuhr's ideas go back, after reading the books, to their original position; others find, as Br'er Rabbit did with Tar Baby, that what they have grasped is not so easy to shake.

In general, the books are directed neither to the rigid believer nor the rigid unbeliever, but to the open-minded person who might describe himself as an uneasy believer, or a troubled doubter, or even a commuter between these two positions. For although the Existentialists, following Kierkegaard, keep advising us to make a "leap of faith," they rarely advise us how to avoid finding ourselves having secretly leaped back again. Niebuhr, when pressed for a specific answer, once told a young troubled doubter that he saw no reason why faith could not be bought "on the installment plan." On the other hand, Niebuhr has frequently and forcefully insisted that the demolition of alternative beliefs, in and of itself, will never persuade people to embrace Christianity. And he agrees with Tennyson, that

> There lives more faith in honest doubt,
> Believe me, than in half the creeds.

On a Sunday morning in the nineteen forties when Niebuhr preached in the little chapel near his then summer home in Heath, Massachusetts, his friend and neighbor, Supreme Court Justice Felix Frankfurter, stopped on the way out to shake hands: "I liked what you said, Reinie, and I speak as a believing unbeliever."

"I'm glad you did," Niebuhr answered. "For I spoke as an unbelieving believer."

Niebuhr's own faith, as one of his teaching colleagues has said, "is in constant dialogue with doubt." Yet so deeply is this faith imbedded in the roots of his being that he unequivocally agrees (in a footnote in the first volume of his Gifford Lectures) with the statement of John Baillie:

> No matter how far back I go, no matter by what effort of memory I attempt to reach the virgin soil of childish innocence, I cannot get back to an atheistic mentality. As little can I reach a day when I was conscious of myself but not of God as I can reach a day when I was conscious of myself but not of other human beings.

At the same time, Niebuhr does not talk about his faith unless people make it clear that they want him to—either by asking questions or by attending a church service or a seminary lecture. Some people are fooled by this reticence on Niebuhr's part into thinking that his faith is peripheral in his life—or even nonexistent. "Don't tell me Reinie takes that God business seriously," said a journalist who has worked with Niebuhr on political matters for years. When this remark found its way back to the vice president of Union Theological Seminary, he is reported to have laughed and said, "I know, some of my friends think I teach Christian Ethics as a sort of 'front' to make my politics more respectable."

Other people are not fooled by Niebuhr's reticence about religion. Said one agnostic, "I still marvel at Niebuhr's appeal to those of us who do not share his overwhelming sense of the existence of God." And a thoughtful but nonpracticing Jew stated simply, "Reinie is my rabbi."

Actually, Niebuhr's readers as well as his friends include every possible coloration of religious belief or lack of it. There are passionate atheists and relaxed agnostics, devout Catholics and Jews, Protestant liberals and fundamentalists. There are secular liberals who approve his politics but shy away from his theology; there are religious devotees who admire his theology but deplore his left-of-center politics. There are people who have disagreed with him both politically and theologically, but still consider him one of the most important influences of our time. Walter Lippmann, for example, today places Niebuhr "in the very highest ranks of thinkers in this country during this century."

While Niebuhr's two avocations have been circuit riding to the colleges and political activity, his two vocations have been ministering for thirteen years in a Detroit parish, and teaching for a third of a century at Union Theological Seminary in New York.

Union is a nondenominational Protestant seminary affiliated with Columbia University. Built in Harkness-style Gothic, it stands on the west side of Broadway, extending from 120th to 122nd Street. On one side, it is cater-cornered from the Jewish Theological Seminary and, at the lunch hour, learned gentlemen can be seen jaywalking in both directions. On the other side, it faces toward the red brick science building on the Columbia campus where the Manhattan Project led to the development of the atom bomb.

In addition to having been vice president of the seminary, Niebuhr was Charles A. Briggs Graduate Professor of Ethics and Theology. But Niebuhr always disclaimed the "theology" part of it. As he wrote in the Living Library Volume,

> It is somewhat embarrassing to be made the subject of a study which assumes theology as a primary interest. I cannot and do not claim to be a theologian.

The implication of this disclaimer is that Niebuhr has never attempted to develop a full religio-philosophic system of his own; nor has anyone ever accused him of being a *systematic* theologian. But since Niebuhr has spent his life teaching and writing in the field of religion, he must, for want of a better word, still be categorized, as least for the layman, as a theologian.

Theologian is not the only word used by the academics that has a somewhat different meaning to the layman. Anthropologist, for example, may mean not a scientist who studies cultures, but a theologian who works up logically from man's creation to God. Or "The New Israel" may mean not the fledgling nation but the Christian Church. In addition to these words whose technical meaning is different from their ordinary one, there are ordinary words whose meaning has been raised, so to speak, to a higher power by the theologians. One such noun is "myth" which no longer means fairy tale or "prescientific myth," but "myth of permanent validity" (like the Garden of Eden story). One such adjective is "moralistic" which, in the hands of a minister, one might assume would be a compliment; Niebuhr and others hurl it like an epithet, implying conventionality and overreliance on the form, as against the content, of religion.

Lastly, there are a few words that Niebuhr himself uses in a special sense. Although he often deplores the attitude of the person he calls an "idealist" because it is too utopian, he applauds the attitude of the person he calls "sensitive." (Indeed, the phrase, "sensitive spirit," is often a tip-off to a bit of masked autobiography.) For Niebuhr, moreover, "optimism" implies over-optimism; at the same time, he hates to be called a "pessimist." As he wrote once to a friend, "ordinarily a 'pessimist' is a person who does not think life is worth living. That is why I object to the term, even when qualified by the adjective, 'Christian.' "

In regard to "liberalism," Niebuhr distinguishes, as Robert Good has pointed out, between its spirit, which implies openness to change, and its creed, which implies the "perfectibility" or progressive (and relatively painless) improvability of man.[2] While lauding the spirit of liberalism, Niebuhr disapproves its creed, calling it "sentimental," an adjective that for him bears the extreme emotionalness of the noun, "sentimentality."

Several of Niebuhr's faculty colleagues reacted with shock to the suggestion that Niebuhr uses even these few words in a special sense. But others thought it undeniable that he does, and thus contributes to the originality of his style. Could anyone, no matter how favorably biased, describe El Greco and not mention that he elongates the faces and limbs of his subjects?

The Niebuhr books vary not only as to difficulty but, also, as to their relative degree of autobiography. Some, like *Faith and History,* give little hint of Niebuhr the man, while others, notably the early *Leaves From the Notebook of a Tamed Cynic,* give a vivid picture. Yet *Leaves* was the book that Niebuhr refused for thirty years to allow to be reprinted, despite fervent appeals from both sides of the Atlantic. The British pastor, D. R. Davies, for example, in his charming, short *Reinhold Niebuhr: Prophet From America,* wrote about *Leaves:*

> This is a book of priceless wisdom for theological students . . .
> An English edition would probably save them from many of the

[2] "The Contribution of Reinhold Niebuhr to the Theory of International Relations" was the title Good gave to his excellent Ph.D. thesis for Yale in 1956.

> errors and pitfalls in which the Christian ministry of all denominations so amply abounds.

Finally, in 1957, after secondhand copies of *Leaves* had risen above eight dollars in price, Niebuhr relented, and the book is now available in hard cover and paperback.

Niebuhr's reluctance to reveal himself in his books puzzles some people, because it is accompanied by such ruthless honesty about what he does reveal. Also, it is accompanied by a typically New England (part of his education was at Yale) reticence about emotion in general. According to H. Richard Niebuhr, Sterling Professor of Theology and Christian Ethics at the Yale Divinity School, a gentler, more scholarly, and, some experts think, more profound, theologian than his brother Reinhold, "You don't get from Reinie's *books* his great sense of the goodness of God."

Even when Reinhold Niebuhr writes about the keystone in the arch of Christian values, the kind of selfless love called *agape*, he shies away from any description of it in terms of emotion (see Chapter 16). As he said in a letter to an undergraduate:

> You amuse me about your very shrewd remark that anything one says about agape sounds soupy. It is quite true. Agape represents in my opinion a very ultimate principle of ethics, but it is certainly not a principle of social ethics; therefore in the realm of economics and politics in which I am particularly interested, I always insist that love must be translated into justice in order to be effective. Of course I have carried on a warfare with Christians who think they can solve everything by love.

He has also carried on a warfare with all people who think they can solve contemporary social or political problems with any one-shot solution. "The field of politics is not helpfully tilled by pure moralists," he says. And too-simple solutions to complex problems are likely to cause harm rather than good, since they "prevent rather than encourage a consideration of the real issues." One reason he is called a pessimist is that he devotes so sizable a part of his books to blasting the illusions and oversimplification of his contemporaries.

His potent and inspiring defense of democracy, *The Children of Light and the Children of Darkness*, written during World War II but still so applicable that it has been reissued in paperback fifteen years later, blasts the "illusion" that democracy is itself an *ultimate* value. Niebuhr would willingly die for it: "Our cherished values of individualism," he wrote in *Irony of American History,* "are real enough; and we are right in preferring death to their annulment." But Niebuhr would also be willing to die rather than place a relative or contingent or proximate value where the ultimate ought to be. Putting something less than God at the center of life, he maintains, is, in the individual realm, idolatry, while, in the collective realm, it is a clear and present danger: "Every absolute devotion to relative political ends (and all political ends are relative) is a threat to communal peace." This is true not only in regard to the Western democracies, but also to the Soviet Union whose absolute devotion to its own "covert religion" of communism Niebuhr started criticizing as early as 1930, during a trip to Russia.

Another reason Niebuhr leaves so much of himself and his life out of the books may simply be the momentum of his thought. Like a juggler with five balls in the air, he cannot stop to explain which event led to what idea: all he can do is to get a quick grip on each before its related ideas, each accompanied by further related ideas, bear down upon him. So well thought out beforehand, however, is the relationship between the various ideas, that Niebuhr rarely needs to revise his shorter works. One day while I was talking to Mrs. Nola Meade, Niebuhr's secretary for twenty-five years, I noticed on her desk a Niebuhr article, self-typed, with only the minimum of revisions. "What number draft do you suppose that was?"

She looked up in amazement. "Why his first, of course. He almost never does more than one."

As for Niebuhr's longer works, if one can judge by the speed with which he turned them out during a period when he was engaged in a staggering variety of other activities, they must also have needed but little revision.

Some people have said that the books would have profited from more editorial blue-penciling and rewriting. Certainly, it is true, as William Lee Miller pointed out in his penetrating article in *The Reporter,* January 13, 1955, that Niebuhr is not a "definitional" writer. Niebuhr rarely stops to define his terms, and when he does, the definition may not be identical with that in some other book.[3]

John Bennett, Dean of Union Seminary and a sympathetic colleague of Niebuhr's, who by no means, however, always agrees with him, says that Niebuhr starts each book afresh, as if he had never written a word before. This makes for a certain amount of inconsistency *among* the books but for a surging vitality *within* them.

His style of writing also varies from book to book. In *Leaves,* it is colloquial; in *Faith and History,* it is scholarly. And most of the books contain within themselves considerable stylistic variety. Niebuhr can punch out the short, declarative sentence: "The self is free to defy God. The self does defy God." And some of his balanced epigrams are on their way to becoming classics: "Man's capacity for justice makes democracy possible; man's inclination to injustice makes democracy necessary." But when his sentences try to establish relationships between too many ideas at the same time, the reader feels as if all the juggler's balls had come tumbling down upon his head. The following king-sized example from *The Self and the Dramas of History* (page 189) is almost a parody:

> If we take Luther's complete rejection of the relevancy of the pinnacles of the Christian ethic of love to any special situation, involving permanent structures, on the one hand, and, on the other, the conviction of liberal Christianity that love is a simple norm for communal integration and the similar conviction of the French, and subsequently of the Russian Revolution, that liberty or equality, either or both, are simply attainable norms for society, we have the moral predicament of Western Christian civilization about the integration of its communities in a nutshell.

And quite a nutshell it turns out to be.[4]

Yet most of the time Niebuhr's sentences are as clear as the complexity

[3] What Niebuhr means in different places by the word "reason," for example, has called forth inquiry from Protestant leaders as different in viewpoint as Paul Tillich and Henry Nelson Wieman, from Catholic and Jewish theologians, and from secular philosophers such as Sidney Hook (see Chapter 18).

[4] Another nutshell reference was that of Charles Burton Marshall in *The New Leader,* August 15-22, 1960: "The involutions of Niebuhr's thought are matched only by the somewhat Teutonic complicacy of his syntax. The nutshells into which he puts his ideas are often the prototype of a black walnut—hard digging for rich meat."

of his material allows, and his paragraphs are so tightly interwoven that it is almost impossible to elide them for the purpose of quoting. They cry out to have the expunged phrases put back in. Yet, once back in, these phrases may cry out for further elucidation.

Niebuhr's reticence about himself, evident in his books, carries over even to projected books about him. Professor D. B. Robertson, who had lovingly compiled a bibliography of Niebuhr's fugitive writings, met with difficulty in obtaining their author's permission to combine some of them into the two volumes of essays that have now finally been issued (*Love and Justice,* and *Essays in Applied Christianity*), and when the editors of the Living Library Volume asked Niebuhr for the customary autobiographical first chapter, they received "an intellectual autobiography" that was far more intellectual than autobiographical.

Once, in a general conversation, the subject of Niebuhr ever writing an autobiography was raised, and he reacted with characteristic vigor. "Dishonest," he said. "At least most of them are. They begin with a dishonesty because they are usually consciously humble, but this conscious humility cannot hide the fact that you consider it worthwhile to record your own little story." When asked whether he would object to someone else writing a book about him—a sort of introduction to his life and thought—he brushed it off as "all right, I suppose," but promptly added that the life part could be reduced to one page.

When I later sent word that I was serious about attempting such a book, he immediately tried to divert me into expanding a recently published article of mine on the Middle East. When I countered by reminding him that Mrs. Roosevelt had just published a book on the area, he brushed that argument aside: "If I let books by famous people deter me, I would never write anything. You are too overawed by Mrs. F.D.R."

Since Niebuhr clearly did not approve of people being overawed by famous people, this opened the way for me not to be overawed by him, but to attempt a book that would include not only his thought but also the chief events of his personal life and such events of national or international life as had evidently influenced him. The chapters on Niebuhr's thought, therefore, alternate with the chapters on his life and times. Those on his thought contain his thought *today* (on the "optimistic" assumption that this will still be his thought tomorrow); while those on his life contain not only the important events of the past, but also those of Niebuhr's responses to these events that seemed valid, at the time, but that he has since discarded as being the kind of remedy that is worse than the disease. Pacifism was one such remedy; Marxism another. Indeed, on April 26, 1939, in a *Christian Century* article called "Ten Years That Shook My World," Niebuhr admitted, with the kind of rueful honesty that is one of his trademarks,

> Even while imagining myself to be preaching the Gospel, I had really experimented with many modern alternatives to Christian faith, until one by one they proved unavailing.

To decide not to be overawed by Niebuhr was one thing, but to continue day after day, against his inclination, was quite another. Yet, in a paradoxical way, it was he who imparted the courage necessary to defy him. Other people have noted this double effect Niebuhr can have on you: on the one hand he may induce "fear and trembling," and on the other, he may stiffen your spine. For so convinced is he of the value of individual freedom, that you end up refusing to let even him impinge upon your own.[5] Two of his favorite texts, in his life as well as his thought, are St. Peter's: "We must obey God rather than man"; and St. Paul's: "It is a small thing to me to be judged of men . . . He who judges me is the Lord." The result, in Niebuhr's case, has been a lifelong willingness to take unpopular stands, combined with an insouciance toward the opinion of his fellow mortals that is particularly striking in this period of "other-directedness" and "togetherness."

His fellow mortals, on the other hand, do not always appreciate this attitude on Niebuhr's part. There is no question that his enemies feel as strongly about him as do his friends. As Arnold Hearn has written on the back of the LP recording of Niebuhr's lecture, *Humanism and the Christian Faith,* "No one who has read or heard Niebuhr feels neutral about him."

And the better one becomes acquainted with Niebuhr and his thought, the easier this is to understand.

[5] Nor would he, of course, seriously try; he did not, for example, kill this book at its inception by the simple expedient of vetoing it.

PART I

A Double Exposure

"For him, truth was no single element, but a gem of many facets, each capable of different, even contradictory appearance. It was impossible to grasp the whole from a single point of view; and, conversely, every honest point of view achieved an aspect of the truth. That any act of vision depends as much upon the situation and the circumstances of the seer as upon the object seen . . . was the theme which ran consistently throughout his life and works."

MICHAEL ST. JOHN PACKE
Life of John Stuart Mill

3

The Man

WHEN strangers used to visit Union Theological Seminary's Professor of Christian Ethics, the receptionist would tell them, if it was near the lunch hour, to go down the hall to the Social Room.

"But how will I know which one is Niebuhr?"

"That's easy. Just look for a crowd of students. He'll be the man in the middle of it."

His ideas, his personality, his power to evoke new thinking still bring the students crowding around. The bench—a hard and slippery one—outside his fourth floor office is usually filled with students, not only from Union and Columbia but from universities all over the country, and from Europe and Asia as well.[1] Some of the people have appointments; others have only patience. If they do not see Niebuhr one day, they will see him the next. For his door is always open. As one of the students said,

> A lot of other professors talk about being sorry not to see more of the students. But they go off to their offices and close the door. Reinie's door is always open—and he's always being stopped in the hall by someone.

Niebuhr, in turn, thrives on the exchange with the students. The tension of dialogue is for him an invigoration, and he has the born teacher's ability to revive his own enthusiasm over familiar material. When he went to Princeton, in 1958, for a year at the Institute for Advanced Studies where there is no teaching, he reported to his close friend, James Loeb,

[1] These students for the academic year, 1961-62, will be at Harvard rather than Union, since Niebuhr will be teaching there part time, in the Government Department the first semester and in the Divinity School the second.

Jr., now United States Ambassador to Peru, that he missed his students even more than he had anticipated.

Not only Niebuhr's students, but also the people who come to hear him preach, have no way of knowing whether the material Niebuhr is expounding is new to him that morning or something he has dealt with for years. As Professor Paul Scherer writes in the Living Library Volume, Niebuhr often delivers what he has to say

> as if he had just arrived at it by some happy inspiration, and doing it with an explosive abruptness that seems to be the result of a kind of spontaneous internal combustion! . . . He seems to be thinking on the spot—thinking his own way into what is still for him an unsolved problem. Not that Niebuhr does not know precisely what he is going to say . . . but to a degree unmatched by other preachers he does identify himself on the spot with what he is saying.

His identification with his subject is so manifest in every facial expression that one old lady in Bennington, Vermont, says that her nieces travelled miles to hear Niebuhr preach because of "his wonderful grimaces." His facial expressions have, apparently, always been volatile: there exists a youthful photograph that looks like a slim, visionary, blond Byron; yet a newspaper picture taken shortly thereafter resembles nothing so much as a thug on his way to the clink. And old-timers around the campus recall that Niebuhr was the best Mephistopheles that ever trod the boards at Union Seminary.

His gestures today are more muted than formerly. His hands are broad and strong fingered—"a farmer's hands," according to Harvey Breit—yet their grace of motion could still win the approval of a Balinese dancer. In younger days he used to wave both arms so much when preaching that a friend commented, "Reinie doesn't tilt at windmills: he *is* a windmill." Even today, with his left arm immobilized by a series of small strokes in 1952, his pulpit maneuverings would delight Abraham Lincoln who is reputed to have said, "When a man preaches, I like to see him fight bees."

Yet Niebuhr is anything but revivalist in his preaching. His approach is deliberately to stir the mind rather than the emotions of his listener. At the same time, he himself feels so deeply about the complex subjects with which he deals that the listener must respond. "He really snowed me," said a medical student after Niebuhr's annual chapel service at Harvard in 1958. So "snowed" indeed was this young man that, despite his medical training, he never even noticed that Niebuhr's left arm was out of commission. A high school girl who attended the same service said, "I was all a-tremble for the rest of the day."

Some people complain that Niebuhr spends so much of his sermon taking Humpty Dumpty apart that there is little time to put Humpty Dumpty together again. Others complain that he deals so thoroughly with the problems of society that there is little time for the individual. Still others say that he stimulates so many questions that there is little time for answers. Nonetheless most of these people keep coming back.

Certainly the ground he covers is vast: as Paul Scherer says:

> His metier is to work not with miniatures but with murals. In them one has to deal with the spread of some vast engagements on many fronts, with the impacts of worlds, with the panorama of a civilization, with maps of centuries and continents in high relief.

In his lectures Niebuhr also roams, with the air of a man quite at home there, over the centuries and the civilizations, over the religious world and the secular. Students emerge dazed; as one of them said, "I have to keep reminding myself of Emerson's saying, that it's better to watch a big fish jumping, than to catch a string of minnows." Others complain of writer's cramp, or charley-horse of the brain. Often the ideas Niebuhr voices are so provocative, and so quickly followed by equally provocative ideas, that it is all you can do not to shout, "Stop! Please. Let me think about that a minute." But his momentum is far too great for him to stop. Bombs fell, in 1939, in Edinburgh during his Gifford Lectures, and according to report, he did not even look up.[2]

John Gunther, author of the famous "Inside . . ." books, has said that interviewing Niebuhr was like tossing paper airplanes into an electric fan. And it is true that even in casual conversation, Niebuhr's words come at you like machine gun bullets. In addition, he distracts you either by tugging on one of his ears or by pulling his nose or by smoothing

[2] He was the fifth American to be invited to give these lectures; he was preceded by men as illustrious as William James and John Dewey, and was followed by men as illustrious as Paul Tillich and Karl Barth.

his bald spot or by ramming a pipe between his teeth or by extricating a pipe from between his teeth or by thoughtfully putting his forefinger to his lips in a sh-shing gesture yet talking right through it. But when he sits quiet and listens, his intentness is so great that you feel as if a vacuum cleaner were at work on your mind.

As he strides in or out of the classroom building—his everyday brown shoes have heavy rubber soles, and he walks like an ex-athlete—he is constantly being buttonholed by a colleague or a student. Often this person, like a scrap of debris swept in to the wake of a speeding train, finds himself accompanying Niebuhr in some direction he had no previous intention of going.

The same kind of thing is likely to happen in the late morning, and midafternoon, when Niebuhr for the sake of his own health and his poodles' comfort, puts on his beret and in all weathers walks the dogs along Riverside Drive.

The poodles are both female, a serene brown one named Vicky, after Victoria Romig, a one-time secretary to Mrs. Niebuhr; and a pixillated black one, named, for some complex Niebuhrian reason, after Winston Churchill, and called Winnie. They are as intelligent as all poodles are supposed to be and as spoiled as none of them is supposed to be. During their walks, however, they do know what it is to put up with frustration, particularly when some biped recognizes their master and comes over to talk to him. Then the poodles find that no sooner do they settle themselves for the chief business of their day than they are yanked forward. The impetus of their master's dialogue has moved him off at an energetic pace and he, of course, is wholly oblivious to their predicament.

Their time for revenge comes when he is in his study. Then they bark and play hide and seek—and, in 1959, Winnie went so far as to produce four puppies who added their shrill small voices to the general untheological atmosphere that has beguiled students and other visitors over the years.

The Niebuhr apartment is sunny, book-filled, and decorated mostly in blue. During 1952-54, Niebuhr's ill health forced cancellation of the traditional "At Homes" for students. But as soon as possible these were resumed; where formerly it had been Beer in the Evening, now it was Tea in the Afternoon.

Doctor Niebuhr tends to run with the conversational ball, but Mrs. Niebuhr, in addition to seeing that everyone's cup and plate are repeatedly filled, often deliberately trips him with a flying tackle of wit or reminiscence. Slim and blue-eyed, she has kept her excellent figure, her delicate British complexion, and most of her British accent, despite developing, over the past quarter century, a passionate concern for her adopted America.

As chairman of the burgeoning Religion Department at Barnard—across 120th Street from Union Seminary—she has amassed an impressive erudition. But the burden of teaching and administering can no more weight down her natural lightness of spirit than her characteristic dove-grey or black attire can mask her real and continuing beauty. In a unique manner she combines laughter and sweet seriousness, irreverence and firm conviction.

There are two Niebuhr children, Christopher, a tall, blond, enthusiastic Groton and Harvard graduate who is reputed to keep a copy of the New York Legislative Manual on his bed table and who can juggle facts and figures faster than Univac; and Elisabeth, a slender, graceful Chapin and Radcliffe graduate whose feminine charm is as striking as her intelligence.

Brought up to speak their minds, the children take issue with their father or mother with gusto—and then the chase is on. Their father, his arsenal stocked through years of omnivorous reading and the practice of sly debaters' tricks, is unrelenting in pursuit: if an argument of theirs is not thought through, it will be demolished. But at the same time, there is affectionate amusement behind his eyes—and you get the impression that he is far more interested in having the children feel free to contradict him than in having them be correct.

There is no denying, however, that Professor Niebuhr has "a low boring point." If a student at a tea is slow in expressing an idea, or if the idea is unoriginal, the student may find that the conversation has swept past him. Niebuhr tries to suffer fools gladly, but the effort it costs him is sometimes visible. Similarly, if a student comes out clearly with a problem, Niebuhr will be full of sympathy; but if the student is hesitant or given to circumlocution, Niebuhr may not have sufficient empathy to sense the existence of the problem and help the young person to communicate it.

The expressions on the faces of students emerging from Niebuhr's office are therefore likely to range from that of Parsifal when he first caught sight of the Holy Grail, to that of a bull when he first catches sight of the red cape. But most of them look relieved: their step coming out is lighter than in going in, and they are prone to engage the first person they see in conversation, almost as if they were spilling over with all that they were stimulated to think or feel.

Yet Niebuhr never wants his students, in class or in private, to accept what he says unless they agree with it. At the end of each lecture, he purposely leaves time for questions from students, and further questions from himself to the questioner. "How do you know?" is one of his favorites. Being literally a man from Missouri (he was born in Wright City), he wants to be shown, and he expects his students to return the compliment.[3] Although their questions—or their problems—may sadden him, it is unlikely any longer that they will surprise him.

The only student reaction he does not like, or at least does not know how to cope with, is praise. At the end of the final lecture of the year the students always applaud the professor. In the case of Niebuhr the applause is tremendous and prolonged. He looks up, perennially startled, grabs up his papers any old way, and strides off rapidly down the aisle, his face down, and the pinkness of the back of his neck a telltale of his embarrassment. As a human being, he cannot, presumably, avoid being pleased at finding himself appreciated, but as a theologian, he cannot, presumably, avoid being displeased at this threat to his supply of humility.

In any event, he genuinely does not like overpraise or adulation. As Arnold Hearn has stated, "he has borne the adulation of disciples," for to Niebuhr it clearly is a burden. Perhaps because he has been given so much adulation in recent years, or perhaps because some of it smacks of "sentimentality," he drinks in the affectionate debunking by family and friends with an almost visible thirst. When Mrs. Niebuhr interrupts a headlong hurtling of his thought with a smiling, "Oh darling, what utter nonsense," or when Christopher scolds him for political naiveté for remaining in the Liberal Party when he could perfectly well join the Democrats, or when Elisabeth tells him he has simply missed the whole point of the

[3] The few words he still pronounces with a Middle Western accent include America, moralistic, guarantee, and embarrassed.

latest Graham Greene play, he bursts out laughing and encourages them to go on. (Several years ago he cheerfully defined the parent of a teenager as the one person in the world who cannot do anything right.)

Although Niebuhr may be benign in private disagreements, he is not always benign in public ones, particularly with people who, he thinks, should know better. And Mrs. Niebuhr is so ferociously loyal to her husband that she has been reported as cutting dead certain people who disagreed publicly with him. One minister remembers that some years ago Dr. Niebuhr hung up on him when the minister phoned to explain why he had written an article critical of Niebuhr. A formidable opponent in debate, Niebuhr has left many a head both bloody and bowed. If he wants to cut a man short, he can do it. Sarcasm, ridicule, interruptions, overpowering voice, all are weapons well-honed by use. Robert Bendiner attended meetings of the Fellowship of Reconciliation with Niebuhr for several months, in 1929, without having the slightest reason to suspect that the man who always cut off irrelevancies and kept the discussion right to the point was a minister. Robert E. Fitch, a one time student of Niebuhr's and his temporary replacement at Union during his illness, wrote of him in *The Pacific Spectator*, Summer, 1950:

> Among other things, he has the Hebrew prophetic talent for fierce polemic, for sharp ridicule, for incisive and satirical portraiture: some of his critics, when they take hold of him, recoil as though they had grasped a stinging nettle . . .

Niebuhr may ride other people hard, but not as hard as he rides himself. Paul Tillich, Niebuhr's fellow giant among American theologians, who credits Niebuhr with having saved his life and that of his wife at the time Hitler came to power, has worried for years that Niebuhr was riding himself too hard. Tillich thinks that the description of Sigmund Freud, in the first volume of Dr. Ernest Jones' definitive biography, applies as much to Niebuhr as to Freud:

> . . . beyond doubt someone whose instincts were far more powerful than those of the average man, but whose repressions were even more potent. The combination brought about an inner intensity of a degree that is perhaps the essential feature of any . . . genius.

Niebuhr does not flex the biceps of his will power, but you sense the impressive strength that he has developed in them through constant exercise. So high a degree of control without such powerful instincts might be stultifying; such powerful instincts without so high a degree of control might be anarchic. The combination is a burning intensity that is both creative and consuming.

While Niebuhr is a tough and unyielding opponent, he can also be sensitive, easily hurt, and immediately ready to make amends if he finds himself to have been mistaken. Indeed, if he feels he has done his opponent an injustice his contrition is overwhelming: it overwhelms not only Niebuhr but also the person toward whom it is directed. A colleague who has engaged in controversy with Niebuhr over the years says, "It's not easy for Reinie to say he's sorry, but when he says it, he really means it." An old friend emerged from Niebuhr's office clutching his brow. "My God," he said. "By the time Reinie gets through suffering over what he's done to you, you're suffering more *for* him than you ever did *from* him. Son of a gun. How can you help forgiving him?"

Others, however, have not forgiven Niebuhr—and never will—for the attacks he has made on them or the causes they consider sacred. One ordinarily mild-mannered couple long associated with the Social Gospel (see Chapter 4) stiffen visibly at the mention of Niebuhr. The wife's criticism is direct: "Niebuhr has a Jehovah complex." The husband, a minister, is less direct and rather more devastating: "if I *have* to have contact with Niebuhr, I would rather listen to him preach than read one of his books; because when he speaks, he has to bear in mind the beginning of his sentence, but when he writes, all he has to do is flip back the pages." (The cattiness-quotient of many ministers, like that of many psychiatrists, appears to equal that of many women, perhaps because these two professions demand an unusual degree of acceptance, without hitting back, of other people's hostility.)

Niebuhr's own attitude toward controversy was epitomized in the open letter he wrote before World War II to Richard Roberts, a pacifist, with whom he had engaged in a notably unpacifistic debate:

> You say that the charge of self-righteousness "is a boomerang" and convicts the one who uses it of being "too sure of the position which he is defending." Perhaps you are right. I have never

> known a controversy between human beings in which the contestants are not more certain of the righteousness of their cause than they have a right to be.[4]

It is, moreover, Niebuhr says, through maintaining the tension of opposing points of view that the truth is most likely to emerge. This tension is necessary within the secular world, the religious world, and between the two. Much as he favors people holding strong convictions, he equally favors having these strong convictions challenged by those of other people. As he wrote in the *Religious News Service* (August 14, 1948), at the time of the first Ecumenical Conference in Amsterdam, when representatives of Protestant and Orthodox Churches all over the world were foregathered,

> It is not . . . moral and religious relativism which persuades many of us in America to espouse freedom of speech and press. We believe rather that even religion, or perhaps particularly religion, becomes corrupted by pretension if the chastisement of both fair and unfair criticism are not levelled against its thought and life. Sometimes there is a considerable grain of truth even in an unfair criticism.

Certainly Niebuhr is anything but a relativist. He believes that there is truth, but that "we must never confuse our fragmentary apprehension of the truth with the truth itself." Our fragmentary apprehension must always stand under criticism, remain open to new facts, and be subject to debate. If it is not thus maintained in tension with opposing points of view and with doubt, it may slacken into untruth or harden into fanaticism.

The tension of vigilance has long been known to be the price of freedom; for Niebuhr it is also the price of truth.

[4] *Christianity and Society*, Summer, 1940

4

The Method

THE truth for Niebuhr can never be plotted on a nice, neat, straight line.

Yeats speaks of the importance of "the crooked way of life," as distinguished from "inorganic, logical straightness." Robert Frost speaks of the need in poetry for "doubleness" and the "form that falsifies no ambiguities." Niebuhr says frankly, "I'm a nincompoop about modern poetry."[1] Nonetheless he practices in his prose what Yeats and Frost have preached.

In Niebuhr's writings, therefore, as well as in his sermons and lectures, the important ideas about God and man, society and history, do not march ahead like the proverbial Indian, in single file: instead, they deploy and dart in upon their objective from several points at once. This double (or triple) pronged method of approaching truth Niebuhr sometimes describes as paradoxical, sometimes as dialogic, and sometimes as dialectical, although it does not follow Hegel's classic pattern of thesis and antithesis, resolving at last into synthesis. Nor is it to be confused with the "dialectic of history" of the Marxists. Instead, Niebuhr makes the challenging demand upon his reader that he postpone the synthesis indefinitely: like a modern composer, he must hold two dissonant notes in his mind without allowing them to resolve into comfortable harmony.

Chief signposts to the reader that this doubleness is approaching are, "on the one hand," and "on the other"; indeed, Niebuhr might well agree with the philosopher quoted by Gilbert Highet who said that these were the two most important bits of language ever invented. Other signposts include the age-old "however," "on the contrary," "at the same time,"

[1] There must be considerable poetic license in that statement, since one of the Niebuhrs' closest friends is W. H. Auden, and since Dr. Niebuhr, particularly in his early years, made frequent use of poetry in his sermons.

"but," and "yet," as well as the three modern terms, "dialogue," which often refers to the tension between points of view, "encounter," which often refers to a tension between persons so great as to result in the change of one or both, and "drama," which often refers to the tensions between historic forces.

Once alerted, the reader needs to summon resources of faith or intellectual discipline or sheer doggedness, in order to prevent his mind from allowing the tension to slacken between the two poles of Niebuhr's thought. As with that old game of diabolo, where you held two sticks in the air with a cord between, it is only by maintaining the tautness that the toy of truth can be balanced aloft.

Ideally, therefore, Niebuhr's basic ideas would be presented on the right and left hand pages of the book simultaneously, or sung in duet. For he deals deliberately with "both-and" rather than "either-or," not in order to be perverse or difficult, but because this is progressively how the truth about the incongruity of the human situation and the irony of history have appeared to him. Indeed, if one could fairly make an oversimplification of Niebuhr's thought, it would be that he is forever at war with oversimplification.

He agrees with his old friend and colleague, that cheerful Wagnerian demigod, Professor Paul Tillich, when the latter rumbles Germanically that "r-reality *iss* dialectical." And Niebuhr explains, in the second volume of the Gifford Lectures, that his own "seeming defiance of logic is merely the consequence of an effort to express the complex facts of existence."

Niebuhr has great respect for logic and all the other appurtenances of reason (see Chapter 18). As more than one writer has pointed out, Niebuhr does not merely defend reason: he uses it. At the same time, Niebuhr says that "no ultimate sense of the meaning of life is rationally compelling." For example, "the question of whether life is worth living is a reasonable question. But reason alone cannot give the answer." We must continue to use reason, but not allow "rational coherence" to become a Procrustes' bed on which the whole of life, history or society is either mutilated or lethally stretched. It is better, he claims, in matters of ultimate importance to be logically untidy than factually inaccurate, and we must also be sufficiently empirical to admit the whole of our experience even when this admission imperils our rational scheme. Sometimes this rational scheme of ours will seem to split in two, and then we must resist the temptation automatically or "prematurely" to fuse the parts together again. For the difference between a contradiction and a paradox is that in a paradox the two sides do *not* cancel each other out.

Because this fissile doubleness of Niebuhr's thought was well described in a *Time* cover story (March 8, 1948) Niebuhr gave the story his approval:

> Niebuhr . . . sees in paradox not the defeat of logic but the grist of an intellectual calculus—a necessary climbing tool for attempting the higher peaks of thought. The twists and turns of his reasoning and his wary qualifications are not hedging, but the effort to clamber after truth . . .

The story was written, although of course not signed, by a writer better known today than at the time, Whittaker Chambers. It is ironic that less than five years afterward, Niebuhr felt impelled to disapprove Chambers' own book, *Witness*, precisely on the ground that it subscribed to the "either-or," rather than the "both-and," principle in regard to religion.

Whether or not Chambers intended it, one implication of his book was that if only everyone would join hands and become good Christians, the communist and every other serious menace to peace of the world would eventually come under control. This was too much for Niebuhr. In regard to the Chambers book, he reminded an acquaintance in a letter, "I have fought consistently against the "either-or" proposition in religion and the faith that the Christian faith will redeem us of all evil."

Certainly Niebuhr's feet are strongly planted against the "either-or" proposition in religion, whether this takes the form so aptly described by Mr. Justice Jackson, in the Zorach "released time" case, as "compulsory godliness" or the form currently practiced in the Soviet Union that could be described as "compulsory atheism."

That Niebuhr should have been misunderstood by both sides, the religious as well as the secular, is therefore not surprising. Perhaps, indeed, if there must be misunderstanding, he prefers having it come from both sides rather than only from one. Certainly the double or paradoxical view of life, inherent in his early writings, became more and more explicit until today the reading of one of his profound statements is like meeting one of a pair of twins on the street: you feel constrained to inquire after the missing one, and nine times out of ten the missing one is thriving and expected to appear at any moment.

Sometimes, however, this appearance is postponed—by intervening paragraphs or by dint of the reader having laid down the book—and then the relationship between the two points may be obscured. One has to get up early in the morning, so to speak, *not* to quote Niebuhr out of context.

Paradox, moreover, is a method of exposition that has been, and can easily be, abused. The ease with which it lends itself to pyramiding is exemplified by Dickens' famous opening of *A Tale of Two Cities*. And often, in lesser writers, paradox serves as a mask for indecision, murky thinking or even deliberate obscurantism. If consistency is the hobgoblin of little minds, paradox may well be the refuge of lazy minds. The comparison between a Niebuhr on the one hand and a befuddler-by-paradox on the other is reminiscent of the remark made by a European thinker, that there is all the difference in the world between Faust saying at the end of a long life spent pursuing knowledge, "I now see I can nothing know," and a freshman saying the same thing on his first day in college.

A great mind can labor to find consistency between two apparently conflicting concepts, like the wave and the particle theory of light, for example, and finally be forced to conclude, as did Niels Bohr in his Principle of Complementarity, that both concepts are essential. Or a small mind can use paradox to avoid thinking through to a decision, as when someone says, "Well, I do and I don't agree with your plan," thus leaving you in doubt as to whether to count on his support.

In this sense Niebuhr stands out in stark contrast. For in addition to pointing to the often hidden second horn of a dilemma, he also often demands that the reader jump down from both horns in order to take the best action available. That this action may not be an ideal one, he is well aware. At the same time, in the political realm at least, he sees inaction as being at times an even less ideal form of action—indeed as a form of irresponsibility. In the middle of World War II, for example, in *Christian News Letter*, August 25, 1943, he expressed his view in terms which stunned some of his friends in the ministry but reassured some of his friends in public office: "Political expediency is nothing to be ashamed of when the future peace of the world is at stake."

There are other dilemmas however upon whose horns the reader must make himself as comfortable as possible, since there is no escape from either one or both. The relation between mercy and justice is one such; the "grandeur" and "misery" of man another. As to the relation between time and eternity, Niebuhr approves William Ernest Hocking's phrase that "man both lives within time and has time within him." Man, by his power of memory, foresight, and conceptual thinking, can transcend time even while being immersed in it. Thus a person who lays down his life for his fellow is performing an act which has both temporal (immediate) and eternal (ultimate) significance; and neither cancels the other out:

> So it is with the great antinomies that through the ages have organized yet disunited man's experience: the antinomy between the ceaseless change and wonderful novelty, and the perishing of all earthly things, and the eternity which inheres in every happening.

The above quotation comes not from a man of the cloth, but a man of the laboratory: Robert Oppenheimer in *Science and The Common Understanding* (p. 87). Nor is this nuclear physicist unique in having been forced by the events of recent years to a more profound awareness of the complexities of both physics and human affairs. Secular philosophers, too, since the start of the twentieth century, have been teaching that the world is not so simple as the eighteenth and nineteenth centuries had assumed. For example, in the preface to *Reason And Nature,* Morris Raphael Cohen wrote:

> Particular attention is directed to the principle of polarity, the principle that opposite categories like identity and difference, rest and motion, individuality and universality, etc., must always be kept together though never identified . . .

This process of keeping-together is not only an uncomfortable one but also an affront to the post-Enlightenment mind which assumes that basic certainties exist, that these can be demonstrated by logic or science, and that the contradictions between them can eventually be resolved. Welcome to modern readers, therefore, is the reassurance by the genial and thoughtful humanist, Joseph Wood Krutch, in *Measure of Man* that

> they have all along been living with other irresolvable paradoxes which did not trouble them simply because they had been for so long accepted.
> To the human mind it seems, for example, that both space and time must be either finite or infinite. Yet it is quite impossible for that same mind to see how they can be either . . . Beside these two ancient paradoxes the paradox of light which is both corpuscular and undulatory, or even the paradox of a human will which is relatively free yet seems bound to obey some statistical law is relatively easy to accept.

This latter paradox is one which has also fascinated Niebuhr. In *Christianity and Society*, Spring, 1939, his puzzlement exploded:

> How curious a creature is man: so bound by circumstance that you can interpret his mass actions in terms which suggest a problem in physics . . . yet . . . so free that the actions of an in dividual can never be predicted.[2]

To Niebuhr it is man's freedom rather than man's virtue that is the basis of man's dignity; yet this freedom is never isolated in Niebuhr's thought. Always it is in a relation of tension with man's finiteness; and the two together are in tension with the freedom and finiteness of other individuals; and with the freedom and finiteness of society; and ultimately with the freedom of God and the "self-imposed weakness" of his love.

When Niebuhr writes, "how curious a creature is man," there are, moreover, other paradoxes he is bearing in mind. There is the psychological paradox called "ambivalence"; the theory that deep within any strong emotion may lie the repressed and paradoxical core of its opposite: within love, hate; within aggression, dependence; within faith, doubt, and vice versa. There is also the paradox Niebuhr has observed in his own life and that of other persons, as well as in the lives of churches and nations, to which he often refers, but never by any one name. It might be called the by-product theory. The situation from which it perenially arises, Nie-

[2] Although the individual person and the individual atom are alike in being unpredictable, the cause of their unpredictability is wholly different, since the inert atom's behavior is random and accidental, and the live person's is at least in part the result of his own conscious and unconscious choices.

buhr says in *The Self and the Dramas of History,* is this "curious" structure of the self: what this involves

> can be validated by common experience. It is that the self is bound to destroy itself by seeking itself too narrowly, that it must forget itself to realize itself, but that this self-forgetfulness can not be induced by the calculation that a more ultimate form of self-realization will flow from the forgetfulness.

This was the kind of paradox that bedeviled the early Christian saints when they went out alone into the desert to achieve humility. Either they never achieved it or, if they did, they became so pleased with themselves that they promptly lost it again. Said Pascal, from whom Niebuhr derives some of his most piercing insights, "discourses on humility are a source of pride to the vain."

A common example of the by-product theory is a scientific discovery made, not deliberately, but as a corollary to some wholly different investigation. Says the physicist, Harrison Brown (italics added):

> The large-scale release of atomic energy was made possible by a long series of discoveries and scientific developments, *not one* of which was prompted by the desire to make an atomic bomb or by thoughts that atomic energy might eventually be released in usable quantities.

Why should this be? We do not know. Sometimes a by-product in the world of history turns out well for mankind, in which case Niebuhr may refer to it as providence; sometimes it turns out badly for mankind, in which case he may refer to it as judgment (see Chapter 20). Certainly what is true of the world of the atom, where human freedom is irrelevant, is doubly true of the world of history where human freedom is thoroughly relevant: there, inevitably, in addition to the results we can plan, there are results we cannot. Sometimes the latter are logically explicable by hindsight; sometimes they remain paradoxical. Most irksome of all, perhaps, is the discovery that the chief prizes in life do not come primarily by planning. Whether it is happiness or self-realization, love or virtue, that we seek, we find that it is less likely to come as a result of direct effort than as a by-product of devotion to something else. This paradox, according to Niebuhr, is often less accidental than it appears to be:

> It is this very constitution [of selfhood] which prevents the self from ever finding virtue or happiness or self-realization by seeking them too directly or insistently.

One explanation, perhaps, is that the achievement of any of these goals involves the attitudes and actions of other people; and other people have sufficient freedom not to be subject either to our complete prediction or our coercion. As Niebuhr said in a sermon at Harvard, in 1951 (using the terminology of the Jewish theologian, Martin Buber),

> No "I" can be an "I" without the encounter with a "Thou." In this way we grow into selfhood . . . But if a man says by way of calculation, "I need to fulfill myself by finding a mate," he can hardly do so.

He can perhaps find somebody to act as mate, but he cannot create in himself or in the mate that unself-consciousness of love that brings fulfillment. This must come by grace or by accident or by luck: the one thing it does not come by is conscious act of will. Indeed one person's calculation may set up a reaction in the other person that destroys the potential of love. Niebuhr deliberately uncovers various forms of what he calls "imperialism" in personal life, whether parental, marital, or ministerial. And the conscious or unconscious effort to manipulate other people under the guise of love must often, he says, be resisted in the name of justice.

He also uncovers the imperialism of groups, which is usually more obvious (see Chapter 14). Still, even nations or churches, industries or labor or farm organizations, are less likely to reveal their power drive in all its nakedness than to attempt to clothe it in high-sounding and partially relevant ideals. (If the clothing of ideals does not fit at all, it may fall off at an embarrassing moment.)

Niebuhr has also written against political candidates whose ambition was so obvious that it set up a counter-reaction in him and other voters.[3] The by-product theory seems to work in politics almost as in courtship:

[3] In addition to scoring the visible ambition of some politicians, Niebuhr also gives them a back-handed compliment. In *The New Republic*, Feb 27, 1961, he admits that "in most professions and vocations, we are not called upon to seek the office we desire. We therefore indulge in the fiction that we did not desire the eminence but merely accepted it as the inevitable fruit of our excellence. . . . Politicians are both tougher and more honest than the rest of us."

the maiden must be genuinely just reluctant enough for the wooer to feel that his decision to favor her is his own free choice and not one foisted upon him by her previous plots and machinations.

In both individual and social context, however, the attempt to manipulate people under the guise of love, Niebuhr points out, is not a true paradox: it is a contradiction in terms. For the attempt to manipulate another person for one's own ends is a form of self-love; while affectionate respect for the freedom of the other person contains at least a seed of selfless love.

This selfless love, or agape, *is* a true paradox: this was the kind of love Jesus knew God's love to be. (Hosea in the Old Testament was bold enough to compare it to the love of a faithful husband toward an erring wife.) And Jesus voiced the heart of both paradox and by-product when he said, "he who seeketh his life shall lose it, and he who loses it [for the sake of selfless love] shall find it." (The words are, "who loses his life for my sake," but in the context of Jesus' life, teaching, and death, this "my sake" can scarcely be interpreted as meaning anything so purely selfish.) The kind of love Jesus "incarnated," is what Niebuhr sometimes calls "heedless love," because it is heedless of the self. It is a love in which the paradox of justice and mercy is finally resolved—but not wholly within the bounds of time and history: "the paradox of self-realization and sacrifice is resolved in the Cross," he says, but "it takes us beyond this life."

Niebuhr refers to the Cross both as an event and as a "symbol." The word symbol, and the word myth, are sometimes used by him together and sometimes interchangeably. The result of his applying them to the New Testament as well as to the Old, and to historically verified events as well as to imaginary ones, has led to some dramatic clashes between him and his more orthodox confrères (see Chapter 22). Niebuhr's conviction is that "we must take the Bible seriously but not literally." The Bible, in his view, contains the profoundest truth about man and man's "dialogues" with himself, with his fellows, and with God; but this truth, even while conveyed by events that occur within time, is not bound by time; even while appearing within history, goes "beyond history"; even while leading to tragedy, goes "beyond tragedy."

These are difficult concepts for the modern mind to catch hold of: particularly to the person without religious training, it is like trying to grasp a marble with a pair of tweezers: you wonder why you ever started. Whether Paul Tillich's characterization of "symbol" in the second volume of his *Systematic Theology* is helpful or not, people debate. His statement was that "everything religious people say about God is symbolic except the statement that 'everything we say about God is symbolic.' "

Whether Niebuhr's characterization of myth is helpful or not people also debate. In a *New York Herald Tribune* Sunday book review, July, 1937, he wrote:

> The ultimate, though revealed in the historical, is never exhausted in it. To express this relation between the eternal and the temporal, the ultimate and the immediate, is the real function of great myth . . . Only in mythical terms can the idea be expressed that the temporal world is essentially good and yet existentially evil, thus allowing ethical tension to express itself.

Curiously, it was a man who rejects the validity of both myth and paradox, the secular philosopher Sidney Hook, who demonstrated in a *New York Times* book review on January 29, 1956, one of the clearest understandings of Niebuhr's use of myth:

> Niebuhr uses the language of religion to suggest the complexities and ironies and irrationalities of human behavior that escape the simple pieties of religious faith and popular science alike. To hold him to a rigorous analytic discourse would be like imposing a proper logical syntax upon a poem.

Still, this comment appears more complimentary to Niebuhr on the surface than it is underneath. For Hook's own world view appears to be divided into two realms: the one, of ultimate importance, being the world of intelligence, scientific method, "rigorous analytic discourse" and courageous political action on the basis of these; the other being a realm of delight but not quite first importance. This second is the realm of woman and emotion, of poetry and art, of religion and psychoanalysis.[4] Niebuhr, thus, appears to be demoted, although Hook in the same article pays tribute to Niebuhr's own political action that has paralleled Hook's although it sprang from entirely different presuppositions.

[4] Freud was a modern scientist who also felt compelled to use myth as a means of communicating his discoveries about the individual (Oedipus) and his conjectures about history (the primal father).

Regardless of Hook's intent, Niebuhr would not quarrel with Hook's characterization of Niebuhr's own "poetic" use of "the language of religion." On the other hand, Niebuhr warns in *An Interpretation of Christian Ethics* that this language must always be used with great care:

> The mythical symbols of transcendence in profound religion are easily corrupted into scientifically untrue statements of historic facts.

One can almost see Professor Hook nodding agreement. But Niebuhr has only given one side of his two-pronged story. He goes on to warn that

> . . . the scientific description of historic sequences may be as easily corrupted into an untrue conception of total reality.

Surely not, Hook might answer, if the scientific description is scientifically accurate.

But "science," Niebuhr would retort, as he did in *The Nature and Destiny of Man*, "which is only science cannot be scientifically accurate."

And the book in which you wrote that, Hook might reply, as he did in his *New Leader* review of it on Nov. 11, 1941, "is eloquent and rhetorically impressive, but its argument will not stand logical analysis for a moment."

Logical analysis, Niebuhr might patiently, or not so patiently, explain again, is all very well in its place: we could not do without it in science or on the surface of life, but its reach, like that of science, is not sufficiently high or deep to grasp man's freedom which is so unique as to be termed "radical."

In contrast, Niebuhr says in *An Interpretation of Christian Ethics:*

> It is the genius of true myth to suggest the dimension of depth in reality and to point to a realm of essence which transcends the surface of history, on which the cause-and-effect sequences, discovered and analyzed by science, occur . . . Therefore the great religious myths deal with creation and redemption. But since myth cannot speak of the trans-historical without using symbols and events in history as its forms of expression, it invariably falsifies the facts of history, as seen by science, to state its truth. Religion must therefore make the confession of St. Paul its own: "As deceivers and yet true . . ." If in addition religion should insist that its mythical devices have a sacred authority which may defy

> the conclusions at which science arrives through its observations, religion is betrayed into deception without truth.

As a young man Niebuhr must have cringed at the obscurantist attitude of those Protestant groups that insisted everything in the Bible must be accepted as literally true, and the harder to believe the truer. The Scopes trial, after all, occurred as late as the middle twenties. At the same time, Niebuhr soon grew to see that modern culture's refusal to take seriously the profoundest myths of the Bible was not as objective and scientific a decision as modern culture assumed:

> It was apparent neither to modern culture nor to modern Christianity that the unconscious moral and religious complacence of the bourgeois soul was as influential in discrediting religious myth as the scientific criticism of religious mythology. Modern culture is compounded of the genuine achievements of science and the peculiar ethos of a commercial civilization. The superficialities of the latter, its complacent optimism, the loss of the sense of depth and of the knowledge of good and evil (the heights of good and the depths of evil) were at least as influential in it [as] the discoveries of science.

These heights of good and depths of evil are in perennial tension with one another. Niebuhr, who is credited with seeing the evil in good people, is not always credited, as he deserves to be, with seeing the good in evil people:

> The issue between grace and sin is drawn on different levels in different lives; but there is no righteous life in which there is not a measure of sin; and no sinful life in which there is not a point where grace may find lodgement.

Nor, he says, will there ever be a period in history when good and evil are not admixed, despite all hopes to the contrary by the advocates of either-or. "The parable of the wheat and the tares," he said in a sermon at Harvard, "is an offense to the simple moralists . . . and the horticulturists." And in more serious vein, he refers to the biblical myth of the Anti-Christ as indicating that good and evil will still be battling at the end of history.

Good and evil, moreover, are admixed not only in the individual and his relationships to other individuals but also in his relationship to society, and its relationships to other societies. Yet if there was onc attitude upon which American culture, both religious and secular, was agreed, it was the refusal to recognize the possibilities of evil in collective life. As Niebuhr wrote before World War II,

> Failure to recognize the heights led . . . to an equal blindness toward the darker depths. . . . There has been little suggestion in modern culture of the demonic force in human life, of the peril in which all achievements of life and civilization constantly stand because the evil impulses in men may be compounded in collective actions until they reach diabolical proportions . . .[5]

"Demonic?" "Diabolic?" From what dusty attic had such words been unearthed? Was not the United States, in the first half of the twentieth century, the most advanced nation, the most prosperous nation, the most idealistic nation?

Niebuhr's warnings to his fellow Americans came by way of the myth called parable. One such was the Tower of Babel which Niebuhr recalled in the land where skyscrapers were probing ever higher into the sky and an ever greater multitude of tongues was being spoken. The foundation of America's tower was weak, Niebuhr said, not because it ignored the laws of gravity (as revealed by science) but the laws of man (as revealed in the Bible and in history).

Because of these warnings Niebuhr was assailed for his pessimism. Yet perhaps the crowning paradox of the prophet's role is that although hurt when reviled, he cannot be satisfied that he is doing his job *unless* he is reviled.

In all events, Niebuhr refused to go along with modern culture, the culture he characterized as having "endowed life with meaning by setting it within the framework of a simply meaningful history." He thus doomed himself to a lifetime of tension with major sections of his his own society.

For there was no pre-existing group that fully agreed with him: if his ideas were too orthodox for the liberals, they were too liberal for

[5] The above mentioned "Ten Years That Shook My World," in *Christian Century*, April 26, 1939, is not only the source of most of these quotations but is one of Niebuhr's most pregnant articles.

the orthodox; and if too secular for the religious, they were too religious for the secular. The integral connection, moreover, between his dual ideas was not always visible to the casual eye. Instead it was like the stem of a tuning fork that has been buried in the ground with only the separate tines visible from the surface. Those people who wished to dig hard could find the underlying stem, but most people either had no wish to make the effort or were busy doing other things.

The other things they were doing, moreover, were often extremely useful to society. And Niebuhr could in no way be certain that the by-products of his own double-edged criticism would be as creative as those of the optimism he was trying to puncture. He could only forge ahead, prodigally expending his energy and brain-power, and prayerfully following Jesus' advice about putting first things first: "Seek ye therefore the Kingdom of God and all these others shall be added unto you."

There is a real life parable (it happens to be true) that illustrates Niebuhr's attitude toward "all these other" by-products. A student came to him and said, "All right. If, as you claim, what we want most in life is likely to come, not directly but as a by-product of our biblical faith, what is to stop us from simply drumming up some biblical faith in order to get, indirectly, what we want most in life?"

The horizontal wrinkles cascade upward on Niebuhr's brow when he is amused.

"Why don't you try it?" he suggested.

PART II

Flashbacks and Close-ups

"Who can decide offhand which is absolutely better, to live or to understand life? We must do both alternately, and a man can no more limit himself to either than a pair of scissors can cut with a single one of its blades."

WILLIAM JAMES
Some Problems of Philosophy

5

The Freedom of Boyhood

IN Wright City, Missouri, on the first day of summer, 1892, a third son and fourth child was born to the wife of the young pastor of the Evangelical synod.[1] No comets shot across the sky; only song birds flew from leafy tree to leafy tree (there were as yet few telephone poles), and bees hummed among the flowers that Mrs. Niebuhr always planted near the parsonage although there was an ever-present chance that before they had time to bloom her husband might have moved her and the family to another church in another town.

Through the open windows of the parsonage, the sound of a newborn's vigorous squalling must have made the neighbors smile as they trudged past on the unpaved street.

So uncomplicated was the birth that Lydia Niebuhr remembered nothing to distinguish it from those of the other children. From the beginning the baby enjoyed an excellent appetite. Within a few months he was gowned in white handkerchief linen and christened Karl Paul Reinhold.

In the nineties, the whole world was enjoying a period of peace that people assumed would last forever. Internally, America was burgeoning. Although the physical frontier had just been closed, the economic one was only beginning to open. That same summer of 1892, two brothers, Charles and Frank Duryea, created a gasoline buggy, the first of its

[1] This basically Lutheran church, an offshoot of the Prussian Church Union, was transported to the U.S. Middle West as the result of an early nineteenth century immigration from Germany. Many years later, in 1934, it joined with a Calvinist group to become the Evangelical and Reformed, and in 1956, it began its official merger with the historic denomination of the Puritans, the Congregational Christian Churches. The two groups together are now known as The United Church of Christ.

kind to be persuaded to run. Horses shied, cattle lowed, farmers cursed, as the noisy, smelly vehicle churned up dust along the country roads. No one surmised that by the time the blond, rosy baby with the bright blue eyes had reached sufficient maturity to take on his first pastorate, the horseless buggy would have reached sufficient maturity to be mass produced, thereby changing not only the face of America—gasoline stations would soon spring up like dragon's teeth—but also creating economic and social problems throughout the nation, particularly in the city of that pastorate.

In 1892, there were already a few premonitory warnings of the kind of complications that lay ahead. Two weeks after the baby's birth, the steelworkers went out on strike in Homestead, near Pittsburgh, and a battle raged between them and the three hundred Pinkerton guards the company had hired to break the strike. By the time the National Guard arrived to put the town and mills under martial law, eighteen people had been killed and many more wounded.

Wright City, some fifty miles northwest of St. Louis, lay far from industrial strife. So remote from the rest of America did its small population feel that many people did not bother to learn English. They preferred the German of their own or their forebears' pre-immigrant status. Services in the Evangelical Church were conducted wholly in German. Nor was Pastor Gustav Niebuhr unusual in this regard. As one of his much younger colleagues in the Evangelical ministry, the Rev. Paul Schroeder, recalls, "ours . . . was a small and unknown group in the total picture of American church life. . . . All its congregations were German speaking or at best bilingual. This German origin constituted a kind of voluntary and also involuntary social and religious segregation." The German Evangelical Synod of North America, moreover, ran the church in a more hierarchical fashion than was customary among most Protestant denominations. Young men straight out of the Seminary, for example, had no choice as to where they would be sent at the meagerest possible salary.

Wright City was Gustav Niebuhr's second post. He had arrived in the United States at the age of seventeen. His family was still living in Hardissen bei Lage, Lippe Detmold, in the northwestern part of Germany where his father, a *Gutsbesitzer*, or substantial landowner, had some twenty-five people working on his *Hof*. The lad was in rebellion primarily against his father's typically Prussian ways, but also against the prospect of having to spend several years in the rigid German military service. As soon as he had completed the *Gymnasium,* or High School, he took off on his own for the new world.

Years later, his son Reinhold wrote to a distant relative:

> My father regarded the tyrannical father as symbol of the whole German system and was rather more than most immigrants who arrived after 1848, ideologically oriented. The 1848ers were the rebels against the conservative reaction in Germany dominated by Metternich. Carl Schurz, one of the 1848ers, was his hero. Schurz had become a general in the Civil War and through him my father gained a great interest in Lincoln. The passionate devotion to Lincoln lasted throughout his life. When I first became conscious of politics my father was an admirer of T. R. [Hulda Niebuhr remembered that her father was also a great admirer of William of Orange.] He was deeply religious and I inherited interest in religion or rather religious conviction from him. . . . Incidentally when he came to this country he hired himself out to a German farmer who had much to do with sending him into the ministry. Perceiving his religious nature and his desire for learning he persuaded my father that it was foolish to carry his rebellion against his father too far. He sent him to our denominational theological seminary in St. Louis. My father died before the outbreak of the first World War. He was therefore saved the ordeal of the Germans of the middle west who overnight were changed from honored citizens to suspected traitors. On the other hand, he might not have suffered, for he changed his loyalty much more explicitly than most of the Germans of my acquaintance.

Hummermeyer was the name of the German-American farmer who thus encouraged young Gustav Niebuhr, and he lived near Freeport, Illinois. The Seminary was Eden Theological, now in Webster Groves, Missouri, just outside of St. Louis.

As soon as Gustav Niebuhr completed his studies, he was assigned, by the Evangelical Synod, to assist in establishing a "home mission"[2] in the post-frontier town of San Francisco. Its minister was the Reverend Edward

[2] as distinguished from "foreign mission." It means a church, still supported by the parent church, that is trying to establish itself in a part of the country where no church of that denomination yet exists.

Jacob Hosto, a second generation German-American, who had originally come from Breese, Illinois. No sooner did the Rev. Mr. Hosto succeed in training his young assistant than he himself was sent to establish a still more remote "home mission" in the foothills of Mount Shasta. But his slim, bright-eyed, vivacious eighteen-year-old daughter, Lydia, soon left Mount Shasta to return to San Francisco and become the bride of Gustav Niebuhr.

Born to them while still in San Francisco was first, Hulda, who subsequently became Professor of Christian Education at McCormick Theological Seminary in Chicago, and died in 1959. Her warmth, thoughtfulness, and humor extended to the writing of stories for young people (*Greatness Passing By* is the best known) and also to the encouraging of visitors to feel completely at home.[3] The second child was Walter, a handsome boy of vivid charm and notable intelligence who became a newspaper publisher, a pioneer in the production of documentary films, and a businessman who made and lost several fortunes before his death in 1946. The third was Herbert who died at the age of six weeks. "My first memory," Hulda said, "is of mother crying and father trying to comfort her."

Perhaps Lydia Niebuhr, like many another parent who has lost an infant, did not feel fully comforted—despite her husband's best efforts and her own profound faith that "whether we live or die, we live unto the Lord"—until she held another infant in her arms. Reinhold, the replacement, born soon after the family had moved to Wright City, was thus doubly welcome.

But his season in the sun was a short one. He was less than two years old when the baby of the family, Helmut Richard, then called "Hem," and subsequently, Richard, was born. No doubt Reinhold had never been able to command his mother's full attention anyway; for there were not only his older sister and brother to be cared for, but also endless numbers of guests, some of whom Hulda recalled were hoboes who knocked at the door and asked the minister for a meal or a night's sleep. When Lydia Niebuhr gently remonstrated, pointing to the fact that these

[3] Her theological interests in combination with those of her brothers, Reinhold and Richard, and of Richard's son, Richard Reinhold, led *Time* to refer to the Niebuhrs as "The Trapp family of theology."

guests might bring lice and other hazards to the children, Gustav Niebuhr said he would never refuse a hungry man a meal or a weary man a bed, and he never did. Fortunately, Lydia Niebuhr had so much energy, so much laughter, so much expertness in cooking, sewing, and toy-making, that her large and unpredictable household did not overpower her.[4] Even in her mid-eighties, she was a Pied Piper to the children on the McCormick Seminary Campus who visited her several times a week to paint and carve, to sew and make designs out of stained glass, to cook and eat.

Hulda's most vivid memory in connection with Wright City was three-year-old Reinhold's reaction to a dead horse he saw being carried in a spring-wagon out of the woods behind the parsonage. At the slightest encouragement, Reinhold would lie down on his back on the floor and stiffen his arms and legs in an imitation of the horse. Hulda also remembered this was the first occasion she realized that "grown-up interest in children could be superior amusement rather than straight interest." To the chief actor of the drama, however, any old form of interest was good enough.

Soon after Richard's birth, the Niebuhr family moved to St. Charles, Missouri. They stayed there eight years. As Hulda recalled,

> We had a large domain: arbors of various kinds in which to set up all sorts of enterprises, heritage of a Swiss pastor family who raised grapes wherever there was any room. There was an enormous apple tree with a sandbox under it—a crabapple tree into which we could crawl with favorite books. There was also a "Gartenhaus" with a built-in table and benches all around where I used to sew doll clothes with my friends, but the boys spent more time in the school yard adjoining. Still, the little house was used by all for lemonade and cookie handouts. The school yard where Reinie spent many hours playing "steps," etc., had a new layer of cinders quite often; hard on shoes and the budget.

Mrs. Niebuhr's recollection of the school next door was less the injury it did to the shoes and trouser-knees than to the peace of mind of her imaginative and dramatically inclined third child. Reinhold could not sleep the night after the teacher described in class how Judas had hanged

[4] She recalled that a favorite toy of the future self-styled "circuit rider" was a hobby-horse she made for him out of an old broomstick.

himself. The swollen tongue, the swinging body, the torments of soul, all returned to haunt the child. The death of a horse was something he could act out and absorb, but the death of a man, self-inflicted because of guilt, was too much for him. Fortunately his mother remembered from her own childhood how devastating such stories could be, and devoted hours to soothing him.

Fortunately Gustav Niebuhr too could remember back to how it felt to be a little child. Bishop William Scarlett[5] tells the story of the red sled with wooden runners which was eight-year-old Reinhold's favorite possession as long as he stayed on the hill near the parsonage in St. Charles. But one day, he ventured further afield. He discovered the big hill where the older boys were shooting down so fast that their momentum carried them way across a frozen pond. Reinhold, in his homemade leggings and jacket, his hand-knitted cap and mittens, threw his well padded form down on his little red sled and kicked off.

Ignominy.

No matter how hard he kicked and strained, he could not make the wooden runners carry him out onto the pond. While he struggled, the other boys on their metal runners passed him, with laughs and jeers.

Trudging home through the snow, his round cheeks made redder by the cold and his tears, the small figure was overtaken by a large bewhiskered one. "Was ist los?" asked a familiar deep voice. "Warum weinst Du?"

The whole woeful story flooded out: the shame of being outdone; the recalcitrance of those hateful wooden runners; the longing for a sled like the other boys'. How mixed the father's feelings must have been: the yearning to equip his child with the best that money could buy; the anxious figuring with the few dollars left after a family of six had had been fed and clothed on $1200 a year; the question of the justice involved in giving one child out of four a present that could not be duplicated for the others.

Fortunately Gustav Niebuhr was a man of common sense as well as erudition. Besides, like anyone involved in the political scene, he had

[5] This Episcopal Bishop, now retired, has long been a close friend of Reinhold Niebuhr's, and is a spiritual, if not literal, descendant of his own namesake, Robin Hood's merry helper.

contacts. One of them was the village blacksmith. So, along they went, man, boy, and little red sled, to the clanging, spark-filled workshop where, for an explanation and a pittance, the great smudged hands attached a set of metal runners.

"What a blessed thing genteel poverty can be," Reinhold Niebuhr later said. "I felt that Father was doing something special just for me. If he'd had less money, he couldn't have done it; if he'd had more money, it wouldn't have meant so much."

The minute school was out the next afternoon, Reinhold headed for the big hill. By the time the other boys arrived, he was ready for a race. With laughter they accepted his challenge; and with chagrin they saw him speed past—far out onto the ice.

Other times, however, the genteel poverty appeared less blessed. Food was adequate but not abundant at the Niebuhr table, while the guests were likely to be more abundant than adequate, at least from Mrs. Niebuhr's point of view. One evening a young Helmut noted guest after guest arriving for dinner when his favorite food, sausages, was being served. By the time the plate reached him, it was empty. Another time, Reinhold, who loved cheese, was served early, but in his hurry, he reached for it with his left hand. His father, who was trying to break him of left-handedness, rapped him smartly over the knuckles. The boy interpreted the gesture as meaning he was not supposed to have that much cheese. In a rage, he stormed out of the dining room. After the meal his mother came upstairs, and Reinhold complained that his father wanted to starve him. "I'm going to get rich some day! I'm going to buy myself all the cheese I want! and I'm going to buy *you* all the cheese *you* want!" When she reported the misunderstanding to her husband, he promptly went and talked to the boy, and apologized for such part of the misunderstanding as was his fault. The example of honest contrition was a part of Reinhold Niebuhr's life from early childhood. Fifty years later he told a young man thinking of entering the ministry,

> If my father had not had grace, I would not have been a Christian—or if he had been secular, and without grace, I might have rebelled and become a Christian. But who knows? That's human freedom.

Another time he conjectured that if a minister has grace, his sons will be tempted to follow him into the ministry, while if he does not, they will be tempted to choose a career as remote from the ministry as possible.

Gustav Niebuhr, according to his children, made a conscious effort to be as different as he could be from his own autocratic father. As one of them recalled,

> We all had our chores to do. Father's was to clean the stove at night and carry the ashes out. One of the boys offered to do it for him. Father said no, that the boy had his own chores to do and this was one that Father was capable of doing. But in saying this, Father wasn't purposely showing a good example. It went deeper than that.

This was, after all, the period when children were supposed to be seen and not heard, but Pastor Niebuhr thought otherwise. Florence Denger, the daughter of a neighbor, was in her mid-teens when the Pastor started giving her individual catechism instruction. One day she summoned courage to tell him of her doubts about God. Gustav Niebuhr listened carefully and then confessed that he too was still subject to doubts, so much so, in fact, that at times he considered himself a Doubting Thomas. This admission from an adult, and a minister as well, was so reassuring to the girl that half a century later she remembered it and credited him with having helped her establish faith enough for a lifetime.

To his own children, Gustav Niebuhr's faith was communicated less by explicit instruction than by implicit assumption. Taken for granted, for example, was the daily recognition by parents with their heads bowed of the source that was higher than they.

Half a century later Reinhold Niebuhr wrote to a young agnostic couple who were troubled about whether or not to give their children a religious upbringing:

> I must tell you an interesting story about your general problem. We had an anthropologist over at Columbia who was thinking his way from the extreme secularism of his discipline to a Christian position. In the process he remembered his youth and the family prayers. And it suddenly came to him that what was left

> of all the conventional religion in his life was the memory of his father and mother praying to a God who was greater than they were. This, he said, was the one thing that a child needed in the period of disillusionment when it realizes that parents were not as powerful nor as good as they had seemed to the child in his early childhood.

Pastor Niebuhr, however, had no interest in having his children behave according to conventional religion just to please the community. When a delegation of the conservative members of his congregation paid a call to suggest that the Niebuhr boys not be seen playing tennis on the afternoon of the Sabbath, he listened carefully, and the boys went right on playing tennis.

A man, then a student spending the night with the Niebuhrs, wrote, "I sensed that the home was a happy and harmonious home, not puritanical but wholesome with acceptance and enjoyment of the experience of family ties." A minister who also visited, about this time, said that he had been particularly interested in Gustav Niebuhr's "give and take at home," having previously been warned that Niebuhr's "wife and daughter could twist him around their little finger."

But try as Gustav Niebuhr might to be the opposite of his own father, he had absorbed too many of the Prussian assumptions to be able to free himself entirely of them. There are family memories of mildly erring sons being sent to stay for protracted periods in the downstairs washroom—once Pastor Niebuhr forgot he had thus incarcerated Walter, and went off on an errand; Walter always remembered, not so much the hours in the washroom, as the extent and depth of his father's woe when he returned and found what an injustice he had unintentionally perpetrated. And in regard to his only daughter, it simply never occurred to Pastor Niebuhr that a girl might be interested in the kind of professional training he was planning for the boys. As Reinhold Niebuhr tells his classes today, "we must never forget how powerful our unthinking assumptions are."

Reinhold's relation with his father was perhaps the most congenial of all the sons. Hulda recalls that "Father talked to Reinie quite early about the problems of the ministry." As Reinhold Niebuhr told the interviewer of the Oral Research Center of Columbia University,

> Father had a great passion for American egalitarianism and American freedom, which for him particularly meant freedom in the family. . . . I have a very vivid memory of the impression he made upon me as an adolescent boy in consulting me about whether or not he should accept a call to a church in another town.

The call to Lincoln, in central Illinois, had come in 1902, the year that Henry Ford's Motor Company was established, and the year also that a ten-year-old boy chose his career. He was walking home with his father after a local celebration in which Gustav Niebuhr had taken a leading part.

"Have you thought, Reinhold, about what you want to be?"

"Yes."

"What?"

"A minister."

"Why?"

"Because you're the most interesting man in town."

There may have been a smile hidden among the plentiful russet whiskers, but Gustav Niebuhr's answer was serious. "Then you must study Greek," he said. "We'll have a lesson every Saturday morning."

Gustav Niebuhr himself read Greek or Hebrew every day, in his *Polyglot Bible.* He also often read Macaulay, partly because he was interested in history, and partly because he had been told that Macaulay's style was worth emulating. A Macaulay epigram whose double edge may also have influenced young Reinhold was that "Nothing is so useless as a general maxim."

The town of Lincoln, Reinhold Niebuhr told the Columbia Oral interviewer in 1954, was, like the other small Middle Western communities of the time,

> heavily German-American. The German farmers were usually very competent and prosperous. The farmers I knew were all second generation. Their fathers had reclaimed the prairie. What happened was that this Illinois farm land, which was very rich, was rather a morass until it was tilled. It was too moist to produce good crops. Somebody came along and taught them how to drain off the moisture. So very suddenly the prairie was re-

> claimed. They bought this land at very low prices. . . . These families all had a poor immigrant in their history . . . but they were all very competent and very wealthy. . . . They had the ambition to work out a farm for each of their sons. If they couldn't buy Illinois farm land, they would shop in Iowa. . . . Our town, like all these Illinois towns that I knew, was populated by these retired farmers. They weren't, incidentally, a very heroic or very lovable type. They were extremely conservative. They had made their pile and they were going to hold on to it. They were always opposed to community improvements which required taxes. . . . My father . . . spent a good deal of time trying to beguile them from their rather unconstructive conservatism.

The parsonage of St. John's Church in Lincoln was a rambling porch-enclosed house with a large yard and a barn or buggy shed. Mrs. Niebuhr gave the boys heavy ropes to hang from the barn rafters and old mattresses to tumble upon. Particularly exciting for the children, Hulda recalled, was the one night a month when both parents attended the Board meeting of the Deaconess Hospital, and the children were free until all hours to play "Circus," or "World's Fair" (modelled on St. Louis), or "Chautauqua."

> Walter was the leader, but Reinie was the actor. He loved to perform "weddings" and "baptisms" with gestures adopted from a certain Father Vaughan. "Behold." Up would go one arm. "Here is a flower." Up would go the other arm. "I shall give you one of its petals." Hurling motion. "I shall fling it."

Looking back, Hulda smiled. "I'm sorry for children today who have to play under supervision. Our school work was set, with lots of memorizing, but our play was free."

For Reinhold, the memories of the barn fused with the rote-learning at school to form an unusual bit of autobiography in *Beyond Tragedy:*

> I remember how wonderful was the experience of my boyhood when we ran to the barn, warned by ominous clouds of an approaching storm, and then heard the wind and the rain beating outside while safe and dry under the eaves of the haymow. The experience had actual religious overtones. . . . The words of the Psalmist, committed to memory . . . achieved a sudden and vivid

> relevance: "Thou shalt not be afraid for the terror by night; nor for the arrow that flieth by day. . . . There shall no evil befall thee."

Certainly no child of the television age could begin to imagine the excitement in the small midwestern community for the ten days when the real Chautauqua—termed by Theodore Roosevelt "the most American thing in America"—came to town. Those were, by all accounts, the top ten days of the year.

A contemporary description appears in *The Lincoln Herald* for August 12, 1904:

> The Chautauqua grounds presented a most beautiful appearance Thursday afternoon when the third annual assembly was begun. To those who had not recently visited the grounds, the transformation into a small city of tents, with here and there a permanent cottage building, and the large commodious and tastily decorated auditorium, capable of seating at least four thousand persons, was a matter of surprise and wonder. Scores of exclamations, such as, "How beautiful," "I had no idea that so much work had been done," "Well, isn't that grand," were heard on every side. . . .

The season ticket for an adult cost $1.50; for a child, $.75. This entitled the holder to see plays, hear concerts, perform gymnastics, thrill to great speakers like William Jennings Bryan and others "of the educational, inspiration, entertainment and religious type."[6] The flag-decorated auditorium contained long wooden benches where every seat was so uncomfortable that people brought cushions and where no seat could be reserved.

One youth, with his blond hair slicked down, must have arrived early on the day when Fighting Bob La Follette was scheduled to speak, for the youth was seated in the very front row. The speech was a fiery one. Toward the end of it, La Follette's son went up on the stage and whispered in his father's ear. "My son Robert," La Follette announced, his hand resting on the young man's shoulder, "who is in charge of my engagements, has just told me that I am already late for my next appointment. I don't

[6] The quotations about the Chautauqua come from V. Deacon Lile's 1938 M. A. thesis, written for the State University of Iowa, entitled "History of The Lincoln Chautauqua Association of Lincoln, Illinois."

want to leave here at all, but . . ."—a pause and a smile—"he's the boss." The crowd clapped its amusement and approval; the La Follette boy turned red with pleasure, and the Niebuhr boy turned green with envy. Yet even as he yearned to change places with the youth on the stage, he recognized that this was nothing more than a clever political trick.

Years later, when Reinhold Niebuhr was at Eden Seminary, he was briefly but seriously tempted by the offer of a political career for himself. Carl Vrooman, who had gone to Washington, in 1912, to take part in the first Woodrow Wilson administration, offered him a job in the Agriculture Department with a salary that looked astronomical. "But by then," Niebuhr told Scarlett, "my religious commitment was too great."

Religious he was, but not particularly bookish. Hulda recollected the not untypical time that "Walter and Reinie were so inspired by reports of a man who had walked all the way across the United States that they themselves walked all the way from Lincoln to Pulaski (twelve miles away)." Closer to home there were other means to express exuberant energy. Said Hulda: "In his teens Reinie was a member of a *Posaunenchor*, a trumpet band, led by an immigrant miner in the basement of our church. All three of my brothers and all their closest friends were in the group. It broke up when the leader persisted in a ban on marches or any other music except hymns."

Extracurricular activities at school were also important to Reinhold. In the eighth grade he reached the finals of the Debating Contest. His father went to hear him, and came home vastly amused. In the heat of argument Reinhold referred disparagingly to his opponent, Paul Cannon, as "that blue-eyed son of a preacher." There was no apparent awareness that the description applied equally well to himself.

He excelled also in writing, and won a local contest with a short story about a bull chasing a little boy. The episode upon which the story was apparently based occurred on the large Hosto family farm in Alhambra, Illinois. Reinhold and Walter and a young neighbor, Henry Dinkmeyer, used to amuse themselves by hiding in the big watering trough and, when the cows came to drink, leaping up and frightening them. There was a bull in residence, but he was not ferocious, and the fence was sufficiently near at hand so that when one cow did chase them, they were easily able to escape. In the story, the cow suffered a sea-change into a ferocious bull and the fence was moved far enough away for the boy to be suspensefully endangered. "As Deceivers Yet True," is the name of the opening sermon in *Beyond Tragedy,* written some thirty years later; and in it Niebuhr notes that art, like religion, "describes the world not in terms of its exact relationships [but] falsifies these . . . in order to express their total meaning."

As a boy, he was already sufficiently sensitive to the meaning of words to register objection to their misuse. One afternoon Adam Denger, in whose grocery Reinhold worked after school, noticed an unusual degree of grit and dust underfoot.[7] "Hey Reinie," he called. "What about you getting out the broom and throwing it across the floor?"

The boy nodded, crossed to where the broom rested against the wall, picked it up and then literally threw it across the floor. Dust and laughter flew high that afternoon.

This same genial Adam Denger was finally forced to close his store. During a recession in the early part of the century, he had extended too much credit to the miners who were then unemployed. Embarrassed by his generosity and unable to pay him back, many of them stole out of town without even saying goodbye. Mr. Denger kept believing that God would protect him if he did what was right. But God let Adam Denger go bankrupt, and his young assistant grew up to preach against sentimentality and reliance on special providence.

From the high school in Lincoln, Walter went to Illinois Wesleyan in Bloomington, Illinois, and Reinhold and Richard went to Elmhurst, a small denominational college offering special scholarships to parsons' sons but no recognized B.A. It was not for considerable time, until Richard Niebuhr became president of Elmhurst, that the college was fully accredited.

After four years at Elmhurst, the two Niebuhr boys went on for three years to Eden Theological Seminary which has also, since that time, vastly improved its standards. One of Reinhold's roommates believes that

> our very inadequate and almost totally unrelated theological training must be heavily discounted as an environmental factor in Reinie's development. Reinie and I were more fortunate than the students who preceded us in that Dr. [Samuel] Press had been added to the faculty a very short time before we arrived.

[7] Subsequent after-school jobs included one in a shoe store and, in summer, picking berries and selling books from door to door.

About Dr. Press, Niebuhr felt equally enthusiastic. He wrote, in his introductory chapter to the Living Library Volume:

> The seminary was influential in my life primarily because of the creative effect upon me of the life of a very remarkable man, Dr. S. D. Press, who combined a childlike innocency with a rigorous scholarship in Biblical and systematic subjects. This proved the point that an educational institution needs only to have Mark Hopkins on one end of a log and a student on the other.

So impressed, in turn, was this particular Mark Hopkins with his student Reinhold that he started saving his letters from the beginning.[8] Forty years later he generously shared them and also volunteered to write to some of Reinhold's erstwhile classmates to see what recollections they might have of him. From South India, the Rev. M. E. Seybold wrote Professor Press:

> I am sure you and the other professors who taught our class would agree that Reinie was easily the best student in our class both at Elmhurst and Eden, and it would be hard to find a better one among all who passed through those institutions. From the first we recognized that a brilliant mind had come among us. Had he cared to, he might have carried off all the prizes offered from year to year. As it was, he had so many and varied interests that he made no effort to do so. That gave some of us lesser lights a chance to garner a few. Talking about interests I remember Reinie taking part in most anything that came along and usually leading the groups taking part. He just naturally stood out, and again, not because he sought positions of leadership, or acclaim, he was just a few strides ahead of others, always.
>
> He always had many questions to ask and was ever ready to argue a point. Probably quite stimulating to his teachers at times, and at other times, he was probably a bit of a headache to them. Even in those days I remember saying that Reinie asked these questions because he thought of things that did not occur to the rest of us, or recognized implications of statements made that others failed to see. He went right on doing that later, too, and so he is where he is today. . . .

[8] At the time Reinhold Niebuhr was at Eden, Professor Press was the first resident full-time professor to teach theological courses in English instead of German.

> And can we ever forget the great debate? I note that you remember it too, till this day. I do not remember the subject debated, but I shall never forget how Reinie led Eden to victory. In preparation for this debate with Concordia, we had a preliminary debate at Eden. Reinie led the side which had to support the subject as assigned to Concordia. I was a member of the opposite side. Well, Reinie's team won and so was to represent Eden. That meant that Reinie had to support the opposite side of the question from the one which he had argued in the preliminary debate. The result was that Reinie knew all the arguments pro and con and Concordia had lost before the debate began. Dr. Becker[9] left very early in the proceedings, so after an enthusiastic home-coming, all of us singing all the way back in the streetcar, we called on Dr. Becker. He answered the door and asked us what we had come for. We told him that we had good news, Eden had won. "Didn't you see me go out?" he said. "I knew we had won at that point, so felt I would only be wasting time by remaining longer." Mrs. Niebuhr was a proud mother that night, for she was there and enjoyed our singing and our enthusiasm.

Dr. Paul M. Schroeder, another classmate, does recall the subject of the debate:

> I believe the choice of the side to be defended was given to the Concordia team, which chose the negative side of the subject: "Resolved that international arbitration is an effective method of eliminating war as an instrument of settling international disputes." That debate was in 1911 or 1912 when optimism regarding the dawn of universal peace was running high. As a consistent idealist I was elated to defend the affirmative position. Reinie however had his misgivings and in his heart preferred the negative position on this subject. His keen mind was able at that early age to detect the unreality of the idealistic utopianism that dominated the Christian thought of that era. How absolutely right subsequent events proved him to be.
>
> One other incident stands out clearly in my mind, indicating Reinie's recognition of qualitative values in Christian thought. We were in Eden at the time of the sinking of the *Titanic.*

[9] Dr. William Becker was then President of Eden Seminary.

> We were deeply shaken by this tragedy in which more than a thousand people perished. I was moved by the sheer numbers of this awful tragedy. Reinie kept commenting on the loss of some of the leaders in the realms of art and science that went down with the ship. I protested that all men are equally precious in the sight of God. But he insisted with his passion for realism that the loss of men and women who are making a great contribution to the welfare of their fellowmen is infinitely greater than the loss of the rank and file of the human family. For me democracy and religious concern for human personality were equated with a kind of hazy egalitarianism, but Reinie's keener insight recognized an aristocracy within the framework of democracy, namely an aristocracy of character and service to humanity.

As Niebuhr himself confirmed much later, in an Oral Research interview, "life is hierarchical, and against this hierarchical tendency of life you've got those transcendent principles of justice [equality and liberty] which try to prevent these hierarchies from becoming vexatious." The reason they are bound to become vexatious unless rigorously curbed is that "wherever there is great disproportion of power, there's bound to be injustice, no matter how idealistic people are."

Reinhold was still at Eden in April, 1913, when his father suffered an attack of diabetes, went into a coma, and died. Discovery of the insulin that would have saved his life came but a short time later.

Yet there was no bitterness when Lydia Niebuhr and her children discussed this small and crucial time-lag, despite the fact that it deprived them not only of someone they deeply loved who was in the prime of life, but also of their financial security and the many kinds of freedom they had up to then enjoyed.

6

The Concept of Freedom

Because of human freedom, Niebuhr says, man is the most incongruous creature in the world. Not even the lemming, which periodically joins with its fellows and swims so far out to sea that he cannot return, is as incongruous as man.

For man, too, can commit mass suicide—or mass murder—and view himself doing it, and wonder why he does it, and erect whole systems of value upon the doing, or the not doing, of it. Man, says Niebuhr, is never wholly at one place at one time, for he is always capable of viewing himself as being at that place at that time, and thereby gaining a vantage point not wholly encompassed by either place or time. Man thus has freedom to rise above himself, and above the self that has previously risen above the self, "indeterminately."

Man also has the capacity, because of this freedom, to enlarge the scope of every desire he shares with the rest of the animals. A lion kills in order to eat, and stops killing and eating when he is sated. Man often does not. His memory of past hunger, his fear of future hunger, his yearning for security, of which food is both a part and a symbol, may combine to create an insatiability unknown in the animal world. Upon this human insatiability, moreover, the arts of civilization rest. For it is man, the only animal who is known, during health, to foresee his own death who unremittingly tears down and builds up in order to prevent the day of hunger and postpone the day of death. Man, furthermore, Niebuhr notes in *The Children of Light and The Children of Darkness,*

> being more than a natural creature, is not interested merely in physical survival but in prestige and social approval. Having the intelligence to anticipate the perils in which he stands in nature

> and history, he invariably seeks to gain security against these perils by enhancing his power, individually and collectively.

The time limit of a man's death, therefore, may not mark the limit of his desires: for the sake of his descendants, his own posthumous reputation, or his fellow citizens he is willing to snatch life from others or to offer up his own. No simple limit can ever be placed beforehand, Niebuhr says, on the creativity or the destructiveness that stems from human freedom: "man is the kind of lion who both kills the lamb and also dreams of the day when the lion and lamb shall lie down together."

Man's unique freedom includes not only the power to rise indeterminately above the present self, but also to encompass much of the collective as well as individual past, and to imagine part of the future. (Just as our fathers wait for their justification in our lives, Niebuhr says, so do we wait for our justification in lives not yet in being.) In recording the behavior patterns of the past, and the exceptions to these patterns, we can sometimes choose whether in the future to fit ourselves into such patterns or to rebel against them; Niebuhr thus agrees with Santayana that those who do not study history are those condemned to repeat it. It is important, moreover, to study which factors in ourselves and in history are variable and which are perennial, and to remember that man's freedom, which Niebuhr calls man's "essence," partakes of both.

Essence that it is, man's freedom is inextricably bound up with man's finiteness. "Man," booms Niebuhr in the opening salvo of the Gifford Lectures, "is his own most vexing problem." Man is vexing because, on the one hand, he is "a child of nature, subject to its vicissitudes . . . and confined within the brevity of the years which nature permits its varied organic form," and, on the other hand, he has sufficient freedom to "stand outside of nature, life, himself, his reason and the world." It is the paradoxical combination of freedom and finiteness that makes in large part for man's incongruity and inner tension:

> Man's very position in the universe is incongruous. . . . Man is so great and yet so small, so significant and yet so insignificant. . . . The incongruity becomes even more profound when it is the same man who assumes the ultimate perspective from which he finds himself so insignificant.

Because of his incongruous position man is often unpredictable. This unpredictability is something Niebuhr is likely to practice as well as preach. Nor does he expect even the highest development of the social and psychological sciences to result in its eradication. The individual, he believes, is too complex and too paradoxical for the sciences to do more than explain afterward which of many possible motives prompted a particular action. In his early *Does Civilization Need Religion?* Niebuhr wrote that

> The importance of hypotheses increases with the complexity and variability of the data into which they are projected. Every assumption is an hypothesis, and human nature is so complex that it justifies almost every assumption and prejudice with which either a scientific investigation or an ordinary human contact is initiated.

Niebuhr's own firm hypothesis is that largely because of human freedom the individual has uniqueness.[1] And Niebuhr ties this freedom and uniqueness of the individual to the creator of man's freedom and uniqueness:

> When the Bible speaks of man being made in "the image of God," it means that he is a free spirit as well as a creature; and that as spirit he is finally responsible to God.

Man is finally responsible to God, so to speak, in a vertical dimension; while he is also responsible, in a horizontal dimension, to his fellow man. He can, therefore, never take total refuge from blame by loading it onto causes outside himself:

> The Christian faith cannot deny that our acts may be influenced by heredity, environment and the actions of others. But it must deny that we can ever excuse our actions by attributing them to the fault of others, even though there has been a strong inclination to do this since Adam excused himself by the words, "the woman . . . gave me of the apple."

[1] Ignazio Silone says: "We must recognize the uniqueness of [the individual's] inner life in the same way that society recognizes the uniqueness of fingerprints." Important as this recognition has always been, it is perhaps even more important in an age when the sciences statistically stress what everyone has in common rather than what is unique.

And the woman, of course, went on to blame the serpent.

Man's indeterminate freedom, in short, means that man bears an indeterminate responsibility. This is an added—indeed essential—factor in man's continual inner tension. And man's awareness of this freedom and responsibility then sets him in a further situation of tension with his society. This is the fact even when his is a "good society, a society dedicated to the upholding of human freedom." For, as Niebuhr wrote in *Christianity and Society* during the soul-searching period of the second World War,

> The simple fact is that an individual rises indeterminately above every community of which he is a part. The concept of "the value and dignity of the individual" of which our modern culture has made so much is finally meaningful only in a religious dimension. It is constantly threatened by the same culture which wants to guarantee it.

And it is threatened by our culture, whenever we assume that man is "no more than an object in nature which it is possible, scientifically, to 'manipulate.'" It is also threatened whenever we assume

> that individual desires, hopes and ideals can be fitted with frictionless harmony into the collective purposes of man. The individual is not discrete. He cannot find fulfillment completely within society. . . . Insofar as he finds fulfillment beyond every historic community, he lives his life in painful tension with even the best community, sometimes achieving standards of conduct which defy the standards of the community with a resolute "we must obey God rather than man." Sometimes he is involved vicariously in the guilt of the community when he would fain live a life of innocency. He will possibly man a bombing plane and suffer the conscience pricks of the damned that the community might survive.

Every adult American was, to a degree, responsible for the slow death and painful disfigurement and genetic corruption of civilians in Hiroshima and Nagasaki, even as we and our children are beneficiaries of the quicker end to the fighting that resulted from our use of the atom bomb. Yet many Americans felt, and feel, no uneasiness about this collective act, nor do they understand why the dropping particularly of the second bomb has made us hated and feared in many of the uncommitted nations of Asia and Africa where dark-skinned people suspect that we never would have repeated so decimating an act had our enemy been of the white race. Some Americans defend themselves against this atomic guilt by pointing out that they were never consulted. This is true—yet what Niebuhr wrote in the *Atlantic*, May, 1927, almost twenty years before the atom bomb, also seems true: that "there is an increasing tendency among modern men to imagine themselves ethical because they have delegated their vices to larger and larger groups."[2]

When our group performs an unethical act in regard to other groups the individual citizen usually goes along, either out of inertia or ignorance or impotence. The prophet, on the other hand, must rise in his indeterminate freedom above the nation or the church he loves in order to voice what he feels to be God's judgment upon it. When the prophets warned the Children of Israel that God was displeased with them for being a stiff-necked people, this stiffness of the neck was considered wrong in relation to God, but not necessarily in relation to society or to its leaders. The prophets themselves were unbending, sometimes to the point of death, and in our own time Niebuhr has applauded various stiff-necked individuals who defied a dictator or a slave society to the point of death. He fully sympathized, for example, with the German Army officers who rose against Hitler on July 20, 1944; and after the war he wrote a *Christianity and Crisis* editorial called "A Visit About Historical Symbols" that defended Jan Masaryk's suicide in defiance of the communist coup d'état in Czechoslovakia as being "neither wrong nor meaningless." There are, thus, occasions when either a murder or a suicide for the sake of freedom may be demanded of the stiff-necked individual.

At the same time, Niebuhr warns we must never deify freedom. It is not God. It is not even "an absolute value," but a contingent one which may conflict with other contingent values such as justice and stability. In *The New Republic*, in 1956 he said, "We only seem to think [that freedom is absolute] because we take the values of justice and stability for granted. But these values have been made compatible with freedom by very slow processes of history in the West."

[2] In only too prophetic a vein, Niebuhr continued, "Yet the groups are not large enough to give moral unity to mankind, and the whole process may simply tend to make the next war an intercontinental war, a real world war, instead of merely a Western World War."

The very slow processes of history are most likely to be effective when there is freedom for the society as well as for the individual: "The community requires freedom as much as does the individual." Neither kind of freedom is strengthened, however—indeed it may be weakened—by the assumption that predominated in the latter part of the nineteenth and early part of the twentieth century: that man's freedom can be scientifically disproved.

Since that time, there has been a radical change in the thinking of many people. The historian, Allan Nevins, says that never in the history of the world has there been such a thorough change in viewpoint as occurred in the second quarter of the twentieth century. It may, therefore, be necessary to recall for a moment what people did believe, especially since many who lived through that period still claim that no one born later can even begin to imagine how glorious it was.

Those were the halcyon years, when the world was so completely at peace that travellers could move from country to country without so much as a passport, when ideas moved freely too, and most of them were hopeful. Who could dispute the evidence that mankind was on the march, physically through science, intellectually through reason, and morally through education? "Give us a million dollars," said one of the secular reformers, for there were, it was true, still a few areas for improvement, "and we will solve the problems of the human race." Nor was this glowing attitude any less characteristic of the religious world than of the secular. According to the Protestant minister, James Freeman Clarke, in the latter part of the nineteenth century.

> The progress of the human race is fixed by laws immutable as the nature of God. The fidelity of man may hasten it; the wilfulness of man may retard it; but Divine Providence has decreed its certain issue.

This "optimism" of the secular and the religious world was accentuated by the world of the printed page. Only a few congenital pessimists allowed any hint of man's incongruity to besmirch the atmosphere of sweetness and light. Indeed one criterion for literature was the avoidance of such besmirching. According to the *Ladies Home Journal*, in 1890.

> A good book is one in which the bright rather than the dark side of life is shown . . . one that glorifies virtue in women and

> honor in men. One in which the good are rewarded and the wicked are made to suffer. One which convinces you that the world is filled with good men and women.

At least James Freeman Clarke admitted the fact that man has "wilfulness"; at least the *Ladies Home Journal* admitted the fact that "the wicked" exist; it was not so much that the facts were hidden as that their significance was belittled.

When children read fairy tales, they were assured that deliberate cruelty had departed from the world together with the wicked witches who once were believed to inflict it; when youngsters read history, they were assured that war, like the knight in armor, was a thing of the past; when students read novels, they were assured that the slum-born viciousness described by Dickens or Zola would disappear as soon as the slums gave way to new, inexpensive apartments (the word "housing" came into vogue only later). A few young people read Marx, but they were assured that the gross injustices of the early industrial revolution that had caused Marx to predict the collapse of capitalism were rapidly being corrected. A few read Freud, but they were assured that Freud's alarming discoveries about man's reason—that it was subject to influence by repressions—were nothing to get upset about, since Freud's discoveries also heralded a whole new era when children would be brought up without repression and would, therefore, be more reasonable and better equipped than anyone in previous history to live at peace with themselves and the world.

Niebuhr criticized not the entire substance of these beliefs; they held, he felt, a partial truth. But this partial truth was vitiated by the serious flaws in the two presuppositions that underlay them. One was the presupposition of man's "perfectibility," a theory dating from the Enlightenment that ascribed all forms of evil to some specific cause that itself was eventually correctible. The other was the presupposition that there was no free will, and that man, therefore, by way of science, was himself becoming predictable. Since man was wholly the product of his heredity and his environment, the reasoning went, a manipulation of these for the better would automatically result in a better man, a better society, and a world at peace.

Charles Fechner, in his book on Jacques Maritain, the distinguished

Catholic theologian who is an older contemporary and friend of Niebuhr's, noted that around the turn of the century,

> a belief in free will was so odd and naive . . . that anyone adhering to it was regarded, at the very best, as either a reactionary or a mystic.

Niebuhr, like Maritain, has been so regarded, and it makes him angry. Niebuhr hit back in the Living Library Volume: "It is incidentally one of the minor trials . . . to be described on occasion by ignoramuses, including even college presidents, as a 'neo-fundamentalist.' One cringes at such a description, for it shows that our culture knows of no distinctions short of the difference between the modern credo and a graceless and obscurantist version of Christian orthodoxy."

The modern credo had understandably assumed that the methods of science that had worked so dramatically in solving the problems of nature would work equally well with the problems of society; and its proponents did not doubt that as each problem was solved, there would automatically follow an improvement in society. Fechner continues his description of that period:

> these two ideas are rarely encountered one without the other: there can be no progress without science, and each fresh scientific discovery offers new proof of man's steady march to perfection.

Paradoxically, Niebuhr, in the process of attacking man's perfectibility, did not debase man, since he gave back to man the freedom and uniqueness that many modernists were denying. Copernicus, in a sense, had truly dethroned man when he insisted that the earth was not the center of the universe; Darwin, in a sense, had truly dethroned man when he insisted that human beings once shared a common ancestor with the primates;[3] but Niebuhr, who appears to dethrone man by insisting that man is not "perfectible," immediately re-enthrones him by insisting that one corollary to man's freedom is his responsibility.

Arthur Koestler, who does not agree with Niebuhr's presupposition that man's responsibility, in the ultimate instance, is to God, nonetheless

[3] In his posthumous *The Phenomenon of Man*, published in the United States in 1960, Pierre Teilhard de Chardin, S. J., appears to re-enthrone man to some extent by re-applying some of Darwin's theories in a way different from their originator's.

makes a telling point in this connection. In *The Invisible Writing,* Koestler explains why modern man was so reluctant to take back into the nest of his beliefs the doctrine of free will that had been wandering homeless since the growth of deterministic science. Writing on his own youth which came a little later than that of Maritain and Niebuhr, Koestler said:

> Determinism was already a lost position in my crumbling world. . . . But to abandon Determinism . . . did not necessarily mean that one had to accept the postulate of Free Will. There were several ways out, such as replacing the laws of causality by the laws of probability. . . . For to accept the concept of Free Will meant to accept ultimate responsibility for all one's actions. . . . It meant to accept an unbearable load of guilt and shame—without the comforts of an ethically neutral science.

Niebuhr had never known the comforts of an ethically neutral science. But he had, since early childhood, known the comfort of God's forgiveness, and through his parents, he had seen how faith in God's forgiveness makes possible the risk of action, and makes bearable the load of guilt that may follow from that action. The ethically neutral natural sciences, moreover, were never the thorn in Niebuhr's flesh that the social sciences came to be. The natural sciences, after all, were dealing with inanimate matter, plants, animals, and man in his dimension of finiteness, while the social sciences were attempting to deal with man in his dimension of freedom and with history which, for Niebuhr, includes this factor of freedom. His appellation of "wise men" when applied to the social scientists, therefore, usually denotes a flick of sarcasm. In *Christianity and Society*, Spring, 1949, for example, he wrote:

> The wise men of our day insist that human nature is flat. They run about with little measurements which can measure whatever is irrelevant but do not touch the heights and depths which are relevant. If we should ever fall into the deep abyss of an atomic conflict, we may be quite certain that on the night before the conflict begins some psychological association will bestow a medal upon an outstanding scientist for having found the key of eliminating aggressiveness from human life.

In return, the social scientists have defended both their scientific method and the ethical neutrality of its application to man and society. One of the best-written of the return attacks was in a review of Niebuhr's *Irony of American History* in *The Saturday Review,* April 5, 1952, by Frederick Burkhardt, then President of Bennington College:

> Dr. Niebuhr's philosophical convictions about human nature . . . enable him to make repeated thrusts at the social scientists. He seems to believe that because there are many aspects of human activity which are irrational, to seek rational, scientific insight into man's nature is therefore inane. He does not jibe at social science because it has produced so little, but because it is attempting the impossible. This is an attitude which is tenable only for those who are convinced they have access to a higher truth. Dr. Niebuhr's assurance on this score is apparent. This makes his book really an exercise in applying a set of fixed dogmatic beliefs to the contemporary human predicament. Since his dogmatism is roomier and subtler than most, it produces a number of interesting and worthwhile pronouncements.

One of these pronouncements by Niebuhr appeared in a paperback symposium called *Freud and the 20th Century,* edited by Benjamin Nelson. Niebuhr raised the question not about Freud's determinism as such but about Freud's individualism which Niebuhr felt underestimated the enormous variety of social pressures upon the modern person. According to Niebuhr, the self's freedom

> is of course not absolute. Retrospectively it is always possible to establish scientifically what pressures prompted the self to certain actions. It is only prospectively that the self is free. The moment it has acted, its actions become one in a chain of cause and effect. Freud is not to be criticized for his determinism as such, though probably for the consistency of his deterministic assumptions. But the primary problem of his determinism is that he finds the causative factors in a too narrow range of subconscious motives. Meanwhile the self acts in a large arena of events and forces in which the action may be prompted by any combination of causes on many levels of economic, cultural, ethnic and other interests. The freedom of the self is in fact partly due to its ability to choose between the pressures which seek to prompt its actions.

In one sense, therefore, the cave man had less freedom than we—because his choices were so limited—yet, in another sense, he had more freedom than we—because there were so few compelling "economic, cultural, ethnic" or other pressures upon him. Niebuhr is less interested in the person who conforms to society's pressures than in the person who does not. He might well say, with Dr. Zhivago, that "to run true to type is the extinction of a man." Among the people who refuse to conform to society, he points out, are those who rise above the standards of society as well as those who fall below them. Because Jesus rose above both the best system of law (Roman) and the best religion (Jewish monotheism) of his day, he was felt as a threat to the stability of society. It was no accident, therefore, that he was crucified between two thieves:

> So nations crucify their moral rebels with their criminals upon the same Golgotha, not being able to distinguish between the moral idealism which surpasses, and the anti-social conduct which falls below that moral mediocrity on the level of which every society unifies its life.

Niebuhr, therefore, also disagrees with Freud's theory that the superego is an almost automatic incorporation of the values of our society by way of our parents. The role of conscience, Niebuhr thinks, includes many more dimensions than Freud envisages. Freud "does not understand how the individual is creatively involved in the historic situations of which he is also the creature . . ."

Niebuhr furthermore takes a cheerful pleasure in the discovery by some psychiatrists that they themselves must rely on a form of free will in their patients which they have left no room for in their philosophy. In *The Self and the Dramas of History*, Niebuhr writes that "the emphasis put by modern psychiatry upon the voluntary cooperation of the patient and the futility of forcing submission to therapy" is but "another indication of . . . the reality of the freedom which has been denied."

Freedom has been denied by many psychological scientists, but not by all. Indeed some psychiatrists question whether Freud was as much against free will as his biographer implied. A strong case for belief in man's freedom was made by the psychoanalyst, Dr. Carl Binger, in *Pastoral Psychology*, December, 1955:

> Psychoanalysis, like the other biological and social sciences, operates, of course, on the principle of determinism. It strives to discover antecedent influences which will explain today's difficulties . . . But we must not deduce from this fact that psychoanalysis undervalues the subjective feeling of freedom which men experience when they are able to make choices and to carry out their intentions. On the contrary, it recognizes this feeling as an important hallmark of mental health. As was pointed out brilliantly by Dr. Robert Knight in 1946, the opposite of *determinism* is not free will at all, but *indeterminism* or pure chance, accident, unpredictability, in short, chaos. "Free will," says Dr. Knight, "is not on the same conceptual level as are these constructs" (i.e., determinism and indeterminism). "It refers to a subjective experience, and to compare it to determinism is like comparing the enjoyment of flying to the law of gravity."

Whether or not there is a feeling of freedom, there is, Niebuhr insists, a fact of responsibility. Biblically speaking, man is a coworker with God and as such bears responsibility for the results of his own actions, whether these results come directly or as by-products. This places a heavy burden upon man—and is one of the reasons why Niebuhr's version of biblical religion is anything but an "opiate."

Legally speaking, too, man bears responsibility for the results of his own actions although his motives may also be taken into account. Manslaughter, for example, is differentiated from murder, not because the victim is any the less dead, but because the motives of the perpetrator were different. On the other hand, to act as lookout during an armed robbery in which someone gets killed, is legally as much a capital offense as to pull the trigger. Thus, by and large, the courtroom assumption is that the accused unless insane must bear responsibility for the results of his actions, just as the judge and jury must bear responsibility for the results of their verdict.

The age-old paradox of freedom and responsibility is brought up to date by Professor Jerome Hall in *The Yale Law Journal*, May, 1956. If, he says, your purpose is to evaluate human conduct, then "some degree of autonomy is a necessary postulate." If, on the other hand, your purpose is not to evaluate but to understand human conduct, then "determinism is a necessary postulate." The scientist in the laboratory can operate on the hypothesis of no freedom, but if he is acting as advisor to the court, or as a jury member, he must operate on the hypothesis of some degree of freedom—and responsibility.

Niebuhr, in his life as well as in his thought, has operated on the hypothesis of both freedom and responsibility, starting at an early age.

7

The Anxious Student

DURING the spring and summer of 1913, after the death of his father, Reinhold Niebuhr returned from Eden Seminary every weekend to take charge of the Sunday services in Lincoln. The Church invited him to stay on permanently as pastor, but instead, with his mother's and sister's blessings, he applied for a scholarship to the Yale Divinity School. As his mother recalled, "taking on the Church and the duties at the Hospital would have been too much for him at that time. And besides, he needed to study. But," she added with firmness, "Yale was where he *had* to make good."

Reinhold Niebuhr's recollection of those days was recorded by the Columbia Oral Research interviewer:

> Our little denomination had the rule that upon graduation from the seminary we were to be sent to any congregation to which the synodical president might assign us, partially in payment for the free education which we had received.... It required months of negotiation to extricate myself from this implied promise and get the permission to postpone the fulfillment of the promise and go to Yale. . . . The standards of Union Theological Seminary were too high for me[1]. . . . Yale, at that time, had indifferent ones because the divinity school was building itself up numerically . . .
>
> At Yale University, of course, I got my first taste both of eastern life and of university life. I was thrilled by it. . . . It was also very thrilling to have good library facilities.
>
> I remember being conscious of the fact that the Easterners

[1] He therefore did not even bother to apply.

> would detect my Middle Western accent, which was at that time a little more marked than it is today. . . . I was glad to find that at Yale people were drawn from all parts of the country so that there was no typical New England accent that would mark us as Middle Westerners. Both at Yale and Harvard, the "college man" was set off from the "university man" . . . and the undergraduates had a proper scorn for the divinity students, partly because we were divinity students, and partly because we were drawn from these nondescript colleges all over the country. That didn't bother one very much when one was thrilled with the general university atmosphere.

But is must have bothered him a little, since he still remembers the inherently not-so-memorable fact that Archibald MacLeish was then chairman of the "Lit," and one of the golden boys on campus.[2] Nor are there many creatures more awe-inspiring to the young than the typical successful Ivy League college senior: usually tall, often good-looking, dressed with elegant casualness, sufficiently athletic to be graceful, well traveled, adept with the opposite sex, able to drink like an Elizabethan, if not an eighteenth century, gentleman, blessed with numerous friends among the equally successful, and confident, with an unfeigned masculine arrogance that is comparable to a newly unsheathed sword (the coming years may blunt it, corrode it, even snap it, or they may hone it to an extraordinary usefulness, but at the time of its first appearance it is conducive, in other young persons, to feelings of inferiority, envy, or rage).

Niebuhr, however, appears to have remained relatively unaffected. The contrast is striking between his response and that of John O'Hara, for example: O'Hara, also too penurious as a youth to afford Yale College, has continued to be haunted by its campus hierarchies to the point that most of his novels include at least one reference to Skull and Bones.

Why, at one time of life, is deprivation a wound, and at other times a spur? For Niebuhr it may be relevant that his early youth was spent within a joyous family of which he was a lively and appreciated part; and within a homogeneous community of which his family was a lively and appreciated part. Genteel poverty for a minister was not only no

[2] Others of these, besides MacLeish, with whom Niebuhr later became acquainted include Dean Acheson and Averell Harriman.

disgrace: it was, if anything, a badge of honor. Gustav Niebuhr, moreover, was not merely "the most interesting man in town" in the eyes of his son, but also one of the most respected men in town in the eyes of the whole community. Mrs. Niebuhr, too, was loved and admired. The world of a child is not a broad one, and within its confines Reinhold's position was that of a prince. On his own, furthermore, in school and college, he was effortlessly a leader, and so recognized by his contemporaries. The shining sword of his youthful confidence was probably in need of a good buffing by the time he got to Yale. And the switch from being a leading member of the majority to an unimportant member of a minority is a form of buffing from which people appear to profit more easily than if it were the other way around.

There were several minorities of which Niebuhr suddenly and simultaneously found himself a part. There was the minority of Middle Westerners in the heart of the insular East; there was the minority of penny watching in the heart of dollar insouciance; there was the minority of being partly second and partly fourth generation American in the heart of a New England community whose leading families were descended from the original settlers; there was the minority of being religious in the heart of a primarily secular institution; there was the minority of being in a graduate school when the majority were in the college; and most painful, perhaps, was the minority of Germanism in the heart of an area where German was almost unknown, and at a time when the very word, because of the Kaiser, was becoming more and more synonymous with enemy.

Even today Niebuhr does not respond with discernible enthusiasm when people, judging him by his Germanic name (one reader of an early article insisted that the name must be a nom-de-plume: it was too Germanic to be true), dart up to him with German phrases on their lips. And he almost winces when his name is, on occasion, mistaken for Niemöller's. On the other hand, his writings on Germany over the years have been remarkably objective.

His attitude toward Yale, too, seems to have remained objective: he has neither resented it for giving him what must have been some sad and lonesome hours, nor glorified it, as did his subsequent chief, the President of Union Seminary, Henry Sloane Coffin. In the late forties, for example, when an influential alumnus approached Niebuhr for permission to put up his name for consideration for President of Yale, Niebuhr was interested, but not tremendously so. He is reported to have said he would consider the offer most carefully, but thought it unlikely to materialize. His judgment turned out to be correct.

During the two years he was a divinity student, the Yale professors who most impressed him were Douglas Clyde Macintosh, Frank C. Porter and Benjamin Bacon.[3] As he told the Columbia Oral interviewer:

> I stayed on in the second year for graduate work, beyond the B.D. degree. . . . I applied for matriculation in the Graduate School . . . the Dean of the Graduate School, who was a German, said, after looking at my record, that he was sorry to have to tell me that if he would follow [only] my record he would advise me to enter as a sophomore at Yale College. . . . I had skipped from a classical high school to a seminary without having what we call liberal arts training in the sciences and literature. The deficiences were all as the head of the Graduate School said . . .
> However, this was 1914. He was a German. He went over to Germany for his vacation and he got caught up in the War. When I came back to Yale he was no longer there. Wilbur Cross [later, Governor of Connecticut] was Dean of the Graduate School. I went to him in the Fall, not telling him of my previous experience, and made another application. I awaited the answer with great anxiety. To my surprise, Dean Cross said . . . "I'll make a bargain with you. If you can maintain an A average, I'll enroll you as a special student and I'll matriculate you after you have maintained the A average."[4]

Despite holding down a part-time job in a small church in nearby Derby, Connecticut, Niebuhr did maintain the A average. But he none-

[3] Niebuhr did not always agree with Macintosh. At a dinner honoring Macintosh on his 60th birthday, Niebuhr suggested that Macintosh's next article be entitled, "My Former Students And Other Battlelines." In the Living Library Volume, however, Niebuhr voiced his gratitude to Macintosh for having "opened the whole world of philosophical and theological learning to me, lent books . . . out of his own library, and by his personal interest inspired a raw and timid student who had made his first contact with a great university."

[4] Some thirty years later when Niebuhr was given an honorary Doctor of Divinity by Yale, he walked in the academic procession with Governor Cross, who had not remembered the episode but was delighted to be reminded of it.

theless only stayed one more year: "Epistemology bored me . . . and frankly the other side of me came out: I desired relevance rather than scholarship." Also, "I received a letter from the President of my church who reminded me of the promise that I had made, asking if I wasn't about ready to take a church then. I decided to turn my back on teaching and go into the ministry. This was quite a serious decision . . . I was hesitant . . . but I made the decision."

The hesitancy, and the decision, and the young student's reliance on his perennially favorite professor, all appear in the yellowed packet of letters which Dr. Samuel Press saved for forty years: some are handwritten, some are typed, and only one carries the full date. The story they tell helps to put them in chronological order—and the year in which they begin is 1914:

Yale, March 2

Dear Professor:

Please excuse this old paper. I happen to be out of paper and wishing to answer you immediately I shall use it. Was very glad to hear from you. . . .

Of course I had intended staying here two years if possible but the thing looks doubtful now. You know I had just about enough money to get through this year and next year I could have taken a congregation but now since my illness cost me $300, I am just that much in debt and I don't see how I can carry that over next year. Of course my brother [Walter] is willing to help me and he makes enough to do it, yet I don't feel that I could accept his help. For while he earns a great deal he is in debt to the extent of thousands having bought his business without capital. I feel therefore that any help he gives me is retarding his growth and independence which he needs for his life's calling . . .

Another reason that seems to have made my stay inadvisable is that I am forgetting my German fast not because I don't read but because I never speak it. I'm afraid I won't have any German left by the end of next year. But at that I've about made up my mind that I will have to do most of my work in English. I'm tired of this halfway business. In Eden I was constantly conscious of the fact that I could speak neither English or German decently. I think I have improved my English a little but of course at the expense of the German. I've made up my mind that I *must* master one language to some degree at least . . . I have therefore applied myself to the English classics quite diligently lately. What do you think of my desertion?

Am glad to hear you say or see you write that two of our men should study every year. I heartily agree with you. The more I see how highly scholarship is prized in other denominations the more the penny-wise attitude of our church makes me sore. But what we need more than several special students is a *college* education for all of our students. The more I look at the thing the more I see that I have been cheated out of a college education. Elmhurst is little more than a high school. I thought once that I lacked only the B.A. but I have found since that I lack the things that make up a B.A.: philosophy, ethics, science and a real course in English. Everywhere around here they not only assume that you have a B.A. but they assume a fundamental knowledge of these college courses. I have bluffed my way through pretty well by industrious reading but I feel all the time like a mongrel among thoroughbreds and that's what I am.

I don't know if I'll ever have a voice in our church but if I will have, it will never be silent until our ministry receives an adequate education. I read recently the report of the synodal praeses before the general conference. It almost made me wild to think that the head of our church should in attacking modern theological science make the statement, that we who believe have long known all the books of the Bible to be genuine. This substitution of piety for critical inquiry shows where scholarship stands in a great part of our church.

I hope you will excuse this all too vehement an attack but it's been boiling in me so long that it had to come out some time.

It may have started boiling even before Niebuhr came to Yale, but certainly nothing at the University would have served to cool it down. In 1913, as George Charles Keller points out in his Ph.D. dissertation, the Yale Divinity School was trying hard to to make Christianity relevant to the twentieth century.[5] Biblical study was expected to be scientific and contemporary social conditions were analyzed in courses called

[5] Keller's dissertation for the Department of Public Law and Government at Columbia University is titled "The Political and Social Ideas of Reinhold Niebuhr."

"The Systematic Science of Society" and "The Modern Labor Movement."

Among the books Niebuhr was reading, he singled out for Professor Press the following as being "very good":

Sebatier (*sic*)	Outlines of a Phil. of Religion (the best of them all)
James	Varieties of Rel. Ex. (think you have this)
James	Will to Believe
Hocking	Meaning of God in Human Experience
Royce	The Problem of Christianity (just out)
Browne	Theism
Martineau	Types of Ethical Theories
Huba (*sic*)[6]	Psychological Study of Religion (very negative)

The next letter appears to have been written in 1914.

Yale University
April 6

DEAR PROFESSOR:

If I am not mistaken it is my turn to write and since I now have a typewriter I will write you a letter with less of the feeling that I am burdening you by making you read my scribble. The year is fast drawing to a close and I am very busy writing the various theses . . . These theses which they require in almost all graduate classes are splendid to make you do original work. For my B.D. thesis I have read I believe about fifty books. Am writing on "The Validity of Religious Experience and the Certainty of Religious Knowledge." . . .

Hope you will not think it traitorous if I tell you that I was somewhat tempted by an offer I received last week through recommendation of the Dean here. It was for assistant rector at the First Church of Meriden, Conn. at a salary of $1500 . . . I have of course no desire to quit [our] church and have often expressed contempt for men who did but when the offer came to me that may be better than I can have after years of labor in our church it made me think for a moment. But I will say nothing more of such things. They cannot interest you . . .

[6] Probably Leuba.

Niebuhr's worry about "such things" turned out to be well founded, as a letter, written probably in 1915, indicates:

The Courier-Herald Co.
Walter Niebuhr, Pres.
Lincoln, Illinois
June 11

DEAR PROFESSOR:

Thanks very much for your letter. I have not yet written to X. since hearing from Detroit. . . . I am so uncertain that I don't know what to write him. That I will have to take care of my mother seems now to be almost certain. Walter will probably never again settle down in Lincoln when he returns. He will leave his interest in the paper here in the care of subordinates and go out into the general newspaper world. This makes it essential that I take care of my mother. The place in Detroit pays $900 and this would of course be enough for me but not enough to take care of the family . . . Even if they would give me a thousand I could not make enough to pay my debts and support the family. It makes one feel very desperate to be so impotent after having spent two years in preparation. I rather feel that this extra preparation ought to entitle me to something a little better than the ordinary but that may be due to bad eastern influence. Perhaps I have been badly influenced by having several positions offered me which would make it possible to fulfill my obligations to my family. Now I am thrown into a curious complication of ethical considerations, duty to family, duty to church and friends. I shall do the best I can . . . I am burdening you again simply because I must unburden myself to someone.

The need to unburden himself further came within a month:

The Courier-Herald Co.
Walter Niebuhr, Pres.
Lincoln, Illinois
July 1

MY DEAR PROFESSOR PRESS:

I've been wanting to write you ever since I returned from school but did not know how to reach you . . . I received the M.A. degree as you may have heard though just exactly how it was done I am still unable to figure out. They turned down men with perfectly A.B. degrees though not of the highest class and gave the degree to me without anything that might be called a college education. I made pretty good marks but I did not think that it would pull me through . . .[7]

I am a good deal worried about my future. In the first place, as you may know, I have not gone for two years to Yale without absorbing a good deal of its liberalism. I have enough confidence in myself to believe that I did not simply fall prey to my environment. In fact I found that there is no distinctive Yale theology. What is being taught there is being taught in all the big schools of the country, Union, Oberlin, Yale, Andover . . . Now I am a good deal worried that my liberalism will not at all be liked in our church and will jeopardize any influence which I might in time have won in our church . . .

At present I am also worried about finances. X told me that he thought Detroit paid $900 a year. Since then I have heard that they only intend to pay $600. I will be frank enough to tell you that I will not accept a place for $600. I realize that I owe a good deal to our church, not to the church so much as to some of you individually who have done so much to help me. Any emphasis on finances may therefore seem to be the worst kind of ingratitude. But my two years at Yale have cost me a great deal of money. Most of it I earned, . . . but as you know I have debts. Besides these debts I will now have to carry some of the burdens at home. Since my father's death my brother has very nobly carried the financial burdens of our family in spite of the fact that he was deeply involved trying to establish a large business without a cent of his own to begin with. He has of course made a great deal but he has also needed a great deal. Now I feel that I owe it to him and to the family to . . . earn to the limit of my earning capacity . . .

I hope you have had a nice vacation after your strenuous year. I am about worn out from my year in Yale. I put in the hardest year of my life . . .[8]

[7] These "pretty good marks," according to his agreement with Dean Cross, must have been straight A's.

[8] In addition to his studies and his part-time jobs, Reinhold Niebuhr also entered an essay in the Church Peace Union's student essay contest, and won the prize: a hundred dollars.

During the summer Niebuhr may have had some rest, but soon he took on the burdens and challenges involved in his first parish:

> Detroit, Mich.
> Nov. 3, 1915
>
> DEAR PROFESSOR PRESS:
>
> It has been some time since you have heard from me and since I have heard from you. In the meanwhile, I went through quite a scrap with the Mission board. I was very sorry that I had to begin my work in this way. I was sent here under false pretenses but forced them to make good the promises they made to me. I was very sorry that thereby I was placed in the position of demanding something that has never been given to a young unmarried man before. But even for a man just graduating from Eden, $600 is too little for a metropolis where over half has to go for board. Perhaps it is a good thing therefore that I forced them to break this rule. They are now giving me $800 and the district board $100.

But out of that $900 he was forced to pay $540 in rent. "How could you *eat?*" a young minister asked years later. Niebuhr shrugged, "We couldn't, much."

There are no more letters from this period, but *Leaves* gives a vivid and continuing picture of the fledgling minister—he was only twenty-three at the outset—attempting in his first church, in his first great urban center, to battle the forces of injustice and depersonalization. In the process, he learned more than some people do in a lifetime about the depths and the heights, the danger and the glory inherent in that most paradoxical of earthly creatures, the human self.

8

The Anxious Self

NIEBUHR is far more patient with people who deny the existence of God than with people who deny the existence of an integral human self. These people, whether sociologists or psychologists, economists or political scientists, are guilty, in Niebuhr's eyes, of a serious mutilation of reality. It is to them he refers when he provocatively insists that although biblical religion tells many small lies in the interest of a great truth, science tells many small truths in the interest of a great lie.

One aspect of this great lie is the denial of man's free will; another is the denial of the individual's uniqueness; and both are included in the denial of the self's integral unity. Here Niebuhr's view is much like that of Jacques Maritain who wrote:

> The notion of personality . . . involves that of totality and independence; no matter how poor and crushed he may be, a person, as such, is a whole and subsists in an independent manner. To say that man is a person is to say that in the depths of his being he is more a whole than a part and more independent than servile.

In contrast, Niebuhr disagrees with Gardner Murphy, the well-known psychologist at the Menninger Clinic, who is quoted by Niebuhr in *The Self and the Dramas of History* as asking, and answering, the fundamental question about the self in a wholly different manner:

> Should the student of personality, at the present stage of research, posit a non-empirical entity, distinct from both organism and its perceptual responses to form and symbols, which is called a "self"? . . . A tentatively negative answer to this question seems advisable.

Tentatively negative, indeed. Niebuhr starts his counter-barrage slowly: "Mr. Murphy is too much of a realist to give more than a 'tentatively negative' answer." But soon the big guns are rolled forward. "The standards of [Mr. Murphy's] science will not permit any but a negative answer, though he promises that another answer might be given when 'the present stage of inquiry' is more advanced." Such a promise by Murphy cannot but mislead, Niebuhr continues, since it is evident that

> no advance in the inquiry will ever enable his type of empiricism to find the free and responsible self. It may be known in introspection and in dramatic encounter but not by methods of empiricism which make the self an "object" of empirical inquiry. It is a "non-empirical entity" only in the sense that it can not be seen through the spectacles of an empiricism, derived from the natural sciences. It is of course not distinct from either its "organism" or its "perceptual responses," i.e., its mind; but neither can it be equated with either.

How then, does one characterize this self that can only be known in introspection and dramatic encounter? "The self," Niebuhr says in the opening chapter of *The Self and the Dramas of History,* is "a creature which is in constant dialogue with itself, with its neighbors, and with God."

Knowing that the latter assertion will stick in the craw of many moderns, Niebuhr is willing to make what he calls

> some preliminary concessions to the spirit of contemporary empiricism and say merely that the self imagines itself in an encounter with the divine. For surely the persistence of this imagination is an empirical datum about the self.

What this "encounter with the divine" has meant to some people for some millennia in terms of grace, contrition, and awareness of sin, appears in Chapter 10; here it may be of interest simply to quote Martin Buber, the modern promulgator of "dialogue," to whom Niebuhr acknowledges his debt in *The Self and the Dramas of History.* Said Buber in *At the Turning:*

> The only element in the historic religions which the world is justified in calling upon is that intrinsic reality of faith which is

> beyond all attempts at formulation and expression but exists in truth: it is *that* which constantly renews the fullness of its presence from the flow of personal life itself. This is the one thing that matters; the personal existence, which gives actuality to the essence of a religion and thus attests to its living force.

In his own book, Niebuhr starts out by describing the self's dialogue with itself:

> Its accusations and defences of itself are quite different from those in which it engages in its external dialogues. The self pities and glorifies itself as well as accuses and excuses itself.

How does Niebuhr know? By doing intensive field work in the subject: by observing his own self with an eye so honest, so relatively objective, so filled with wry humor and dismay, that his thirteen year diary, *Leaves from the Notebook of a Tamed Cynic,* is well on its way to becoming a classic. At the time of its publication, in 1929, it was received with critical acclaim, and John Haynes Holmes in *The New York Herald Tribune,* offered its author a fine bit of indirect praise by saying it was a "pity" Niebuhr "should have been betrayed into giving a title to his book which does him such gross injustice! Dr. Niebuhr is not and never has been a 'cynic'; he is not, and I believe never will be, 'tamed.' "

In *Leaves,* ironically as it turned out, Niebuhr sometimes berated himself for indulging in the very kind of introspection that provided him with grist for his later analysis of the self and its various dialogues:

> If I were physically anaemic I never would be able to escape pessimism. This very type of morbid introspection is one of the symptoms of the disease. I can't justify myself in my perilous position except by the observation that the business of being sophisticated and naive, critical and religious, at one and the same time is as difficult as it is necessary.

Already the tension of being at the same time critical and religious was beginning. A quarter century later, in *The Self and the Dramas of History,* he further elucidated this tension:

> The dialogue within the self proceeds on many levels. Sometimes it is dialogue between the self as engaged in its various responsibilities and affections and the self which observes these engage-

> ments. Sometimes the dialogue is between the self in the grip of its immediate necessities and biological urges, and the self as an organization of long-range purposes and ends. Sometimes the dialogue is between the self in the context of one set of loyalties and the self in the grip of contrasting claims and responsibilities.

Even the most normal person therefore is constantly divided, though not split, into a minimum of two parts, the one, as Niebuhr calls it, the "engaging" (or acting) self; the other the "self-transcendent" (or viewing) self. Sometimes one part dominates; sometimes the other; but always, potentially if not actually, unconsciously if not consciously, they are in dialogue. Whether such steady internal dialogue exists in any other part of the animal kingdom, Niebuhr refuses to conjecture.[1] As he tactfully wrote to an old-lady poodlephile,

> In regard to the capacity of animals to conduct an internal dialogue, I am completely without ideas except that I think it is quite obvious that domesticated animals have taken over a great deal of the human dimension. I think my family would agree with you that this is particularly true of Poodles.

A simple example of dialogue in this "human dimension" might be the following.

If I am riding on the bus talking in a friendly way to my seatmate, and he mentions that he is coming down with a cold, my engaging-self will, almost automatically, pull away. Later I may realize that I hurt his feelings. I may then either rationalize my action by thinking I had no right to take home a germ to the family, or I may contritely resolve to use more self-control next time. In the latter instance, one could say that the self-transcending self was being less sinful than the engaging self. Yet, as Niebuhr shrewdly points out in *Discerning the Signs of the Times*, there is an immediate further danger:

> We judge the action of yesterday wrong in the contrite contemplation of today. But if that should give us an uneasy conscience we may regain our self-respect by the observation that what we are today must be virtuous. Otherwise we could not

[1] As depth analysis of dreams would indicate, our inner dialogue continues even—or particularly—when we are asleep.

> have found the action of yesterday contrary to virtue. Thus we never know anything against ourselves ultimately . . .

An example of the opposite would be the soldier who sees his buddy in danger and flings himself forward to rescue him. That would be the acting self at the pinnacle of agape or self-sacrificing love, a pinnacle that the viewing self may equal but never surpass. Indeed, in this case, it may not even equal it. For no sooner does the soldier return with his buddy in his arms than he may begin to look about in hopes that someone in authority has witnessed his action and will promote or otherwise reward him.

Thus the self-transcendent self can be a source either of contrition or corruption. There is no guarantee that by taking thought we can add one cubit to our moral stature. Sometimes, in fact, we may diminish it, as for example when we start congratulating ourselves on our selfless devotion to some great cause and quite forget that one of the reasons we consider this cause so great is that it is *our* cause. In addition, therefore, to the simple grasping selfishness of the primitive id, and the involuted self-centeredness of the superego, both of which Freud so graphically charted, there is also, Niebuhr says, an indefinitely expanding self-centeredness of the ego which Freud did not sufficiently explore. Indeed, what Freud called the "ego," as Niebuhr points out in *The Self and the Dramas of History*, can use all its various powers of reality-testing and of reason

> to justify its ends as well as to judge them . . . The chief difficulty in the Freudian analysis of the self is that it is blind to the resources for both love and self-love at the very heights of the human personality, rather than in a pleasure-seeking id.

Nor did Freud, in his theory of rationalization, see as clearly as did Marx, in his theory of ideology, that the self is also "blind to the resources for both love and self-love" in the values of its own society (some of which the self has incorporated). Niebuhr combines aspects of Freud's rationalization and Marx' ideology in his concept of interested reason (see Chapter 22). In simplest terms, this means that "the self is always the master, and not the servant, of its reason." At the same time, the self also feels itself

> under the necessity of seeking what it desires by proving that the desired is really desirable; or that what the self wants is in accord with some wider system of values than the self's own interest. These hypocrisies are the most telling refutations of one-dimensional views of selfhood.

They are hypocrisies, moreover, that tend to fool the self more often than other people. As Nietzsche noted, "the most common sort of lie is that by which a man deceives himself: the deception of others is a relatively rare offence." A particularly virulent form of the self's hypocrisy, Niebuhr says in *Discerning the Signs of the Times,* has been that of the religious leaders who identified their own system of values with the will of God:

> . . . we must not claim too much for our knowledge of God and His judgments. When we do, we merely make God the ally of our interested position in the scheme of things. Christian faith must contritely admit that the Christian, as well as every other religion, has frequently accentuated the fury of party conflict and increased the measure of human pretensions. It has done this to such a degree that secular idealists . . . have sometimes shamed the community of the faithful and have introduced more charity into the human community than they.

Not only were some religious leaders overly rigorous in imposing their doctrines on other people, but they were overly rigorous in applying these doctrines, without adequate qualifications, to the complexities of modern society. An accusing finger was pointed by Niebuhr at the leaders of the Christian church during the twenties when the ranks of labor, not yet organized, still included men who were working from twelve to fourteen hours a day, women who were jammed into sweat-shops, and children, tender in age and stunted in size, who were daily forced into the mines:

> A strong emphasis upon the doctrine of self-sacrifice has again tempted the church into a critical attitude toward the assertion of rights on the part of the dispossessed, on the ground that this represented an expression of selfishness.

Church leaders, in other words, must recognize that there are times when social justice can be more important than individual selflessness. And a quarter-century later Niebuhr wrote:

> We believe that Christians must be concerned not only with the integrity of individuals and with the spiritual quality of individual lives but with the structure of the human community on every level, from the local through the national and international community. We do not believe that individual goodness automatically solves any issue of social justice. The moral quality of a community is partly determined by the integrity and the moral concern of the individuals who comprise it; but it is also determined by the actual structures and systems through which its economic, social and political life is ordered.

Intelligent, discriminate judgment, therefore, is as necessary as moral fervor, particularly in economic, social and political relations. "Discriminate judgment," Niebuhr told a group of budding politicians during the Christmas vacation of 1953, "is the goal of education." And in a technical society, the self's dialogues need to be well-informed not only about the self, but also about the structure of the world in which the self is to play its responsible part.

To be well-informed about the self, Niebuhr believes, means to bear in mind the self's intermittent if not continuous anxiety. This anxiety stems from the basic incongruity of man's doubleness, from the fact, as Niebuhr says in an oft-quoted passage from the Gifford lectures, that

> man is both strong and weak, both free and bound, both blind and far seeing. He stands at the juncture of nature and spirit; and is involved in both freedom and necessity. His sin is never the mere ignorance of his ignorance. It is always partly an effort to obscure his blindness by overestimating the degree of his sight and to obscure his insecurity by stretching his power beyond its limits.

The anxiety that develops out of this insecurity may be temporarily assuaged: we gain all sorts of particular securities, of wisdom or virtue, of wealth or power, but none is ever quite enough, nor does it last. In regard to the security that comes from wisdom and virtue, Niebuhr writes,

> Man is anxious because he does not know the limits of his possibilities. He can do nothing and regard it perfectly done, because higher possibilities are revealed in each achievement . . .

And in regard to wealth and power, Niebuhr writes,

> There is no level of greatness and power in which the lash of fear is not at least one strand in the whip of ambition.

Anxiety, moreover, like Proteus, makes its reappearance in a multitude of forms. As Christopher Fry wrote in *The Dark Is Light Enough:*

> One always thinks if only
> One particular unpleasantness
> Could be cleared up, life would become as promising
> As always it was promising to be—
> But in fact we merely change anxieties.

This change, on the other hand, may be felt as a vast relief. Someone has defined a vacation as "a change of worries": others have found that facing up to their own anxieties meant changing these into more manageable forms. Niebuhr has done much to help people recognize the various forms that anxiety takes. He would agree, moreover, with Paul Tillich's statement that

> Religion now sees that having to live and die creates enough anxiety for man—and the problem should not be compounded with neuroses induced by condemnatory religion.

Actually Niebuhr would be the first to escort someone with a neurotic anxiety to the nearest good psychiatrist. He is well aware, as Dr. Paul Hoch has written, that a gross change in the *quantity* of anxiety becomes indistinguishable from a change in its *quality*. One of Niebuhr's frequent quotations is St. Paul's definition of the normal human condition as "perplexed but not unto despair." Although everyone may have ample grounds for perplexity and anxiety, it is rare, even in the turmoil of the mid-twentieth century, that anyone has realistic grounds for that unrelieved feeling of un-faith, un-hope, and un-love that psychiatrists call severe depression and laymen call despair.

According to some Christian dogma, despair is a serious form of sin in that it presupposes lack of adequate faith in God, and the act of suicide on the basis of despair is the unforgivable sin. In Niebuhr's view, suicide is wrong, except in unusual cases like that of Masaryk, because it assumes a Godlike omniscience on the part of the perpetrator, whereas the fact is that human beings who only "see through a glass darkly" can no more predict all out ruin than all out success. The assumption that they can, therefore, is likely to be a form of the sin of pride.

When Niebuhr uses the word despair he is referring to the miserable apathy or frenetic casting-about by normal people; he is not referring to despair as a symptom of mental illness.[2] His years of pastoral counseling have made clear the paradoxical effect religious faith can have on people suffering from serious depression: it sometimes accentuates their guilt for succumbing to despair (a despair that may be stemming from buried guilt) since they believe they ought to be feeling more faith than in fact they can.

Despair, moreover, even in normal people, Niebuhr says, can be a source of danger: it was partly the despair of the Germans following World War I that caused them to grasp at, and then cling to, the false gods offered by Hitler. At the same time, despair may be less dangerous to a nation than is the kind of overoptimism that prevents people from seeing, and thereby correcting in time, the flaws in their society that may be leading it toward catastrophe.

Niebuhr, therefore, warns against the phenomenon that psychiatrists too are constantly on guard against, namely, what appears to be too little anxiety, or anxiety too well-disguised. In its social form Niebuhr calls it optimism. In its individual form he calls it complacency or self-righteousness, and he points to its corrosive effect, not only on its host, but also on other people. For complacency may lead to indifference to the needs of others, and self-righteousness may lead to indifference to the freedom of others. Both involve a too inactive—or a too well-hidden—internal dialogue.

Thus a minimal degree of inner tension or anxiety, like a minimal degree of muscle tone, would seem to be necessary for the optimum functioning of the self. Anxiety, Niebuhr repeatedly says, is "the basis of all human creativity . . . as well as the precondition of sin. The destructive aspect of anxiety is so intimately involved with the creative that there is no possibility of making a simple separation between them."

No peace of mind, in other words, should be so complete that we

[2] The figures for mental breakdown among ministers appear to be rather high. Union Seminary, like many seminaries today, carefully screens its applicants and also offers a variety of courses in psychology.

cease our internal dialogue or our efforts to act responsibly in history. "Sin bravely," was Luther's advice, "and, more bravely still, believe." We can never be certain that our best efforts will result in good, but this is no excuse for remaining an observer when the times cry out for participants. To sit on one's hands is not a becoming posture for a free man in a free society.

To be an observer rather than a participant is also to avoid "encounter" —that form of dialogue wherein one or both persons are changed. Life is full of such encounters—and anxiety-arousing as they sometimes are, we must not, Niebuhr believes, except for short periods of recuperation, try to avoid them. For we are made to be in dialogue not only with ourself but also with our fellows, and ultimately with God. The Bible, in fact, is the record, not of a monologue on the part of God or man, but of a spirited exchange between them. The plants and animals were created docile and monological, but man was created with sufficient power of reason, freedom, and integrity to enter into a covenant (or two-way commitment) with the God of the Bible who must, Niebuhr says, "be defined as a person since he embodies both structure and a transcendent freedom." Thus, the Bible, in Buber's terminology, is a description of dialogues between an "I" and a "Thou," between God and man. God is defined as the "other," the "divine other," but not the "wholly other"; as being neither so impersonal as to be called an "It," nor so remote as to be unaffected by the actions of man. Man, in turn, is defined both as an individual and as a member of a group or "people."

In both dimensions, man has sufficient freedom to defy God and to deny God. Niebuhr does not agree with *The Hound of Heaven* analogy of God pursuing man "down the labyrinthine ways" until man is caught. Man, on the other hand, is also free to keep searching for God, even though his search appears to lead down a blind alley. Indeed, says Niebuhr, the man who tries to pray, and has, as did Lloyd George, "the feeling that there is no one at the other end of the line," may be closer to God than was the Pharisee who in prayer thanked God for making him "not as other men." The Pharisee clearly assumed that his prayer had put him into dialogue with God, but the Bible's words are, "he prayed thus with himself." The Pharisee's self-righteousness and complacency were unshaken by the experience of prayer, whereas the message of the Bible, as Niebuhr says, is that "the true God can be known only where there is some awareness of a contradiction between divine and human purposes."

Saul too was self-righteous and complacent when he set out for Damascus to reorganize the persecution of the Christians. But along the way he was confronted by God-in-Christ in an encounter so shattering that he revised his life, his religion and even his name.[3] From that experience the sickly Paul also received an infusion of strength sufficient to take his ailing body to the four corners of the then world despite physical and spiritual hardships culminating in martyrdom.

Thus the encounter with God which leads to new life may also lead to shedding some aspects of the old life or the old self. As Niebuhr says in *Discerning the Signs of the Times,*

> The self is always righteous in its self-analysis and secure in its self-esteem until it feels itself under a more ultimate judgment than its own . . . The only moments in which the self-righteousness is broken are moments of genuine prayer. Yet something of that broken spirit and contrite heart can be carried into the contests of life.

"Broken spirit and contrite heart" were the psalmist's words. To the modern mind that sees no cause for man to bend the knee to God or anyone else, these words might seem less objectionable if they were recognized as being the prelude to a new self-knowledge and wholeness that the self may never achieve by forgiveness of itself. Indeed the self's forgiveness of itself may lead to a greater self-righteousness or monologue, while the experience of God's forgiveness may lead to a new openness of the self to further dialogue with God and man.

It was, for example, not a man who had forgiven himself but one recently risen from agonizing prayer who summoned the courage to defy friend and foe, society and church, in order to defend each individual's right to search the Bible for himself, without mediation by clergy, and thus perhaps be "encountered" by God. "Here I stand," were Martin Luther's words: "So help me God, I can do no other."

Half a millenium later one of Luther's followers was described by one of *his* followers in these terms:

[3] Biblical scholars point out how frequently God emphasizes the uniqueness of the individual by asking for his name.

> One thinks of Niebuhr, in the first instance, as a present day spiritual and intellectual heir of the Old Testament prophets, St. Paul, St. Augustine, Luther, Calvin, and Kierkegaard.

With such a fine resounding quote a chapter could end, but not a chapter on Niebuhr, especially not a chapter on Niebuhr's view of the anxious self and its various dialogues. The quotation is therefore continued:

> And yet, Niebuhr has also been much concerned to do justice to the genuine insights of the Renaissance and humanistic liberalism. He is debtor not only to the biblical thought of Augustine and the Reformers, but also to the modern thought of Marx, James, and Freud. He characteristically works out his own position through a constantly critical intellectual dialogue with other thinkers of the past and the present.

And he started this outward dialogue with the members of his very first congregation.

9

The Man of God

DURING the thirteen years of Niebuhr's pastorate there, from 1915 to 1928, the city of Detroit grew threefold, from half a million to a million and a half, and Bethel Evangelical Church grew proportionately even faster, about tenfold. Of course, its congregation did start, as Niebuhr recalled in a Columbia Oral History interview, at a fairly low level:

> I had a rather amusing experience there. This was a very small little flock. When I came there they wanted to impress me . . . they invited the children from the neighboring orphanage and also the old people from a nearby home . . . I thought, "well, this isn't a bad congregation, except that the composition is a little curious." The next Sunday I awoke to the reality that this wasn't that kind of congregation at all, but just a little handful of twenty people. It was a handful of twenty people for some time. [This "twenty people," in effect, meant eighteen families, as *Leaves* makes clear.]

"For some time" was not very long. Within four years, the congregation was able to stand on its own feet financially and no longer needed missionary aid from the Central Church.[1] Within seven years, Bethel had moved from its small lot and chapel costing $8500 to an imposing new edifice on West Grand Boulevard costing more than $128,000. And by the time Niebuhr left, according to the religious magazine, *Advance*, Bethel's

[1] And one year later, in 1919, the congregation voted to discontinue the use of German in the services, being the first in the Michigan district of the Evangelical Synod to do so.

congregation had grown from 65 to 656, its annual expenses from $957 to $18,397, and its benevolence from $75 to $3889.[2]

Of inestimable help to the young pastor was his mother who moved from Lincoln to Detroit at the beginning of his term. As Niebuhr told the Columbia Oral Interviewer,

> My mother . . . was a remarkable person who was kind of an assistant to my grandfather and then to my father, and subsequently to me . . . In my parish in Detroit, she was, in effect, a parish deaconess. She also ran the women's meetings. She had great organizational skill. She made life rather sufferable for me as a young parson who didn't like to do this organizational work. I started very early to . . . give lectures in the colleges, all of which was made possible by the fact that my mother was, in effect, assistant pastor.

Mrs. Niebuhr, remembering these days, said, "the one place I'd like to go back to is Detroit."

That her son appreciated her help not only in retrospect but also at the time, is indicated by the first *Leaves* entry in 1915:

> Difficult as the pulpit job is, it is easier than the work in the organizations of the congregation. Where did anyone ever learn in a seminary how to conduct or help with a Ladies Aid meeting? I am glad that mother has come to live with me and will take care of that part of the job. It is easier to speak sagely from the pulpit than to act wisely in the detailed tasks of the parish. A young preacher would do well to be heard more than he is seen.

The problem of being *heard* turned out to be difficult too. After three months he was admittedly discouraged.

> Now that I have preached about a dozen sermons I find that I am repeating myself. A different text simply means a different pretext for saying the same thing over again. The few ideas that I had worked into sermons at the seminary have all been used, and now what?

It took some five years—until 1920—before a solution to this problem was recorded:

[2] This was a period of general church growth in the United States. According to W. W. Sweet in *The Story of Religion in America,* 1950, there were more costly churches built in the ten years following World War I than at any previous time.

> I am really beginning to like the ministry. I think since I have stopped worrying so much about the intellectual problems of religion and have begun exploring some of its ethical problems there is more of a thrill in preaching. The real meaning of the Gospel is in conflict with most of the customs and attitudes of our day at so many places that there is adventure in the Christian message, even if you only play around with its ideas in a conventional world.

In finding the nonpreaching aspects of the ministry difficult, Reinhold Niebuhr was not at all unusual, according to his mother. His early problems may have been standard, but from his point of view, they were still a source of distress:

> I am glad there are only 18 families in this church. I have been visiting the members for six weeks and haven't seen all of them yet. Usually I walk past a house two or three times before I summon the courage to go in. I am always very courteously received, so I don't know exactly why I should not be able to overcome this curious timidity.

Later, as his congregation and his self-confidence both grew, his approach became much speedier. One parishioner claims he could always tell when Pastor Niebuhr was coming to call. First would come the sound of a car screeching to a stop, then the sound of running feet on the porch, then the sound of the doorbell, and only after these, the sound of the car door slamming. The calls, though hurried, made a lasting impression on many a family, for Niebuhr's powers of memory and concentration enabled him to pick up the conversation where it had left off on the previous visit.

He came to be on intimate terms with a number of his families. Their reliance on his deep interest in them was symbolized by the small lad who called out in church, as the pastor was ascending the pulpit, "*Here* I am, Dr. Niebuhr."

Another child who saw the pastor only in church nonetheless felt so at home with him that he ran up in the street one day, and asked, "Where is your big black bathrobe?"

Niebuhr recorded his own feeling about this garment at the time:

> I found it hard the first few months to wear a pulpit gown. Now I am getting accustomed to it. At first I felt too much like a

> priest in it, and I abhor priestliness. I have become reconciled to it partly as a simple matter of habit, but I imagine that I am also beginning to like the gown as a kind of symbol of authority. It gives me the feeling that I am speaking not altogether in my own name and out of my own experience but by the authority of the experience of many Christian centuries.

On the other hand, he still strips off the gown at the first opportunity. While other ministers remain robed at least until after they have shaken hands with the departing congregation, Niebuhr somehow disposes of his gown before stationing himself at the church door.

While his sermons for adults were delivered only from short notes or none at all, his sermons for children were soon delivered only from a complete and carefully worded text. The possibility of misunderstanding by children became apparent early. One Sunday he tried to dramatize the power of habit by asking one of the boys, Frederick Ruttman, to come up front. After tying a string around the boy's two raised hands, Niebuhr told him to break it. With the string tied once, twice, even three times around, the boy was able to break it. But the fourth time, the string was too strong. The analogy to the force of habit, the pastor felt, was thoroughly clear.

After lunch the parsonage phone rang. "What did you do to Frederick this morning?" Mrs. Ruttman asked. "The children will do nothing but talk about the tricks the pastor did with Frederick."

Often Niebuhr turned the children's sermon over to his sister, Hulda, whose gifts lay noticeably in that direction. But he always kept his young men's Bible Class even though it too at first was discouraging. After a full year, he wrote:

> The young fellows I am trying to teach in Sunday school don't listen to me attentively. I don't think I am getting very close to where they live. Or perhaps I just haven't learned to put my message across. I am constantly interrupted in my talk by the necessity of calling someone to order. It is a good thing that I have a class like that. I'll venture that my sermons aren't getting any nearer to the people, but the little group of adults I am speaking to in the morning service are naturally more patient or at least more polite than these honest youngsters, and so I have less

> chance to find out from them how futile I am. But that doesn't solve the problem of how to reach those fellows.

Four years passed before the problem of how to reach them was on its way to solution and the pastor was on his way to learning the art of creative listening:

> I had a great discussion in my young men's class this morning. Gradually I am beginning to discover that my failure with the class was due to my talking too much. Now I let them talk and the thing is becoming interesting. Of course it isn't so easy to keep the discussion steered on any track. Sometimes we talk in circles. But the fellows are at least getting at some of the vital problems of life and I am learning from them. Disciplinary problems have disappeared. The only one left is the fellow who is always trying to say something foolish or smart in the discussion.

He found it easier, apparently, to deal with the problems of the young than the aged members of the congregation. For one thing he was himself still very young. For another, he could join their Sunday afternoon activities of soft-ball, tennis, or basketball.

There is disagreement among the observers as to the pastor's skill, but none as to the vast amount of energy he expended.

Even so, he had energy to burn. Otto Pokorny remembers that Reinhold and his mother

> were at our home very often for dinner, and on one of these occasions, he boasted of his physical prowesses, and then would attempt to show me that he was stronger than I, and we would wrestle right in the dining room. During one of these "bouts," his foot hit a glass panel in the china cabinet and cracked it. We never replaced it, often joking with him about it, and in later years, he still boasted that he could "take me on."

The problems of the very old and the hopelessly ill, unfortunately, do not lend themselves to solution via high spirits. Indeed the pastor often found himself both debilitated and frantic at the slow but irresistible approach of death:

> This sickness of Miss Z's is getting on my nerves. I can't think of anything for the rest of the day after coming from that bed of

> pain. If I had more patients I suppose I would get a little more hardened. Talk about professionalism! I suppose men get professional to save their emotional resources. Here I make one visit in an afternoon and get all done up. Meanwhile the doctor is making a dozen. He is less sentimental, but probably does more good.

"Probably does more good," but not certainly; for in addition to the areas of life where faith seemed of little or no account, other areas appeared where faith seemed of crucial account:

> A young woman came to me the other day—and told me that my talk on forgiveness . . . several months ago has brought about a reconciliation between her mother and sister after the two had been in a feud for five years. I accepted the news with more outward than inward composure. There is redemptive power in the message! I could go on the new courage that came out of that little victory for many a month.

The help the minister is able to offer his parishioners is perhaps less important than the manner in which he goes about offering it. Professor Press recalls an example of Niebuhr's manner that is, he says, virtually unique among ministers:

> To me it stands out as a most precious characteristic of a genuinely Christian pastor. His predecessor in the pastorate of Bethel Church told me that from time to time he would receive a communication from Reinhold Niebuhr, informing him of serious illness or a death in the home of a parishioner of Bethel and asking him as former pastor to write a message of comfort applicable to the situation.
>
> This trait of unselfishness in a pastor's relationship to his parishioners and, possibly even more, the mark of courtesy toward a predecessor is so rare, sad to say, that the action has few parallels.

The other chief recollection by Professor Press of Niebuhr's years in Detroit was that "his mind was always open and he was willing to learn from simple people as well as from world events."

World events were beginning to cast an ever longer shadow over the land.

War had erupted in Europe in July, 1914, shortly before Niebuhr came to Detroit, and every year the neutrality of the United States was further challenged, until finally, in April, 1917, we were at war. In 1918, Niebuhr was sent by the Church to visit some United States training camps:

> I hardly know how to bring order out of confusion in my mind in regard to this war. I think that if Wilson's aims are realized the war will serve a good purpose . . . but it is easier to talk about the aims of the war than to justify its methods.
> Out at Funston I watched a bayonet practice. It was enough to make me feel like a brazen hypocrite for being in this thing, even in a rather indirect way. Yet I cannot bring myself to associate with the pacifists . . .

He was pushed closer to the pacifists by the Versailles Treaty whose aims were, at least partially, the achievement of revenge, and whose means were, at least partially, more secret and selfish than the American people had suspected possible:

> Gradually the whole horrible truth about the war is being revealed. Every new book destroys some further illusion. How can we ever again believe anything when we compare the solemn pretensions of statesmen with the cynically conceived secret treaties? Here was simply a tremendous contest for power between two great alliances of state in which the caprice of statesmen combined with basic economic conflicts to dictate the peculiar form of the alliances.

The climactic push toward pacifism came in 1923 when Niebuhr was invited to join one of Sherwood Eddy's traveling seminars and, together with Will Scarlett and Kirby Page, visited the Ruhr. At first they had trouble, Scarlett recalls, obtaining an entry permit—the French in retribution against the Germans had sealed off the Ruhr—but finally, by dint of their United States passports and their eloquence, they were able to cross the border one evening around supper time. So did a Russian communist with a very heavy suitcase. They did not like being followed by him as they walked through the strange and rapidly darkening countryside. They stepped up their pace. At first he huffed and puffed and tried to keep up. But their youth and long legs and relative unencumberedness were too much for him, and he finally fell back, a perspiring symbol of many another Marxist who would try in later years to follow Niebuhr's reasoning and be forced to choose between dumping his ideological baggage or being left behind.

The three Americans stayed in Essen several weeks. They had a letter to the head of Krupp who was, according to Scarlett, so facinated by the American minister with the flawless German that he kept reinviting them. Partly as a result of the young men's urgent report, the American Red Cross in Berlin was alerted to the desperate need for food of the Germans in the Ruhr. At the same time, Sherwood Eddy joined James H. Causey, a banker from Denver, in forming a committee to raise $500,000, in order, as Eddy later described it, "to keep trainloads of food flowing into the distressed area by a system of revolving credits . . . We fed the Ruhr during the entire French occupation."

From Essen which was under French control, Scarlett and Niebuhr went on to Cologne which was under the British. From there the two intrepid voyagers set off for London by air, neither having flown before. Pale of visage, according to Scarlett, they solemnly shook hands with each other before boarding the same plane. Once aloft, they forgot their fear in the fascination of watching the earth change as they were lifted above it. Niebuhr still uses the analogy of an airplane to exemplify the self's transcendence over its past self, at the same time that it is neither wholly transcendent over its present self, nor wholly blended into what the mystics call the ineffable, wherein all earthly and historic distinctions disappear.

Niebuhr's own view of the Ruhr visit appears in *Leaves:*

> I have been spending a few days with S and P in the Ruhr district. Flew back to London from Cologne by aeroplane. The Ruhr cities are the closest thing to hell I have ever seen. I never knew that you could see hatred with the naked eye, but in the Ruhr one is under the illusion that this is possible. The atmosphere is charged with it. The streets are filled with French soldiers in their grey-blue uniforms. Schools have been turned into barracks. Germans turn anxious and furtive eyes upon every stranger. French officers race their automobiles wildly through the streets with sirens blowing shrilly. If you can gain the confidence of Germans so that they will talk they will tell you horrible tales of atrocities, deportations, sex crimes, etc. Imagination fired by

> fear and hatred undoubtedly tends to elaborate upon the sober facts. But the facts are bad enough. . . .
> This is as good a time as any to make up my mind that I am done with the war business. Of course, I wasn't really in the last war. Would that I had been! Every soldier, fighting for his country in simplicity of heart without asking too many questions, was superior to those of us who served no better purpose than to increase or perpetuate the moral obfuscation of nations. Of course, we really couldn't know everything we know now. But now we know. The times of man's ignorance God may wink at, but now he calls us all to repent. I am done with this war business. I hope I can make that resolution stick.

The resolution, however, never fully stuck. Even at the height of Niebuhr's pacifism, he wrote an article for the *Atlantic Monthly* (May, 1927) which included serious criticism of the pacifist position, noting, for example, how much more appealing pacifism was in the "have" nations than the "have not."[3] And when he subsequently became chairman of the pacifist Fellowship of Reconciliation, he was never in full accord with their ideas, and soon resigned (in the early thirties). As Scarlett recalls, "it took Reinie about ten years to change his mind. It was the cumulative events in Europe leading to Hitler that made him reject his pacifist position." Yet even after rejecting it, Niebuhr was able to recognize pacificism's perennial value as the far pole of religious perfectionism. In *Radical Religion*, Autumn, 1937, he wrote:

> Though, as is generally known, this journal does not accept pacifism . . . it is nevertheless obvious that pacifism in the modern church has something of the same functions as asceticism in the medieval church . . . the church would be the poorer and its counsels in greater danger of corruption by popular hysteria if it lacked the pacifist testimony. War is such a terrible catastrophe in modern life that anyone who participates in it ought to do so only with a very uneasy conscience; and his conscience ought to be kept uneasy by the influence of those who find it impossible

[3] During that same year he noted ruefully that "perhaps my pacifism is related to the pacifism of the beast of prey whose maw is crammed." (*Christian Century*, December 15, 1927).

> to reconcile war with Christ. In that sense pacifists are not fools to be tolerated . . . but witnesses which must be heard.

It was in 1933, ten years after the young men's trip to the Ruhr, that Hitler came to power. Dean John Bennett of Union Seminary believes that Niebuhr's break with pacifism came slightly earlier and "in the context of political coercion in the class struggle rather than in the context of international war." (Knowing Niebuhr's penchant for duality, it seems safe to assume it came from both.)

Bennett also includes an interesting conjecture as to why Niebuhr was attracted to the extreme position of pacifism to begin with:

> I have always wondered if one element in his own feeling about life . . . is not a hidden disappointment that the perfect goals are not within reach . . . It may be true that the vigor of Niebuhr's attacks on perfectionism comes partly from the fact that he has always been much tempted by it. He preserves the perfectionist element in Christianity in his own statement of the nature of Christian love . . . and in the tribute that he pays to the perfectionist forms of pacifism which make no claims for the applicability of pacifism to political life.

One application of thoroughly modified pacifism to political life was that of Gandhi in India. Gandhi's passive resistance against the British overlords was as much resistance as it was passive. And as Niebuhr pointed out, it worked as well as it did because the British had reachable consciences. It would presumably not have worked against the proconsuls of a fanatic like Lenin or a criminal like Hitler.

Domestically, pacifism found its optimum application to political life, Niebuhr felt, in the Alabama bus-boycott of 1955-56. In *Christianity and Society*, Spring, 1956, Niebuhr wrote the lead editorial in praise of its organizer, the local leader of the Fellowship of Reconciliation, Martin Luther King:

> [King] scrupulously avoids violence and calls his strategy the "way of love." It is the most effective way of justice. Those of us who are nonpacifists[4] will be quick to admit that whenever pacifism . . . is not preoccupied with moral scruples about guiltless-

[4] Nonpacifist seems a mild term for one who has been described by others as "the sharpest critic of pacifism in the American Church."

> ness . . . whenever it does not occupy itself with the problem of contracting out of responsibilities of justice in the name of perfection. . . it becomes impressive.
>
> In the case of the Montgomery boycott the most obviously effective way of bringing pressure for the sake of justice has been adopted. Violence in any local situation is not only wrong but self-defeating. In the case of a Negro minority in a white society it would be suicidal. The boycott and the strike are recognized forms of pressure in a free society, but the boycott is unfortunately not as widely recognized legally as the strike. Hence the court proceedings against the Negro boycott leaders. But it is very obvious that even in a just and free society there must be forms of pressure short of violence, but more potent than the vote, to establish justice in social relations.

The need for establishing a minimal form of "justice in social relations" was laid, like a foundling, on Niebuhr's doorstep in Detroit:

> We had a large Negro population which grew tremendously with the automobile industry . . . I subsequently became the chairman of the mayor's committee on racial relations. We had a rather long struggle to provide what one might call elemental justice to a growing Negro group, emphasizing equality in jobs, housing, and so forth.

As a result of Niebuhr's efforts on the racial front, four Negro families came regularly to his church. They were professional people, and most members of the Bethel congregation were pleased to have them.[5] But the Negroes maintained positions of responsibility in their own churches, and both they and their churches rejected the idea of their officially joining Bethel. Niebuhr took up with his official board the question of such membership. The board was willing, but the Negroes never came to be.

[5] D. R. Davies, in his otherwise accurate small book on Niebuhr (*Reinhold Niebuhr: Prophet from America*, London: J. Clarke & Ltd., 1945), deduced from Niebuhr's sympathy with the laboring class that his church membership must have been primarily "workers." This statement caused some eyebrow-raising among the professional and business people who in truth had made up a large part of Niebuhr's congregation. There were, of course, laboring people too, but the majority was middle class. Among the business group, several were very well off and one was a multimillionaire. So great was this man's generosity that Niebuhr felt forced on one occasion to ask him to reduce his gift lest the other donors feel their participation dwarfed by comparison.

It was therefore the general racial situation in Detroit, rather than a particular one in his church, that brought about Niebuhr's involvement in the world of practical politics:

> The Mayor who appointed me [chairman of the Committee on Racial Relations] was a rather unsavory politician who combined what has subsequently become rather apparent in American municipal politics—that is, liberal attitudes on racial and economic affairs, with a certain lack of scruple in the mechanics of politics. I greatly shocked some of my Christian friends—pastors and others—in accepting a position under this rather unrespectable political figure . . .
> The vice chairman of my commission was a Jewish lawyer . . . Through him I established contacts with the Jewish community and from him I learned another aspect of American democratic life—the cooperation across a religious line. I learned, incidentally, the very great resources that the Jewish community has in its passion for practical justice.

This lawyer, Fred Butzell, was an important influence on Niebuhr during the Detroit years. As Niebuhr recalled in the unpublished *Later Leaves* thirty years afterward:

> Butzell was the most remarkable man I have ever known. He could combine a gentle cynicism with the spirit of charity because he knew himself as well as other people. He knew what made people tick. But his almost clairvoyant knowledge of human character was free from malice because he was so little self-deceived . . . Butzell and his brother, Judge Henry Butzell of the Michigan Supreme Court, [had established] a law-firm, most of the junior partners of which had been put through college by Fred. Fred instructed the Principals of all Detroit High schools to put him in touch with the brightest Jewish lads in the graduating class. Fred thereupon made a proposition to these lads. He offered to "invest" in their life. He told them he would lend them enough money for college and graduate school, and they could repay him when they were professionally established. Most of Fred's investments went to the Harvard Law School, and a goodly number of them subsequently became his partners. Fred's practice was large but mostly unremunerative . . . His waiting room was always filled with poor people, or mostly poor people.

Another person who was of great influence on the young Evangelical pastor was the Episcopal Bishop of the Diocese of Michigan:

> Bishop Charles D. Williams was . . . a man of extraordinary integrity and courage and he dared to insist that workers required collective bargaining in a city in which all the new industrialists were insistent that the future of the auto industry required the kind of autocracy which had grown up with the rising industry. Some of the wealthy men of the Diocese, being very uncomfortable under a Bishop who insisted in speaking about problems of justice in industry, declared the boycott on the missionary budget. The Bishop challenged with his resignation, which the Diocese could not afford to accept without advertising the subservience of the Church to "big business."

Here, in the eyes of some observers, was an indication that power must, on occasion, be challenged if justice is to prevail. Although the Bishop had no intention of using his resignation for any ulterior purpose, his threat to resign may have had the effect of a one-man strike. In all events, the workers about whom he was so concerned were in a pitiful state, as Niebuhr was steadily growing more aware: "Thousands in this town are really living in torment while the rest of us eat, drink and make merry." Niebuhr therefore supported the labor leaders and also the political candidates who were trying to bring about better working conditions through government action.

In 1924, Jane Addams asked Niebuhr to chair the large Detroit meeting for La Follette for President. At last the small boy on the Chautauqua front bench could mount the stage and speak out. It was Niebuhr's first involvement with politics on the national level; he was never, thereafter, to withdraw from that involvement.

Niebuhr's energies were expanding in several directions at once. In addition to the growing work of his church, and the growing fight for social justice, there were steadily more invitations to speak in the colleges and universities, to secular as well as religious groups. His acceptance of these out-of-town invitations was made possible largely by Sherwood Eddy, a leading figure in YMCA, who once heard Niebuhr speak and was so impressed that he contributed sufficient money to Bethel Church to hire an assistant and thus free Niebuhr to be a roving ambassador from the religious community to the academic one. Certainly Niebuhr was an enthusiastic ambassador. He enjoyed the contact with young minds, the clash of argument, the chance to see new places. In 1926 he voyaged to Harvard for a preaching engagement. His salary by that time had risen to $3000 a year, but out of it he was expected to pay a Sunday pulpit-substitute for Bethel. All told, his expenses came to considerably more than Harvard's $25 honorarium. He was out of pocket, but not out of sorts: "I didn't mind," he told Scarlett, "because the greater the university, the more it could count on prestige rather than cash to get the people it wanted."

His prestige as a writer was also increasing. His first article in a national magazine (*The Atlantic Monthly*) was published in 1916; his chief recollection: "Sixty dollars looked so big." During the next twelve years he published some forty articles, mostly in *The Christian Century, The World Tomorrow,* and *The Atlantic,* as well as unsigned editorials for *The Christian Century;* his recollection of that type of assignment: "There was nothing I wanted so little as anonymity."

Anonymity was well on its way out of his life, but not bachelorhood. *Leaves* contains a few wistful references to his longing for a family of his own. But his financial situation was not conducive to taking on added responsibilities, and no likely candidate presented herself; nor was there time for him to go a-searching:

> The old Methodist preacher who told me some time ago that I was so cantankerous in my spirit of criticism of modern society because I am not married may be right. If I had about four children to love I might not care so much about insisting that the spirit of love shall dominate all human affairs. And there might be more value in loving the four children than in paying lip service to the spirit of love as I do.

In addition to insisting that the spirit of love should dominate human affairs, Niebuhr was probing some of the reasons why it did not. And much of this probing led back to God the Creator, who had given to man freedom sufficient to love himself inordinately and thereby to accomplish evil as well as good.

10

The God of Man

IF Niebuhr's dual method of paradox can be compared to a pair of railroad tracks running parallel until they appear to meet in the distance, Niebuhr's conception of faith can be compared to a full circle.

He himself refers to the circular relation between faith and repentance. For unless a person has some initial faith in God's forgiveness, he is unlikely to face up to the depth of sin in himself; and unless he faces up to the depth of sin in himself, he is unlikely to feel the repentance which can result in God's forgiveness and the grace of a "new life." Somehow, as it were, the climactic tension of the self's dialogues with itself, with its fellows and with God, is dissolved into a momentary blessedness and a renewal. To those who have experienced it, even once in their life, it is as unforgettable as it is inexplicable: the self feels itself simultaneously taken out of itself and also most truly itself, while God is simultaneously known as judge and forgiver, not only of the individual but also of the whole human enterprise within which the self must lose itself to find itself.

Niebuhr is never very explicit about this experience of God, although to him it is presumably of central importance. To those who have themselves experienced it, he can easily communicate; to those who have not, he perhaps feels he cannot convey its essence in words (and in the interest of privacy, he has no desire to try). Yet he did not in any way criticize the short attempt at describing it by E. A. Burtt in the Living Library Volume, while he did criticize other aspects of Burtt's chapter. Said Burtt,

> To the individual who passes through it it is indeed a new birth. He feels himself to have been saved from the death that is the inevitable consequence of unresolved inner conflict . . . what we

> have here is a human transition from a state marked by conflict, feelings of guilt, a sense of helplessness (perhaps even despair) to a state of release from guilt, of achieved integrity, of strength, of happiness.

Before there is the release, however, there must have been the buildup: the self must first and painfully have searched itself and all of its resources and found something vital lacking. As Niebuhr says in *Faith and History*, "God must be experienced as 'enemy' before he can be known as friend." So excruciating is the experience of God as enemy that it can scarcely be included in the atheist's rubric that religion is but wishful thinking on man's part. For no man but a masochist would wish on himself such an experience. At the same time, Niebuhr believes, this experience is a necessary one. Or, as Paul Scherer writes, "for Niebuhr there can be no justification by faith until optimism breaks down and men cease to trust in themselves that they are righteous." Not merely are one's best efforts—and one's nation's best efforts—felt to be shamefully inadequate, but seemingly impossible demands for the future may be felt to be imperative. Some of the greatest Old Testament prophets responded to the Lord's felt command by an impassioned plea to be released from it. And Jesus' words in the Garden of Gethsemane were, "let this cup pass from me"; he was forced to wrestle with himself all night before he was ready to say, "Thy will not mine be done."

On the other hand, the experience of being judged and found wanting by God almost presupposes some faith that the God before whom all hearts are open will not only understand but also forgive. John Bennett minces no words about Niebuhr's attitude in this regard:

> If one faces the truth about the human situation, about oneself, with full honesty and realism along the lines suggested by Niebuhr's doctrine of man, it is difficult to live with what one sees unless there is some understanding of justification or forgiveness.

It may therefore be the lack of such "understanding of justification or forgiveness" on the part of many moderns that keeps them from facing the truth about the human situation and about themselves along the lines suggested by Niebuhr's doctrine of original sin.

On the other hand, those religious people who consider God's forgiveness to be a secure possession, to which they renew their own title each time they obey a commandment or go to church, are more wrong, Niebuhr believes than are the secularists. He blasts the complacency of the kind of believers whom Buber calls "the happy possessors," and agrees with him that, instead, the life of faith must be a life of "holy insecurity."

This holy insecurity in Niebuhr's own life has been described by a colleague as a "continual inner dialogue between faith and doubt." Niebuhr himself traces its beginnings to the first years in Detroit. In 1956 he wrote to a young man considering becoming a minister:

> There were years in my early ministry where I did not have specific experiences of doubt but a rather general experience pervading everything, which I expressed scripturally in the words, "I believe, Lord, help Thou my unbelief." I did not find any rest for this condition in which all the young people in my generation found themselves until it became clear to me that by the nature of the human and the divine self there cannot be a "rational" validation of religious experience. Religious faith must remain to the end, on the one hand, in Pascal's phrase, "a great gamble while it is on the other hand a certainty based on an accumulation of experience." Pascal, living in a rationalistic century dominated by Descartes, was incidentally my best guide as he has been the guide for many in our generation.

Just because religious experience cannot be rationally validated, however, is no excuse for God to be clutched as a secure possession or for reason's questioning to be ignored. In the Living Library Volume, Niebuhr points out that in this direction false faith, or idolatry, lies:

> We must confess the significance of the long history of religious fanaticism, and must admit that a religion which has triumphed over idolatry in principle may in actual fact be made an instrument of partial and interested perspectives. Without such admission the humility of a genuine scientist and the measured common sense of the man of affairs, who knows his ends to be in conflict with other legitimate ends, are superior to the wisdom of Christians.

Fanaticism is one hazard; another is the conventional piety against which Kierkegaard fulminated. Kierkegaard quoted the scriptural passage where God's attitude toward man's faith is described in these terms: "Oh, that thou wert either hot or cold, but since thou art lukewarm, I shall spew you out of my mouth." *Hot* can be applied to the person overflowing with the new life of faith; *cold* can be applied to the person who simply cannot find evidence that God either created, or cares about, a poor small creature on a poor small planet; but *lukewarm* means something quite different. To Niebuhr it means monologue, an unwillingness to ask questions lest the answers be too upsetting, a retiring into religiosity. To Kierkegaard, these "philistines," as he called the conventionally pious, were unreachable by true faith because they were convinced they already had it—or, in Barbara Ward's telling phrase, "men rarely learn what they think they already know."

Since unidolatrous faith comes in such large part by grace, Niebuhr is inclined to credit the Holy Spirit when people achieve it, and not to blame the people who do not. As he wrote to an agnostic friend in 1955,

> I have never worried too much about the non-believing saints, that is, I haven't worried about the fact that their saintliness was not related to an explicit faith. I think it is part of "the hidden Christ." Life is a very mysterious thing and some have found the key to it without explicitly knowing it, while others have found explicit keys which are so filled with illusion as to make them less graceful than the unbeliever.

This concept of the "hidden Christ" appears, almost hidden, in a footnote of the Gifford Lectures (Volume II, p. 109). There, Niebuhr says:

> A "hidden Christ" operates in history. And there is always the possibility that those who do not know the historical revelation may achieve a more genuine repentance and humility than those who do. If this is not kept in mind the Christian faith easily becomes a new vehicle of pride.

His emphasis, therefore, is not on saints without faith, but on sinners with faith. And counting himself among their number, he explains the implications of the "truth in Christ":

> In every experience of life, Christ appears in many guises to the believer. He is the judge in comparison with whom I am found to fall short and to be an unprofitable servant. He is the redeemer

> who gives my life a new center of loyalty and a new source of power. He is, however, also the law, the logos, the essential structure of life which I must seek to obey, even though I fall short in my obedience. He is what I am essentially, and therefore what I ought to be.

Thus a single experience of faith, crucial as it may be, may also, in the long run, be less significant than "a life that is based on faith." As Niebuhr wrote to the same young man, who finally decided he would go into the ministry,

> Experiences are fleeting. Sometimes one has a strong awareness of the ultimate mystery of the divine, and sometimes one is troubled by what mystics call periods of dryness. For me the main point is that the experience of faith is a total attitude toward the mystery of God and life which includes commitment, love and hope.

At the Seminary he has been heard gruffly to complain about "some of these first-year students who expect the experience of God every time they get down on their knees." Other times, he grows impatient with people whose religion is so moralistic, or whose rationalism is so inclusive, that all mystery for them is banished from life and history. These people, different as are their preconceptions, agree on neatly correlating what *does* happen in life and history with what, according to their version of "law," *should have* happened. Niebuhr counters them by insisting that God is not limited to what makes sense to human reason. Indeed he agrees with Augustine that a God wholly comprehensible to man would not be much of a God.[1] At the same time, he believes that God is not, on that account, wholly mysterious to man: God is *Deus Absconditus*, but he is also *Deus Revelatus;* God has disclosed through his encounters with individuals and peoples, and through significant events of history, an intention that is real and perennial. This intention can be apprehended not by man's reason alone but by man's whole self:

[1] Niebuhr said in *Faith and History*, "The idea of a source and end of life, too transcendent to the desires, capacities, and powers of human life to be either simply comprehended by the human mind or easily manipulated for human ends, represents the radical break of Biblical faith with the idolatrous tendencies in all human culture."

> If the disclosure [by God] is . . . apprehended in repentance and faith it will . . . lead to a reformation of life. It cannot be apprehended without repentance, because the God that stands against us . . . cannot be known if we do not abate the pretension of reaching God by our thought or of regarding His power as an extension of our power.

On the other hand, Niebuhr insists, human reason must not be jettisoned in favor of uncritical acceptance of whatever is handed down by some religious authority. Niebuhr is likely to be most impatient with people who misquote Tertullian and say, "I believe because it is absurd."[2] On the other hand, what appears to man as absurd may not always be false. We need the whole of our experience in order to judge which absurdities to reject and which to go on living with. For example, it appears quite absurd that all the world, ourselves included, should be made up of colorless, odorless particles. Yet, modern technology is based upon that assumption. Similarly, there are absurdities in the Bible that we may reject, and others upon which we may base our life. Among the latter, for Niebuhr, is "the absurdity of a suffering Messiah":

> This absurd doctrine of the God-man Christ contains the whole essence of Christian faith—its belief that God transcends history and yet makes himself known in history; that history as measured by Christ is tragic and ends tragically for it crucifies Christ; that only God is able to resolve the conflict in which all men stand; that God cannot do this by simply wiping out history and transmuting it into eternity, but by redeeming history, but that the redemption of history involves more than persuading man to follow the law of God. It involves God's taking upon himself the inevitable violation of the law.

"Absurd" as is the doctrine that God thus suffers, people still need to use their faculty of reason to distinguish between the false and true versions of this doctrine: "Rational discrimination," says Niebuhr, is a "resource in distinguishing religious visions which are in the service of human pretensions and the 'word of the Lord' which punctures all human vanities."

[2] Tertullian's words have a somewhat different connotation: "Certum est quia impossibile est."

The puncturing of human vanities is felt subjectively; but its results may be visible objectively: they reveal themselves, Niebuhr says, in a "humility and charity . . . an absence of pride and pretension." These qualities are, however, more discernible in the simple decisions of personal life than in the complex decisions of communal life. Niebuhr smilingly quotes a Dutch theologian he met at the Ecumenical Conference in 1948, who said that the religious quality of a Christian's life can be seen in his marital and business relationships more clearly than in his political judgments, since the former are likely to be trustworthy and the latter not necessarily so.

Reason is essential too, Niebuhr believes, in discerning the majestic dramas of history through which God's judgment and mercy become manifest to the eyes of faith. These continuing collective encounters with God are precisely what refute the belief of those pious individualists, or dogmatic rationalists, who see in every event a neat rewarding of personal virtue or intelligence, or an exact punishment of personal sin or stupidity. In rebutting them, Niebuhr likes to quote the passage from Luke, 13:4, in which Jesus asks a rhetorical question and answers it with vehemence:

> . . . those eighteen upon whom the tower in Siloam fell and killed them, do you think that they were worse offenders than all the others who dwelt in Jerusalem? I tell you, No.

And to the class graduating from Union in 1957, Niebuhr said,

> We build falsely on true foundations if we try to mediate the grace of the Christian faith through slogans and clichés or if we try to quiet anxious hearts through spurious appeals to special providence which is supposed to protect the faithful. For the Gospel gives no special securities or exemptions from the frailties of men and the tragedies of life.

This was the special providence William James derided when he spoke of "lobbying in the courts of the Almighty for special favors," and which Lillian Smith colorfully described as "shaking a tin cup in the face of God." Niebuhr likes, in this regard, Lincoln's profound observation during the Civil War: "Both sides pray to the same God, and the prayers of neither have been fully answered."

One reason why appeals to special providence are rarely answered in full is that no man is an island. The tower of Siloam does not twist in the air in order to fall only on the wicked. Each person is involved not only with the fate of his group but with all the people who are acting during his lifetime in all the various dramas that were set in motion by the persons and groups that preceded them.

Another reason is that some appeals to special providence fly in the face of nature's laws, the laws according to which God created the universe; and the God of the Bible, as Richard Beebe has said, is "not a God of caprice." One can scarcely expect God to turn off the laws of gravity even when a pious person is falling, nor will it do us one bit of good to pray about the weather. As Niebuhr once wrote to an old friend:

> I would never think of praying for a change in weather, but I have frequently done what you have done and prayed for someone I loved who was in danger . . . Prayer in this instance is an expression of concern and love on the ultimate level. I think the whole mystery of personality is expressed and revealed in it.

And to a student who pressed Niebuhr for his views on special providence, Niebuhr answered:

> You say, "there have been times in medical history and in many people's lives when a person who is loved survives by dint of something over and above the doctors' highest skills and his own survival impulse. Now this may just be human love at work or it may be God's love at work." That states the issue precisely except that I would leave out the word "or." I think that human love at work is an instrument of divine grace and I think that Buber is quite right in insisting that divine grace is an overtone of all our interactions with one another. To believe in God is to believe that the universe has a mystery of grace in it beyond the conscious designs and contrivances of men. The orthodox doctrine of special providence assumes a divine interference with the various causal sequences of nature and of history. I do not think there is any evidence for such interference, yet I have as a pastor many times witnessed what you say in your sentence, "there have been many times in medical history . . ."

Thus the establishment of nature's consistent and predictable laws is one example of God's self-limitation. Another is his creation of man with freedom to discover nature's laws and break them, to discover the law of his own nature, the "law of love," and break it, and then perhaps to repent and be forgiven and thereby develop the power to forgive others. Such self-limitation on God's part confronts man with a basic paradox. Niebuhr wrestles with it in a sermon called *The Power and Weakness of God*:

> If God is all powerful He must be the Creator of evil as well as of good. All the suffering of the world would seem to be finally attributed to Him. If the suffering is due to disharmonies in the order of the world, which God has not mastered, and to recalcitrant forces which He has not subdued, the goodness of God becomes more sharply defined; but His power is called into question. This rational contradiction lies at the heart of faith's apprehension of the Holiness of God. It is never completely resolved.

At the same time, Niebuhr goes on to say, all the ages of Christian faith have found one luminous point which does make sense out of the rational contradiction. The luminous point is God's third form of self-limitation: the willingness to suffer with and for man, in the act of forgiving man. God took action in history to heal the breach between man and God, not through a flaunting of divine power but through the offer of forgiving love. As Niebuhr wrote in *Christianity and Power Politics*:

> The good news of the gospel is not the law that we ought to love one another. The good news of the gospel is that there is a resource of divine mercy which is able to overcome the contradiction within our own souls, which we cannot ourselves overcome. The contradiction is that, though we know we ought to love our neighbor as ourself, there is a "law in our members which wars against the law that is in our mind," so that, in fact, we love ourselves more than our neighbor.

This "grace of God which is revealed in Christ" is not only pardon (or justification); it is also a form of power. Yet is appears to many people so absurd as to be what Niebuhr calls a scandal. The German name for this scandal is *Einmaligkeit*: literally, one-time-ness, which is translated by Niebuhr as "the scandal of particularity."[3] Why, in other words, should

[3] "It is a scandal for all rationalistic interpretation of history that the idea of a universal history should have emerged from the core of a particular event, whether that event be the covenant of God with Israel, or, as the New Testament conceives it, the 'second covenant,' instituted by the coming of Christ . . ."

God have chosen one man, in one place, at one time, to reveal the essential nature of God and of man? Many moderns consider that since a just God would not have played favorites, and since a democratic God would have showed himself to everyone, everywhere, at all times, the God of the Bible must either be very ungodlike or not exist at all.

In the Bible, however, as the psalmist reminds us, "God's ways are not our ways." And "the preaching of Christ crucified" which appeared, as St. Paul admitted, "unto the Jews a stumbling block and unto the Greeks foolishness," has subsequently appeared to countless generations as an indication that the God who notes each sparrow's fall and by whom the hairs of each head are counted, both finds uniqueness as important as universality, and has set through Christ's uniqueness, a universal pattern.

Part of this pattern, as Niebuhr says in *Discerning the Signs of the Times,* is that only in God is the paradox of power and weakness, of judgment and mercy, finally resolved:

> The weakness of God's love is not the weakness of goodness striving against the recalcitrance of some "given" stuff of creation . . . The justice and the "wrath" of God can prevent any human rebellion from developing its defiance to the point of ultimate triumph. The devil, according to Christian myth, is able to defy God but not absolutely. The divine order is supported by the divine power. . . . But . . . justice and wrath have a negatively redemptive effect. They prove to men and nations that there are limits beyond which their rebellion can not go. But punishment may prompt men and nations to despair as well as to repentance. There can indeed be no repentance if love does not shine through the justice. It shines through whenever it becomes apparent that the executor of judgment suffers willingly, as guiltless sufferer, with the guilty victim of punishment. If it does not shine through . . . childish recalcitrance may harden into adolescent rebellion and mature despair. Because such love seldom shines through the punishment which "righteous" victors exact of the "unrighteous" vanquished, the repentance of vanquished nations is extremely difficult. . . . The place in history where it shines through most clearly is the cross. The crux of the cross is its revelation of the fact that the final power of God over man is derived from the self-imposed weakness of his love . . . His mercy is the final dimension of His majesty.

Few things are so worthless, Niebuhr says in the second volume of the Gifford Lectures, as those for which people have not yet felt a need. This is particularly true of mercy: when we know we are in need of it, nothing is more precious; when we do not know we are in need of it, the offer of it may appear as the worst kind of insult. It is therefore only after we have faced up to the destructive self-centeredness in our own life and that of our group or nation that we begin to feel the need for mercy; yet without a hint that such mercy may be available, we may never face up to the destructive self-centeredness of our own life and that of our group or nation. These two dimensions of self and group or nation always go together, Niebuhr says, and God's judgment and mercy apply to both. If anything as circular as faith can be paraphrased, these are the three main items:

(1) God can be known in individual encounter.

(2) God can be known through his "mighty acts" in history (which Niebuhr defined at Kent in 1956 as "the particular events of history which point beyond themselves to the ultimate . . . mystery and meaning which give significance to our existence").

(3) It is the same God in both instances:
"The revelation of God to man is always a twofold one, a personal-individual revelation, and a revelation in the context of social-historical experience. Without the public and historical revelation the private experience of God would remain poorly defined and subject to caprice. Without the private revelation of God, the public and historical revelation would not gain credence . . . Private revelation is the testimony in the consciousness of every person that his life touches a reality beyond himself, a reality deeper and higher than the system of nature in which he stands . . . The experience of God is not so much a separate experience, as an overtone implied in all experience.[4]

"God's mighty acts" occurred not only in biblical times, but in modern times, not only as a form of judgment but of mercy. As to judgment, Niebuhr writes:

[4] Niebuhr's interpretation of "revelation" appears in Chapter 20.

> For biblical faith, God is revealed in the catastrophic events of history as being what each individual heart has already dimly perceived in its sense of being judged: as the structure, the law, the essential character of reality, as the source and center of the created world against which the pride of man destroys itself in vain rebellion.

An example of such judgment in modern times could be Hitler's *Götterdämmerung,* brought about by his own overweening racial, national, and personal pride and also by the armed might of the nations who felt threatened by this pride. Yet the nations by whom he was brought low were guilty of lesser but analogous forms of the same pride. For example, the type of racial arrogance the Allies criticized in him is one reason the British, the French, the Dutch, the Belgians, and ourselves are today hated in many colonial and postcolonial parts of Asia and Africa.

As to the acts in history which reveal God's mercy, Niebuhr said in a letter to a student (May 20, 1955):

> I would say anything is Providential which is not by human contrivance. Butterfield speaks of "secular providence." This is, those events in history which are beyond human contrivance and which people must believe in even if they do not believe that all the effects are under a Divine rule. They are patterns of history above and beyond what people intend . . . For instance, the fact that we have, in the international situation, a certain hope derived from our very hopelessness is a Providential working in history which nobody could have anticipated or contrived.

There have been other occurrences that unexpectedly brought good out of evil and confounded the most meticulous and optimistic planners. An example Niebuhr often uses is the way religious liberty developed in the American colonies: the original fighters for religious liberty wanted it for themselves alone; they had no interest in helping rival creeds. But the rival creeds wanted liberty too. The result was that all of them got what none of them had been far-sighted and large-hearted enough to try for. On the other hand, as Niebuhr warns in *Irony of American History,* once we start to congratulate ourselves on our good fortune it is but a small and human step to start thinking we deserved it, and thus to build the very kind of pride that has led throughout history not to good fortune but its opposite, not only in individuals but in nations:

> From that day [of the Puritans] to this, it has remained one of the most difficult achievements for our nation to recognize the fortuitous and the providential element in our good fortune. If either moral pride or the spirit of rationalism tries to draw every element in an historic situation into rational coherence and persuades us to establish a direct congruity between our good fortune and our virtue and our skill, we will inevitably claim more for our contribution to our prosperity than the facts warrant.

Niebuhr goes on to say with his tongue only half in his cheek:

> If it is not possible for modern man to hold by faith that there is a larger meaning in the intricate pattern of history than those which his own virtues or skills supply, he would do well to emphasize fortune and caprice in his calculations.

Niebuhr's belief that there is a larger meaning in the intricate pattern of history was quoted by Sidney Hook in his review of the Living Library Volume; and on the basis of it, Hook termed Niebuhr a "cosmic optimist," a name which Niebuhr is said to have laughed at but not denied. (The italics represent the part of Niebuhr's statement quoted by Hook):

> *The Christian faith holds out the hope that our fragmentary lives will be completed in a total and larger plan than any which we control or comprehend,* and that a part of the completion is the forgiveness of . . . the evils into which we fall by our frantic efforts to complete our own lives or to endow them with significance . . .

Around this passage Niebuhr had woven an unusual bit of autobiography:

> Two old ladies were dying shortly after I assumed charge of the parish. . . . One old lady was too preoccupied with self, too aggrieved that Providence should not have taken account of her virtue in failing to protect her against a grievous illness, to be able to face death with any serenity. She was in a constant hysteria of fear and resentment. . . . The other old lady had brought up a healthy and wholesome family, though her husband

> was subject to fits of insanity which forced her to be breadwinner as well as homemaker . . . I stood weekly by her bedside while she told me what passages of Scripture to read to her; most of them expressed gratitude for all the mercies of God which she had received in life . . . she faced death [from cancer] with the utmost peace of soul.
>
> I relearned the essentials of the Christian faith at the bedside of that nice old soul. I appreciated that the ultimate problem of . . . existence is the peril of sin and death in the way that these two perils are so curiously compounded; for we fall into sin by trying to evade or to conquer death or our own insignificance, of which death is the ultimate symbol. As for the difference between the faith of the two old ladies, outwardly so similar until submitted to the ultimate test, we in the churches ought to admit more humbly than is our wont that there is a mystery of grace that none can fathom. . . . The Church is a curiously mixed body consisting of those who have never been shaken in their self-esteem and self-righteousness . . . and of true Christians who live by "a broken spirit and a contrite heart." Whether we belong to this latter group, which makes up the true but invisible church, no one but God can know.

High among those who were not "shaken in their self-esteem" was one Detroit churchgoer who held virtual power of life and death over thousands in his city, whose prestige throughout the nation was so great that many people wanted him for President of the United States, and whose reputation for humanitarianism had spread throughout the world.

Niebuhr saw no reason not to try to shake this man's self-esteem. He did so by speaking and writing what he discovered to be the truth about the pitiful condition of the people whose livelihood depended upon this man.

Henry Ford, in turn, disapproved of the young pastor's stepping outside the bounds of his parish. There was never a personal dialogue between the two—but each, in varying degrees, became for the other a source of tension.

11

The Sin of Ford

"I CUT my eyeteeth fighting Ford."

Such was Niebuhr's characterization of his Detroit years, from 1914 to 1927, when the rapidly industrializing city was still, as he recalled it, a "frontier town."

Even before Niebuhr's arrival the town had become known, according to Allan Nevins' *Ford: The Times, The Man, The Company*, as "one of the open shop capitals of the land." The hostility of its industrialists to unions was famous, and among its other characteristics were the large pool of immigrant labor, the widespread use of adolescent workers, the scant attention paid to safety, and the prevalence of piece work.

Henry Ford differed from his fellow industrialists in his disapproval of piece work. In its place he developed the assembly line which has since been adopted for mass production all over the world. But Ford was never content with his own assembly line's production; he always wanted more and faster production, and to that end he hired efficiency engineers who devised various, and cumulative, forms of the speed up. Workers were analyzed and directed as if they were machines, except that no provision was made for the depreciation of *these* machines: since they were human, Mr. Ford decided, the problems of aging and injury were theirs, not his.[1]

Mr. Ford was not deliberately being cruel: he was simply trying to get the price of cars down so that more people, including Ford workers, could buy them. To that end he increased not only production but also wages, and when he needed capital for expansion, he cut dividends rather than

[1] The rate of industrial accidents, Nevins points out in his book on Ford, were far higher in the United States at that time than in either Germany or Great Britain.

wages, thus involving himself in a law suit brought by his fellow entrepreneurs, the Dodge brothers.[2]

This attitude on Ford's part was praised to the skies. As late as 1959 the praise was still pouring in, with R. L. Bruckberger writing in *Image of America,*

> I consider 1914 a momentous year in history . . . the year in which Henry Ford, by . . . more than doubling wages at one stroke, finally freed the worker from "proletarian" servitude and lifted him above the "minimum subsistence wage . . ."

And Henry Ford, whose pre-Madison Avenue public relations were unexcelled, himself added to the praise by announcing to the press, on January 5, 1914, that "the greatest and most successful automobile company in the world" was, under his direction, inaugurating "the greatest revolution in the matter of rewards for workers ever known in the industrial world."

The press took his announcement—as it then took all his announcements—at face value. Nevins points out that "nine tenths of the newspaper comment was favorable, much of it . . . ecstatic."

The nation too accepted Ford's pronouncements without question. What he *said* was that he intended to build human material, with cars being only the by-product, but what he *did,* according to the young minister on West Grand Boulevard, was so to concentrate on building cars that ravaged human beings were the by-product. At the time, in *Leaves,* Niebuhr recorded that

> young men were fed into the assembly line, and soon they were exhausted, both physically and emotionally.

So terrible, indeed, was the pace of work, combined with tension and boredom, that strong men in the prime of life, despite Ford's bruited five-

[2] Ford took other actions that, in the light of history, were forward-looking and that, at the time, were condemned by many of his fellow entrepreneurs. One such action was to hire white and Negro people to work together; another was to hire handicapped workers and people who had been in jail. When Ford finally resigned from the conservative Employers' Association, of which he had been a leading member, the Association called him what Franklin Roosevelt later was called, "a traitor to his class." Typical activities of this Employers' Association had been to lobby against Child Labor Laws, factory inspection bills, and provisions for safety measures.

day week, were so exhausted that they had to spend most of every weekend in bed.

Niebuhr also noted Ford's summary dismissal of men in middle age, with no provision for pensions. Nor did Mr. Ford believe in contributing to the Community Fund that tried to help these people:

> Ford said he believed in justice rather than charity. The institutions of the Community Fund meanwhile found a goodly portion of their case load among the Ford workers.

But worst of all, Niebuhr felt, were Ford's "retooling periods" which lasted anywhere from four months to around a year. During these times the workers were unemployed in such large numbers that most of them could not possibly find other jobs. In 1927, when Ford discontinued the Model T and closed the factories to prepare for the Model A, sixty thousand men were out of work, and when they were finally re-hired, they were treated as new employees and forced to start again at five dollars a day.

"Ford," said Niebuhr bitterly, "was celebrated throughout the world as a great humanitarian and undoubtedly regarded himself as one." But the workers, and the minister who climbed the rickety steps of their crowded fire-trap dwellings, had a different perspective on this famous humanitarianism:

> Mother and I visited at the home of ——— today where the husband is sick and was out of employment before he became sick. The folks have few connections in the city. They belong to no church. What a miserable existence it is to be friendless in a large city. And to be dependent on a heartless industry. The man is about 55 or 57 I should judge, and he is going to have a desperate time securing employment after he gets well.

The realism with which Niebuhr recognized the near-hopelessness of the man's predicament did not, however, dull his feeling of personal responsibility:

> I promised . . . I would try to find him a job. I did it to relieve the despair of that family, but I will have a hard time making good on my promise. According to the ethics of our modern industrialism men over fifty, without special training, are so much junk.

Machines that are worn out lie on the scrap heap rusting quietly, but human scrap cries out, and occasionally some one listens. Niebuhr, presumably, approached one of the automobile executives who was a member of his congregation and found him sympathetic. For the diary goes on to qualify the heartlessness of "the ethics of our modern industrialism":

> It is a pleasure to see how such an ethic is qualified as soon as the industrial unit is smaller and the owner has a personal interest in his men. I could mention quite a few such instances. But unfortunately the units are getting larger and more inhuman.

Nor was there any way to prevent the growth of these units: production of an item as complex as the automobile demanded largeness, and the people of America demanded the automobile. Not even the young minister was above sharing their enjoyment of it:

> I love nothing so much in the realm of physical pleasure as the sense of power which comes from "stepping on the gas" when ensconced in a big car.

And the cars in those days were really big. The Model T, with its top up, stood seven feet tall, with its driver, as recalled by E. B. White, "a man enthroned."

Niebuhr liked driving the Ford cars but he did not like the way they had been financed. Ford gave out a statement that producing the Model A had cost him about a hundred million dollars, but that his reserves were still about a quarter of a billion.

Niebuhr had a fondness for figures, and no fondness for Ford. As he wrote in *Leaves*,

> I have been doing a little arithmetic and have come to the conclusion that the car cost Ford workers at least fifty million dollars in lost wages during the last year. No one knows how many hundreds lost their homes in the period of unemployment, and how many children were taken out of school to help fill the depleted family exchequer, and how many more children lived on short rations during this period. Mr. Ford refuses to concede that he made a mistake in bringing the car out so late. He has a way of impressing the public even with his mistakes . . .

Niebuhr was not only unimpressed; he was aghast:

> What a civilization this is! Naive gentlemen with a genius for mechanics suddenly become arbiters over the lives and fortunes of hundreds of thousands. Their moral pretensions are credulously accepted at full value. No one asks whether an industry which can maintain a reserve of a quarter of a billion ought not make some provision for its unemployed.

This was years before the Wagner Act enabled unions to organize without undue interference from employers, years before the industrial unions arose to take the place of the craft unions in mass production (the C.I.O. was not organized until 1938), years before child labor was forbidden by law, and years before unemployment compensation was provided, together with the welfare payments and surplus food that today keep unemployed workers and their families from starving. Niebuhr meanwhile could not sit still. He had to expose the facts.

One of the magazines for which he regularly wrote was *The Christian Century*. He had become a contributing editor in the early twenties and, as he told the Columbia Oral investigator,

> I proceeded to express my dim views of the Ford empire in various editorials. Some of my parishioners had gathered evidence proving that the Ford annual wage was very low, when the various lay-offs were considered. I finally put this study of wage and living standards under my own name. This led to a curious, and on the whole, heartening experience. One of the members of my Church Board was a retired manufacturer of Ford parts. He received a letter from Ford's secretary informing him that his young parson who evidently did not know much about the auto industry was being corrupted "by one of the most vicious anti-Ford journals in the country." Thus I was accused of corrupting myself. My parishioner showed me the letter, and before I could react, he pulled his own answer from his pocket and said, "I thought I would give this answer if you approved." The letter said, "I am sorry to hear about my pastor's offence to the Ford Motor Company. I have talked to him about the article and he instructs me to say that if there are any inaccuracies or misstatements in the article he will correct them."

There was no reply from Mr. Ford—or his secretary.

It may be significant that Niebuhr's brave parishioner was a *retired* manufacturer of Ford parts. For the heavy club of Mr. Ford's displeasure was felt not only by his workers but also by his executives, and by the executives of companies that did business with Ford. Whether Ford's frequent dismissal of his own executives was caused by jealousy or by reluctance to have power move too far from his control, Niebuhr was not certain, but he was quite willing at the time to suspect Ford of both motives.[3] As he later recalled,

> Mr. Ford typified for my rather immature social imagination all that was wrong with American "capitalism." I became a socialist in this reaction . . . I became a socialist in theory long before I enrolled in the Socialist Party and before I had read anything by Karl Marx. I became the prisoner of a very cute phrase which I invented, or it seemed to me at least, to be "cute." The phrase was, "when private property ceases to be private, it ought no longer to be private." The phrase which was prompted by the unprivate character of these great motor companies . . . does not seem to be so astute in the light of subsequent history in which justice was achieved by balancing various types of collective power.

Of these types of collective power it was with labor, the then-underdog, that Niebuhr identified himself. This form of sympathy, within the Protestant Church, was still a relatively unusual one. At the end of the nineteenth century, according to Carl Degler's *Out of Our Past,* the Protestant churches had, as a rule, "no following among the working men"; their congregations were made up primarily of business, professional and farming people. A turn of the century study of Pittsburgh, for example, showed that although business and professional men made up only 10 per cent of the population, they made up 60 per cent of the Protestant Church membership. Said a typical worker, "The rich folks build their churches for themselves, and they keep them for themselves, and I ain't never going to interfere with that arrangement."

[3] Ford's top assistant, Harry Bennett, is quoted by Murray Kempton as having said about Ford's executives, "They knew what side their bread was buttered on and did as they were told."

But some people *were* beginning to interfere with that arrangement. In 1892, the year Niebuhr was born, complaints about the church were voiced from within the ranks of labor: Said Terence Powderly of the Knights of Labor, "You can count on the ends of your fingers all the clergymen who take any interest in the labor problem." And from within the ranks of the church also, action began to be taken. In that same year, seven Protestant seminaries, for the first time, offered courses in social ethics and Walter Rauschenbusch of the Rochester Theological Seminary led a group of Protestants to pledge assistance in the "practical realization in the world" of the Kingdom of God which they understood specifically to include the marching hosts of labor.

Rauschenbusch was a leading spokesman for the Social Gospel, a post-Civil War movement that had become simultaneously religious, socialist and perfectionist, in the sense that it believed progress to be inevitable. It preached the "service motive" rather than the "profit motive," and insisted that since evil was socially caused, evil was therefore socially alleviable. The clarion call of Rauschenbusch was that "our inherited Christian faith dealt with individuals; our present task deals with society."

The Social Gospel's leading spokesman in Detroit was Niebuhr's friend and mentor, the Episcopal Bishop, Charles Williams. To Niebuhr the Social Gospel appeared, at the time, to be a valid reaction not only against the cruel abuses by *laissez faire* capitalism and its particular form of individualism: "each man for himself and the devil take the hindmost." It also appeared as a valid reaction against the Protestant Church and *its* particular form of individualism: "let every one develop a pious attitude toward God, and society will be redeemed."

It was not long, however, before Niebuhr began to see flaws in the Social Gospel. It seemed to him to plumb the depths of sin neither in the individual nor in society. And by the early thirties the uncritical enthusiasm expressed by some of its leaders for the accomplishments of the Soviet Union caused Niebuhr to do battle against what he called their naïveté.

Meanwhile, in Detroit, Niebuhr could see at first hand not only the sufferings of labor, but also the spiritual blindness of the successful industrialists.[4] Ford was the most extreme of these—but he was not the only one, nor was the form of blindness he exhibited the only one.

The wealthiest man in Niebuhr's congregation was a pious, naïve gentleman whose path in business had been paved with gold because he was a boyhood friend of Henry Ford. As Niebuhr recalled for the Columbia Oral Interviewer:

> That was the only basis for his wealth because Ford was sentimental about his friends. . . . He did this job only for four or five years and he made a fortune in that time. . . . He was embarrassingly generous with this. He had the old-fashioned evangelical . . . notion that he got his money because he had tithed since he was a little boy. The Lord had prospered him because he had been a tither. He felt that he would have to return this money to the Lord's cause.

Some ministers might have been glad simply to receive the money and honor the donor. But Niebuhr was troubled. He could see that the man had prospered because of knowing Ford, not because of tithing. The man's religion, in addition to spurring this generosity, was also blinding him to the facts of economic life. Here was the mirror-image of Adam Denger, the grocer of Lincoln, who had assumed that God would prosper him because he had been generous to the unemployed miners. God's ways, Niebuhr suspected, were not that simple, nor were the ways of a technical society. Thus a naïve idealism could be a hazard in the complex modern world either to the self (as with the complacent tither), or to those for whom one was responsible (as with Denger's family), or to those over whom one held power (as with Ford's employees). In *Leaves,* Niebuhr had described Mr. Ford as naïve; in the unpublished *Later Leaves,* 1954, he was more explicit:

> Ford was an idealist . . . and as many an idealist, completely lacking in self-knowledge . . . He could not understand that power impulses may be subtly compounded with idealistic impulses.

[4] Niebuhr's friend and colleague at Union Seminary, the late Professor David E. Roberts, told of the tycoon who said to Dr. Joseph Parker, "I'm a self-made man, you know." Dr. Parker's answer was, "Sir, you have lifted a heavy burden of responsibility from the shoulders of the Almighty."

Niebuhr's opportunity to place himself publicly on the side of the underdog came at a time when most ministers were tacitly on the side of the top-dog. As Niebuhr had written in a *Christian Century* article called "The Church and the Middle Class," published just before Christmas, 1922, it was difficult for ministers to be effective champions of social justice when the victims of this injustice were not part of their congregation and when the beneficiaries of the injustice paid the church's bills. Niebuhr's own church, on the other hand, had always stood loyally behind him and did so again when the time came to be counted. This was in 1926. The American Federation of Labor had arranged a convention in Detroit in the vain hope of attracting the industrial workers to its own craft unions.[5] Niebuhr recalled for the Columbia Interviewer how

> the business community of Detroit, which had always breathed sweetness and light, showed its fangs. The Board of Commerce had all kinds of meetings in which they decided how they were going to stop this. Meanwhile the Federal Council of Churches . . . sent a secretary to Detroit to ask . . . what churches . . . would invite labor speakers to their Sunday evening exercises. . . . I, of course, together with about a dozen other parsons, submitted this to my board and was enthusiastic about its acceptance. So we invited these labor speakers.
>
> Whereupon the Board of Commerce let out a tremendous blast and shrewdly sent committees that would be most influential in each particular church situation to the pastor and to the board members to ask for the withdrawal of these invitations . . . The fact is that all of the churches withdrew their invitations in a rather abject way. That made me a little sick about the obvious subservience of the churches to the business interest. The only

[5] A full decade passed before these workers were organized in industrial rather than craft unions. Walter Reuther who subsequently became one of the key leaders in the UAW:CIO had arrived in Detroit at the age of nineteen shortly before Niebuhr left. As Reuther recalls: "I learned to know Reinie later on and I was much impressed and attracted to him as a person by his ability to relate religious, ethical and moral standards to practical, political and social problems. I grew up in a family where applied Christianity and brotherhood were the core of our family philosophy and Reinie Niebuhr's high sense of social idealism as applied to the challenging problems of our times spoke the language that I understood during my formative years and the years when I was involved in the early beginnings in the United Automobile Workers."

two churches that refused to withdraw were my little church and the Unitarian Church.

Another person sickened by the tactics of the Detroit "business interest" was Rabbi Stephen S. Wise of New York City who entrained for Detroit and, at the invitation of William Green, president of the American Federation of Labor, addressed the convention. He also met one of the two ministers who had resisted the business interest and thus started a friendship which lasted until Wise's death in 1949, and included many occasions when Niebuhr addressed the Free Synagogue in New York.

In 1927 Niebuhr's first published book, *Does Civilization Need Religion?* appeared. He gave copies to his own Church Board. "My God," one of them confessed to Niebuhr's assistant, "I read the first page and didn't understand a word."

Actually the book is not difficult, but the Board member was perhaps expressing a feeling which Niebuhr and others were beginning to share, that the intellectual interests of the young pastor were exploding beyond the confines—and demands—of a single parish. Bethel Church had been like a flower pot in which the bulb of his self and ideas could safely grow. But now he was sprouting in too many directions for the pot to hold him much longer, and his roots had developed too great a thirst for the watering of new ideas, new disciplines, new challenges.

At Sherwood Eddy's instigation, Niebuhr had spoken before a Student Volunteer Convention in Detroit in 1923. In the audience was Henry Sloane Coffin, later President of Union Seminary, who sent a note up to Niebuhr asking to see him. They became acquainted, and in time Coffin offered Niebuhr a teaching post at Union. (Sherwood Eddy reports in *Eighty Adventurous Years* that he was privileged for three years to contribute money for Niebuhr's salary until an opening in the regular faculty appeared).[6] When Niebuhr asked what on earth Coffin considered him equipped to teach, Coffin said simply, "you can't teach anything but just what you think." As a result Niebuhr has always taught just what he thought in the field of Applied Christianity. As he wrote in *Later Leaves:*

[6] This opening occurred through the death of Professor Gaylord White. But even before that event, Yale had offered Niebuhr a full professorship. Niebuhr thus completely vaulted over the stage of assistant professor and remained an associate professor only for three years.

> I had come to the pastorate with simple Christian "liberal" moralism. I regarded love as the answer to every moral problem. It is, indeed, in the sense that we are so created that we can not realize ourselves within ourselves but must go out from ourselves into the lives of others. But in the process of building communities every impulse of love must be transformed into an impulse of justice.

Justice—how to define it and how to achieve it? If its component parts were order, liberty and equality, how were these related to each other? When was reason more important than love to their achievement? And when was the use of power an unavoidable necessity? These were typical questions of Social Ethics to which Niebuhr devoted years of research—on a practical as well as theoretical basis.

Not only did Niebuhr believe that "justice must be the instrument of love," but he also believed that justice must be guarded against all well-meaning powerful men whose lack of self-knowledge was combined with self-righteousness, yet whose creativity was one of society's most valued resources.

In Detroit, Niebuhr had challenged the pretensions to virtue of Henry Ford. In New York he went on to challenge the pretensions to virtue in every man—himself included.

12

The Sin of the Individual

No aspect of Niebuhr's thought has been as widely and as passionately misunderstood as his revival of the classical Christian doctrine of Original Sin.

Charming reference to the fact of this misunderstanding was made by William Temple, Archbishop of Canterbury, after Niebuhr had been lecturing in Swanwick, England:

> At Swanwick, when Niebuhr had quit it,
> Said a young man: "At last I have hit it.
> Since I cannot do right,
> I must find out tonight
> The best sin to commit—and commit it."

The term, original sin, tends to be associated with St. Paul and those of his professional Christian followers who preached distrust of human agencies in this world, and hell fire in the next. It also has a fleshly connotation, as suggested by the limerick's choice of night as the time for sinning. The term, therefore, was not a wholly fortunate one for Niebuhr to use, yet in a way he was forced to use it, since there was no other that harked back to the Fall of Man as recorded in the Old Testament. Says Rabbi Abraham Heschel, whose thought regarding these matters is closer to Niebuhr's than that of many ministers:

> It is the prophets who teach us that the problem of living does not arise with the question of how to take care of rascals [but] with the silent atrocities, the secret scandals which no law can prevent.

Certainly Niebuhr has shown little interest in rascals, and in the scandals which laws can prevent. He is perfectly willing to leave overt crimes to the laws enforcers. And he is less concerned with the three per cent of American youth who are delinquent than with the ninety seven per cent who will grow up to be good citizens. He therefore almost never writes about what most people think of as sin, original or otherwise. One hunts long in his writings before finding mention of murder or theft, for example, and when these do appear it is likely to be in their collective, rather than individual form: Nazi murders, or Soviet thefts of neighboring lands.

As for the ancient Seven Deadly Sins—pride, covetousness, lust, anger, gluttony, envy, and sloth—pride is the only one to which Niebuhr pays prolonged attention. Anger, in fact, he says is not always a sin at all, but "the proper attitude toward evil." As such it is far preferable to "an emotional detachment from the issues of life," since we *should* respond to the Hitlers with anger sufficient to gird ourselves against them. At the same time, we must remain on guard lest this righteous wrath degenerate into hatred or vengeance which Niebuhr calls the "egoistic corruptions of anger." (He defines vindictiveness as anger, not that injustice has been *done*, but that it has been done to *us*.)

Nor need we be sinless, Niebuhr believes, in order to rise in wrath against gross sin in others. If there was any group that aroused Niebuhr's own wrath to towering proportions, it was the prewar pacifists who insisted that Americans had no right to criticize Nazi murders of millions because we had three lynchings a year ourselves; or their postwar counterparts, the fellow travellers who insisted that Americans had no right to criticize Soviet capture of satellite nations because in 1898 we captured Cuba ourselves. Precisely because Niebuhr is so excruciatingly aware of the mote in his own, and his own nation's eye, is he able to point to the need for action also to remove the beam in the eye of others.

When Niebuhr calls anger the proper attitude toward evil, he is referring more to historical evil than natural evil. Historical evil is defined as the "bloodshed, slavery and social misery . . . of the world" brought about by the sinful misuse of human freedom. Natural evil, on the other hand, is typified by a child's death from disease. In *Faith and History,* he writes,

> natural evil represents the failure of nature's processes to conform perfectly to human ends . . . Death is a simple fact in the dimension of nature; but it is an irrelevance and a threat of meaninglessness in the realm of history.

The problem of death, moreover, is compounded with that of sin. (That is the implication, Niebuhr says, of St. Paul's often misinterpreted statement that "the wages of sin are death.") For death, besides being a simple fact in the dimension of nature, is also the final symbol of man's insignificance. In attempting to deny this human insignificance, man in his freedom may rise to heights of creativity or sink to depths of destruction or do both at the same time. The historical evil that stems from man's misuse of his freedom is, Niebuhr says, the kind of evil with which the Bible is primarily concerned, while natural evil is a subject in which the Bible is "only obliquely interested."

In regard to the further deadly sin of covetousness, Niebuhr does not mention it often, but when he does, he calls it "the besetting sin of bourgeois culture," by which he means primarily American culture. With covetousness, he would probably lump envy which he mentions even less often. And the sin of sloth he never mentions at all. (It is probably one to which he has never personally felt tempted.) Thus it seems fair to say, as did William John Wolf in the Living Library Volume, that

> Niebuhr's categories fail adequately to account for the sins of the weak man as they do so forcefully for those of the strong man.

The strong man who is recognized to be *wise* or *powerful* or *good* is the person whose tendency to pride Niebuhr most often attacks, perhaps because the sin that exacerbates him most is the one that strikes closest to home, or perhaps because he has seen, in the technically advanced and interrelated modern world, the preventable and terrible damage done to thousands by the pride of one.

The *wise* man, by whom Niebuhr usually means the professional thinker and teacher, the philosopher or social scientist, is punctured by Niebuhr for overrating the extent and applicability of his own wisdom. All knowledge about human affairs, Niebuhr says in the first volume of the Gifford Lectures, is not merely incomplete but also unconsciously influenced by the thinker's time in history, his place in society, and the securities and traumas of his personal life:

> All human knowledge is tainted with an "ideological" taint. It pretends to be more true than it is. It is finite knowledge gained from a particular perspective; but it pretends to be final and ultimate knowledge.

The professional thinker way well admit this limitation in principle, but nonetheless fail to recognize its evidence in his own thought:

> A particularly significant aspect of intellectual pride is the inability of the agent to recognize the same or similar limitations of perspective in himself which he has detected in others.

The *powerful* man, by whom Niebuhr usually means the social, economic, religious or political leader, is punctured for the imperialism he exhibits in his denial of freedom and justice to others. This tendency may start at the level of the family:

> Have we not all known loving fathers and mothers who, despite a very genuine love for their children, had to be resisted if justice and freedom were to be gained for the children? Do we not know that the sinful will-to-power may be compounded with the most ideal motives and may use the latter as its instruments and vehicles?

In the wider field, the combination of will-to-power with ideal motives may lead to ruthless fanaticism, as in the Spanish Inquisition and the French and Russian Revolutions:

> Man is always most inhuman not when he is unconsciously driven by natural impulse, but when he imagines his natural impulses and his relative values to be the instrument of some absolute good.

As for the *good* people, they are punctured by Niebuhr for compounding their personal aims with the idealistic causes to which they devote themselves. One reason for their doing so is that

> man cannot love himself inordinately without pretending that it is not his, but a universal interest which he is supporting.

Yet one result of their doing so is that much good work gets done that might not otherwise be done. At the same time, Niebuhr warns, much good work is *un*done and much confusion is engendered when too great a claim is made for the purity of the person's motives:

> We are not only not as good as our ideals but we tend to use our ideals as weapons of prestige, failing to recognize that the ideals are not as good as we pretend they are.

The business man who passionately insists that freedom is the primary value is no different from the labor leader who passionately insists that equality is the primary value. In both cases there may be more self-interest than the speaker is willing to admit and therefore less primacy to his particular value than he is willing to recognize.

Even the person who has no economic, or other ostensible stake in the values he upholds does not get away without puncture. Niebuhr who has attended numerous public dinners points out that

> Pride is a subtle form of self-love. It feeds not on the material advantages which more greedy people seek, but on social approval. [Jesus'] strictures against the Pharisees were partly directed against their social pride. "All their works they do for to be seen of men . . . and love the uppermost rooms at feasts and the chief seats in the synagogue and greetings in the markets."

As for the minister whose own job, Niebuhr says, is to puncture pride and self-deception, including his own, he of all men is the most prone to hidden pride:

> The worst form of intolerance is religious intolerance, in which the particular interests of the contestants hide behind religious absolutes. The worst form of self-assertion is religious self-assertion in which under the guise of contrition before God, He is claimed as the exclusive ally of our contingent self.

Thus Niebuhr spends most of his time denouncing, not the visible sins of wicked people, but the invisible sins of good people. And many good people have wondered why he bothered. Since everyone knows that man is not perfect, why not laugh off the little imperfections, particularly those of people who are trying to be creative? Why not be grateful for their efforts, and let well enough alone?

Because, Niebuhr's answer would be, well enough is no longer good enough. In the days of the cave man, one person's pride and lack of self-knowledge could ruin the life only of his own family, but in the days of Henry Ford it could and did ruin the lives of tens of thousands. (And today it might ruin life for everyone on earth, and for those—if any—to come.) Hidden pride had been, in Niebuhr's eyes, the besetting sin of Ford; in time, Niebuhr found so many evidences of it in himself and others that he promoted it into being the besetting sin of man.

He could not, moreover, in the thirties find much that was well enough to be let alone, with the Depression growing at home and Dictatorship abroad. The feel of this period was given by Hugh MacLennan in *The Watch That Ends the Night*, a novel termed by Niebuhr "a masterpiece":

> There are few people who passed through the thirties who even dare or can recall what that time was really like or what it did to human beings . . . there was poison in the air then . . .

How had the world reached such a state, especially after the high hopes based on continuing progress? There were secular answers, both liberal and radical, to the problem of historical evil, but to Niebuhr, after a time, these answers did not go deep enough (see Chapter 18). There were religious answers, both liberal and neo-orthodox, but to Niebuhr, after a time, the liberal ones did not go deep enough, and the neo-Orthodox ones went so deep as to become irrelevant (see Chapter 24). Finally, in the mid-thirties, Niebuhr started seriously pondering the writings of St. Augustine. As he recalled in the Living Library Volume:

> I am surprised to note in retrospect how late I was in studying the thought of Augustine carefully. The matter is surprising because the thought of this theologian was to answer so many of my unanswered questions.

Augustine wrote about superbia, or pride. Niebuhr had detected its telltale fingerprints at the scene of every personal, social, and economic injustice. He even suspected, to a degree Augustine had not, that its corruption extended into the very Church whose job, in part, is to uncover such corruption.

For pride, Niebuhr decided *was* a corruption, a corruption of human freedom. "It is not by nature but in freedom that man sins." And the sin of pride, as Niebuhr described it in the first volume of his Gifford Lectures, is "the quintessence of sin" because it alienates man not only from God but from his fellow:

> Man is at variance with his fellow man by the force of the same pride which brings him in conflict with God.

This pride also alienates man from parts of himself, those aspects of his freedom for which "love is the only law":

> Man is an individual but he is not self-sufficient. The law of his nature is love . . . and . . . this law is violated when man seeks to make himself the center and source of his own life.

This law of love is, of course, not the kind of law that is enforceable. Enforceable laws deal with the actions of rascals, not with the hidden motives of law-abiders and law-enforcers. Thus, in view of Niebuhr's writings, one could argue that the person who breaks one of the Ten Commandments may well end up less sinful than the person who self-righteously denounces people who break a Commandment. For the commandment-breaker at least knows whereof to repent, while the commandment-enforcer would be stunned if asked to repent.

Niebuhr often contrasts what was said by Jesus to the woman taken in adultery and to the men about to stone her to death for her transgression. To the frightened woman, he said simply, "Go, and sin no more," while to the righteous pillars of the community, he said, "Let him who is without sin cast the first stone." Jesus furthermore did not limit sin to overt acts, but included dwelling upon self-serving thoughts. Niebuhr pays particular attention to the kind of self-serving thoughts that the thinker himself does not always recognize as such because they concern the wider rather than the narrower self:

> There are indeterminate possibilities of relating the family to the community on higher and higher levels of harmony. But there is no possibility of a family escaping the fault of regarding its own weal and woe as more important to the whole than it really is. There are unlimited opportunities of relating "our" nation more harmoniously to the lives of other nations; but there is no possibility of doing so without some corruption of national egoism.

Thus original sin, in Niebuhr's view, is basic to the world's woe, even though it springs from the same unique human freedom from which the world's weal also springs. "We are condemned," he says, "not for being ego's, but for being egotists." And in the collective as well as individual realm he agrees with Pascal who wrote about the doctrine of original sin:

> Nothing offends us more shockingly than this doctine; and yet without this mystery, the most incomprehensible of all, we are incomprehensible to ourselves.

The Christian Church, Niebuhr could see in the thirties, was doing parlous little to combat the sin of pride. Fundamentalist ministers were busily denouncing the overt sins of rascals, thus stirring pride in themselves and their congregation for not sharing in these particular forms of sin. "The Church," said Niebuhr in exasperation, "must have special grace to be able to withstand the boredom of the moralistic sermons preached from its pulpits." At the same time, liberal ministers were busily assuring their middle or upper class congregations that as soon as everyone practiced "the love method" in his personal life, the economic and social ills of society would be cured. This, Niebuhr felt, tended not only to augment the "pride of the established" which he terms complacency, but also the "pride of the advancing forces of society" which he terms ruthlessness. Thus he noted at the time that

> since liberal Protestantism is, on the whole, the religion of the privileged classes . . . it is not surprising that its espousal of the ideal of love, in a civilization reeking with social injustice, should be cynically judged and convicted of hypocrisy by those in whom bitter social experiences destroy the sentimentalities and illusions of the comfortable.

Niebuhr's criticism of the church extended beyond its leaders to those members who were paying such strict attention to the letter of Christian law that they forgot its spirit. In the Living Library Volume he refers to the "excessive conventionality . . . frantic respectability and . . . devotion to the minutiae of propriety" on the part of some church members, and he once made a devastating prediction about their behavior (quoted by Robert Moats Miller in *American Protestantism and Social Issues*):

> If there were a drunken orgy somewhere, I would bet ten to one a church member was not in it. But if there were a lynching, I would bet ten to one a church member was in it.

Another aspect of the church Niebuhr criticized was its desertion of the healthy Hebraic tradition in the direction of the ascetic Hellenic tradition. For the distinction between a supposedly bad body and good soul was a Greek one, very different from the Hebraic assumption that the self was a unity of body, mind, and spirit. Certainly in Genesis it is made clear that this unique human self-in-a-body was the self that God created and loved:

> Male and female created he them . . . and God saw everything he had made, and behold, it was very good.

Much damage to sensitive souls, Niebuhr felt, had come from a "graceless Christian legalism" and from a Christian asceticism based upon Greek dualism.[1] On the other hand, as he made clear in the Gifford Lectures, a healthy attitude toward sex does not include approving the sin of sensuality. This he defines as the idolatrous placing of a single function of the body at the center of life, thereby destroying the harmony of the whole. Like pride, therefore, the sin of sensuality is basically an abuse of man's freedom:

> The sex impulse is never purely as biological in man as in the brute. It is creatively related to the artistic impulse and lies at the foundation of family organization, which in turn is the nucleus of larger organizations of the human community. But sex can also become the perverse obsession of man because he has the freedom to center his life inordinately in one impulse, while the economy of nature preserves a pre-established harmony of various vitalities.

Animals stop eating when sated, and they make love only when nature signals at specified times of the year. But man has the freedom to worship the flesh or, by way of the flesh, to try to escape from the freedom-based anxiety of the self:

> The self is seeking to escape from itself and throws itself into any pursuit which will allow it to forget for a moment the inner tension of an uneasy conscience. The self finding itself to be inadequate as the centre of its existence, seeks for another god amidst the various forces, processes and impulses of nature.

Thus civilized man may try to return to the Garden of Eden but the gates are barred. The state of nature can be defined as paradise, Niebuhr says, because in it there is neither freedom nor responsibility, and hence

[1] Sometimes he jokes in class about this: "Since young men tend to commit sins of the body, and old men, sins of the mind, it is no accident that the church, which is run by old men, has concentrated its strictures on sins of the body."

no uneasy conscience. But man cannot go back to being wholly a child of nature because in his freedom he is also a child of God. Even, therefore, when his sin is most sensual, it is not wholly sensual:

> The freedom of his spirit causes him to break the harmonies of nature and the pride of his spirit prevents him from establishing a new harmony . . . his sin is therefore spiritual.

In New York City in the late twenties there were a number of gifted and intelligent people engaged in seeking "for another god amidst the various forces, processes and impulses of nature." They sought it in the speakeasies and in the rumble seats. Fun was the order of the day, and glamor was one of its by-products; but so was despair, as Scott Fitzgerald poignantly showed.

No one reading Niebuhr's writings of this period would surmise that Niebuhr was living in the jazziest city during the naughtiest age. He was aware of what was going on—it would have been impossible not to be—but his interest was engaged by what seemed to him a form of evil far more important to combat than sensuality.

To make an unlikely conjecture, what would have happened if Ford had established a love nest in Detroit and spent the better part of his time there? His own family would have suffered, but *sixty thousand* families would not have suffered as they did in the retooling period (in point of fact, Ford was meticulous about avoiding sins of the flesh—he neither drank nor smoked and even forbade his workers to). When Niebuhr later said that "not much evil is done by evil men," his next sentence was, "most of the evil is done by good people who do not know that they are not good." And one by-product of this ignorance is that their victim too is sometimes fooled. An important step in achieving justice, therefore, is to reveal to the victim the source of his woe. This step in itself is a form of arming him against the evil, and it is a step which Niebuhr has hopefully and frequently taken.

To make another unlikely conjecture, could one not claim that the gangster, Al Capone, ended up doing less damage than Ford? Of course Capone did nothing creative, as Ford did. Capone was an almost wholly evil man, and society finally protected itself against him. But to go a step further, as Niebuhr did once in class: Hitler, too, was a grossly evil man, and his philosophy was so uncreative and dangerous that the world rose in righteous wrath and destroyed him. Lenin, on the other hand, was not purely evil: he was a fanatic idealist who directly, and indirectly through his followers, liquidated as many millions of people as did Hitler. But Lenin's theories of economic justice have been sufficiently creative to spread, not only to the adjacent lands where the Red Army stands ready to enforce them, but also to many distant lands of Asia, Africa, the Middle East and Latin America where the concurrent dangers of these theories—because partially hidden—have not yet been fully understood. In the long run, therefore, the damage caused by a Lenin may surpass even that by a Hitler.

There is of course no measuring rod for social damage, any more than there is for pride. One can only conjecture. And Niebuhr's conjecture is that, over and above all the specific causes of evil in the world, there is a general cause at the heart of man. This assumption on his part has infuriated the people whose faith in the efficacy of improved social institutions had no ceiling on it. To them it seemed as if Niebuhr was denying the worth of their—and his own—endeavors to improve these institutions. Why should he insist that a new form of evil was likely to appear even in their new and improved state? As Donald Burton Meyer said in a footnote of his perceptive Ph. D. thesis,

> Unfortunately Niebuhr himself never explicitly, once and for all, insisted that plasticity in human nature was not at stake; inherent sin did not mean fixed forms of sin.[2]

And it is true that Niebuhr does not deal with plasticity as such. But he does state that no form of individual sin is fixed: it is the tendency to sin, not any particular form or intensity of sin, that is perennial. In *Christian Realism and Political Problems,* for example, he said:

> Good and evil are not determined by some fixed structure of human existence. Man, according to the Biblical view, may use his freedom to make himself falsely the center of existence; but this does not change the fact that love rather than self-love is the law of his existence in the sense that man can only be healthy

[2] This thesis, written for Harvard in 1953 was published in 1960 by The University of California Press as *The Protestant Search for Political Realism.*

> and his communities at peace if man is drawn out of himself and saved from the self-defeating consequences of self-love.

Man's perennial tendency to sin thus involves a breaking of the love commandment, that two-pronged edict that Jesus said summed up all the law. Niebuhr agrees with Martin Buber about the creativity of this synthesis by Jesus of the two formerly separated Old Testament Commandments, "thou shalt love the Lord thy God with all thy heart and all thy soul and all thy mind," from Deuteronomy, and "thou shalt love thy neighbor as thyself," from Leviticus. Yet, as Jesus also taught, love which is in essence not subject to being commanded must be experienced before it can be understood. And Niebuhr suggests in *An Interpretation of Christian Ethics* that this same love must be experienced before *sin* can be understood:

> The love commandment stands in juxtaposition to the fact of sin. It helps, in fact, to create the consciousness of sin.

Niebuhr who had experienced the grace of love since earliest childhood has not only shown an acute consciousness of sin but he has also shown an acute consciousness of the difficulty of pointing to sin without falling into it:

> The temptations to false prophecy are so ubiquitous that any sensitive teacher of the word may well be driven to the edge of despair. It is so easy to condemn flagrant pride and to condone a subtle form of it; to outlaw overt injustice and to sanction a covert form of it; to condone the security of power because its tentative necessity is recognized . . . or to encourage men to the illusory hope that they may build a world in which there is no power, pride or injustice. How can all these temptations be avoided? They cannot.

At the same time Niebuhr, whose life as student, minister, and teacher has not been conducive to contact with grossly evil people, seems to take for granted a degree of virtue in the average sinner that would make many such a one feel he should be sprouting wings.

Niebuhr assumes, for example, that there is no unbridgeable hostility within the family but an underlying and abiding love. Yet even this, he says, is not enough:

> Love within the bounds of consanguinity and intimate community is . . . devoid of special merit. "For if ye love them which love you, what thanks have ye? Do not the publicans do the same?" An all embracing love is enjoined because God's love is like that.

Niebuhr also assumes that people give, not rarely or skimpily, but often and generously to worthy causes. But this too, he says, is falling short of the law of love since what they give is of their surplus while those to whom they give it are lacking in basic necessities. At a World YMCA conference in Cleveland in 1931, he said,

> Religious idealism . . . encourages worth-while philanthropies but has difficulty in realizing that philanthropy may frequently be a veil behind which injustice lies.

Where then, does Niebuhr draw the line on selflessness? Where, please, may we rest on our hard-won laurels? Nowhere in history, according to to the second volume of the Gifford Lectures. Man's freedom is so great that "no fixed limits can be placed upon either the purity or the breadth of brotherhood for which men strive." Nor can the person who has sinned and been forgiven consider himself as remaining in a state of sanctification:

> The possibilities of new evil cannot be avoided by grace; for so long as the self, individual or collective, remains within the tensions of history and is subject to the twofold condition of involvement in process and transcendence over it, it will be subject to the sin of over-estimating its transcendence and of compounding its interests with those which are more inclusive.

He therefore defines original righteousness, the opposite of original sin, as "not a reality but an intention;" it is "perfection before the deed." As soon as we act, and act eventually we must if we wish to be responsible, there will be some form of self-centeredness revealed in that action. Even St. Augustine, Niebuhr points out, fell into the sin of pride in the process of writing a book about it. Augustine claimed that in the City of God, the sins of the City of the World would be overcome. But Augustine went on to identify the City of God with the Christian Church, of which Augustine was a member. Thus, Niebuhr concludes,

> The Church, as well as the state, can become the vehicle of collective egoism. Every truth can be made the servant of sinful arrogance, including the prophetic truth that all men fall short of the truth.

What then is the point of trying? If man can do nothing perfectly, why bother to do anything at all?

Because, Niebuhr would say, first of all it is man's duty; secondly it is part of man's nature, and thirdly there have been, and will again be, occasions when one person's imperfect actions are completed by others, or when his mistake turns out to be a useful one, or when by-products emerge that could never have been forseen and even afterward can only be explained as having happened "by the grace of God."

"A Nahum, or Prophet of Doom, among American philosophers," was the description of Niebuhr by John A. Mackay in the March, 1934 *Intercollegian.* Yet Mackay went on to say that "grace is a strangely lost word which Niebuhr restores to religious writing in this country."

There can be no comprehension of grace, Niebuhr believes, without a comprehension of sin; no sense of what forgiveness can mean, without a sense of how deeply man stands in need of it. He agrees therefore with Luther that "the final proof that man no longer knows God is that he does not know his own sin." Perhaps Niebuhr has also been working on the converse theory, that if man *does* come to know the depth and pervasiveness of his own sin, he may also come to know the grace of God. In all events, whatever the by-product, Niebuhr felt it his responsibility to point out the sin that exists not only in the religious world of which he was a part, but also in the secular world of which he was rapidly becoming a part.

13

The Seminary and the City

NIEBUHR's life in New York was, if anything, even more hectic than it had been in Detroit.

He continued to preach, travelling every single weekend of the academic year to colleges and universities around the country; he continued to take part in an ever-increasing number of religious and secular organizations; and, for the first time, he started full-time teaching. This latter activity, he recalled in the Living Library Volume as

> a hazardous venture, since my reading in the parish had been rather undisciplined and I had no scholarly competence in my field, not to speak of the total field of Christian theology. My practical interests and the devoting of every weekend to college preaching prevented any rapid acquisition of competence in my ostensible specialty. It was therefore a full decade before I could stand before a class and answer the searching questions of the students at the end of a lecture without the sense of being a fraud who pretended to a larger and more comprehensive knowledge than I possessed.

In the late twenties, New York City was hectic too. The pre-Beats were staying up all night making whoopee, and the stock speculators were staying busy all day making money. The fashionable businessman wore a small round gold ornament on his watch chain bearing the pre-Peale positive thinking of the bearded Dr. Coué: "Every day in every way I'm getting better and better." From the point of view of their profits, this was exactly right.

Then, in September, 1929, the bottom, as they said, dropped out of the market. In *Leaves* two years before, Niebuhr had criticized the evils of stock manipulation, singling out "stock dividends, watered stock and excessive rise in stock values" as part of the "pure legerdemain" by which "millions in property values" were being created. But neither he nor most other people foresaw the extent and duration of the depression that followed the crash.

The early thirties were a time of terrible poverty, and terrible contrasts: the contrast between what people used to have and be, and what they now had and were; the contrast between the productive capacity of the world's wealthiest nation and the paucity of its output.

On the same day that millions of unemployed workers were wearing out their last pair of shoes trudging hopelessly in search of a job, a wealthy financier sent word to his Sunday luncheon guests please not to wear hard soles lest they scuff the decks of his new $250,000 yacht. Children cried for food, first lustily and then weakly, only blocks from where overfed adults put more on their plates than they could eat. Men of former stature in the community pulled down their hat brims to hide their faces as they stood for hours in the breadline. "Brother, Can You Spare A Dime?" reached the then-equivalent of the Hit Parade.

Even nature seemed to be conspiring against the less fortunate members of society. Unusually cold winters made the gloveless fingers of street-corner apple vendors turn a mottled blue. And summers were bedeviled by drought. Thousands of small farm owners in the Middle West were forced to leave home as dust storms blew the eroded top soil away. The famous Land of Opportunity was offering not only less opportunity but less land as well.

The suffering in the cities was portrayed by Clifford Odets in *Waiting for Lefty;* the suffering in the hinterland by John Steinbeck in *Grapes of Wrath;* the suffering of the whole nation by John Dos Passos in *U.S.A.* Magazine articles by experts condemned the economic and political system that permitted such suffering to stem from such injustice. Three days before the first inauguration of Franklin Roosevelt as President of the United States (March 4, 1933), *World Tomorrow* published the words of Reinhold Niebuhr that he has since publicly eaten: "capitalism is dying and . . . it ought to die."

Nor was this point of view unusual at the time. As Murray Kempton recalled in *Part of Our Time,* 1955,

> It is already hard to remember that only a generation ago, there were a number of Americans, of significant character and talent, who believed that our society was not merely doomed but undeserving of survival, and to whom . . . its institutions seemed not just unworthy of preservation but crying out to be exterminated.

To many of these people, whether liberal or radical, religious or secular, the palliative measures taken by the New Deal seemed to be mere patchwork ("whirligig reform" was Niebuhr's term) and therefore grossly inadequate. What was needed was not a shoring up of the old system but its fundamental reconstitution. In *Christianity and Society,* Autumn 1953, John Bennett recalled

> the situation in which many of us lived twenty years ago. That was the period of the great depression and at the time labor was mostly unorganized and whether organized or unorganized it was helpless to defend itself against unemployment . . . It was natural for Christians who were concerned about Social Action during that period to become convinced that nothing short of socialism was an adequate goal. . . . Often it was enough to say: "Young man go left." A straight line to the left of the place where we were seemed a clear path of advance.

Long were the arguments within the political and academic groups of which Niebuhr was a part. Should the change in society be revolutionary, as the Communists and extreme Socialists insisted? Or should the change be evolutionary, resorting not to widespread bloodshed but to other forms of power-wielding in the interest of justice? And how, after the change had been accomplished, could the new society be prevented from developing different—and perhaps equally terrible—forms of injustice? Says Bennett who already was working closely with Niebuhr:

> A large part of Niebuhr's thought about the application of social ethics . . . is concerned with the relation between justice and power. The strength of the egoism of all social groups is such that the power of every group needs to be checked by the power of those of whom it is tempted to take some advantage. The struggle for justice consists largely in the effort to increase the

1. Hulda, Reinhold, Walter (in Wright City, Missouri, on the day of Reinhold's christening.)

2. Reinhold, Mother, Richard, Hulda, Father, Walter St. Charles, Missouri

3. The parsonage and the church in Lincoln, Illinois

4. Reinhold, Walter, Hulda, Richard
Lincoln, Illinois

Hulda and Reinhold, Father and Mother Niebuhr in front of church in Lincoln, Illinois—c. 1912

6. Ursula Keppel-Compton shortly before her marriage

7. Reinhold, as he looked when he first went to New York City. PHOTO BY BACHRACH

8. Reinhold Niebuhr in New York City, about to take off for Europe —again. PHOTO BY LILO KASKELL

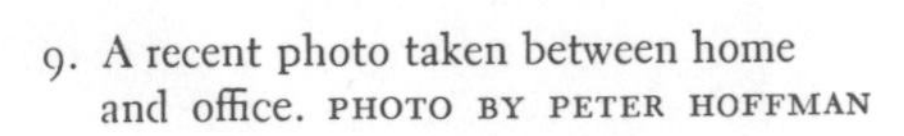

9. A recent photo taken between home and office. PHOTO BY PETER HOFFMAN

power of the victims of injustice. But the victims themselves will always be tempted by their new power.

Niebuhr had arrived in New York still pacifist in his leanings. In 1928, the *Fellowship for a Christian Social Order* of which he, Sherwood Eddy, and Kirby Page had been guiding spirits, merged with the equally pacifist *Fellowship of Reconciliation* of which John Haynes Holmes and Henry T. Hodgkin had been guiding spirits. For several years Niebuhr was its chairman and wrote an editorial column, *Ex Cathedra* (no less), for the magazine, *World Tomorrow*, which, although not the official organ of the F.O.R., mirrored its views. But by the beginning of the thirties he was ready to move on.

His move was in the direction of a modified socialism that excluded pacifism but did not favor violent revolution. On the other hand, it did not exclude revolution as the absolutely last resort. As Niebuhr wrote in 1932, "once the principle of coercion and resistance has been accepted as necessary to the social struggle and pure pacifism has been abandoned, the differences between violence and nonviolence lose some of their significance." But the violence of the extreme Marxists continued to repel Niebuhr, and in 1930 he helped to found the *Fellowship of Socialist Christians* whose purpose, as John A. Hutchison recalled in *Christian Faith and Social Action*, was "to explore and express a form of social Christianity independent of both pacifism and Marxism."

This group practiced its principles by pressuring its members when their income rose higher than $1400 a year to contribute generously to special projects. In spite, or because, of this the group continued to grow. In time it included original thinkers as varied as Paul Tillich and H. Richard Niebuhr, Will Herberg and Liston Pope. It met a few times a year, for a few days at a time, systematically to discuss some problem of importance to contemporary society. The group seems also to have discussed frequently and unsystematically the adapting of its own name to conform with the changes in its ideas. Starting as the *Fellowship of Socialist Christians* and carefully explaining that emphasis should be placed upon the noun, Christians, rather than upon the adjective, Socialist, the group then changed its whole title, after World War II, to *Frontier Fellowship*, until it merged, in 1951, with *Christian Action*.

At the same time, the group's magazine, which had started out, in 1935, as *Radical Religion*, changed its name, in 1940, to *Christianity and Society*, and finally merged, in 1956, with *Christianity and Crisis*, another Niebuhr-led production. (Since then the magazine has been busy changing not its name but its format, and under Wayne Cowan's thoughtful direction has expanded its coverage to include literature, theatre, the arts, and humor.)

But dropping the name "Socialist" from the group's title, and "Radical" from its magazine, did not imply, Hutchison makes clear, that the members had "ceased to be radically critical of social institutions;" what it meant was their "conclusion that Socialism in any precise sense of the word was no real cure for the ills of society."

Niebuhr personally, at the very height of his Marxism, always had reservations about it. His position at that time, in the early thirties, might have been summarized something like this:[1]

Where he agreed with Marxism	*Where he disagreed with Marxism*
¶ he was in favor of abolishing private ownership of the means of production (in Detroit he had already concluded that "private property that is no longer private should not be private").	¶ he was never in favor of abolishing all private property, such as small farms and businesses.
¶ he accepted the concept of "ideology" and agreed that our relation to property helps to determine our system of values. "Optimism" therefore seemed to him to be a typically bourgeois attitude based on the notable economic and social progress of the middle class.[2]	¶ he rejected the concept that our relation to property is the only, or even the chief, determining factor of our system of values; the individual in his freedom is capable, he maintained, of rising at times above all values of his class (or nation).

[1] This was the one page that was shown to Niebuhr and it met with his immediate approval; indeed he read it so fast that there exists some doubt that he could have read it at all. Some people *can* take in a page at a glance—and this is one quality that their slower reading friends find it difficult to forgive.

[2] In 1956 he still maintained that "what we think of man and God, of sin and salvation, is partly prompted by the comparative comforts or discomforts in which we live."

Where he agreed with Marxism	*Where he disagreed with Marxism*
❡ he was in favor of strengthening the workers against the business oligarchs.	❡ he never thought that the proletariat would be as sinless after the abolition of private ownership of the means of production as the Marxists claimed. Property, he felt was *not* the only cause of sin.
❡ he agreed that an unjust civilization was dooming itself to destruction by its own excesses.	❡ he felt that the extreme catastrophism of Marxism left too little room for God's freedom or man's.
❡ he felt that the economic theory of history made sense in ways that previous theories of history had not.	❡ he felt that Marxism's giving of economic power to the very people who already held political power was more dangerous than any previous theory of history.
❡ he admired an "idealism vigorous enough to condemn the [existing] social system in the name of a higher justice."	❡ he considered it idolatry to believe that humans could fully blueprint and bring forth the Kingdom of God on earth.
❡ he agreed that the Christian Church sided too often with the business interests and thus endowed the business cause with religious sanctity.	❡ he noted that the political oligarchs who suppressed the Church in Russia were themselves being endowed "with the religious sanctity which primitive priest-kings once held" (The *Atlantic*, April, 1931).
❡ he agreed that the Christian promise of rewards in the next world for submission in this world had been abused by power-mongering clerics, landlords, and political leaders, to the point where talk of selfless love and forgiveness was suspect.	❡ as early as 1930, during his visit to the Soviet Union, he noted the terrible "brutality" of the new system, and the following year he wrote that in this new "religion" there was "no sympathy or pity for human life as such and not any forgiveness."

Together with his political activities, Niebuhr continued his religious ones. He was active on three commissions of the Federal Council of Churches, namely, "Research and Education," "Racial Relations," and "Goodwill between Jews and Christians." He also served on the administrative committee of the ruling body of his own denomination, the

Evangelical Synod. And he took part in the *Theological Discussion Group* founded in the middle thirties by Henry Pitney Van Dusen.[3]

Yet his religious and political aims did not always coincide. In 1926, Niebuhr had been one of the founders of the *Emergency Committee for Strikers' Relief*. This committee included a number of devout Quakers as well as other pacifists. As Niebuhr recalled, the group decided "not to offer relief, if the relief were merely for the strikers. They wanted to offer relief to both strikers and non-strikers." To Niebuhr this appeared to be a self-defeating gesture since the nonstrikers were being more of a help to the employer than to their striking coworkers. An all-inclusive charitableness that ignored the factors of power in modern society could thus have results the opposite of those intended. Nor could purity of motive insure validity of result. The law of love, he was beginning to see, could never be carried over in an unqualified way into the social struggle.

The book in which Niebuhr first seriously grappled with the problem of where the law of love was applicable, and where it was not, was *The Contribution of Religion to Social Work*, the Forbes Lectures of 1930 published in 1932. In it Niebuhr insisted that there were areas of life where rational discrimination was more valuable than the purest religious idealism:

> The virtues of a rational morality are . . . sobermindedness and balance. Religion, on the other hand, is an affair of the emotions . . . it always involves a potential danger to a balanced view of a moral problem. If it is a sublime emotion . . . the religious devotee . . . may achieve a nobility which the rationalist can never encompass. . . . But emotion may disturb the cool judgment which is . . . necessary to high morality. It may lead to extravagances which emphasize one value . . . as against all other values. . . . Where a moral duty is simple but difficult, religious impulse is required to furnish the necessary dynamic for its fulfillment. But whenever a moral problem involves a complex situation with many conflicting and competing values, religion is usually not a helpful ally.

[3] This group underwent an unavoidable name-change, since it had started out as "The Younger Theologians." It met twice a year for a weekend and served as an important meeting ground for the theological liberals, the neo-Orthodox and the Religious Naturalists. It still meets on a once-a-year basis.

In that same year of 1932, Niebuhr also published *Moral Man and Immoral Society*, a book whose title in order to be accurate, he said jokingly, should have been *Im*moral Man and *Even More* Immoral Society. For its thesis is that sinful as is the individual, society is even more so. The book put Niebuhr on the intellectual map, and despite general critical acclaim, it also caused passionate controversy.

Among those who attacked it most unlovingly were the stalwart defenders of the law of love; among those who attacked it most unreasonably were the stalwart defenders of human reason. Niebuhr's attempt to maintain a dialectic tension between the soberness and balance of reason and the nobility of religiously inspired altruism was either not understood, or it was understood and firmly rejected. The secular liberals and radicals rejected Niebuhr's obscurantism (see Chapter 17), while the Protestant liberals and followers of the Social Gospel rejected Niebuhr's pessimism. Alan Richardson recalled, in the Living Library Volume, that

> *Moral Man and Immoral Society* seemed to many Christian leaders, especially to those of the older generation, to be the outpouring of a cynical and perverse spirit, very far removed from the benevolent and sanguine serenity which was held to be the hall-mark of a truly Christian mind . . . Their dearest assumptions concerning man's perfectibility, his kinship with the divine, his natural goodness, all were demolished with a ruthless iconoclasm.

As for the secular liberals and radicals, Niebuhr was both attacking their presuppositions and collaborating ever more closely with them in political causes. Whereas in Detroit he had learned through practical experience the resources for social justice among the Jews, in New York he learned the resources for social justice among the secularists. Some of the most irreplaceable workers in the vineyard of the Lord turned out to be those who cared not a rap for the Lord's proprietorship.

So relaxed were many of these secularists on the subject of religion that they never gave it a thought. Others were refugees from a rigid religious upbringing; for them atheism held so central a place in life that they were called the "believers in No-God who worship *him* with devotion." To both groups a minister appeared as some bare-chested priest of Amon Ra who had re-emerged to suggest that modern man take up seriously the worship of the sun.

To Niebuhr, in turn, the hardheadedness and humor of these secularists must have seemed like a cold shower after a Turkish bath. For as a liberal minister, and subsequently as a pacifist, he had been repeatedly exposed to the steamiest kind of sentimentality. In all events, he made no effort, by voice or pen, to lead his secular friends in the direction of religious faith. Nor did he explain to them what a valuable abrasive to Christianity they were unwittingly providing by that same hardheadedness and humor. Niebuhr was discovering how "God maketh even the wrath of man to praise Him." And he was also learning that while many in the religious world wanted to know what the secular world was thinking, the secularists did not necessarily return the compliment.

In 1929, the secular *League for Independent Political Action* had been formed, largely at the instigation of Professor Paul Douglas of the University of Chicago.[4] John Dewey, America's greatest living philosopher, was the League's chairman, and Niebuhr was a member of its Executive Committee. If Niebuhr did not write the League's first call to action, he must surely have been in full agreement with it:

> A political awakening is coming. No discouragements of the past should blind us to the fact that the Republican-Democratic alliance can never endure. An opposition party must arise . . . Progress is always made by the conflict of ideas.

The opposition party envisioned by Paul Douglas was "a vigorous party of the farmers and workers," interweaving the Middle West and Far West with the Eastern Seaboard, and the white collar workers with the manual ones. This party was to replace the moribund Republican and Democratic parties and would institute the following reforms: regulation of public utilities, progressive taxation, social security, protection for labor unions, and aid to farmers through farm credit and crop insurance. Ironically, within a decade the two old parties had resuscitated themselves sufficiently to embrace not one, but all these reforms; and the same Paul Douglas who then was saying the destruction of the Democratic Party "would be one of the best things that could happen in our political life" has now for years been one of its most effective standard bearers in the U.S. Senate.

[4] *Common Sense*, edited by Alfred M. Bingham and Selden Rodman, was the unofficial organ of the LIPA.

Actually there did exist a third party at the time the *League for Independent Political Action* was established. This was the Socialist Party whose leader, Norman Thomas, the League supported for President of the U.S. in 1932. But instead of embracing the proletariat in its membership, the Socialist Party embraced the middle class, especially the college-educated; and instead of embracing the country as a whole, it tended to center on the Eastern Seaboard. Its qualified Marxism appeared "pink" to the conservatives, but to the radicals the group appeared, in Leon Trotsky's supposed phrase, as "a party of dentists." Norman Thomas, the tall ex-Presbyterian minister with the sharp wit and the sweet smile was, however, indefatigable in pushing its program. And he courageously maintained labor's right to organize right in the teeth of the company police.

Thomas ran several times for President of the United States on the Socialist Party ticket. As he recalled in 1959, "I had rather be right than President—but I wouldn't have minded being both." Niebuhr supported him in 1932 and 1936. But by the second half of the thirties, Niebuhr was drawing more and more away from the Socialist Party because of its pacifism and isolationism; his formal resignation in 1940 represented several previous years of violent disagreement which left some hard feelings on both sides.

The Socialist Party was at the peak of its influence in the thirties. It had, as Arthur Schlesinger, Jr. relates in the first volume of his *Age of Roosevelt*,

> by far the largest following among the Marxist parties. But the Socialist appeal lacked qualitative intensity. . . . Paralyzed by internal squabbles, the Socialist Party did not take effective advantage of the depression. Where the Communists courted the unemployed by mass meetings and riots, the Old Guard Socialists shrank from such provocative methods. The party concentrated instead on research, education and persuasion.

In 1930, the Socialist Party candidate for Congress on the upper west side of New York City was Reinhold Niebuhr. "The winning candidate," Niebuhr recalls, "was the powerful Sol Bloom, and I think the only votes I got were from Columbia academics, or slightly more than that because I got a couple of thousand." Actually Niebuhr had been surprised to find himself running at all. Maurice J. Goldbloom, then an active member of the Socialist Party, remembers it well:

> In 1930 Niebuhr did run . . . quite against his will. What happened was that the Socialist Party filed a designating petition for him, and he didn't send in his declination until after the legal deadline (I think he was in Europe).[5] So in order to give effect to his declination, the party named Donald Henderson to replace him and sent a letter to all enrolled Socialists in the district telling them to write Don's name in on the primary ballot. Don . . . assumed that everything had gone according to schedule. He therefore embarked on a vigorous, not to say frenetic campaign . . . papering the district with pictures of himself and spending something like a thousand dollars of his own rather meager funds (and I believe a good bit of his friend Corliss Lamont's money as well). It was therefore more than a mild surprise to him . . . when the Board of Elections published the official list of candidates, and the name on it was Niebuhr . . . What had happened was that Charlie Webber who was then teaching at Union Seminary, and later became C.I.O. Regional Director for Virginia, organized the boys at Union to vote for Niebuhr in the primaries, and Niebuhr therefore was nominated against his will.

That it was also against the will of many Union Seminary trustees, Henry Sloane Coffin soon discovered via a constantly ringing telephone. Years later President-emeritus Coffin enjoyed the remembrance of furor past.

He smiled as he told of the occasion when Niebuhr consented to sit as judge of a Columbia student mock trial which was to "try" Columbia University President, Nicholas Murray Butler (in absentia), for the extreme conservatism of his political ideas. About the depression Butler was quoted as saying: "much of the talk of mal-distribution of wealth is sheer invention . . . mischievously devised by radicals." And about the growth of dictatorship abroad Butler had intimated in 1931, after Mussolini (and Stalin too) had come to power, that dictators were likely to be more impressive people than leaders of democracies. Butler's reputed admiration for Mussolini was part of the campus scuttlebutt.

[5] He probably *was* in Europe. Four dispatches which he wrote from Russia for *Christian Century* appeared in September and October of 1930.

When Coffin, however, explained to Niebuhr what a public embarrassment Niebuhr's mock trial appearance would be to him, Coffin, and to the Seminary, Niebuhr withdrew his name. "He tried to make amends," said Coffin, "as he always did when he felt he had been in the wrong." Thoughtfully Coffin paused, and then concluded: "Reinie has changed from being a violent social reformer to being a theologian. He has come a long way—I think he went around to a lot of political meetings and got fed up. The people were too naïve, too simple."

Union Seminary contained some naïve and simple people too. They and others were spellbound by one of its most challenging professors, Harry F. Ward, a leader of the left wing of the Social Gospel who, by the early thirties, was looking upon the events in Soviet Russia as being, in many ways, a constructive experiment in social Christianity.

Just as the pacifists appeared to Niebuhr too absolutist as to the means they approved, so the left wing of the Social Gospel appeared too absolutist as to the ends they approved. But to the young and inexperienced student there was something appealing and exciting about Ward's denunciations of the status quo and his radical hopes for the future. One student remembers him as the best teacher he ever had. Another remembers him as

> a gloomy, almost a morose person, who looked as if there were no hope at all. Since he was a professor in a Christian seminary, I decided he must be like Jeremiah, a prophet of gloom.
> My wife took a course under him . . . primarily a study of Marxism. She thought, naturally enough, that it would be given from the Christian standpoint, with a proper critique of Marx' ideas. But apparently it was taught as if the doctrines being studied contained all the truth one needed to know.[6]

Ward himself was able to reconcile many truths in Marx with many truths in the Bible, but some of the students were not. Bull sessions lasted far into the night, and sometimes bit irrevocably into the soul. One young man relinquished his faith in God and left the Seminary;

[6] According to Professor Ward in 1961, "My basic course in all the years I taught was the 'Social Teaching of the Bible,' and as other Christian scholars have done, and are doing, I am compelled to recognize that, because of their historic origin, there are some things in Marx which coincide with the ethical imperatives of Jesus and the 8th century prophets."

others sweated it out, sometimes veering toward the god of dialectical materialism; sometimes toward the God of Christ; sometimes thoroughly hung-up between the two.

On May Day, 1934, a few students climbed to the roof of Union Seminary and substituted the Red Flag for the Stars and Stripes. President Coffin was so infuriated that he talked of expulsion. Niebuhr was torn between loyalty to Coffin and to the students, some of whom were *his* boys rather than Ward's. The then-president of the student body, Carl Hermann Voss, said banteringly to Niebuhr, "You're partly responsible too, you know." But the grace of humor quite deserted Niebuhr that day and he solemnly nodded: "I know. Many of us are responsible."

At that time the hideous injustices of the Soviet system were still relatively well camouflaged, while the injustices of laissez faire capitalism were screaming from the headlines. There was no unemployment in Stalin's Russia, for example, while there were fifteen million unemployed in Roosevelt's United States.

Nor were the corrective measures taken by the New Deal always of a kind to instil faith in the recuperative powers of American society. A government order to slaughter baby pigs while human babies were starving was enough to drive to desperation those who hungered after righteousness as well as those who hungered after food. A group of forty-five religious leaders, including Niebuhr, John Haynes Holmes, Robert Searle, and others, wrote to President Roosevelt, in 1935, to say that there would be no permanent recovery in the United States as long as it depended upon palliative measures within the capitalist system.

In 1934, two years after *Moral Man,* Niebuhr published *Reflections on the End of an Era.* As he told his class twenty years later: "I thought I had outgrown my Marxist catastrophism, but it is clear by the title that I had not." The book was a selection of the Religious Book Club and it can still be read, like Vachel Lindsay's *Congo,* out loud, to the muffled beating of a drum:

> History is . . . like nature, slow to destroy what it has found useless or dangerous, and even slower to inter what it has destroyed.

Boomlay, comes the echo from the Detroit past:

> No feudal squire ever beat down rebellious serfs more ruthlessly than the industrial oligarch does when he finds his reign imperilled by the men who run his machines without respect for or loyalty to his power.

The contemporary picture, on the other hand, was not wholly dark. A bourgeois culture had not been entirely without creative results:

> The most outstanding achievement of a bourgeois civilization is its discovery and affirmation of the rights of the individual.

And one can hear overtones of a soft British voice in the point that follows:

> The emancipation of women, historically related to the struggle for universal franchise, is another achievement of bourgeois individualism.

These freedoms were not only enormously precious but they were being mortally threatened. The decadent features of capitalism, Niebuhr and many writers of the time believed, were leading straight toward fascism. *Reflections on the End of an Era* was catastrophic not merely in its title, but in its prognostication that "the drift" toward fascism "is inevitable."

Arthur Schlesinger, Jr., in his Living Library chapter, says of Niebuhr during that period, that in

> rebounding from the liberal belief in the inevitability of progress [he] was all too susceptible to an equally extreme belief in the inevitability of catastrophe. The recurrence of the "end of an era" formula in his writings of the thirties suggests his shocked fascination with the possibility of some basic turn, some drastic judgment in history.

The concept of drastic judgments in history, Niebuhr said as early as 1930, was "closer to the genius of Hebrew prophecy than liberalism, either secular or religious." In fact, if one could rightly read between the lines of the censored dispatches from the lands where capitalism had already "drifted" into fascism, some drastic judgments could soon be expected. And within a year after *Reflections*, Niebuhr was in personal touch with people who knew at first hand what the censored dispatches had left out.

Niebuhr had warned against Hitler's rise before 1933—and immediately afterward he went to work to help rescue Hitler's victims. Paul Tillich was the first of many distinguished refugees from fascism whom Niebuhr helped to settle in the United States. But at the same time, Niebuhr also kept in touch with the anti-Nazis who stayed inside Germany. Richard Day, serving as a chaplain in Europe after D-Day, was told that Niebuhr was *the* contact for the German Underground in the United States. This may have been something of an exaggeration, but the fact was that Niebuhr had stayed in touch with German underground through both religious and secular channels.

On the religious side, his chief contact was with Dietrich Bonhoeffer, a German Lutheran pastor who came as a post-graduate student to Union Seminary in the pre-Hitler thirties. Bonhoeffer who already had a book to his credit was firmly convinced of the Lutheran doctrine of "the two realms."[7] In one of Niebuhr's seminars Bonhoeffer was challenged by the young American students (whose lack of sophistication Bonhoeffer rather scorned) to explain how this doctrine would work in political life. Bonhoeffer said that if a Communist arrived at his house fleeing from the police, Bonhoeffer, in his capacity as private person, enjoined by God to love all men, would save the Communist; but if the police arrived, Bonhoeffer, in his capacity as loyal citizen, enjoined by the state to support law and order, would give the man up.

This rigid and automatic dichotomy sat not well with the students—nor, for that matter, with their professor. In time, ironically, it sat so ill with Bonhoeffer that he joined the group of rigorous Christians who, together with the Prussian Army officers, not only defied, but attempted to destroy, the head of the German state. During the 1944 attempt on Hitler's life, Bonhoeffer was caught and imprisoned, and on the night before the Allied forces liberated his prison, he was executed. Before then he had gone through several stages in his thinking, during which he had stayed in touch with Niebuhr. One stage which Niebuhr disapproved, and which Bonhoeffer subsequently abandoned, was the plan of going to India to study nonviolence under Gandhi. Another was the plan, in the early summer of 1939 (when Bonhoeffer predicted war would come by September, which it did), to leave Germany in protest against the gov-

[7] This doctrine is based on the scriptural edict to "render therefore unto Caesar the things which are Caesar's and unto God the things that are God's."

ernment's appalling actions. This plan brought him unexpectedly to the Sussex village where the Niebuhrs were living, prior to the Gifford Lectures. Niebuhr cabled President Coffin of Union Seminary who promptly cabled back to Bonhoeffer with an offer to teach in the Summer School. Bonhoeffer went to New York but later decided to return to Germany. "I made a mistake," he told Niebuhr the last time they saw each other. "The Christians in Germany will have to decide whether they wish to see the victory of Germany at the expense of civilization, or the victory of civilization at the expense of Germany. I would be a coward if I didn't take part."

On the secular side, Niebuhr's chief contact with the German underground came in 1935, when Mary Fox of the League for Industrial Democracy introduced him to Karl Frank, alias Paul Hagen.[8]

This sensitive and courageous man in his late thirties had been secretly going back and forth to Germany from the time Hitler achieved power. By 1935, however, armed resistance within Germany was no longer possible: the Nazis were too strong and they had killed or driven into exile too many potential insurrectionists. But Paul Hagen nonetheless thought it worth risking not only his life but the most hideous death in order to stay in touch with an underground group of several hundred members of the noncommunist left. He brought them news and money from the outside world and helped them to continue educational work among the labor people. After the end of the war, there turned out to have been other such isolated pockets of resistance, on the conservative as well as the liberal side, but at the time it was too dangerous for anyone to make an overture to anyone else of whose anti-Nazism he could not feel absolutely certain.

Hagen's group succeeded in smuggling out of Germany many people who otherwise would have been tortured or killed. But its main emphasis was on staying put and surviving if possible.[9] The group also maintained some contact, largely through Hagen, with fellow noncommunists of the Left in Spain.

[8] It was Hagen, in Richard Wagner's *Niebelungen Lied,* who finally succeeded in killing Siegfried, thus bringing about the *Götterdämmerung* or decline of the Teutonic gods.

[9] After the war, many of these survivors were in a position to be of crucial help in the re-establishment of democracy in Germany.

In Spain, Hagen, who assumed that his ability to be shocked by human cruelty had long since been exhausted by witnessing the Gestapo, found one further dimension of horror. For in the course of the Civil War, the Spanish Communists, Anarchists, and even a few of the Socialists copied their enemies, the Falangists, those Spanish allies of the Nazis, in simply and daily making use of murder in order to silence anyone who disagreed with them. Said Hagen years later:

> The greatest shock of my whole life was the idea of mass terror occurring as a matter-of-fact thing that people do every day, like something you have for breakfast. There was a complete change of morals. It was like mass paranoia. The idea of mass terror and murder was introduced in Spain by the Russian cadres. But others did follow.

Within the New York group of Socialists and independent liberals Niebuhr was a leading figure; as Hagen recalled in 1954, "Reinie was a hundred per cent helpful and self-sacrificing." But in reporting to this group, Hagen concentrated on the German rather than the Spanish problem:

> My job was not to report on the bad situation in Spain, but in Germany. I may even have been shy about mentioning the Spanish thing to Reinie. Not that a person like Reinie is shockable—but murder would have made it more difficult for him. And you must remember that murder was not an essential characteristic of the Left—only of a few cadres. I had the feeling, why grieve Reinie unnecessarily.

Although Niebuhr shared Hagen's hope of a resurrection of freedom in Germany, Hagen did not share Niebuhr's biblical basis for such a hope. Hagen's disinterest in Christianity was, however, no more of a drawback to Niebuhr than that of Fred Butzell had been. From the reverse point of view, moreover, Hagen felt the same way about Niebuhr:

> I hardly ever think of a time when there was any difference of opinion between us. I had the feeling of complete identity with him even though we have different philosophies. There is no use attacking a dogma. We were polite with each other. Whatever you may think about his thinking, he has the greatest integrity I have ever seen.

In political affairs, however, their presuppositions were identical. James Wechsler in *Age of Suspicion* described Hagen in words that apply equally well to Niebuhr:

> What he had learned was that there were few simple answers and slogans, and that man may fight best if he is fully aware of the complexity of the struggle.

The struggle was complex, Niebuhr felt, on the domestic front as well as the foreign one. The evils from which America was suffering did not of course compare with those in Germany, but they were terrible enough. And there was the danger of their leading to something worse. What could one do?

Work day and night, was Niebuhr's answer, and pray.

For although drastic judgment was part of the biblical message, so was providence. History was ultimately under the dominion of a good God, the creator of human freedom; and although evil would flourish to the end of history, it would not do so unchallenged and uninterrupted.

A prayer written by Niebuhr in the heart of the depression (and reprinted by Howard Chandler Robbins in *The Way of Light*, 1938) gives a picture of his dialectic feeling at the time:

> Oh God of grace and truth . . . mean though we are, we are not wholly so. . . . We are sick of the injustice and cruelty of which the whole world groans; we hear the cries of the oppressed and remember the desperate anxiety of those who face the future without employment, victims of the world's greed. Give us wisdom and grace to establish justice between men. . . . Help us as we worship thee to come to a closer knowledge of ourselves.

"Closer knowledge of ourselves." Here again lack of self-knowledge is tied to sin. For it was in the depths of the self, as well as in the depths of the economic and political structure, Niebuhr felt, that the basic causes of human cruelty and injustice were to be found.

A European scholar, Hans Hofmann, reports in his *Theology of Reinhold Niebuhr* a personal interview in which economic injustices were traced by Niebuhr to depths within man that modern man was refusing to recognize. Hofmann writes:

> It is highly significant that Niebuhr finds the origin of evil and the seed of the decline of the capitalistic era . . . in a false

> view of man. This opinion he never abandons. Not only can he trace to the wrong view of man all the failures and disasters of that form of society . . . What is still more important, he is led to the conclusion that a new era of humanity can be victoriously attained only with a new and definitive view of humanity. The effort to attain such a view . . . appears in all the years of creative work that follow. We have here come to the inner turning point of his development, as he himself once expressly affirmed.

But Niebuhr's view of humanity, as *Moral Man* had made clear, was never limited to the individual; it also included society. "Man," as Niebuhr says, "is the kind of creature who cannot be whole unless he be committed." And one of the towering paradoxes of the human scene is that the large group, like the nation, to which the individual commits himself—often with selfless devotion—is likely to be less moral than he.

14

The Sin of Society

EVERYONE knows that the mob is likely to be less moral than the individual. But until *Moral Man and Immoral Society* was published in 1932, few people knew that society—by which Niebuhr meant any large group such as the nation, class, large corporation, or labor union—is also likely to be less moral than the individual.

Many of Niebuhr's piquant ideas, such as those about original sin, were admittedly grounded in the Bible or other classic writings, but his ideas about society are quite unique. They are, furthermore, as persuasive to the secular world as to the religious; although the ideas originated out of Niebuhr's biblical presuppositions, they make sense without these—they are, in fact, verifiable by anyone by way of history books and daily newspapers and engagement in political action.

If these ideas are so patently valid, why did no one discover them before? Perhaps because the technological complexity of modern society has recently dramatized them as never before. The current instances are new, but the principles they exemplify, Niebuhr says, have been there all along.

"Society," he wrote in *Moral Man*, "is as primordial as the individual."

The individual, therefore, is a self tied in with its community, as it is a self tied in with its body. If there is anything Niebuhr has less interest in than a disembodied soul it is a desocialized individual.

In the Old Testament, the social dimension of man was deemed so important that salvation was pictured for the community rather than for the individual. For some Old Testament prophets this saved community consisted of Israel; for some, only Israel's remnant; and for some, the whole world. This latter universalism stemmed from Amos, but was also a part of several Eastern religions before being adopted by Christianity.

Certainly its cogency appears to be accentuated rather than diminished in the cobalt age.

The community to which an individual gives his primary allegiance varies from person to person and from period to period. For some people it is the family, for others the church, the class, the region, the race. In the days of the Roman, and also the Holy Roman, Empire, Niebuhr says in his recent book, *The Structure of Nations and Empires*, the core of loyalty was the empire; today it is the nation. For some moderns this devotion to their nation includes concern for the rest of the world; for some it excludes such concern. But either way, patriotism is a highly prized quality: "my country, right or wrong," is held up to school children as the model to follow; and its opposite, treason, is punishable by death[1] in the democracies as well as in the dictatorships. So potent, indeed, is patriotism that it takes for granted the willingness of the individual to lay down his life for his country. As Niebuhr points out, even a bourgeois country like the United States which historically emphasized the qualities of prudence and calculation, has nevertheless also paid homage to the heroic heedlessness of its national and regional martyrs.

Such heroic heedlessness is a form of agape, of selfless love, and it stands at the very peak of Christian values. But at the same time, Niebuhr points out, the nation for which the individual gives "the last full measure of devotion" is never as unselfish as that individual:

> The paradox is that patriotism transmutes individual unselfishness into national egoism.

And the patriot himself is likely to be the last to note how selfish his nation is being in relation to its fellow nations:

> The ethical attitude of the individual toward his group easily obscures the unethical nature of the group's desires.

Sometimes, in fact, Niebuhr questions how ethical the individual's attitude toward his group or nation really is. In *Christian Century*, April 22, 1926, he suggested that "nationalism is simply one of the effective ways in which modern man escapes ethical problems." And two years later,

[1] Niebuhr came out in favor of commuting the death penalty for the Rosenbergs to life imprisonment (see Chapter 26).

April 27, 1928, he concluded that World War I had been "made inevitable not by bad people who plotted against the peace of the world but by good people who had given over their conscience into the keeping of their various political groups."

The large political group is bound to be more immoral than the moral individual for a number of reasons. One reason is that the large group is incapable of agape or selfless love. As Karl Löwith has pointed out, there has never in history been a sacrificial nation. Nor is there likely to be one, Niebuhr says, no matter how virtuous the nation's leaders. For virtue includes responsibility, and responsibility to those within the nation precludes completely sacrificial action by its leaders.

Another reason why nations are less ethical than the individual is that nations have less power of self-transcendence. A prophet—or even a small group—can rise in judgment over the nation, but the nation itself has no organ of self-transcendence; its response, indeed, to the prophet's judgments has been such that Jesus' words continue to apply: "A prophet is not without honor save in his own country."

Nations, furthermore, are incapable of being, as is the individual, "encountered" by God as Judge. For the individual

> the knowledge that we are sinners and that inordinate desires spring from a heart inordinately devoted to itself, is a religious knowledge which, in a sense, is never achieved except in prayer.

Although this knowledge can be carried by the individual into his actions as a citizen, the nation itself when it tries to pray is more than likely to offer up what Niebuhr calls "liturgies of self-congratulation."

Not only is the nation incapable of selfless love but even of what Niebuhr calls "mutual love," the kind of love which is historically justified. The highest norm for any large group is, therefore, justice, although there is always the ideal possiblity that justice may be raised to a higher level by love. Nations are, to be sure, capable of friendship, kinship, and other kinds of organic and historic bonds, but the fact of power is never irrelevant to their internal unity or to their external alliances:

> The relationship between groups must . . . always be predominantly political rather than ethical, that is, they will be determined by the proportion of power which each group possesses at

> least as much as by any rational and moral appraisal of the comparative needs and claims of each group.

But power is not the whole story of their relationship either. As Niebuhr writes in *Daedalus*, Winter, 1959, another key factor is prestige. And between these two, the relationship is paradoxical. For as the nation's power grows, so does its prestige; yet as the nation's prestige grows, its need to flex its power diminishes. There is, furthermore, a complex relationship between its need to exercise power internally and externally; by and large, the less the need for internal exercise of power, the greater the nation's external prestige. Khrushchev's reduction of the Stalinist terror within Russia has enormously enhanced Russia's appeal to the neutralists. Or as William Phillips says, "a liberalized communism is far more difficult for the West to combat than the kind that relies on the knock on the door in the middle of the night."

The prestige of a nation, Niebuhr points out, depends partly on the *truth* about it, in terms not only of its power but of its ideals and the degree to which it incorporates these. But the prestige of a nation also depends partly on the *un*truth about it, in terms of exaggerating its worthy aspects and playing down the unworthy ones. Such exaggeration is a fact of life in the political realm, for it provides an important method of winning, without coercion, the support of the nation's own people and its allies. "The dishonesty of nations," Niebuhr says, "is a necessity of political policy"; and sometimes he quotes La Rochefoucald's maxim, "hypocrisy is the tribute that immorality pays to morality." Perhaps, like the proverbial woman who dresses as much for herself as for others, the nation must dress up its ideals and the extent to which it incorporates these, for the sake of its own people and its allies.[2]

For its own people, these ideals may develop a central significance that Niebuhr calls religious. But for the nation's allies and neighbors, the degree to which it lives up to these ideals may seem doubtful. Niebuhr likes to quote the Mexican philosopher who confessed to him:

> You will scarcely understand how much patience is required to be the national neighbor of a nation which is at once so powerful and so innocent.

[2] Recently the four tiniest and most helpless states of Europe banded together to dress up their joint policy for the atomic age. The slogan of Monaco, San Marino, Lichtenstein, and Andorra: "Peace through Tourism."

Niebuhr's frequent trips abroad and his wide reading of history have helped to give him a perspective on his native land less innocent than that of many other equally patriotic people. It is, he says, no accident that a rich *have* nation like the United States should stand for peace and for the type of economic and political freedoms that we have been able to afford but that the new *have not* nations may not be able to afford. Nor is it an accident that they should stand for national freedom (a form of autonomy for which they may, or may not, be ready) and for a type of equality between small and large nations that we may not always be able to afford to let them have. Our reluctance to see certain cold war impasses brought before the UN General Assembly, where the many small *have not* nations have the same vote as the few giant *have* ones, is but one realistic expression of the power factors upon which our national existence and our economic and political freedoms depend.

Niebuhr's sense of how mixed are the ideals and power factors in large-group relations started after World War I. This was the war the United States had entered in order "to end war." Americans believed passionately in this ideal and felt a terrible disillusionment (in which Niebuhr shared, according to *Leaves*) when America's entry into the conflict was shown to have been partially maneuvered for unidealistic reasons by the munitions makers abetted by the British government. The famous photograph of the German soldier cutting off the hand of the Belgian child was shown to be a fake with a British bit-part actor playing the part of the helmeted Hun. Yet during the war Americans believed—and possibly wanted to believe—the picture: since we and our side stood for peace and freedom, anyone who opposed us must necessarily be capable of the grossest depravities. With supreme and terrible irony, such proved to be the case with Nazi Germany thirty years later; but it was not equivalently the case with the Kaiser's Germany.

At the same time, the United States had also entered World War I (as she later entered World War II) for reasons of power not always admitted —or even always recognized. As Walter Lippmann has so cogently indicated, the defeat of Britain in either World War would have meant to the United States that the surrounding oceans were no longer in friendly hands. The century of peace enjoyed by Americans before World War I, and the luxury of neutrality enjoyed by them during the first years of *both* World Wars, were parasitic upon the power of the British Navy. Thus the United States maintained its innocence in terms of motive while displaying a certain irresponsibility in terms of power.

This irresponsibility, however, was outgrown by the United States after World War II. For the balance of power had shifted, and now clearly it was the Americans, rather than the British, who were "the first among equals" in the Western Alliance. The fact that American troops are now stationed in Europe is but one earnest of our intention to fulfill these new responsibilities. Our allies rely on us—in NATO and other ways—as we rely on them. For their power is essential so that together the West can provide a viable counter-force against further Communist aggression.

The Soviets describe their own overrunning of the satellite nations after World War II, not as the naked power grab it appears to us, but as the liberation of the workers of those countries from the injustices imposed upon them by the almost feudal structure that still was being maintained. In some of the countries, notably Hungary, Romania, and Poland, there was just barely enough truth in this assertion for many Russians to believe it, and even for some of the people in the overrun countries to believe it—for a time. But there was no truth in it in regard to Czechoslovakia, which did not of course prevent the Russians from claiming it as justification for their subversion of that formerly democratic land.

We can see the power element in *their* action, but many of *them* did not; *we* did not see the power element in *our* entry into World War I, but the Germans no doubt did.

Today the Russians accuse America of imperialism[3] when we try to help the less developed countries to help themselves. We, in turn, view this action on our part as motivated by unselfishness, or at the least by "enlightened self-interest." At the same time, we view Russian attempts to help these same countries as "imperialism" by way of subversion, while the Russians claim to be building "peace."

As individual citizens, it is, as Robert Burns pointed out, impossible to "see ourselves as others see us." And for a nation, this would take more than "a giftie from some power." For, as Niebuhr says, another aspect of the

[3] According to Marxist dogma, imperialism grows logically out of capitalism and is a key reason why capitalism is supposed to bear within it the seeds of its own inevitable dissolution.

nation's being less ethical than the individual is that "there is less reason" —less of a rational faculty—to guide its decisions:

> Individuals have . . . a rational faculty which prompts them to a sense of justice which educational discipline may refine and purge of egoistic elements until they are able to view a social situation, in which their own interests are involved, with a fair measure of objectivity. But all these achievements are more difficult, if not impossible, for human societies.

These societies, therefore, must stand open to criticism by individuals and groups. One group which historically has criticized society is the Christian Church. Niebuhr recommends that it both continue this role and also avoid offering purely Christian answers to complex collective problems. Having long been against political parties organized along religious lines, Niebuhr says today in regard to mankind's most dramatic collective problem: "When you face a nuclear dilemma, there is no Christian answer."[4]

A more commonplace example of a purely Christian answer being irrelevant to a collective problem was given by Niebuhr in *Christianity and Society*, 1950:

> "A Christian," declared an eager young participant in a symposium . . . "always considers the common welfare before his own interest." This simple statement reveals a few of the weaknesses of moralistic Christianity in dealing with problems of justice. . . . The first error consists in defining a Christian in terms which assume that consistent unselfishness is possible. No Christian, even the most perfect, is able "always" to consider the common interest before his own. At least he is not able to do it without looking at the common interest with eyes colored by his own ambitions. . . . Unfortunately there is no possibility [of complete unselfishness] for individual men; and perfect disinterestedness for groups and nations is even more impossible.

Niebuhr went on to record his frank relief when "a shrewd business man" in the symposium asked a leading question. "What do you mean by common interest?"

[4] Interview with William Rowley, Albany, New York, *Knickerbocker News*, September 18, 1959. Niebuhr's views on atomic problems appear in Chapter 26.

> Does it mean the family or the nation? If I have to choose between "my family" and "my nation," is the Christian choice inevitably weighted in favor of the nation since it is the larger community? And if the choice is between "my" nation and another nation, must the preference always be for the other nation on the ground that concern for my own nation represents collective self-interest?

Obviously no, says Niebuhr. We must always summon reason and discriminate judgment in order to weigh the conflicting claims. It is clearly only common sense to say that

> we cannot, for instance, solve the problem of our conflict with Communism by yielding to it as "the other," to the disadvantage of our civilization because it is our own.

Therefore, Niebuhr sums up:

> A Christian justice will be particularly critical of the claims of the self as against the claims of the other, but it will not dismiss them out of hand . . . A simple Christian moralism counsels men to be unselfish. A profounder Christian faith must encourage men to create systems of justice which will save society and themselves from their own selfishness.

Another reason the selfishness of groups is greater than that of individuals is that the group does not have a biological time limit to its life. Nations, according to Niebuhr, have "pretensions of immortality"; at the same time, they are not likely to appreciate the fellow-nation's fear of obliteration in the empathetic way that an individual apperciates his fellow-individual's fear of death.

Because nations live so much longer than individuals, they also nurse their grievances longer—sometimes until these fester into poisonous hatred. Niebuhr had seen such hatred in the Ruhr after World War I, on the part of both French and German. Certainly France's fear and resentment at the outcome of the Franco-Prussian War of 1870 contributed to her insistence that the Treaty of Versailles, two generations later, contain the punitive war-guilt and reparations clauses that in turn helped to push Germany down into the postwar chaos that laid the groundwork of despair from which Hitler rose to power.

Thus nations do, frequently, "let the sun go down on their wrath." This leads to their being not only less moral than individuals but also less able to live at peace with one another. As Niebuhr sadly wrote in *Moral Man,* seven years before the outbreak of World War II:

> Though human society has roots which lie deeper in history than the beginning of human life, men have made comparatively but little progress in solving the problem of their aggregate existence.[5]

Niebuhr's critique of large groups does not apply to those small groups within a democracy which have no overt power, but considerable prestige, and to whose endeavors individuals—often altruistically—devote much time and energy.

Niebuhr's appreciation for the worth of such groups has steadily grown as has his membership in their number. He points out, however, that the small group, which on occasion may act as the conscience of the large group, is not itself wholly able to transcend the interest of the large group. For its own existence is contingent upon the continuance of democracy within the large group. Were the United States ever to be forced to undergo the process of sovietization—a process, as James Conant has pointed out, that is far more destructive to life and liberty than anything going on in *already*-sovietized Russia today—these small groups would be the first to be liquidated. Thus, although they do not themselves exert power, they are not independent of its exertion.

Small groups, moreover, do exert subtle forms of power, through publicity and through the prestige of their support and the threat of their nonsupport. Thereby they combine spurring an individual to "moral" efforts greater than he might otherwise make, with an "immoral" wielding of power to accomplish these aims. How then shall the moral individual view himself as a responsible member of the several immoral societies of which he is a part?

Niebuhr's answer in *Christian Faith and Social Action* is couched in religious terms, but it applies to the secular citizen as well:

> To know both the law of love as the final standard and the law of self-love as a persistent force is to enable Christians to have a

[5] Niebuhr likes to quote a statement he heard Churchill make in regard to the Allies' attitude toward Germany after World War II: "Let us only remember so much of the past as will help us to be creative in the future."

> foundation for a pragmatic ethic in which power and self-interest are used, beguiled, harnessed and deflected for the ultimate end of establishing the highest and most inclusive possible community of justice and order. This is the very heart of the problem of Christian politics: the readiness to use power and interest in the service of an end dictated by love and yet an absence of complacency about the evil inherent in them. No definitions . . . of justice can prevent these forces from getting out of hand if they are not handled with a sense of their peril.

While Niebuhr was grappling, in the early thirties, with the problems of justice in the collective realm, he was also learning a thing or two in the personal realm about the problems of love. (For what, after all, is love if it, too, cannot be "used, beguiled, harnessed and deflected for the ultimate end of establishing the highest and most inclusive possible community" of two persons in marriage?) *Does Civilization Need Religion?* had been dedicated

To the memory of my Father
who taught me that the critical
faculty can be united with
a reverent spirit
and
To my Mother
who for twelve years has shared
with me the work of a
Christian Pastorate

and *Leaves* had been dedicated to Niebuhr's "friends and coworkers of Bethel Church." *Moral Man,* however, carried a reticent and irreducible dedication that was to reappear in subsequent volumes: "To U.M.N."

15

Love and Marriage

THE romance, of course, had the Seminary on its dignified ear. The setup was almost too Hollywood to be true: the tall, arresting lone-eagle professor in his late thirties, who treated his female students with the same intellectual rigorousness as his male ones—an attitude which some female students took to be a compliment and others did not—yet who colored visibly when a young lady told him she was glad to meet him; and the glorious young British girl with the long blonde hair, round blue eyes, and flawless skin, who had been the first female student ever to win a first in theology at Oxford, and who had been recommended by her professor there, Canon William Streeter, to President Henry Sloane Coffin of Union Seminary as "a maiden erudite as may be."

Coffin himself liked to recall "the arrival of that very pretty English girl who made a great splash with the boys." Ursula Keppel-Compton, the daughter of a doctor and the niece of an Anglican bishop, was, he said, "a first-rate student, though occasionally distrait." The following was his recollection of her interview with him on the subject of her specialty at the Seminary:

Coffin: "What are you going in for?"

Miss Keppel-Compton: "I prefer to browse."

Coffin: "We don't give fellowships for browsing, you know."

Miss Keppel-Compton (dazzling smile): "You're *so* insistent."

Meanwhile, in the Stenographic Pool, daily bets were being placed as to which of the young, and not so young, gentlemen would succeed in taking her to lunch.

The field finally narrowed to three: two professors and one student; and then to two, one of each. Whether the following story is apocryphal or not, it is firmly believed by many then-students:

Time: an afternoon in the spring of 1931—
Place: Riverside Drive, near 120th Street—
Reinhold Niebuhr turning to Ursula Keppel-Compton who was valiantly trying, on legs far shorter than his, to keep up with his long strides: "Well, Ursula, it's inevitable, isn't it?"
Ursula Keppel-Compton (slightly winded): "Yes, dear."

Today Reinhold Niebuhr is known to entertain himself, and those of his guests who have not heard it before, by quoting the statement that "in courtship it is the man who pursues—until the woman catches him." Mrs. Niebuhr, and those of the guests who *have* heard it before, are known to look at each other with a wild surmise and count to ten before continuing the conversation.

A rather more chivalrous description of courtship was given by Niebuhr in the Harvard Chapel twenty years after his own:

> No *I* can be an *I* without the encounter with a *Thou*. . . . Thus it is good to find that a man can only be fulfilled by a woman, a woman by a man. . . . There is fortunately a divine madness which leads men to lose themselves in others.

At the time, that spring of 1931, Niebuhr referred in class to someone in the Old Testament who "took unto himself a wife." A whoop from the students made him stop and realize that the phrase was shortly to apply to himself. Red in the face, he huffed defensively, "Well, it's a normal and natural thing to do."

As soon as classes were over in May, Ursula Keppel-Compton went home to England for a month to prepare for the wedding. Transatlantic cables are reported to have burned on the perplexing subject of vests, which in America mean waistcoats but in Britain mean undershirts. Whether the bridegroom and ushers ended up wearing one or the other, both or none, the then-students never discovered.

The Niebuhrs were married with full Church of England solemnities, and Mrs. Niebuhr has remained a devoted Anglican despite her long-term feminist disapproval of that Church's refusal to ordain women: "Nothing but women's societies," President Coffin remembered her complaint.

Ursula Niebuhr has occasionally preached in the James Chapel at

Union, and also in the little church in Heath, Massachusetts. Her husband credits her with a "far better liturgical sense" than his own, and there has been talk for years about their collaborating some day on a book of prayers.

In addition to sharing her husband's religious interests, she also shares his political ones. She could not, however, bring herself to relinquish her British citizenship until after her beleaguered native land had not only survived the Battle of Britain but had arrived at a harmonious postwar relationship with the United States.

Ursula Niebuhr's first vote as an American citizen was in the national elections of 1956, and she registered, to the delight of her son Christopher, as a member of the Democratic Party, rather than joining her husband in the Liberal Party, or those of her friends who did not join, but were born into, the Republican Party.

In addition to being dedicated "to U.M.N.," *Moral Man* must also have benefited from some bridal proof-reading, since certain British spellings, like organi*s*ing, civili*s*ation, and hum*our*, begin to make their appearance. Outspoken and humorous as she is, she must have enjoyed the book's originality and iconoclasm. Both Niebuhrs, in fact, are so relaxed about irreverent expressions that one visitor forgot himself in their presence to the point of referring to someone he disliked as "a Christer." Mrs. Niebuhr nodded understandingly and Doctor Niebuhr pricked up his ears, not as a minister, but as a collector. "That word, you know, comes from Yale," he explained. "It was coined originally about the Dwight Hall boys."

The word that is used by the Niebuhrs as the signal for the dogs to lie down and wait for their owners' return is "Church." While putting on her coat (she rarely wears a hat) Mrs. Niebuhr speaks the word in holy tones, and the dogs, overawed, lie down near the front door. Perhaps the Niebuhrs *are* on their way to church (they attend services either at James Chapel or at the nearby Episcopal Cathedral of St. John the Divine), or perhaps they are on their way to a meeting, a dinner with students (within one week they were treated to an Indian and a Japanese home-cooked meal) or on rare occasions, to the theatre (the rareness coming from their lack of time rather than their lack of enthusiasm).

Moral Man, furthermore, may not have appeared as iconoclastic to Ursula Niebuhr as it might have, had she spent her first twenty-odd years on this, rather than the other side of the Atlantic. For the various forms of social security that seemed revolutionary in the United States in the early thirties were commonplace in Britain and many nations of Europe. There, old age pensions and unemployment benefits had been in operation for a generation, while here, in 1935, when Roosevelt tried to make them part of the New Deal, the antagonistic reaction was extreme. Said New York's distinguished Representative, James Wadsworth, for example,

> This bill opens the door and invites the entrance into the political field of a power so vast, so powerful as to threaten the integrity of our institutions and to pull the pillars of the temple down upon the heads of our descendants.

The temple of unfettered laissez faire had tumbled in many parts of Europe and so had the temple of optimism. This was the period when Niebuhr, according to Donald Burton Meyer, was busy "instructing America by European example." Niebuhr was not simply trying to "*épater les bourgeois*"; he genuinely felt, on the basis of World War I, the crash and the depression, that "the real fact about our civilization is that it is flirting with disaster." (*Christian Century,* March 23, 1931).

At the same time, Niebuhr was already publicly disagreeing with extreme pessimism, particularly that of Europe's leading theologian, Karl Barth, whose first book translated into English, Niebuhr had reviewed in 1928 (see Chapter 22).

In his attack on Barth, Niebuhr was continuing the Jack-the-Giant-Killer pattern that first became evident in Detroit, only this time it was the leader of Europe's Protestantism rather than the leader of America's industrialism whom he was trying to cut down to size. Nor was this the end of such attempts.

When Niebuhr first arrived in New York, John Dewey was bestriding the Columbia campus like a Colossus. Niebuhr tried from the philosophical, though not the educational, point of view to leave Dewey without a leg to stand on. So impatient was the young teacher to question the basic presuppositions of the old master that he could not even wait to get into the text of his book, *Moral Man*: the attack on Dewey starts right in the Preface.

Dewey, however, did not bother to answer Niebuhr directly during the thirties. But his disciple, Sidney Hook, took up the cudgels in his defense. Thus, in part at least, the young theological brave had his reward: fresh scalps and scars to carry home to his bride.

Life inside the tepee, meanwhile, was having its ups and downs, according to the cheerful recollections of its then-inhabitants. For one thing, a new home needed to be found for Mrs. Gustav Niebuhr who had moved from Detroit to keep house for her son at Union Seminary. (In time she settled with her daughter, Hulda, on the campus of McCormick Theological Seminary in Chicago.) Then, in addition to the ordinary differences between two people, Reinhold and Ursula Niebuhr had a difference of nationality and a fifteen year age gap with which to cope. Both of them now advise young people embarking on matrimony not to be the least concerned if "the first two years are hell." At the same time, Niebuhr says (as he did in a sermon at St. George's in Manhattan, in 1959) that for him the Pope's encyclical on marriage had one serious flaw: it omitted the fact that "marriage is fun." And during the first year of Niebuhr's marriage he published *The Contribution of Religion to Social Work* in which he said,

> Where religion encourages an attitude of mutual forbearance and forgiveness, and where it emphasizes the sacramental character of the family union, thereby assuming its permanence, an atmosphere is created in which difficulties are resolved much more easily than in a purely secular atmosphere. It might not be too strong an assertion to say that religion has achieved its highest triumphs in family life.

In subsequent years Niebuhr frequently called the family "the seedpot of the Kingdom of God"; it is in family life, he says, that the closest approximation of selfless love is usually to be found. And in *Moral Man*, published that same year, he wrote,

> In the sphere of human and moral relations the love of those who are nearest and dearest to us and who do not lose confidence in us in spite of our weaknesses and failings is, and has always been, regarded by the religious imagination as a symbol of the benevolence and the forgiving of God . . . there is a tremendously helpful and therapeutic value in the assurance of religion that

> the past can be conquered and need not tyrannize over the present or the future.

Nor is it exclusively within the family circle that people find the experience of the past being conquered. Religiously, the most dramatic such experience is when the self at its farthest reaches is encountered by God; romantically, the most dramatic such experience is when two people fall in love; and on the level of friendship, an encounter can be so creative that one or both persons are changed and strengthened. Will Herberg, in the *Union Seminary Quarterly Review* of May 1956 described the beginning of one such friendship: it started with his being intellectually confronted by *Moral Man* several years after it had been published:

> My first encounter with the thought of Reinhold Niebuhr came in the later 1930's. I was then at a most crucial moment in my life. My Marxist faith had collapsed under the shattering blows of contemporary history. . . . I was left literally without any ground to stand on, deprived of the commitment and understanding that alone made life livable. . . . What impressed me most profoundly was the paradoxical combination of realism and radicalism that Niebuhr's "prophetic" faith made possible. Here was a faith that transferred the center of its absolute commitment to what was really absolute—the transcendent God—and was therefore able to face the real facts of life unafraid, with open eyes. . . . This "meeting" with Niebuhr's thought—I did not yet know him personally—quite literally changed my mind and my life. Humanly speaking, it "converted" me, for in some manner I cannot describe, I felt my whole being, and not merely my thinking, shifted to a new center.

Herberg's post-Marxist pit of almost suicidal despair was known to other fervent and brilliant men at this time as *The God That Failed* makes clear. One result of being raised from it, in Herberg's case, was that he

> could now speak about God and religion without embarrassment, though as yet without very much understanding of what was involved.

He could also pick up the telephone and call the author of *Moral Man*. "Can I come up and talk to you?"

He came, he saw, and the worst of the past was conquered. Many subsequent conversations resulted, and one day Herberg said, "I hope you won't mind, Reinie, but I've decided against becoming a Christian."

Niebuhr beamed.

He knew by then that Herberg's commitment to biblical faith was so strong that the words could only mean that Herberg was embracing, instead of Christianity, his own ancestral faith of Judaism.

The foreword to Herberg's influential and controversial *Judaism and Modern Man* says,

> What I owe to Reinhold Niebuhr in the formation of my general theological outlook, every page of this book bears witness.

What Niebuhr, in turn owes to Herberg is not only friendship and intellectual stimulation—listening to the two men talk is like watching a tennis match played at triple speed: the observer's head nearly comes off from the strain of having to move it back and forth so fast—but also insight into the profundities of biblical Judaism. Niebuhr had had friends of Jewish background ever since Detroit and Fred Butzell, but either, like Butzell, they attended religious services out of habit rather than conviction ("second rate book reviews" was Butzell's opinion of most rabbinic sermons), or, like James Wechsler, they attended no services at all. Here at last was a sophisticated modern who was at the same time a devoted believer in the Jewish religion. The discussions ranged far, wide, and deep. And before long they had involved the two wives as well.

Ursula Niebuhr, like her husband, is a friend and admirer of Herberg's. She invites him to address her classes at Barnard and teasingly says that he reminds her of St. Paul.

Anna Herberg, Will's late wife, was also a friend of both Niebuhrs, and in their discussions she fulfilled the essential role of one listener among four persons. She said little, and when she spoke, it was softly. Yet she clearly had the reserves of strength that made her a modern counterpart of Ruth in the Bible: spiritually, in effect, she had said to her husband, "wheresoever thou goest, I shall go; thy people shall be my people." Thoroughly involved in Marxism with him, she then also broke with it, and subsequently embraced Conservative Judaism with him and learned to follow its rituals and dietary laws. After he became the Jewish counterpart of Niebuhr—circuit-riding to the colleges and universities—she uncomplainingly travelled or serenely settled for brief times in one unfamiliar place after another.

Thus she and Ursula Niebuhr appear to epitomize the two kinds of wife that men of exceptional leadership-qualities seem to choose: the self-effacing woman whose interest is identical with her husband's, and the dynamic woman with an interest of her own, which gives her a center of gravity slightly different from his, from which to offer him fresh perspective upon his own activities.

There are, of course, exceptions, but the wives of men in public life seem to fall into these two categories. The self-effacing helpfulness of a Mamie Eisenhower stands in contrast to the dynamic helpfulness of an Eleanor Roosevelt (whose career was teaching). Other similar pairs whose husbands also occupied the same position at different times are: Lady Churchill and Mrs. Hugh Gaitskill (whose brief career was medicine); Mrs. George C. Marshall and Mrs. Dean Acheson (whose career is painting); Mrs. Thomas E. Dewey and Mrs. Averell Harriman (whose career was running an art gallery). Both kinds of wife are able to make their respective husbands happy; there is no choice between them except the choice made by the man himself.

Certainly there do not exist many men with the brilliance and forcefulness to have made a suitable spouse for Ursula Niebuhr, just as there do not exist many women with the brilliance and verve to have made a suitable spouse for Reinhold Niebuhr. For him, the spice of life lies in dialogue: at home, in the classroom, on visits to friends, he challenges others to argument and enjoys the process whether he wins or loses.

Niebuhr was once asked for his opinion of a learned and articulate friend whose wife never disputes a point her husband makes and invariably shushes everyone else whenever the Great Man wishes to speak. Niebuhr smiled. "Something must be wrong with a fellow to want a wife like that."

Nor are the subjects the Niebuhrs enjoy discussing always serious ones. Although the National Advertising Council has been telling everyone, including those who do not relish being told such things, that "families that pray together stay together," the Niebuhrs' point of view would more likely be, "families that laugh together laugh together."

One event they still laugh about involved the bridegroom's landing in jail the summer after they were married, and the bride's having to borrow fifty dollars to bail him out ("I wonder if it was worth it," she ruminates in his presence). He, it seems, was driving back to Heath, Massachusetts. Characteristically impatient, although not a speeder, he neglected to notice a new Stop sign that had been posted at a V in the road in Lee, Massachusetts, right next to the Police Barracks. (The original sin of pride at remaining within the speed limit may have prevented him from being sensitive to the presence of troopers.) As he cruised along without stopping, a siren blew. And when he was hauled in, he found he did not have enough money to put up his own bail. So off he went to a barred cell and was kept on the spiritual equivalent of bread and water, i.e., without a typewriter. "I felt like a jail bird for those four hours," he recalls. "Guilty. I went over my life like a drowning man."

The following summer he was equally busy, travelling, speaking, writing. Yet the atmosphere of the home to which he hurried back between engagements can be surmised from the contemporary note from Ursula Niebuhr to Bishop Scarlett:

> Reinhold is pretty fit, though gets very exhausted at times. We're feeling terribly sentimental today, as we've been married two years all save a day, and that somehow seems an occasion.

It was an occasion—for the first most difficult two years were over. And by the time a son, and then a daughter, came to complete the family, Reinhold Niebuhr's understanding of the "vocation" of motherhood—fatherhood he terms but an "avocation"—was sufficient to convince him that the one part of the Bible surely written by a woman is the Magnificat. This hosanna has been echoed in every generation, regardless of the mother's religion or lack of it, when her body first becomes the vessel through which new life is to appear: "my soul doth magnify the Lord . . . for he hath regarded the lowly estate of his handmaiden."

As for fatherhood, Niebuhr is reported as having been quite capable, in his wife's absence, of diapering a baby with one hand and writing a book with the other. Nor did he—at least in summer—leave the household and gardening chores entirely to his wife. For she too, it was clear, needed time to pursue her intellectual interests. And besides, in modern America, how could he have done otherwise, publicly committed as he was to the necessity of justice as well as love?

16

Love and Justice

WHEN Niebuhr was asked by *This Week* magazine to choose the text from the Bible that has meant most to him, his answer was Ephesians 4:32, "And be ye kind one to another, tender hearted, forgiving, even as God for Christ's sake hath forgiven you."

In explanation of this choice, Niebuhr gave two reasons: one, because the text describes "the high point of the Christian ethic, which is forgiving love," and the other, because it indicates that the only way we can achieve the power to forgive is from having, ourselves, been forgiven: "the charity of forgiveness is . . . not possible as a duty. It comes by grace."

Such grace, Niebuhr says, is not limited to Christians or other religious people. In a recent book of essays, *Pious and Secular America,* he notes the

> simple observable fact that we have the capacity to love only as we have the security of the love of others. It is this security which is the real source of grace to most people. It is a grace which can be mediated by anyone, religious or irreligious, who is capable of love.

To people with biblical faith God's love and forgiveness are the highest reality; to people without this faith human love may be the highest reality. Yet human love is connected to God's love in the eyes of faith. "The fruits of the spirit," said St. Paul in a passage Niebuhr frequently quotes, "are love, joy and peace."

Although forgiving love is "the high point of the Christian ethic," it cannot be forced either within oneself or other people. As Niebuhr said in James Chapel in 1956, "There is no power in the sense of duty to compel attitudes of love . . . the law cannot compel the selfish heart to love his fellowman."

We may force ourselves to *say*, "I love you," or "I forgive you," but we cannot force ourselves or anyone else to *feel* love or forgiveness, or to carry forgiveness to its ultimate conclusion which is either genuinely to forget our grievance or honestly to suffer with and for its perpetrator rather than ourselves. Forgiving love, therefore, is the opposite of self-pity. And we become capable of offering this love to others only if we have previously been offered it by someone whose opinion matters to us. Yet the appropriation of such forgiveness, as well as the ability in turn to offer it, is never wholly the result of will power. As Niebuhr said in a Harvard sermon, "It is the fruit of grace which breaks the prison house of self-concern."

In the *Messenger*, June 21, 1950, Niebuhr tried to define this mysterious and misunderstood word, "grace":

> The realm of "grace" distinguishes itself from law as freedom is distinguished from coercion. God's grace is the free gift of his forgiveness beyond his Law and justice . . . Grace in art represents the freedom of the artist above and beyond the instruments and techniques of his art . . . In the Christian life "graciousness" in our personal relations [is] . . . never a substitute for the justice of the Law . . . When we feel we "ought" to do something we are under the law. We set our sense of duty against our inclinations. But there are moments of grace in which duty and inclination are one . . . the most perfect expression of "grace" in human relations is our forgiveness of one another.

One modern technique of such forgiveness is the professional acceptance and understanding offered to patients and parishioners by psychiatrists and pastoral counselors. When the patient or parishioner learns to respond to this acceptance and understanding, he may find a dissolving of that calcified anxiety called guilt which was one of the contributory causes of his exorbitant self-concern, his painful anxiety, or his destructive behavior.[1] The doctors credit transference; the ministers credit grace. As Niebuhr said in a recent sermon (he deals with this subject more in recent years than in the past, and more in sermons and lectures than in books), "It is surprising how similar are the conclusions of the Christian faith and the wisest of the psychiatric approaches to this problem."

Both know that love cannot be legislated; yet both know that we need love from the day we are born, not as a reward for doing the right thing, but as its prerequisite. As one of Niebuhr's favorite masters, St. Augustine, advised, "love and do whatever you wish." For Augustine knew from his own experience that those who loved in the way of agape would *want* to do what was best for others, not out of fear, not out of duty, not out of hope of reward, but freely and joyfully, out of gratitude for God's love and man's. Augustine, moreover, had learned in his own life the difference between remorse which is a despairing regret, and repentance which bears the hope of being forgiven.

On the other hand, Niebuhr sternly warns, there are dangers in trying to overapply the ultimate principle of agape or forgiving love. For one thing, it does not carry over to the relationships between large groups; their highest goal is justice rather than love. For another thing, forgiving love ceases to be love and becomes a weapon when it is deliberately used to manipulate other people. It may still be *called* love, but in fact it is a form of imperialism. And Niebuhr deplored (in *Christianity and Society*, Autumn, 1942) "the poverty of the English language" which includes in the one word, love, "everything from a purely physical desire . . . to the sacrificial passion which ended on the Cross."

Going back to the word's history, Niebuhr recounted how the writers of the New Testament rejected the common Greek word for love, *eros*, and settled instead on the Stoic word, *agape*, and filled it with new meaning. "The Greeks had a word for it," but the English language does not

[1] Unfortunately the word "anxiety" is used theologically for the feeling all men have because of their combination of finiteness and freedom, and psychiatrically for the feeling the individual may have because of his unconscious conflicts and repressions. Niebuhr distinguishes further between the anxiety that comes from lack of faith, and the "fear and trembling" described by Kierkegaard which presupposes faith and awe.

—nor, curiously, does any other modern language. Agape, Niebuhr continued,

> is something more than even the most refined form of sympathy, for it does not depend upon the likes and dislikes which men have for each other. It is not determined by interest or passion. It is not the love which we have for people because we share common ideas with them, or because we are intrigued by the tilt of their nose. . . .
> The love which the gospel demands is justified and validated only transcendentally. We are asked to love our enemies that we may be children of our Father in heaven. An attitude of spirit is enjoined without any prudential or selfish consideration. We are not told to love our enemies because in that case they will love us in return . . . Such a love is not easily achieved. In a sense no one ever perfectly achieves it. But is is, at least, no psychological absurdity. It does not demand that we should be emotionally attached to someone with whom we are in conflict. It does demand that we should desire the good of our enemy. If achieved, it purges us of hatred; for hatred always has an egoistic root. . . .

Yet this Law of Love was precisely what Freud attacked in *Civilization and its Discontents* for being "a superlative example of the unpsychological attitude of the cultural super-ego." The Christians who were promulgating this law, said Freud, were producing "revolt or neurosis in individuals" and making them unhappy. For this law, he said, "is impossible to fulfill."

Niebuhr's answer to these accusations by Freud was given in *An Interpretation of Christian Ethics;* though Niebuhr felt that Freud had misinterpreted the teachings of Christianity, Freud's accusations, nonetheless, had sufficient validity to merit discussion:

> [Freud's] is a perfectly valid protest against a too moralistic and optimistic love perfectionism. But it fails to meet the insights of a religion which knows the law of love as an impossible possibility and knows how to confess, "there is a law in my members which wars against the law that is in my mind" . . .

> [The Law of Love] would be regarded as less dangerous by Freud if he knew enough about the true genius of prophetic religion to realize that it has resources for relaxing moral tension as well as for creating it.

In the person who feels himself to be a forgiven sinner, there may appear what Niebuhr calls "the nonchalance of faith" which he contrasts with "the stinking sweat of self-righteousness" generated by those who work full time at perfecting their own and other people's virtue by means of "strenuous moral striving." As Niebuhr wrote in *The Messenger*, April 24, 1951:

> Christianity is . . . in short not primarily a moral law, so rigorous that no one can keep it. The Christian faith is primarily the assurance of a divine forgiveness toward all who do not pretend to be righteous but know themselves to be sinners.

This divine forgiveness is misinterpreted not only by militant atheists like Freud but also by many pious believers. It is with some of the latter in mind that Niebuhr quotes Pascal's statement: "The world is divided into saints who know they are sinners, and sinners who believe themselves to be saints."

Among the latter, Niebuhr says, are those Christians who not only preach agape as a technique of making friends and influencing people, but attempt to practice it wholesale in regard to groups as well as individuals. This identification of agape, or selfless love, with mutual love, or the "love which is reciprocated and historically justified," misses the whole beyond-history or eschatological dimension of the Bible, Niebuhr feels. The crucifixion, he insists, is *not* a success story within history; it was a tragedy. And it is only from the vantage of beyond-history that its significance is lifted beyond-tragedy.[2] Niebuhr therefore says that the New Testament ethic of agape must not be "reduced to the limits of a prudential ethic, according to which we are counseled to forgive our foe because he will then cease to be our foe." Nor does Niebuhr believe, in the modern world where power factors are often determinative, that

[2] *Beyond Tragedy* was the title he chose for his first volume of sermonic essays, published in 1937.

"if suffering love becomes sufficiently general it will cease to be 'suffering' and change society into a harmony of life in which no one need suffer." Therefore he concludes:

> The relation between sacrificial love and mutual love contains the issue of the relation between the eschatological and the historical in a nutshell. Love, heedless of the self, must be the initiator of any reciprocal love. Otherwise the calculation of mutual advantages makes love impossible. But heedless love usually wins a response of love. That is a symbol of the moral content of history. But this response cannot be guaranteed . . . This is a symbol of the "tragic" dimension of history and a proof that the meaning of life always transcends the fulfillments of meaning in history.

Mutual love, for example, is love in a happy marriage. Each partner loves someone who clearly loves him. Yet each partner also maintains a bit of nonchalance or heedlessness whereby if his spouse appears unloving or positively sour, he does not self-protectively withdraw his own love and the vulnerability that accompanies it. Instead he takes a chance, hoping that his spouse is merely coming down with a cold, and continues offering his own love, though perhaps now reduced (for the sake of his partner) from the "passing gear" of intimacy to the "cruising gear" of cherishing.

Certainly without a hint of agape, mutual love can quickly degenerate into petty calculation: "I won't give my heart to you unless you give yours to me." Anyone who watches small children at play can see and hear what happens when mutual love degenerates into mutual recrimination: sometimes the freedom of the participants must be limited in order to maintain, not love any longer but justice, or perhaps not even justice any longer but order.

Agape stands at the top of the ladder of the individual's values, with mutual love a rung below. Yet mutual love partakes of agape on occasion. Similarly justice stands on the rung below mutual love, and yet it partakes of mutual love on occasion. Justice, at the same time, stands at the top of the ladder of *society*'s values. As Niebuhr said in *Later Leaves:*

> In the process of building communities every impulse of love must be transformed into an impulse of justice. Justice must be the instrument of love . . . Justice means the calculation of rights. It means taking sides for the weak against the strong. It means rational discrimination between competing claims.

"Taking sides for the weak" involves the use of power, and the use of power involves sin. Here is the paradox of social action. As Niebuhr tells his classes, "We cannot be good unless we're responsible, and the minute we're responsible, we're involved in compromise." Nor is personal religion, vital as it may be in individual life, a sufficient guide for the "social and moral perplexities which men of power face." Niebuhr points to Oliver Cromwell who "really wanted to do the will of God, and thought he was doing it. Yet nothing in Cromwell's personal religion could save his dictatorship from being abortive and self-devouring." As a contemporary example, Niebuhr points to the pious American representative at an international meeting whom Niebuhr heard announcing that United States trade policies are based upon the Sermon on the Mount.

When Niebuhr speaks of justice as meaning "rational discrimination between competing claims," he is relying on man's use of reason, which is also necessary for "the calculation of rights." Reason, thus used, must not only be as objective as possible, and also as open as possible to correction by other people. It is a tool to be deliberately used for the achievement of justice, thus differing from agape which is not a tool and therefore should not be deliberately used. All forms of love, in fact, are subject less to deliberate use than to unconscious *ab*use: too often they serve as masks for injustice. The old slaveowner, for example, may have genuinely loved his slaves, and they him, and the very genuineness of their love may have hidden from him, and perhaps even from them, the gross injustice of their situation that was quite visible to outsiders. Thus, as Niebuhr said in *Christian Century*, January, 1958, "love as a substitute for justice is odious, but love as a supplement to justice is an absolute necessity."

Because love is an absolute necessity as a supplement to justice in the social as well as the individual realm, the analogy of the two ladders falls down. Instead, the following diagram was prepared and handed in to

Professor Niebuhr by this writer who was then auditing his course in Christian Ethics:

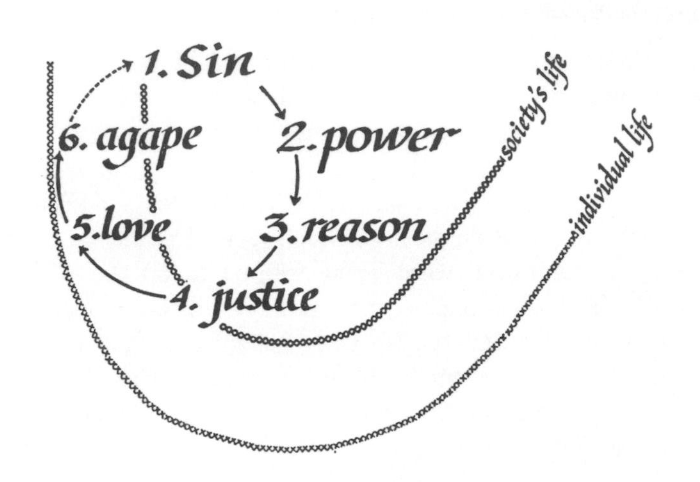

The key:

Starting, of course, with sin, one moves by steps around toward agape. But the last arrow is dotted rather than solid because forgiving love is a form of grace and cannot be predicted or deliberately achieved.

The difference between moral man for whom agape is the highest goal, and immoral society for which justice is the highest goal, is indicated by the two different kinds of line (x-x-x-x-x for the individual, and o-o-o-o-o-o for society). Yet the line for society does not intersect the circle exactly at the point of justice but at some indeterminate point between justice and love.

The steps:

1. Sin is a recurrent profound self-centeredness that exists in every person and even more so in every group;
2. Power is necessary to protect ourselves and our group against the sin in others, and for them to protect themselves against the sin in us;

3. Reason is necessary in the world of sin and power
   a) to recognize these when they are masked,
   b) to decide what the fair thing is,
   c) to find means of carrying it out;
4. Justice is the ultimate goal of power-balancing and of reason's deliberations;
5. Love, however, is also necessary lest justice become static and eventually deteriorate;
6. Agape, the highest degree of love, is relevant to the individual but not to the group; in history it can lead either to the tragedy of love engulfed by sin, or to sin dissolved by the grace of love.

Niebuhr's comments on written assignments by students tend to be relatively gentle. The following was the one elicited by the diagram:

> I like your outline of sin, power, reason and justice very much, though I would regard justice not as a goal of reason but as the goal of love, sin presupposed. That is, granted the fact of sin, or self-love, justice is the only historically possible goal to achieve. Your diagram reminds me of the diagrams which I constantly put on the blackboard and which the students say they don't find as illuminating as my outlines, and I must say I find your outline more illuminating than your diagram.

Far better than the diagram was the paragraph on Niebuhr's social ethics by John Bennett in the Living Library Volume:

> Niebuhr's conception of the relationship between love and justice is extraordinarily many-sided. There is no more fruitful analysis in all of his ethical writings than his discussion of this problem. All ideas of justice are for him both negated and fulfilled by love. Justice is in part an embodiment of love wherever there are complex human relationships . . . justice must always be thought of in dynamic terms. . . . Love makes our consciences more sensitive to the needs of others, especially to the needs of those who have been neglected or exploited. The vast body of social legislation in recent years in many countries is an embodiment of justice. It became possible partly because of the political and economic pressures of groups that have been at a disadvantage, but also because there has developed in society at large,

> even among privileged classes, a more sensitive social conscience. Those who think of Niebuhr as chiefly the great discoverer of sin fail to realize how much credit he gives to the effect of this sensitized conscience upon society. He never thinks of it as working alone, for always its effectiveness depends upon its interaction with . . . political pressures.

Among the well-meaning groups that confuse the relationship between love and justice, between agape as an "impossible possibility" and politics as the art of the possible, was the Oxford Group, now called Moral Re-Armament or MRA.[3] When the group's leader, Frank Buchman, returned from a visit to Germany shortly before World War II, he issued an announcement:

> I thank heaven for a man like Adolph Hitler, who built a front-line defense against the anti-christ of communism. . . . Of course I don't condone everything the Nazis do. . . . But think what it would mean to the world if Hitler surrendered to the control of God. . . . Through such a man God could control a nation overnight and solve every last bewildering problem.

Niebuhr's answer, in *Christian Century* (and reprinted in *Christianity and Power Politics*) was so devastating that some readers remember it best of all his polemic writings. Yet the main point was made without pyrotechnics. It was simply that if the Group would

> content itself with preaching repentance to drunkards and adulterers one might be willing to respect it as a religious revival method which knows how to confront the [individual] sinner with God. [But instead] it runs to Geneva, the seat of the League of Nations . . . or to Hitler, always with the idea that it is on the verge of saving the world by bringing the people who control the world under God-control. . . . This idea of world salvation implies a social philosophy which is completely innocent of any understanding of the social dynamics of a civilization.

For Niebuhr such social dynamics are not only complex but so vast that no dictator, no matter how powerful, is able to create "his dictatorship out of whole cloth." Instead the dictator is "a creature as well as a creator" of history, and the acme of his power can never be a "simple

[3] "Agape," Niebuhr insists, "is *not* a simple possibility for sinful man."

personal force exerted without complexity upon the vast social movements in modern history."

Yet these well-meaning groups were not alone, Niebuhr felt, in their oversimplification of the dynamics of modern society. Many of the social scientists, particularly some psychiatrists, were falling into the same error.

In Niebuhr's view, psychiatry is of inestimable value in treating troubled individuals, among whom Niebuhr "suspects [are the] many pitiful victims of a graceless religious legalism." But at the same time he warns that the methods of psychiatric treatment can neither encompass the whole of the human self nor carry over automatically to a troubled society. As he wrote in *Faith and History:*

> Every discipline of psychology and every technique of psychiatry may be appreciated as contributing to the cure of souls provided the self in its final integrity is not obscured by detailed analyses of the intricacies of personality, and provided its techniques are not falsely raised into schemes of redemption.

The psychiatrist whom Niebuhr attacks most vehemently is the benign, rosy-cheeked Dr. Brock Chisholm, recently chief of the World Health Organization, who often applies the principles of psychiatry to world affairs. As a result, Niebuhr accuses him of trying "to redeem the world by not frightening children." Not that Niebuhr is in favor of frightening children—he thinks, for example, that the Christian concept of God as judge needs to be qualified for those of tender age (see Chapter 26) —but he himself is frightened when he sees people with the intelligence and good will of Dr. Chisholm appearing to ignore the factors of power in society and thus, through oversimplification, rendering its problems even more difficult of solution.

Another example of the specific psychiatric schemes for world redemption that Niebuhr deplores is the suggestion that if Russian babies were not swaddled so tightly in infancy, the Russian nation would cease being so aggressive. Here again Niebuhr is not in favor of swaddling, but he strongly disapproves any redemptive suggestion that blandly ignores the centuries-old imperialist dreams of Russia, together with the explosive dynamism of Marxism, and the resultant need for the West to maintain counterpower in its own defense.

As for the self in its final integrity being obscured by psychiatry,

Niebuhr says of his old friend, the late Dr. Karen Horney, "If, as she claims, man's egocentricity is soluble by adequate psychiatry, then man would have less freedom than I think he has." And he makes somewhat the same point in regard to Harry Stack Sullivan whose ideas he generally approves but whom he criticizes, together with Ashley Montagu, for failing to "conceive of egotism arising in the individual without specific cause."

In regard to Erich Fromm, Niebuhr wrote in one of his frequent reviews of Fromm books, "The point of the debate lies in the difference between the psychiatric analysis of various particular types of insecurity from which particular people suffer and the Christian conception of the precarious situation in which all human life stands."[4]

This precarious situation, moreover, will remain as long as moral man and immoral society remain. It will also lead to creativity, to destructiveness, and to

> abortive attempts to establish a security which is incompatible with the very character of human existence. . . . For the structure of human existence, which the psychiatrist is anxious to define accurately, is compounded of finite elements and elements of indeterminate freedom. Man's sin is not disobedience to a divine fiat, but the idolatry of making himself his own end.

Nor do those who pride themselves on following the divine fiat necessarily succeed any better than the secularists who go about their business of fighting injustice wherever it appears. John A. Hutchison says of the *Frontier Fellowship* which Niebuhr both helped to found and continued to lead:

> Often we found ourselves standing shoulder to shoulder with secular liberals on some issue such as racial or industrial justice. The irony of such situations was frequently heightened by finding traditional religious persons on the other side of the battle lines.

Christianity and Society, Spring, 1948.

17

Working with the Liberals

WHEN Niebuhr likes people, he likes them with élan. Not that he is uncritical about them, but his first reaction is to support them, and only later to question their wisdom.

His loyalty to his liberal friends has led him into strange places and predicaments, particularly since this loyalty has also extended, at times, to his friends' organizations. Professor Press once distinguished between Reinhold and Richard Niebuhr by saying that if an organization was doing *one* good thing, Reinhold would join it, and Richard would not. During the thirties and forties there were many permanent or ad hoc organizations doing "one good thing," and Niebuhr lent his name to more than a hundred of them.

Niebuhr furthermore believed that his position as a man of the cloth made it more, rather than less, imperative for him to involve himself in the battles for racial, social and economic justice. Too many of his clerical colleagues, he insisted, were using piety as a refuge from controversial engagement. As early as 1927 he wrote in *The Christian Century* whose subscription list is high in ministers,

> It is hardly conceivable that God should have interfered in history and should have nothing more to show for his interference but that harmless individual, the modern parson.

One of the areas of deep concern to Niebuhr and other "sensitive spirits" in the thirties was the South. In 1932, Theodore Dreiser had reported from Harlan County, Kentucky, that the coal miners, when working, were earning but eighty cents a day (within one week eight children of miners died of undernourishment), and when these miners struck for higher wages, they themselves were in danger of death (during the strike that year, twelve were shot by deputy sheriffs). The middle class in the area tended to support the mine owners, and the ministers tended to support their middle class parishioners. Niebuhr paid a visit to Kentucky as a member of a church delegation, and his impressions were still vivid a quarter century later (*Christian Century*, August, 1956):

> I well remember a rather pathetic experience . . . in Harlan County, Kentucky, at the time when industrial violence engulfed the county because of a strike by its miners. Their wages were very low because that was the only way the Kentucky mine owners were able to meet the competition of the Pennsylvania coal fields. . . . We met with the ministers of the county in order to convince them that it was dubious for the middle class community to be so indifferent to the plight of the miners, simply because they felt that the community itself was endangered by a higher wage scale.
>
> These calculations in justice, which touched the collective interests and challenged the moral complacency of the . . . churches, were quite beyond the moral comprehension of the Harlan County ministers. We were assured that they had just had a collective revival in the town and would have another one; and that these revivals were bound to generate the kind of Christian perfection which would make the collective sins we spoke of quite impossible.

Worse even than the plight of the Southern miners was that of the Southern share croppers. Said Naomi Mitchison, the British novelist, during the depression in the United States,

> I have travelled over most of Europe and part of Africa, but I have never seen such terrible sights as I saw yesterday among the sharecroppers of Arkansas.

In 1934, Niebuhr travelled south again, to assist in the formation of the liberal "Fellowship of Southern Churchmen." As Robert Moats Miller recalls, "in many respects Reinhold Niebuhr was the spiritual godfather of the Fellowship. He it was who helped the delegates to 'delineate truth from fiction, fact from fancy.' So eloquent were his exhortations that the group dubbed him 'Judgment Day in britches.'"

Southern ministers varied, then as now, from the pietistic, whom Niebuhr scored, to the socially and politically venturesome, whom Niebuhr—and the Fellowship of Socialist Christians—supported. The then-new biracial Southern Tenant Farmers' Union, for example, had fourteen ministers in its Executive Committee. This was at a time when union organizers were being shot and beaten up, and share croppers who dared to join the union were being evicted from their pitiful dwellings. In 1935, Frazier Hunt reported on the violence and terror:

> I talked to some of these men and listened to their tales of how they were being beaten, thrown into jail, hounded and hunted down like runaway slaves. To all intents and purposes they were still slaves.

Another visitor to the area at that time was Bishop Scarlett of Missouri:

> Four or five of us had met in Memphis for a piece of business, and it was proposed that in the afternoon we drive over to Parkin, Arkansas, where a number of Negro sharecroppers had been evicted from a plantation nearby and were camped along the road.

As the group was setting out, Scarlett was sternly admonished by John Rust, who had invented a cotton picking machine and knew the region intimately, to "leave . . . the names of those you want notified in case you do not return." Scarlett had laughed: "Tell me another."

But Rust was not amused. "I'm serious. Those fellows in Arkansas will accept no interference with what they are doing, and you will get into trouble if you go."

"Well," said Scarlett, "if I don't come back in time for the midnight train, please wire the Rector of Emmanuel Church, Webster Groves, Missouri, that his Bishop is in jail and will not show up for the Service of Confirmation tomorrow."

The Bishop did reach home in time for the "laying on of hands," since it happened that no one, in a different sense, had laid hands on him. And one by-product of the expedition was that Sherwood Eddy, moving with characteristic speed and vigor ("the very next day," according to Scarlett), set up a refuge in Mississippi for the evicted share croppers from Arkansas. As Eddy recalled in *Eighty Adventurous Years,*

> We bought a farm on the spot, raised $17,500 in thirty days and paid cash for the 2138 acres which we called Rochdale, located south of Memphis in the Mississippi Delta. . . . Within a few months thirty evicted families were settled on the farm. The Cooperative Farms, Inc. was formed with Reinhold Niebuhr as president, myself as secretary-treasurer, Sam H. Franklin, Jr. as director [and Scarlett as a member of the board].
> The history of the project for the next decade was one of constant struggle in the midst of bitter race prejudice, a mixture of failure and success, and of sacrificial service rendered by volunteer workers from near and far.

These volunteers included young southern ministers between "calls" and students between academic terms. When Jonathan Daniels visited the Delta Cooperative, he wrote in *A Southerner Discovers the South,* 1938:

> The staff of the cooperative seemed to me like Robinson Crusoes washed up by good will on the Delta of the Mississippi where they were applying their city brains and their missionary Christian enthusiasm energetically and ingeniously to the hard problems of the isolated land.

Among the hardest problems were the financial ones: both the raising of funds and their distribution between the farm cooperative and the consumers cooperative. Questions constantly arose as to which item belonged where and which services were donated and which were expenses. One of the crack analysts of the Cooperative's books was its president. "Reinie would have made a superb accountant," Eddy told people. "He could look at a sheet of figures and, at a glance, pick up flaws that no one else had seen."

Another hard problem was the racial one. As Sam Franklin summed up for Jonathan Daniels, "We are upholding the true Christian attitude toward the races, but not doing anything foolish."

Still another problem, unexpectedly, came from the Southern Tenant Farmers' Union. This group, having started as an ally, ended up being a burden. First it demanded the right of having its own representative living on the farm and acting as a "kind of arbiter between manager and people," according to the report of Sam Franklin to the Delta Board. It then demanded, he said, the right of having

> separate locals for the two races which would pass on details of farm operation as the Council now does . . . I told them that I had already tried to show our people that a union was necessary even on a cooperative . . . and that I was glad to deal with locals when necessary, but that I could not agree to the national office supplying that kind of middle men, nor to passing over the function of the Council to the locals.

Lastly, the Cooperative, like Pharoah of Egypt, was bedevilled by plagues. First came the boll weevil, then the flooding of the creek, then illness among the farmers, then mechanical failure among the tractors, then more red ink on the balance sheets, and most unkind of all, the defection of some of the tenant families. As Sam Franklin wrote to the Board,

> Dissatisfaction among the Negro families [has] continued and on Saturday of last week I heard that four more were planning to leave. I have spent a great deal of time, both day and night, discussing the matter, and I would attempt to summarize the cause of their dissatisfaction as follows: first, disappointment at not receiving a bigger cash dividend [it averaged $306 per family for all on the place] plus the natural restlessness of the Negro; second, a feeling that they had not been dealt with quite fairly in some matters, for which in some cases there were probably some real grounds for complaint . . . while in others their ignorance of the working of the cooperative and their deep suspicion were alone responsible; and third, the fact that a local plantation owner, acting as we believe, in accord with an understanding among planters to entice our Negroes away, had come down and offered cash advances to certain men if they would leave us and go to him. Indeed, one very shrewd old Negro, who was not among those leaving, told me that he thought the planters had made it up to entice our Negro labor away and that then they were going to do something to our white people and so break up the farm.

What the planters never quite accomplished America's entry into World War II did. Soon after Pearl Harbor the Cooperative was disbanded and the land sold off to individual owners.

Thus did Niebuhr, without ever being in business, learn some of the managerial headaches to which businessmen are prone; thus did the young man, who had felt that private property should not always remain private, learn that communal ownership does not, of itself, solve the problems of property; thus did the believer in man's freedom learn that freedom leads to insatiability as well as to fulfillment: that the long-starved may have their appetites whetted rather than stilled when offered a share of the fruits of their labor;[1] thus did the theologian learn what the working politician takes for granted, that the people for whom one did a favor last year are precisely those to turn against one this year, with the famous, if apocryphal, question: "What have you done for me *lately?*"

What Niebuhr took longer to realize was that just as the growing power of labor was necessary to challenge the established power of business, so the power of labor itself would need to be challenged. The first issue of *Radical Religion* (of which Niebuhr was editor from the beginning) came out in the autumn of 1935, and it contained a plea for the formation of an American Labor Party. Some twenty years later, Niebuhr wrote in the closing issue of *Radical Religion*'s successor, *Christianity and Society*, that neither he nor the then-young author of that plea had

> anticipated the tremendous expansion of the labor movement . . . forming a powerful united body of fifteen million organized workers. The movement is now so big that one may understand the apprehensions of even some staunch friends of labor about its effect upon our life, though one does not share the prejudiced fears of the NAM.

Labor, however, in the latter thirties (the Wagner Act was passed in 1935), was still the underdog by a vast margin and among those who supported its objectives were people concerned not only with bread and butter but with justice. There were also, numerically speaking, a few people with more nefarious motives who in some unions achieved a disproportionate degree of power. This happened in the College Section of the Teachers' Union in New York City where the Communist minority was battled by such distinguished members of the majority as Reinhold

[1] This is a problem the United States is currently grappling with in many of the less-developed lands where we are giving technical and economic aid.

Niebuhr, George Counts, John Childs, Paul Hays, William Withers, Persia Campbell, and George Hartman.

By 1933, the United States had renewed diplomatic relations with the Soviet Union, and for another fifteen years the possibility did not occur to the average American that to be a Communist might include treason. Of course American Communists were known to be devoted to the Soviet Union, but was not our land of the melting pot full of such dual allegiances? Some Americans are devoted to the land of their forebears, "the auld countree"; others to the historic base of their religion, whether Rome, Jerusalem, or whatever; others to the cultural center of their particular art, Paris for painters, Ireland for poets, Germany for musicians, England for judges; and no one thinks to question their patriotism. Some people, on the left as well as the right, did question the patriotism of American Communists, but their warnings were not widely heeded. On the left, for example, some first-generation American Socialists, who had tried unsuccessfully to work with Communists in Europe, proclaimed its impossibility, as did some native labor leaders who had tried unsuccessfully to work with them at home. On the right, for example, Martin Dies issued blanket accusations of un-Americanism, but by including the whole of the left if not part of the center in his denunciations, and by using methods deplored by Americans concerned with civil liberties, he beclouded rather than clarified the issue.

Meanwhile some of the most public spirited Americans went on working with the Communists and the fellow-travellers, or as Averell Harriman subsequently named them, the fellow wanderers, who could see no wrong in the Soviet Union.

Niebuhr, on the other hand, even at the height of his own Marxism, had always been able to see things wrong in the Soviet Union. As early as 1927, in *Christian Century*, he condemned the Russian attempt "to build a brotherhood of love through a strategy of hate." And in 1930, after a trip there, he reported back to *The Christian Century* (September 24):

> The new Russia is robust and vitally alive but . . . its vitality is shot through with brutality, and the vengeance it takes upon every representative and symbol of the old order must chill the ardor with which one would like to praise its achievements.

Niebuhr continued for a few more years, however, to see validity in some of the basic Marxist concepts. For this he was severely criticized by Charles Clayton Morrison, editor of *The Christian Century*. Good Christians, Morrison wrote in 1933, were being confused by Niebuhr's insistence on economic determinism. During that same period, paradoxically, Niebuhr was also being severely criticized by the Communists. Said one of them in a review of *Moral Man*, good Communists were being confused by Niebuhr's insistence on pouring "the sauce of Christianity" over his valid economic analyses, and thus Niebuhr, in effect, was "worse than a thug."

Niebuhr did not trouble to answer the accusations by the Communists, but Morrison's must have stung. For Niebuhr's reply, published in *Christian Century*, was in his full polemic style: "Your editorial . . . dealing with my . . . views reduces them to what you call a 'skeleton outline,' but I am afraid that in your eagerness to make out a case against me you have left only two shinbones in the skeleton."[2]

To identify the dangerous facets of communism within Russia was comparatively easy, despite the pre-"iron-curtain" (this phrase was coined only after World War II) behind which the Soviet Union tried to hide its internal failures and resultant terrible cruelties. But it was less easy in the thirties to identify the dangerous facets of communism within the United States because these could be not only hidden but disguised.

One form of camouflage was the secret infiltration by Communists of worthy noncommunist groups. In the United States this technique was called the United Front.[3] It had originally been recommended by Lenin when the revolutionary upsurge he expected in western Europe failed to materialize, and later, in July-August, 1935, it was promulgated as world-wide policy by the Comintern. Its success was described by Ben Gitlow, the American ex-Communist, in 1948 in *The Whole of Their Lives:*

> Once the communists get their toes into the narrow opening of a door to an organization, they usually succeed in . . . either capturing the organization or dominating its affairs . . . They

[2] After another year of substantive controversy with its policies, Niebuhr resigned as a contributing editor of *The Christian Century* in 1934.

[3] Technically, in Europe, the "united front" meant cooperation between communists and socialists, as against the "popular front" which also included liberals.

> have thus surrounded themselves with an army of respectable persons . . . who unknowingly are generous contributors to communist causes . . .

Some of these respectable persons have remained eminently respectable. General Dwight D. Eisenhower, for example, lent his name to Russian War Relief in the forties. This organization later turned out to have been dominated by Communists and fellow travellers. Other of these respectable persons subsequently lost their status of respectability when they remained identified with groups widely recognized as being under Communist domination. A notable American example was Henry A. Wallace who, in his attempt to be elected President of the United States in 1948, became head of the Progressive Party. He, in the terse phrase of an anti-Communist politician, "was raped easy." A notable British example was The Very Reverend Hewlitt Johnson, "Red" Dean of Canterbury. He, in the terse phrase of Reinhold Niebuhr, had "a soft heart, a softer head, and an incredible vanity which only the big crowds, delivered by the Communists, can satisfy."

As the thirties progressed, controversial events occurred to which the American Communist reaction was either different from that of the rest of the country, or identical with that of Communists abroad, or both. The first of these controversial events came in 1937, when Radek, Platakov, and other former leading Russian Communists went on trial for treason in Moscow, publicly groveled, and were executed. To the non-Communist world the Moscow Trials appeared as a travesty of justice; to the Communist sympathizers they appeared as a justified response to the dangers Russia faced from the hostile nations surrounding her. Arthur Koestler's *Darkness At Noon* gave stunning insight into what happens when political leaders become convinced that the end justifies the means. And Niebuhr's attitude toward the trials was unequivocally expressed in *Radical Religion*, Spring, 1937:

> Whatever interpretation one may place upon the Moscow trials they are a sorry business . . . Those who are convinced that Stalin can do no wrong assure us that the trials carried conviction among the foreign newspaper correspondents. We beg leave to doubt it . . . The conflict which has broken out in America between the followers . . . of Trotsky and the members and

> liberal sympathizers of the communist party fills us with dismay. One of the questions put by the "liberal" followers of Stalin to the liberal sympathizers of Trotsky . . . was: "Should not a country engaged in building socialism . . . whether or not one agrees with all the means whereby this is brought about, be permitted to decide for itself what measures of protection are necessary. . . ?" In other words, if one believes in the great Russian experiment in general terms, one is also supposed to suppress all critical faculties and accept the official version of a less than convincing trial.

For Niebuhr the chief practical lesson of the trials was the essentiality of maintaining democratic forms in any change toward socialism. The chief ultimate lesson was that no political system—even the most perfect—was to be identified with the Kingdom of God:

> As Christian socialists we assert with a certain measure of self-righteousness that we are glad that we have religious certainties which absolve us of the necessity of finding our religious security in the shifting forces of politics.

The shifting forces of politics in America meanwhile were shifting in all directions, and Niebuhr, together with many liberals, found himself unintentionally embroiled in some of the shifts, and intentionally embroiled himself in others.

One in which he was unintentionally embroiled was the internal fight within the College Section of the Teachers' Union. The disciplined Communist minority had won control, and the anti-Communist majority could not agree on how to win it back. One tactic was to organize a Save The Union Committee, which then elected George Counts and Reinhold Niebuhr as its co-chairmen. But the Committee was unsuccessful and many of its members, including Niebuhr, resigned from the Union. Staying in meant submitting to Communist control; yet resigning meant strengthening that control. It was a mess whichever way you looked at it.

In retrospect James Loeb wrote:

> Our battle in the College Section was especially tough because most of the distinguished members belonged only because of their sentimental feeling about the labor movement. As the fight

> with the Communists got tough, our ranks became thinner and thinner by resignations from anti-communists. We lost the fight in New York but won it nationally and Counts became the first anti-communist to be president of the American Federation of Teachers. I'm still not sure it was a mistake to try to hold the union together. In the United Parents' Association, for example, the same fight took place but the anti-communists (led by Rose Shapiro) won and the organization is still thriving. The mistake is to lose.

In retrospect Niebuhr's feelings, too, were mixed. As he wrote in *Radical Religion*, Summer, 1939, "we cannot speak for Dr. Counts, but, as for ourselves, we are a little dubious about our handiwork."

Another political battle of the thirties, one in which Niebuhr intentionally embroiled himself, started in January, 1938, when Stanley Isaacs, then Republican Borough President of Manhattan, hired an assistant named Simon W. Gerson whose previous experience had been as a newspaper reporter. This unimportant-seeming appointment turned out to have been a major political mistake which injured Isaac's subsequent career and rubbed off to some extent on his friends like Niebuhr who loyally and publicly supported him. Says J. M. Flagler in his *New Yorker* Profile (December 12, 1959) of Stanley Isaacs:

> What made it a mistake was that Gerson's paper happened to be the *Daily Worker* and Gerson himself happened to be a member of the Communist Party. The fact that Isaacs could even consider hiring him is a fair indication of the political climate of those days; neither La Guardia nor any other Fusion leader raised any objection to the appointment of Gerson, who was a familiar figure around City Hall, and by and large, as Isaacs had ascertained, a well-liked one. As most local voters saw it, the peril of the moment was not Communism but Tammany Hall.

Isaac's reason for taking on the young man (who thereafter did his job with exemplary dispatch) was his desire to "have the viewpoint of conservatives, liberals, and radicals, because they were representative of the diverse citizenship of this borough . . . and the needs of which I wanted interpreted to me by those who best understood them." But the outcry against the Gerson appointment began to mount. Political groups, the press, nonpolitical groups and individuals joined in verbal attacks on Isaacs, some of them admitting an itch to attack him physically as well. Even the State Legislature in faraway Albany took cognizance of the Gerson appointment, and held hearings in 1938 and again in 1940, before passing a law denying public jobs in New York State to anyone who advocated overthrow of the government by force or violence.

Isaacs, meanwhile, despite those who advocated *his* overthrow by force or violence, stood by the appointment. As Isaacs says today, "I would never discharge any person appointed by me to a government position if he were rendering service, to my knowledge, with complete loyalty and efficiency. I am sure that was true of Gerson, or I would not have kept him during those hectic days."

People like Supreme Court Chief Justice Charles Evans Hughes, the prominent New York attorney, Charles C. Burlingham, and George Hallett, executive director of the nonpartisan Citizens' Union, rallied loyally to the support of Isaacs. Said a letter, of which Niebuhr was one of fourteen signers in 1938,

> The outcry against Simon W. Gerson because of his membership in the Communist Party seems to us wholly unrelated to any consideration of fitness for public office.

Today the signers, presumably, would not state the issue so flatly: "public office" is too broad a term. At the same time, they might well point out that the job in question was as assistant not to the Secretary of State but to one of New York City's five borough presidents. Had Gerson wished to commit subversion or sabotage in the teeming and vulnerable great port, his lowly berth in its governmental hierarchy would not have helped him to do substantially more damage than can be done by any reckless individual.

Two years after his appointment Gerson resigned. As Isaacs says today, if he had it to do over again, he would not hire Gerson, but having hired Gerson, he still would not summarily dismiss him. As the only Republican member of the New York City Council, Isaacs continues with courage and integrity to take sometimes unpopular stands, with the full consent and approval of his old friend Reinhold Niebuhr.

Yet some of the Gerson-smudge continues to rub off not only on Isaacs but on Niebuhr. As late as October, 1959, Niebuhr was attacked in *American Mercury* by John Benedict in an article entitled

WHAT RELIGION ??????????

DOES REINHOLD NIEBUHR PEDDLE?

IT HAS MORE COMMUNISM THAN CHRISTIANITY

One of the supposedly Communist moves made by Professor Niebuhr who teaches at what Benedict calls the "Rothschild-Rockefeller-financed Union Theological Seminary" was to give his signature "for the (Simon) Gerson Supporters."

In defending the Moscow trials, the American Communists and party-liners had gone against the majority of public opinion in the United States. But when the Hitler-Stalin nonaggression pact jarred the world on August 24, 1939, and was followed one week later by Hitler's march on Poland, the American Communists came into line with much of United States public opinion which, for other reasons, wanted America to stay out of war. Slightly less than two years later, on June 22, 1941, Hitler turned on his erstwhile cosignatory and invaded Russia, thus forcing the American Communists to flip-flop again and now do all they could to get America into the war. Niebuhr who had criticized their extremism in the first instance also criticized it in the second.

The necessity to rationalize these flip-flops drove many people out of the Communist Party. It also thinned the ranks of those who, with curiosity, were watching the party from the outside: "I grew tired of being 'bored from within,'" said Professor Morris Raphael Cohen of City College when asked why he had dropped his subscription to the *New Masses*. The flip-flops also created fissures within the noncommunist organizations which the Communists were trying to use as part of the United Front.

One such organization was the American Students' Union. Niebuhr, at the request of his Young Socialist friend, Joseph Lash, had addressed their first meeting in Columbus, Ohio, at Christmas time, 1935. The Socialist Party had approved the founding of the American Students' Union which grew to include 12,000 dues-paying members, most of whom were still in college, and some of whom were under Communist discipline. All these young people were united—at least temporarily—in their antimilitarism and anti-Fascism; they emphasized personal heroism in helping the anti-Fascists in Spain, but at the same time they tried to block the large increases in armament at home. Being antimilitarist was good Socialist dogma at the time: Roosevelt's high expenditures for ships and arms were looked on as suspect: their purpose was believed to be the bolstering of the national economy by cutting unemployment, and their result was believed to be the hastening of war. Even Niebuhr who by 1938 had thoroughly abandoned pacifism and what he called his "liberal illusions," blasted Roosevelt's naval budget of that year as "the worst piece of militarism in American history."

Yet Niebuhr differed from the young people in the ASU through his awareness of the deliberate subversion by some American Communists—"the black legions of the Soviet foreign office," he called them—and also of the nondeliberate, but nonetheless dangerous, confusion sown by the party-liners.

Among the latter, Niebuhr reluctantly concluded after World War II, were those who set the editorial policy of *The Nation*. He had served for several years as one of its contributing editors, and he stayed on longer than he wished to because of his loyalty to the publisher, Freda Kirchwey, and to his fellow-editors Robert Bendiner and Margaret Marshall. But the editorials flip-flopped once too often, and Niebuhr resigned. Not one word of his resignation was ever printed by the magazine. And soon Bendiner and Margaret Marshall also left; it took about a decade for Freda Kirchwey also to take her leave.

In a magazine the policy line is relatively easy to see. But in a political organization the line can be quite difficult to see. In 1936, largely at the instigation of national leaders of the Democratic Party, the American Labor Party was founded in New York. One aim was to provide a political home for the old Socialists who might then be persuaded to vote for Franklin Roosevelt instead of the perennial Socialist candidate, Norman Thomas. Niebuhr, at the time still a member of the Socialist Party, never joined the American Labor Party, but many of his friends did, particularly those connected with New York City's two great rival clothing unions, the International Ladies Garment Workers, whose president was, and is, David Dubinsky, and the Amalgamated Clothing Workers of America, whose president was Sidney Hillman, and now is Jacob Potofsky.

According to gossip in labor circles at the time, "Hillman and Dubinsky hate each other like two rabbis in the same small town." Not only were the two unions rivals (a raincoat for ladies fell under ILGWU jurisdiction; the identical coat for men fell under Amalgamated's) but their forceful presidents ended up as rivals in the American Labor Party, with Dubinsky in charge of the State organization and Hillman, in co-operation with Vito Marcantonio, in charge of the City organization. Both men had courageously and successfully fought Communist attempts to infiltrate their respective unions. And within the ALP Dubinsky continued refusing to have any dealings with them. But Hillman, like John L. Lewis, then President of the United Mineworkers of America, thought that a political party was sufficiently different from a labor union for Communists safely to be admitted if kept in check. The bon mot of the gossipers was then amended to, "Hillman hates Dubinsky even worse than he hates the Communists."

The showdown came in the Presidential Primary of 1944, when rival slates of district committeemen were presented, one by the ALP State organization and another by the City organization. The City, i.e., Hillman, slate won and a meeting of the defeated group was immediately called at the McAlpin Hotel. Among those attending were Adolph Berle, Alex Rose, George Counts, John Childs, and of course David Dubinsky. Reinhold Niebuhr was invited but could not attend. At the meeting, James Loeb bet John Childs a dollar that its end result would be the founding of a new party. Loeb came out a dollar richer; Childs came out chairman of the new Liberal Party.

Niebuhr who, by then, had resigned from the Socialist Party was elected one of the Liberal Party's vice presidents. He attended meetings of the executive committee for years and was often consulted by phone on issues and candidates. But the Liberal Party never grew very much beyond the City and not at all beyond the State. The American Labor Party, on the other hand, received a spurt of new strength when Henry Wallace ran for President in 1940. But subsequently, as the Americans realized that the Russians had changed from wartime allies to Cold War enemies, and as the Communist influence in the ALP became even more apparent, the party shrank. Finally, in the election of 1956, it no longer had enough registered voters to rate a place on the ballot.

Reminiscing about those years, when people with the best motives did some of the worst things, and people with the worst motives did some of the best things; when the United States was so oblivious to the outer peril that the Draft Act extension passed the Congress, in 1941, by a margin of only one vote, and so oblivious to the inner peril that Park Avenue matrons rose in Carnegie Hall to sing the Internationale, one of Niebuhr's colleagues sighs: "Reinie was ahead of most people not because he was always right, but because he was always ahead of the game in seeing where he was wrong."

Niebuhr takes a dimmer view of his own role: "When you look back, you could kick yourself. You could see *part* of the truth; why couldn't you see the whole thing?"

18

Battling with the Liberals

"PART of the truth" was what the liberals saw, but many of them assumed it was the whole thing.

Niebuhr's philosophic quarrel with some of the intellectuals with whom he worked most closely in liberal causes concerned their attempt to compress man's paradoxical grandeur and misery into categories that science could prove and reason could explain.[1] What they left out, he insisted, was as important as what they included, and the fact that they left it out was itself evidence of their overoptimistic view of themselves and the rest of the world:

> No accumulation of contradictory evidence seems to disturb modern man's good opinion of himself. He considers himself the victim of corrupting institutions which he is about to destroy or reconstruct, or of the confusions of ignorance which an adequate education is about to overcome. Yet he continues to regard himself as essentially harmless and virtuous.

In denying that man was essentially harmless and virtuous Niebuhr knowingly took the chance of puncturing the tires of forward-moving America. For clearly the liberal faith in progress had been serving to energize people. How could idealists sit still when there were so many things to be done for people, things that could be done and if done would contribute to peace and prosperity for all? In *Does Civilization Need Religion?* (1927) Niebuhr had openly wondered whether people

[1] Niebuhr's use of grandeur and misery harks back to Pascal's statement which he often quotes: "The philosophers tell us about the grandeur of man and tempt us to pride, or they tell us about the misery of man and tempt us to despair: where but in the simplicity of the Gospel are the two related?"

might not be allowed to keep some of their optimistic illusions about the individual, and their utopian illusions about society, lest on losing these, they fall into the "enervation of despair." But by the time of *Moral Man and Immoral Society,* five years later, Niebuhr felt forced to reject this temptation: the whole truth as he saw it must be told, no matter how damaging to man's self-esteem, how shocking to man's reason, and how undesirable its possible by-products. Nor was Niebuhr under any illusion as to the chances of this truth being widely understood or appropriated within the foreseeable future. Two years after *Moral Man,* he wrote in *Reflections Upon the End of an Era,* 1934:

> The effort to combine political radicalism with a more classical interpretation of religion will strike the modern mind as bizarre and capricious. It will satisfy neither the liberals in politics or religion, nor the political radicals, nor the devotees of traditional Christianity. These reflections are, therefore, presented without much hope that they will elicit any general concurrence. Perhaps they may help a little to shake the easy faith by which the tragic facts of contemporary history are obscured.

"Tragic" and "tragedy" were two words Niebuhr used more and more as the thirties progressed, as refugees were fleeing Germany, as millions of peasants were allowed by the government to starve in the Ukraine, as children of American share croppers lay listless from malnutrition. Tragedy was a word, however, to which Americans were deeply resistant: there seemed something almost subversive about it. America had never had a Schopenhauer or a Nietzsche and never wanted one; while Europe treasured her pessimists, America drowned hers out with the sound of humming machinery. The fact that Niebuhr's views were appreciated in Europe was a strike against him at home. If he wished to be appreciated on this side of the Atlantic he had better stop being so gloomy and Germanic.

For there was, in the mid-thirties, an upsurge in the national mood. The nation was like a driver whose reaction following a near-accident is not to be more cautious and responsible, but to speed up, out of sheer relief that nothing fatal had occurred. Rich business men were happy to pay for the flossiest debutante parties in history—a Cord car was the door prize at one of them—though they were not a bit happy to pay the taxes for national welfare which they called "killing the goose that lays the golden egg."[2]

The goose, meanwhile, seemed to be thriving. By 1934, the national income had risen above the depths of the depression by more than 20 per cent and the trend was definitely upward. By 1936, as Murray Kempton recalled in *Part of Our Time*:

> There was little talk of boom, but there appeared to be a growing sense that before long things might be as they were when people thought they had been so much happier than they really had been.

The wishful thinking that saw the past as happier than, in truth, it had been was also projected onto the future. And it underlay the easy faith of the liberals which Niebuhr was trying to shake. This was contained in the two words: "if only." For the religious liberals, as Alan Richardson recalled in the Living Library Volume,

> all one had to do in order to be perfect was to obey the simple ethical injunctions of the Sermon on the Mount. "If only" everyone would do unto others as he would be done by, then the Kingdom of God would have come . . .

And for the secular liberals, the "if only," Niebuhr said in the *Gifford Lectures*, lay

> usually in some specific form of social organization. One school holds that men would be good if only political institutions would not corrupt them; another believes that they would be good if the prior evil of a faulty economic organization could be eliminated. Or another school thinks of this evil as no more than ignorance, and therefore waits for a more perfect educational process. . . . But no school asks how it is that . . . essentially good man could have produced corrupting and tyrannical political organizations or exploiting economic organizations, or fanatical and superstitious religious organizations.

On the other hand, Niebuhr never agreed with the secular pessimists

[2] These debutante parties of the thirties remained unequaled for lavishness until the late fifties when the grandson and namesake of Niebuhr's old antagonist, Henry Ford, gave his daughter a debut in Detroit that *Life* estimated as costing $250,000.

who looked upon man as incapable of improving his lot, or with the religious pessimists who saw all human woe as God's punishment for man's sins and therefore neither to be questioned nor combatted. In this sense too, therefore, Niebuhr follows Pascal:

> If any man exalts man, I humble him; if anyone humbles man, I exalt him; I always contradict him until he understands what an incomprehensible monster man is.

Incomprehensible, yes; but worth every effort to comprehend? Yes, too, emphatically. Every fact discovered by science, every connection discovered by reason, must be given open-minded consideration; and Niebuhr specifically praised the true scientists' "humility before the fact" and their ever-present willingness to change their hypotheses when necessary. In this sense he was more than willing to ally himself with empiricism against obscurantism and with reason against irrationalism. As he wrote to a friend:

> I stand in the William James tradition. He was both an empiricist and a religious man, and his faith was both the consequence and the presupposition of his pragmatism.

But this "pragmatism" of Niebuhr's was recognized more by the inner circle of his acquaintance than by the outer one. The dedication by his friend, Paul Hutchinson in *World Revolution and Religion,* for example, was

To Reinhold Niebuhr
Who is not afraid of a fact.

Yet to the outer circle, religious and secular, Niebuhr's view of sin, and his reliance on paradox to explain it, were not only irrational but dangerously obscurantist.

Said Henry Nelson Wieman, the influential leader of the religious liberal group called Religious Naturalists, in his book, *The Growth of Religion,* paradox is

> an evasive ambiguity by which problems are concealed rather than solved, and by which reason is said to be confounded . . . [It is] among the most dangerous practices in the world today.

> In this way men feel themselves free to follow the dictates of blood instead of the brain.

And Sidney Hook wrote in his 1941 *New Leader* article entitled *Social Change and Original Sin: Answer to Niebuhr*:

> I have taken issue with his doctrines not only because they are false but because they are errors that can easily be used to justify social evils against which Niebuhr has so valiantly fought.

And so they could. Yet it is as inconceivable that Niebuhr would permanently water down his doctrines lest they be misused as that a scientist, or Hook himself, would permanently water down the results of research lest *these* be misused. (There may, in the field of both religion and science, be excusable *temporary* holding back of information: the minister at a time of bereavement may "temper the wind to the shorn lamb" and the scientist in time of war may postpone publication of experiments that could be helpful to the enemy.)

Niebuhr's doctrines, furthermore, leave room precisely for this danger of misuse: according to the biblical view of sin and grace, there is no concept, including that of sin and grace, that man cannot twist to his own advantage (and thus perhaps to someone else's disadvantage.) St. Paul records an early such example when he quotes the question by a man who hoped to use divine forgiveness as an excuse for human self-indulgence: "Shall we continue in sin, that grace may abound?"

Starting in the early thirties, Niebuhr's attacks on the leading secular liberal, the "naturalist" philosopher, John Dewey, were based on what Niebuhr called Dewey's "incredible naïveté" about the pervasiveness and subtlety of human sin. "No one," Niebuhr summed up in the *Gifford Lectures*, "expresses modern man's uneasiness about society and complacency about himself more perfectly than John Dewey."

In the late twenties and early thirties, when Niebuhr was relatively unknown and God was still viewed as relatively unimportant, Dewey treated these attacks as an old dog treats the yapping of a puppy: as beneath notice.[3] But after a decade, when Niebuhr was no longer an

[3] A contemporary example of the attitude toward God was the collegiate bon-mot coined while compulsory church-attendance was still the rule: "Please do not rattle the funnies in chapel; remember that others are trying to *study*."

unknown and religion was starting its spectacular comeback ("there are no atheists in the fox-holes"), the old dog turned and growled. In an article for the *Partisan Review,* in 1942, as part of a series significantly entitled "The New Failure of Nerve," Dewey did not refer to Niebuhr by name, but clearly included him among the disapproved:

> I come now to the question of the moral and social consequences that flow from the base and degrading view of nature in general and human nature in particular that inheres in every variety of anti-naturalistic philosophy. I begin with the fact that the tendency of this view has been to put a heavy discount upon resources that are potentially available for the betterment of human life.

Niebuhr, in turn, was trying to "better human life" by dispelling the illusions contained in John Dewey's accelerated form of "if only": this was the "as soon as" Dewey had described in *Liberalism and Social Action.* According to this theory, the profoundest problems of society would lend themselves to solution *as soon as* men applied to them the same "organized cooperative inquiry which has won the triumph of science in the field of physical nature."

To Niebuhr there were several fallacies in this position. One was the assumption that nature, which does not contain human freedom, can be equated with society and history, which do contain it. Another was the assumption that the problems of human society could ever be viewed with the same objectivity as the problems of nature. As he wrote in *Discerning the Signs of the Times*:

> The difference between the knowledge of nature and the knowledge and estimate of our fellow man is this: in the knowledge of nature the mind of man is at the center of the process of knowing; and the self with all its fears, hopes and ambitions is on the circumference. In the knowledge of historical events the self, with all its emotions and desires, is at the center of the enterprise; and the mind is on the circumference, serving merely as an instrument of the anxious self.

Because this anxious self must operate from a particular locus in time, and place in society, Niebuhr said, its judgment about social issues tends to be more biased than the person realizes, and to be presented as less biased than it is. So great, in fact, is man's ability to overestimate his own objectivity, even when he recognizes intellectually that his own social or national or religious interests are concerned, that some of "the worst injustices of history" have arisen "from these very claims of impartiality for biased . . . historical instruments." Dewey's profound underestimation of bias in himself and in men of similar intelligence and good will could itself only have arisen, said Niebuhr,

> in a period of comparative social stability and security and in a nation in which geographical isolation obscured the conflict of nations, and great wealth mitigated the social conflict within the nation.

It could only have arisen, too, in an age when the advances of science and technology were dramatic and beneficial. The resultant uncritical faith in scientific method (or scientism) led to a further fallacy in Dewey's thinking. This fallacy, in Niebuhr's view, was the theory of the "cultural lag," according to which, as Niebuhr wrote in *Christianity and Society*, Spring, 1939;

> we have social injustice because the social sciences have not kept up with the technical sciences. When will our modern rationalists learn that men are not logical, not because they do not know logic, but because they are capable of standing outside, rather than inside, a system of logic, and thus making it the servant of their interests.

Lastly, Niebuhr attacked Dewey's assumption that the intelligent and self-critical methods used to solve the minor problems of society would work equally well with the major ones. In his *Nation* review of Dewey's *Liberalism and Social Action* Niebuhr was perfectly willing to admit that

> many conflicts of interest are . . . arbitrated, at least when the contrast between them is not too sharp and when the contending parties do not absorb the total community and therefore destroy the last remnant of impartiality and neutrality with reference to a particular dispute.

But in regard to the major conflicts of interest, Niebuhr said, feelings would run too high and impartiality too low for any "organized cooperative inquiry" to be fully trustworthy. As he concluded in the Gifford Lectures:

> Not a suspicion dawns on Professor Dewey that no possible "organized inquiry" can be as transcendent over the historical conflicts of interest as it ought to be . . . No court of law, though supported by age old traditions of freedom from party conflict, is free of party bias whenever it deals with issues profound enough to touch the very foundations of the society upon which the court is reared.

In return, Dewey pointed to what he considered fallacies in Niebuhr's way of thinking. One was Niebuhr's reliance on God rather than on man alone; the other was Niebuhr's belief that man's misery accompanies his grandeur at each new level of historic creativity. These were not only incorrect, said Dewey in *Partisan Review*, but they were nonpragmatic:

> In the case of any candid clear-eyed person, it is enough to ask one question: what is the inevitable effect of holding that anything remotely approaching a basic and serious amelioration of the human estate must be based upon means and methods that lie outside the natural and social world, while human capacities are so low that reliance upon them only makes things worse?

And in the same issue of the magazine, Sidney Hook, also writing from the secular, "naturalist" point of view, said:

> To Niebuhr's myth of inevitability and orginal sin, we counterpose the truth that the *human* estate is one in which moral good and evil are achieved by custom, education, training and *intelligent choice.*

But don't you see, Niebuhr might have said, as he did in *Pious and Secular America,* that the person who makes these intelligent choices has a freedom over and above his "training, custom and education?" Don't you see that "the mystery of freedom is greater than the mystery of reason?"

No, I don't, Hook might have insisted, as he does in informal conversation. For "I don't think there exists such a thing as Mystery with a capital M. Instead, there are lots of small mysteries which we should approach as if they were gaps in knowledge rather than unfathomable and unbridgeable abysses."

Approach and observe them any way you like, Niebuhr might say, as he did in *Christian Realism and Political Problems,* but "no empirical observation is possible without a conceptual framework. And every rational framework points beyond itself to some framework of meaning which cannot simply be identified with rational coherence."

And you, Hook, might counterpose, are the last person who ought to be talking about rational coherence. As I have often said,

> logically not a single one of Reinhold Niebuhr's social, political and ethical views can be derived from his theology. This is demonstrable: his theology and metaphysics are perfectly compatible with the opposite of his own views of secular themes.

In fact, Hook might continue, those who approve Niebuhr's view of sin are precisely those who tend to disapprove his view of democracy:

> Who has not heard some apologist of Hitlerism or Stalinism proclaim that, after all, people are fundamentally contrary, that they have to be driven for their own good, that . . . the "Old Adam" in each of us will reach out for all he can take unless he gets a little taste of the rod?
> Of course the logic is weak, but the argument has psychological force so long as the assumption about the fixity and constancy of human nature goes unchallenged.

But wait, Niebuhr might say. You and Dewey both confuse Luther's doctrine of total depravity with the Bible's doctrine of original sin. Man's perennial tendency to sin arises precisely from the fact that his nature is *not* "fixed or constant":

> Sin arises from the corruption of the very spiritual freedom which gives man his dignity . . . the proud and vainglorious pretensions of men, their lust for power, their desire for domination over their fellow-men, their fanatic cruelties . . . all these sins are corruptions of man's unique freedom as a person.

But listen, Hook might say, you're making it sound as if John Dewey and I maintained that man was potentially perfect: instead,

> intelligent naturalism claims neither divinity for man nor infallibility for human judgment. It is conscious of man's limitations and the intractibilities of things without sinking into despair or consoling itself with other-worldly myths. It recognizes the cussedness and cantankerousness of human nature as reflecting the obstinacy of habit, the weight of social inertia, and the tincture of stupidity in the best of men. For it there are problems of evils—always concrete, specific and not necessarily soluble: but there is no such thing as *The* problem of evil except as that is created by arbitrary theological assumptions.

Look, Niebuhr might say, could I ask you one question? There's no use my debating what you call "otherworldly myths" and "arbitrary theological assumptions" because there can be no true dialogue between us in regard to those.

You couldn't be more right, Hook might say. But what was your question?

Simply this, Niebuhr might say, how, according to your theory that scientific intelligence will ameliorate the human condition, did the most ghastly evils in all history arise in a country where the people were educated, not illiterate; scientifically advanced, not backward; and although not rich, certainly less poor than most of the rest of the world? Once the Nazis' premise of a master race was accepted, was it not perfectly *logical* for them to liquidate the twelve million people they considered inferior? Do you, an intelligent man, really think that intelligent men using scientific methods are necessarily more virtuous than simple people? Don't you ever wonder why the great universities of Germany stood not far from the crematoria?

And don't *you* ever wonder, Hook might reply, as he did in his *New Failure of Nerve* article, "why fascism should have arisen in such strongly religious and metaphysical countries as Italy and Germany?" There were churches, too, not far from the crematoria, and some of the German bishops—not all, I grant you—urged their parishioners to support the Führer. Admittedly, there were grievous economic, social, and political errors made inside and outside Germany which led to the Führer's rise, but he also whipped up the German people to a frenzy of destruction through appealing not to logic and reason but to the call of the blood.

And you, who denigrate logic and reason by using paradox, who insist that there are "dialectical truths beyond reason," who beat the drum for the concept of original sin, contribute to the very confusion and despair that lead people to follow dictators.

Not so, Niebuhr might answer. Confusion and despair come when the object of our faith lets us down, or when we can find no object of faith that will not let us down. And the people who run the greatest danger of being let down are those who worship something less than God. Pascal spoke rightly when he said,

> The human spirit believes and loves so naturally that, if it does not have true objects of faith and love, it will have faith and love in false things.

And in our time the false things have been, first, the naïve adherence to the belief in progress, and secondly, the sophisticated

> form of scepticism which is conscious of the relativity of all human perspectives. In this form it stands on the abyss of moral nihilism and threatens the whole of life with a sense of meaninglessness. Thus it creates a spiritual vacuum into which demonic religions easily rush . . . The rise of Nazism . . . was, in one of its aspects, the growth of a demonic religion out of the soil of despair . . . spiritually [men] were ready to worship race, nation or power as god in order to avoid the abyss of meaninglessness.

Well I don't know—Hook's eyes twinkle when he is about to make a personal thrust—whether you consider me "naïve" or "sophisticated" in my atheism . . .

And I don't know—Niebuhr's eyes can twinkle too—whether you are an atheist at all:

> Most forms of ostensible atheism are merely protests against some traditional or conventional conception of the divine. They usually contain some implicit or even explicit conception of the divine in the sense that they have a system of coherence with an implicit or explicit center and source which is not explained but is the principle of explanation. Their god may be "nature" or "reason" or . . .

Go no further, Hook might say. For me, what you call the "explicit center and source" is what I call "the supreme and ultimate authority . . . [which] is the self-critical authority of the scientific method—or intelligence."

So be it, Niebuhr might say. Other people find other "provisional and tentative structures of meaning in nature, life and history," and, like you, they work creatively on the basis of these. It is only "when these seemingly 'eternal' values are shaken that life is threatened with despair or is challenged to a profounder consideration of the meaning of life." Therefore I agree with Professor Demos of Harvard that

> The whole question about whether God exists or not is really the question about whether there is an ultimate meaning of existence beyond any particular and usually idolatrous meaning which we give to life from our perspective.

And I, Hook might smile and add, do not believe there even exists an "ultimate question; only *pen*ultimate ones."

And I, Niebuhr might smile and add, am forced to admit that belief in the God of the Bible does not of itself prevent some people from making this belief into a form of idolatry. As I sometimes tell my students,

> If you arrive at truth and don't recognize the fragmentary character of your own apprehension, you may become a fanatic. But if you believe all truth is relative, you may become a nihilist. For myself, I believe that there is agreement beyond all disagreement and this has been affirmed by the reasonableness of unbelievers from Montaigne on, and by the humility of Christians whose experience of divine judgment and forgiveness is validated by the grace . . . of a new life . . . which issues from this experience.

Unremitting as was Niebuhr's attack on the secular liberals, his attack on the religious ones was even more so. At times, in fact, they accused him of exaggerating their position in order the better to knock it down, and at other times they questioned the applicability of his generalizations. Bishop Scarlett noted with a smile, "the religious liberal Reinie attacks doesn't appear among the people I would call liberal. As for myself, I tell him I'm an unrepentant liberal."

Perhaps Niebuhr has been so critical of the religious liberals because he was once of their number, and there are few people of whom we so strongly disapprove as those whose beliefs we have outgrown. Perhaps he was so critical because they, unlike the secular liberals, had read the Bible and therefore theoretically should have known better than to set up reason or love as God, in place of the Creator, Judge, and Redeemer.[4] Or perhaps he was so rigorous because, prophetically speaking, the judgment of the Lord is supposed to come down first and hardest on the household of faith.

In all events, his attack called forth an equally rigorous response. In 1947, a book was published (by Beacon Press) called *The Religious Liberals Reply*. Nor did the title even bother to include the name of the man to whom the authors felt such need to reply. The leader of these liberals, Henry Nelson Wieman, made the point Sidney Hook also makes, that Niebuhr places insufficient reliance on man's power of reason. Wieman subsequently made the point Paul Tillich also makes, that Niebuhr does not sufficiently define what he means by reason. Said Wieman, "the word 'reason' has many different meanings. Niebuhr constantly refers to it, but to my knowledge never explains what he means by it."

And this is the truth. A student once asked in class for Niebuhr's definition of reason. "Analytic and logical faculty," was the snap answer, and Niebuhr promptly recognized another questioner. Certainly, to Niebuhr, the word means more than this: sometimes it means a kind of intuition; sometimes, the power to form concepts; sometimes the power of self-transcendence; sometimes the linkage of inductive and deductive chains. Wieman surmises that for Niebuhr the word means "the use of observation, inference, prediction and logical coherence." And Charles C. West in his *Communism and the Theologians*, 1958, notes that Niebuhr

> distinguishes between prudential, instrumental reason "which Ulysses shared with the foxes," and that passion for perfect coherence which "Plato shared with the gods."[5] Reason in the

[4] Niebuhr would agree with the modern theologian who said that "although God is love, love is not God."

[5] Niebuhr himself in *Children of Light*, had credited this distinction to Alfred North Whitehead.

> second sense expresses man's capacity for disinterestedness in morality, culminating in the ideal of equality of all other life with one's own. It is the principle of order in history and the instrument whereby man attempts to grasp the coherencies of the world . . . Here both the possibilities and perils of reason as an expression of human freedom become clear. For man uses reason in his freedom on the one hand to recognize this finiteness and on the other hand to erect premature structures of meaning and truth which universalizes his partial perspectives.

The word "premature," or "abortive," often appears when Niebuhr speaks of reason. For reason, to him, is part of the paradoxical self which has, in the words of Browning that he likes to quote, "Thoughts hardly to be packed into the narrow act,/Fancies that break through language and escape." Reason, therefore, when dealing with matters human must neither allow the tension to slacken between "on the one hand" and "on the other," nor the passion for consistency to slam the door before all the facts are in.

Niebuhr's use of reason thus is characteristic of his use of other words connected with human freedom. Like *history* it carries what he calls "tangents of related meanings" and "a penumbra of mystery." The central meaning can be crystallized into definition, but the tangents and the penumbra must be left, so to speak, in solution. For if they are prematurely or abortively lifted from their fluid state, the result may be a distortion of the truth.

As a result, some of Niebuhr's profoundest passages have lacked precision, and both secular and religious liberals have understandably attacked him on this ground. When Sidney Hook feels friendly, he calls Niebuhr's use of words "poetic"; when less friendly, he calls it "oxymoronic." And Charles Clayton Morrison, in *The Christian Century*, accused Niebuhr of using "weasel words" and a "shifty use of language."

The word reason, on the other hand, is so generally confused with reasonable that Niebuhr is by no means alone when he uses the two interchangeably: "Man is more than reason; that is why his actions are usually less than reasonable."[6] Hook does it too: "To speak [as Niebuhr does] of 'the inevitable subordination of reason to interest in the social

[6] *Christianity and Society*, Spring, 1939.

struggle' is to assume . . . that no conflict of interests has ever been reasonably adjusted."[7] Yet according to the Oxford dictionary, the use of reasonable to mean "endowed with reason" is rare; the common definition is "sensible."

An example of a person whose devotion to reason led to an extraordinary avoidance of both sensibleness and reason's orderly categories was James Bissett Pratt who attacked Niebuhr's view of reason in *The Religious Liberals Reply:*

> That reason has the last word is the presupposition of every argument. If a man denies this it will be impossible to prove it to him: but this is because it will be impossible to prove *anything* to him. The man who denies the ultimate authority of reason has, for the time being at least, withdrawn himself from the circle of rational beings—he has yielded to the not uncommon wish to "turn and be as the animals." With such a man it is impossible to argue or discuss. Toward him one's attitude must necessarily be that which one takes to an animal or a young child or a victrola.

Niebuhr, whether in his unlikely role as victrola, young child, or animal, views the relation between reason and justice in a way that might be applied to James Bissett Pratt: "There is no guarantee of justice in man's reason . . . [for] the reason with which we reason about each other's affairs is not 'pure' reason and it cannot be made objective and impartial by any scientific method."

Wieman's attack on Niebuhr, whether in the *Liberals Reply* or the Living Library Volume, was both more reasonable than Pratt's—and also far more telling. Niebuhr, indeed, in his Living Library Volume answer, admitted that "the most substantive differences" were with Professor Wieman. And in answering Wieman Niebuhr came as close as he ever has to defining what he means by reason:

> I have never maintained that the corruption of sin is "in reason." I have asserted that it is in the self and that a self-centered self is able to use reason for its own ends; which is why there is no protection in reason as such against sin. I have also not been scornful of reason in all of its aspects in reaching the truth. I

[7] John Dewey: *An Intellectual Portrait,* The John Day Co., 1939.

> have agreed with Kant in finding logic a provisional instrument of morals insofar as the logical principle in reason may prompt the self to consider its own ends in terms of their relationship with a total and coherent system of ends. Naturally I would not dispense with every analytical power of reason to analyze and chart the coherences and sequences of every type of reality. Professor Wieman has unconsciously misconceived all of these emphases because of a preconception that anyone who is critical of "reason" must be an obscurantist who trusts "blind faith" in place of reason.

Niebuhr also stated that Wieman and the religious naturalists have a "picture of the self and of God, of the world and of history" that is "more 'rational' . . . in the sense that its coherencies are neater and . . . mystery has been abolished from the realm of meaning"; but there is, he points out, one serious flaw in their picture, the same flaw that he detects in the secular liberal picture, namely that it is not true to life:

> . . . all significant truths and facts about man and God, about the nobility and misery of human freedom, and about the judgment and mercy of God, are left out. . . . Thus a culture which prides itself on its "empiricism" obscures and denies every "fact" which does not fit into its frame of meaning.

Another attack on Niebuhr's use, or misuse, of reason comes from those Catholics sufficiently liberal to be willing to enter into dialogue with a Protestant. For example, the great modern Thomist, Jacques Maritain, said of Niebuhr in a letter:

> Sur le plan théologique il y a évidemment bien des différences entre lui et moi (il est protestant, je suis catholique); ce que j'apprécie surtout en lui c'est sa largeur d'horizon et l'esprit de foi avec lequel il aborde les problemes contemporains, notamment les problemes sociaux, et c'est son sens profond des responsabilités du chrétien en matiere temporelle.[8]

[8] In theological matters there are obviously many differences between us (he is Protestant; I am Catholic); what I particularly admire about him is the breadth of vision and the spirit of faith with which he attacks contemporary problems, particularly social problems, and his sense of profound responsibility as a Christian for the affairs of this world.

But there is no agreement between Maritain and Niebuhr on the subject of reason. Says Maritain, "God is accessible to our reason." And for Niebuhr this statement is insufficiently dialectical: God both is, and is not, accessible to our reason. God is accessible primarily to faith, to an engagement of the whole self in which we find ourselves, including our reason, judged, forgiven, and renewed. Reason, however, is essential in distinguishing between the false and valid aspects of that faith. At the same time, reason is not capable of explaining everything. There is, Niebuhr says, "a basic irrationality about the giveness of things." The world of nature, and the fact that man is both rooted in it and able, in his freedom, to move beyond it, such "givens" are the springboard from which reason leaps, but they are not, themselves, logical deductions from the chaos, or the nothingness, that presumably preceded them. As Niebuhr says, "creation is not knowledge: it is where knowledge begins." And even after knowledge has begun, "there is one chink in the realm of meaning and rational intelligibility. That chink is the fact that no previous cause is a sufficient explanation of a subsequent event."[9]

At the heart of knowledge, therefore, there exists unknowns, and perhaps also unknowables (see Chapter 20). This is one reason that faith in God, like atheism, is not *rationally* compelling to someone who starts from the opposite presupposition. Man's presuppositions are, Niebuhr says, so potent and so often disguised that the religious person who asserts that man can find God or discern God's will solely by means of his own rational faculties may, in his pride, be setting these rational faculties in the place of God.

For holding such views Niebuhr is attacked by such Catholic critics as Edmond Darvil Benard of Catholic University, who accuses him of having "a sharp anti-rational bias." The Catholic magazine, *American Ecclesiastical Review*, during the winter of 1944-45, carried a series of

[9] In *Pious and Secular America* Niebuhr gives what he calls "a homely example of this fact." There is, he says, "no scientific explanation for the elephant's tusks or the porcupine's quills or the fact that the skunk has an even more ingenious mode of defense . . . One can give these irrationalities the appearance of rationality by sorting the animals . . . into categories and tracing their lineage and relationships to other types. But the most searching philosopher of the sciences in modern life, Alfred North Whitehead . . . discerns the limits of rationality and posits a 'primordial God,' a kind of X to symbolize the realm of mystery."

articles on Niebuhr, criticizing his Gifford Lectures in general and his view of "Natural Law" in particular. This concept, itself based upon a systematic and detailed use of reason, was succinctly described by the Reverend John Courtney Murray, S.J., in *We Hold These Truths*:

> Its only presupposition is threefold: that man is intelligent, that reality is intelligible; and that reality, as grasped by intelligence, imposes on the will the obligation that it be obeyed in its demands for action or abstention.

Many of these obligations, Niebuhr believes, particularly the major ones dealing with abstention, are clearly to be honored. Every society, he notes, contains some variety of "thou shalt not kill" and "thou shalt not steal," and, he adds, "Most of us would include respect for the person, and not merely his life and property in the moral law." But when the obligation deals not with abstention but with action for the purpose of "organizing the human community in terms of maximum justice and liberty, our moral preferences obviously cease to be universal and are obviously colored by our interest."

At the same time that he sees our interest as coloring our view of the moral law, he rejects complete relativism in human affairs. In *Christian Century*, December 2, 1953, for example, he pointed with scorn to "the absurdity of Bertrand Russell who during the war declared that he abhorred Nazism but could not attribute his judgment to anything more than a 'matter of taste.' "

The moral law, to Niebuhr, is more than a matter of taste, but it cannot be exactly defined, even by human reason, as Saint Thomas Aquinas had assumed. For, as Niebuhr wrote in the Gifford Lectures, human reason both transcends and is servant to man's "interest," a form of interest not merely personal but connected with his time in history and his place in ecclesiastical or secular society. Therefore,

> undue confidence in human reason, as the seat and source or natural law . . . makes this very concept of the law into a vehicle of human sin. It gives the peculiar conditions and unique circumstances in which reason operates in a particular historical moment, the sanctity of universality.

The Gifford Lectures, of course, were themselves delivered at a particular time in history by a man whose loyalty and "interest" lay with the liberals imprisoned in Spanish dungeons by the Franco régime which had recently gained power with the help of the Spanish Catholic Church. Niebuhr's attack on Natural Law at that time, therefore, was in part a reflection of that loyalty and interest:

> The whole imposing structure of Thomistic ethics is, in one of its aspects, no more than a religious sanctification of the relativities of the feudal system as it flowered in the 13th century. The confusion between ultimate religious perspectives and relative historical ones in Catholic thought accounts for the fury and self-righteousness into which Catholicism is betrayed when it defends feudal types of civilization in contemporary history as in Spain for instance.

The ultimate religious perspective of Natural Law, therefore, Niebuhr approves, but he does not approve its relative historical perspectives, especially when these are spelled out in too great detail. In regard to society's life, for example, he questions Natural Law's definition of a just war which "assumes that obvious distinctions between 'justice' and 'injustice,' between 'defense' and 'aggression'" can always fairly be made:

> Contemporary history reinforces the clear lessons of the whole of history upon this point. Not all wars are equally just and not all contestants are equally right. Distinctions must be made. But the judgments with which we make them are influenced by passions and interests.

And in regard to individual life, Niebuhr claims that there are areas of man's freedom where the mystery of human personality as it encounters another personality is too great for any exact rule to apply:

> In Catholic natural law all social relations, including family relations, are precisely defined. *Inter alia* it is maintained that the natural law prohibits [artificial] birth control . . . The prohibition . . . assumes that the sexual function in human life must be limited to its function in nature, that of procreation. But it is the very character of human life that all animal functions are touched by freedom. . . . Freedom in relation to sex may occasion license and it may also provide for a creative relation between the sexual impulse and other . . . more refined

> spiritual impulses. . . . It is not possible to escape the fact that the primary purpose of bisexuality in nature is procreation. But it is not easy to establish a universally valid "law of reason" which will eternally set the bounds for the function of sex in the historical development of human personality.

Niebuhr's insistence on the limits of human reason applies not only, of course, to its use in Natural Law, but also to his own or any man's use of it in criticizing Natural Law. As a result of this attitude, his arguments with Catholic theologians have often resulted in a bond rather than a breach, and a willingness to continue the dialogue. As the learned Jesuit, Father Gustave Weigel, writes in the Living Library Volume:

> Critical though he is, Niebuhr yet shows a friendliness to Catholicism which Catholics do not always perceive in Protestant theologians. With Niebuhr a Catholic-Protestant dialogue is possible because he does not allow bitterness and hostility to poison the air of the encounter.[10]

Indeed, Niebuhr tends first to vent his ire on the household of his own Protestant faith. As he wrote for *Christianity and Crisis* whose 8500 subscribers are mostly Protestant:

> The acrimonious relations between Catholics and Protestants in this country are scandalous. If the two forms of the Christian faith cannot achieve a little more charity in the relation to each other, they have no right to speak to the world.

Niebuhr states, moreover, that Protestantism itself has often erred by adjusting too easily to "every form of popular culture which strikes the imagination as plausible in a particular era and then vanishes again." In modern times, for example, the Enlightenment concept of progress and the perfectibility of man was adopted not only by the secular liberals, for whom the concept of grace had no meaning, but also by the Protestant

[10] Niebuhr's friendliness to Catholicism was shown in the Presidential campaign of 1960 when he made forceful statements on television and radio to the effect that the nation would not be endangered by the election of a Catholic layman. Response to these statements on the part of some Protestants was vitriolic.

liberals who consequently felt that grace had little relevance. (If there was no basic sin, what need was there for grace?)[11]

This serious error the Catholics have avoided, but their concept of grace was also one with which Niebuhr disagreed. For according to their belief, only one institution, the Catholic Church, is capable of dispensing or mediating grace. So special indeed is this institution, founded by Christ through Peter ("You are Peter and on this rock I will build my church"), that its head, the Pope, when defining for the whole church a matter of faith or morals, is believed by his followers to be infallible.

For Protestants, including Niebuhr, no man or institution is infallible. And since grace comes by the power of the Holy Spirit through the Bible, and, indeed, through the historic church, no person can claim possession of it. In Niebuhr's view, therefore, any claim to control grace, rather than to be controlled by it, is sin, whether on the part of an individual or an institution. At the same time he notes that in contrast to the fragmentation of the Protestant denominations, the Catholics have,

> . . . by the assertion of the authority of the Church in all matters of doctrine, maintained a monolithic unity which must be, in some respects, the envy of all Christians.

In other respects, however, this monolithic unity comes at too high a price for Protestants to wish to pay:

> What is at stake is the whole Reformation insistence on the right of private judgment and on the "priesthood of all believers."

Niebuhr therefore sees no real chance that the two forms of the Christian faith will ever come close enough doctrinally to unite. And from the Catholic point of view, Father Weigel states in the Living Library Volume that there could never be agreement with a Protestant point of view such as Niebuhr's which "excludes final authority in anything historical" and insists that everything except God "is finite, Jesus

[11] There is a difference between *common grace*, manifested in family love, for example, and *saving grace* which is manifested in the Mass (for Catholics) and in Communion (for some Protestants). When theologians write of grace, it is generally *saving grace* they have in mind.

of Nazareth was finite, and the Catholic Church or any other church is yet more finite."

As to Jesus' finiteness, Niebuhr agrees with the conclusion by Albert Schweitzer in *The Quest for the Historical Jesus* that Jesus, like many of his contemporaries, was mistaken in the imminence of his eschatological expectations: the Kingdom of God was pictured as coming momentarily. As to the Catholic Church, Niebuhr says, it is not only more finite than Jesus, but its pretense that it is not finite is a temptation to "demonic arrogance." And he disagrees with "the Catholic minded," by which he also means the Eastern Orthodox and Anglo-Catholics, because of their conviction that "the Church is the Extension of the Incarnation and is therefore perfect and cannot repent. They admit that individual members fall into sin but hold to a mystical reality beyond all historic and empiric facts. For Protestants this reality is Christ himself who is head of the Church."[12]

The Catholic concept of the Church, from Niebuhr's point of view, therefore involves lifting

> a historic institution into a transhistoric reality, making the claim of speaking for God, or being privy to the divine will, and of dispensing divine grace . . . No matter, therefore, how much we may admire or envy the Catholic Church, we are prepared to pay the price necessary for the freedom of the individual conscience and the freedom to contradict even a very imposing institution, suggesting that it is in danger of ascribing human prejudices to the divine.

In response, Father Weigel summed up:

> Niebuhr's accusation against the Catholic Church only presents us with the disjunction: either Niebuhr or the Catholic Church is arrogant.

And Niebuhr's answer was directed to this same point:

> Father Weigel neatly brings the whole issue to a head in his statement that either the Church or I am arrogant and one must take one's choice between the pretension of the private individual and that of a great historic institution which has been the

[12] Religious News Service, September 25, 1948, written from Amsterdam, Holland at the time of The World Council of Churches meeting.

> treasury of the "Oracles of God." This is a "palpable hit" which may well leave the private critic reeling.

But not for long. Niebuhr who has stood against the either-or principle in regard to religion continues to insist that all human arguments, including those about the Church, are between self-righteous sinners.[13] As for the wounds he sustains, their pain is worth it, even when, as sometimes happens, they never quite heal. For in regard to all controversy he agrees with his old controversialist, John Dewey, at whose side he fought against injustice and at whose ideas he threw some of his most lethal darts:

> Better it is for philosophy to err in active participation in the living struggles and issues of [the philosopher's] own age and times than to maintain an immune monastic impeccability.

[13] D. B. Robertson says of Niebuhr that "something of the Reformation concept of the invisible church continues to be a meaningful and essential instrument for keeping all particular churches under judgment." The invisible church may thus be related to the concept of the hidden Christ.

19

No Rest for the Prophet

NIEBUHR, says Alan Richardson, "comes to the question of history . . . in the challenging spirit of a Biblical prophet: one will best understand history and its meaning in the effort to change it . . ."

Niebuhr's efforts to *change* history have been personal, organizational, and governmental. On the podium, in the pulpit, through religious and secular publications he personally raised his voice, usually against the prevailing trend of opinion. Organizationally, if there existed a group trying to do what he thought essential, he joined it; otherwise he created it. Since his willingness to join is matched only by his reluctance to withdraw (out of loyalty to his friends who are still involved), the inclusion of his name may mean anything from a heart-like essentiality to an appendix-like vestigiality. Governmentally, he was called in both by the legislative branch, appearing, at the request of the Senate Foreign Relations Committee, as a witness in favor of Lend-Lease, and also by the executive branch, serving at the request of the State Department as an advisor, and being sent by the USO during World War II to visit the American camps in Britain.

Niebuhr's efforts to *understand* history have been based largely on his view of man. Underneath all particular causes of historic events he was always searching for the universal one. As he wrote in *Moral Man:*

> It is important to begin by recognizing that the force of egoistic impulse is much more powerful than any but the most astute political analysts and the most rigorous devotees of introspection realize . . . If it is defeated by social impulse, it insinuates itself into social impulse, so that a man's devotion to his community always means the expression of a transferred egoism as well as of altruism.

While Niebuhr was thus being prophetic in the sense of denouncing sin, few of his contemporaries noted that he was also being prophetic in the sense of foretelling. Not, of course, that he was always correct; in domestic affairs particularly he could have said with La Guardia: "When I make a mistake, it's a beaut." But in foreign affairs since the middle thirties his forthright predictions have had an unnerving habit of coming true.

In 1934, for example, in *Reflections Upon the End of an Era,* five years before Hitler invaded Poland and France, Niebuhr wrote, "it is difficult . . . to see how Hitler's Germany can finally avoid war with either France or Poland." And two years later, in *Radical Religion,* Winter, 1936, Niebuhr supported the League of Nations sanctions against Italy who had invaded defenseless Ethiopia, because, as he said,

> Unwillingness to run some risk of war in the present moment means certain war in the future.

That was the year Hitler reoccupied the Rhineland, without opposition from France. One of the most terrible footnotes to history is the evidence that turned up after World War II that if France, as De Gaulle was urging, had stood firm against this reoccupation, Hitler might then have fulfilled his promise to commit suicide.

Although not a military man, Niebuhr's attitude was similar to that of De Gaulle. As he wrote in *Christian Century,* September 29, 1937:

> The more we fear to resist aggression now by non-military means because we fear that even such means might lead to war, the more certain will we be to meet ultimately a foe who has strengthened himself during our days of hesitation.

The primary foe at this time was Nazi Germany. Niebuhr, be it said, had been in earlier and closer touch with developments in Germany than were most Americans. The Nazis too, be it said, did all they could to disguise the wounds they were inflicting on their political, racial, or religious victims. American students bicycling in Germany in the early thirties came home full of enthusiasm not only for the beautiful scenery but for the clean and friendly people and the beer halls where they had spent happy evenings singing and drinking with the Germans, and even, in fun, occasionally, returning their stiff-armed Nazi salute. Yet the disguised wounds were suppurating; slowly at first, and then in a steady stream, evidence poured out of Germany causing those confronting it to sicken and to question themselves how such a thing was possible.

But many Americans refused to confront it. Torture had been outlawed for centuries; surely these stories were hysterical exaggerations. Or if, by some historical "sport," they were not, then surely nothing comparable could happen in the United States. *It Can't Happen Here* was the bitter title given by Sinclair Lewis to his novel in the mid-thirties about a fictional but not implausible fascist dictatorship in America.

For Niebuhr who tended to see man in universal rather than particular terms, it seemed unfortunately quite possible that what had happened in medieval times could happen again, and that what man could do in Europe he could do in America. So despairing did Niebuhr at first feel after Hitler came to power that he briefly endorsed a position of neutrality and suggested in a 1934 *World Tomorrow* article that perhaps America's role should be to preserve "some islands of sanity in a sea of insanity." But by the following year Mussolini's invasion of Ethiopia demonstrated to Niebuhr, although not to the majority of Americans, that such a role was impossible.

What role America should assume was the subject of heated private and public debate during the mid-thirties. Some loyal Americans, following the memory of Woodrow Wilson, felt that the nation's role should be internationalist: the whole point of having fought World War I was to "make the world safe for democracy," and it was not yet too late for the United States to join the League of Nations and the World Court. Other equally loyal Americans, following the memory of George Washington, felt that the nation's role should be one of neutrality: the whole point of having fought the American Revolution was to "avoid entangling alliances" and consequent involvement in the perennial quarrels between the European powers.

In the later thirties, as the neutrality position hardened into isolationism, and the internationalist position hardened into interventionism, Niebuhr concentrated on attacking isolationism.[1] He attacked it from three points

[1] Not all the self-styled isolationists in America fully deserved the name. Some were still internationalist at heart but considered war itself the worst of all evils; others feared that the United States would lose her democratic freedoms at home in

of view: the *pragmatic* because he thought that against Hitler it would not work; the *psychological* because he thought it based, at least in part, on a reluctance to face the full extent of the Nazi horror lest this horror force responsible action; and the *theological* because he thought isolationism, at heart, was a form of self-love.

In making these attacks, however, he used terminology that from a public relations standpoint was anything but conducive to winning agreement from his fellow Americans. For he equated isolationism with both individualism and self-sufficiency, qualities which have been admired in this country since the inception of Operation Bootstrap in 1620, and in *Children of Light,* he equated these with sin:

> The ideal of individual self-sufficiency, so exalted in our liberal culture, is recognized in Christian thought as one form of the primal sin. For self-love which is the root of all sin, takes two social forms. One of them is the domination of other life by the self. The second is the sin of isolationism.

The responsibilities of a modern nation, like those of the individual, cannot, logically or ethically, be said to stop at the water's edge. Yet Niebuhr was wrenched to his depths by the thought that in the event of war, American young men might again have to die, by the hundreds of thousands, on foreign soil. There was nothing personal in this feeling: he himself was too old, and his son too young, to get into active fighting. Indeed his distress might have been less if he *had* been able to risk his own life: as it was, he was making public pronouncements the effects of which might, for all he could be certain, hasten the holocaust in which others would have to do the suffering and dying. Yet he had to keep saying what he felt was the truth: he himself could neither turn irresponsible by refusing to speak nor self-protective by saying only what his countrymen wished to hear. The Munich Pact, for example, which was temporarily bruited, in Britain as well as in the United States, as having brought peace in our time, did not appear thus to Niebuhr, and

---

the process of fighting for them abroad, and both these groups tended to support the "short-of-war" steps America took to strengthen the democracies. The argument, moreover, that Niebuhr used against the pacifists, that they were refusing to face the full horror of Nazidom, could be turned the opposite way: that the interventionists were refusing to face the full horror of war.

he said so publicly as well as privately. In September 16, 1938, he wrote to Scarlett:

> Isn't the world situation terrible. I am afraid no good will come of the Chamberlain visit. It means selling Czechoslovakia out or war. I hope I am mistaken. . . . I have listened to the radio news constantly. At first I had high hopes after the Chamberlain visit was announced, but as the Hitler demands began to leak out, the hope vanished again.

By the following Spring Niebuhr, driven by inner conflict and outer catastrophe into working even harder than usual, was in such a state of exhaustion and depression that the doctor forced him to cancel most of his engagements.

Yet the catastrophes continued to mount.

And Niebuhr as soon as he was half-well again, continued to write and speak.

Finally in September, 1939, one year after the Munich Pact, Hitler marched on Poland. "Our hopes were wrong," said Niebuhr, "and our fears were right." Britain and France, allies of Poland, honored their commitments and declared war on Germany. In the United States the isolationists banded together in the America First Committee, and the interventionists, including Niebuhr, banded together in the William Allen White Committee to Defend America by Aiding the Allies. This latter Committee differed from the group known as the Fight For Freedom Committee in that the White Committee contained a large number of people, also including Niebuhr, who were not yet certain that American *boys* would have to get into the war: the emphasis was on aiding the embattled Allies by every step short of war and taking the consequences. This was a path by necessity filled with tension and pitfalls. And by the Spring of the following year, 1940, Niebuhr had again worked himself into a state of collapse. As he wrote to Bishop Scarlett on April 5, 1940:

> It is very generous of you to worry so much about my health but you must not do it. I am getting along fairly well, of course at a reduced speed. I have to rest every afternoon and knock off every evening. It was, in fact, this business of working at night which got me back rather close to my condition of a year ago. It

> isn't easy to quit work at seven every evening when there is so much to do.

There was so much to do because the nation was so confused about external affairs and so riven by its internal differences. In some cases, members of the same family stopped seeing each other: the nation had not thus been rent since the Civil War. Niebuhr's exposure to the bitterness came in part through the counterattacks on him by the pacifists and isolationists. "I do wish," Niebuhr said wistfully to Loeb, "that they'd hate Hitler more and me less." Niebuhr's exposure to the confusion was described in an article he published in *The Nation*, June 29, 1940 and subsequently included in his *Christianity and Power Politics:*

> The morning newspaper brings reports of disaster everywhere. The morning mail acquaints me with the confusion created by these reports. My mail this morning, for example, contains four significant communications. The first is a letter from the Socialist Party informing me that my views on foreign affairs violate the party platform and asking me to give account of my non-conformity. The party position is that this war is a clash of rival imperialisms in which nothing significant is at stake. The second letter asks me to support an organization which will bring peace to the world by establishing "world education" and erecting a "world radio." It fails to explain how its world education is to seep into the totalitarian states and wean them from their mania. The third letter is from a trade union under Communist influence asking me to speak at a union "peace" meeting. The fourth is from a parson who wants me to join in an effort to set "moral force against Hitler's battalions," but it fails to explain just how this moral force is to be effective against tanks, flame-throwers, and . . . planes.

Niebuhr's reaction was a combination of anger and sadness:

> I answer the Socialist communication by a quick resignation from the party. I inform the trade union that my views would not be acceptable at the peace meeting. The proposal for a world radio is quickly consigned to a file which already contains eighty-two different recipes for world salvation. I start to answer the parson who wants to set "moral force" against Hitler, but over-

> come with a sense of futility and doubting the ability to penetrate the utopian fog in which the letter was conceived, I throw my reply into the wastebasket. Thus I save some time to meditate upon . . . the vapid character of the culture which Hitler intends to destroy. This culture does not understand historical reality clearly enough to deserve to survive. It has a right to survival only because the alternative is too horrible to contemplate.

For two years and two months after Hitler's invasion of Poland, the United States remained confused and divided. France fell, the Battle of Britain took a terrible toll, many areas to the south of Japan crumbled. Yet, in 1940, both Presidential candidates, Roosevelt and Willkie, campaigned on the promise to keep us out of war. As Niebuhr summed up in *Radical Religion* that summer:

> Just as in the world war, our vital interests are only ultimately and not immediately touched by a possible allied victory. This prevents the whole nation from feeling that coincidence of vital and ideal interests which alone prompts nations to enter such a horrible carnage with comparative unanimity.

His personal conclusion, as he wrote Scarlett, was that because of this division in the nation,

> I don't think we ought to declare war now. I think we ought to convoy and if that brings us into war, all right. But to declare war now is not to understand our internal situation and to aggravate the hysteria of the isolationist block. I believe the President's policy is smarter than that.

For Niebuhr to refer to Roosevelt as smart denoted a real shift in his thought, based more upon Roosevelt's foreign than domestic policy. Niebuhr had started out with a personal distrust of Roosevelt dating back a whole decade to the refusal by Roosevelt, then Governor of New York, to come out in a clear-cut way against Mayor Jimmy Walker despite the obvious scandals in Walker's administration of New York City. Though Walker was eventually forced to resign, lawyers of probity, such as Charles C. Burlingham, kept up their criticism of Roosevelt's wishywashyness. To Niebuhr who admired Burlingham, Roosevelt therefore appeared as a man without principles, and the New Deal appeared as "a form of insulin that can ward off dissolution without giving the patient permanent health."[2]

But after the war in Europe had begun and the danger to the United States grew with each of Hitler's victories, Niebuhr began to realize that what he had thought of as lack of principles on the part of the President was really political skill and timing of a high order. Each time a specific short-of-war measure to help the Allies, such as Lend-Lease or the Destroyer Deal, was pressed, it barely won the consent of the disunited country. Niebuhr voted for Roosevelt for the first time in 1940, and publicly admitted his own "disgraceful slowness" in appreciating the President's pragmatic wisdom.

Niebuhr's feelings about the "insulin" of the New Deal also changed in retrospect. Being finally free of any remnants of Socialist dogma, Niebuhr could see more and more virtues in the mixed economy. And in May of 1940, when Britain's new Conservative government under Winston Churchill (replacing that of Chamberlain) was able, with public support, to raise one of its taxes from 37 to 85 per cent, Niebuhr admitted there was more life in the old capitalist dog than he, and many others, had previously supposed.[3]

It was no accident that Niebuhr's change of heart about Roosevelt's foreign policy carried over to the domestic policy as well. For the two, in Niebuhr's view, were integrally related. And, late in 1940, he helped to establish two new organizations whose purpose was "to wage a two-front fight for democracy at home and abroad."

One was the magazine *Christianity and Crisis* which was directed to the Protestant community, many of whose leaders were pacifist. (In the Methodist denomination at that time, for example, it was estimated that

[2] The dedication of Niebuhr's *The Structure of Nations and Empires*, published in 1959 just before Burlingham's death at the age of 100, was "To Charles C. Burlingham, counsellor of judges and statesmen, civic reformer and pillar of his church, who in the century of his life has shown us how to combine realism with civic virtue and the sense of justice."

[3] These particular tax figures were used by Niebuhr in a 1940 *Christian Century* article, but subsequent research, aided by the British Economic Information Chief in the United States, Richard Miles, failed to identify them. This, Niebuhr was immediately able to do: they were the taxes levied on the Gifford Lectures emolument. They, together with the devaluation of the pound, turned this emolument from a bonanza to barely enough to cover expenses.

more than half the ministers were pacifist.) Present at the founding meeting in December, 1940, in addition to Niebuhr, were Charles C. Burlingham, F. Ernest Johnson, John A. Mackay, Francis Pickins Miller, Henry Pitney Van Dusen, and Charles T. White. Niebuhr was selected chairman of the Editorial Board.[4]

The second organization was directed to the whole American community; called The Union for Democratic Action, it held its preliminary founding meeting in November, 1940. In attendance, in addition to Niebuhr who became its chairman, were Murray Gross, who became its secretary, Lewis Corey, George Counts, Freda Kirchwey, and James Loeb who became its (staff) executive secretary.

The formal founding meeting was six months later, in May of 1941, and Niebuhr was elected chairman. As Loeb recalls, "We had six weeks of grace" before the Germans invaded Russia, thus causing the American Communists, up to then fanatic isolationists, to become equally fanatic interventionists.

The United Front was thus reactivated with a vengeance, but as Loeb recalls, not only did UDA reject all Communists as members, but also "no UDA-er would be involved in Russian War Relief" or any other of the organizations the Communists were infiltrating:

> During those years, we became almost the pariahs of the liberal movement. We were sometimes called the "hang back boys" because we refused to participate in so many "worthy causes" that we knew were run by the communists. They were the thing to do and we refused to do them. We fought at meetings, we pleaded, we warned, and we were damned unpopular. We fought in the Teachers' Union, the labor unions, and all over the place. Tragically for the world, we were right about the way it would turn out, but nobody ever loved Cassandra . . . it would have been better for the world if the fellow-travellers had been right about the Soviet Union.

The Red Army's heroism in fighting the Nazi invader was soon the toast of America, lauded by the isolationists as well as the interventionists,

[4] The Board consisted of John C. Bennett, William Adams Brown, Charles C. Burlingham, William F. Cochran, Henry Sloane Coffin, J. Harry Cotton, Harold W. Dodds, Sherwood Eddy, Frank P. Graham, Rhoda E. McCulloch, John Mackay, Francis Pickins Miller, Edward L. Parsons and Henry Pitney Van Dusen.

by the conservatives as well as the liberals. For if the Russians could knock out Hitler, not only would the Allies win the war but the United States would not have to enter it. "It was hard," said Loeb, "to draw the line between supporting the Soviet Union and not working with the American Communists who started proliferating organizations and being conservative domestically."

Niebuhr meanwhile was working day and night trying to draw for his countrymen the difficult lines of their responsibility. And as a result, in 1941, for the third spring in a row, he collapsed. A letter to Scarlett tells the same alarming story:

> Will, I think you will have to cancel that February engagement in 1942. I hate to ask you to do this but it is dangerous for me to commit myself so far in advance. In spite of cutting down on my engagements I am almost as close to nervous collapse as last year and the doctor is asking me to cancel everything again. I am trying to get by with half-cancellations. There is nothing serious, but I simply can't go through the year. Each year I become so fatigued about this time that I can't sleep and thus get into a vicious circle. . . . The doctor thinks I can get my health back completely if I take a full six months off some time but I can't do that for some time. . . .

Nor did he. Somehow he lasted until the summer, rested a bit, and the next fall went back to his arduous schedule. The strain showed itself not only through physical exhaustion but through a growing irascibility. Those who most aroused his ire were those optimists whose attitude, according to the definition of the acerb Voltaire, included "the madness of maintaining that everything is right when it is wrong."

In the late Fall of 1941, E. P. Dutton published *The Crisis of Our Time* by Pitirim Sorokin, and sent out the following letter to a number of leading clergymen:

> Only once in many years does a publisher have the privilege and responsibility of sponsoring a work of [this] far-reaching nature . . . A many-sided, unified interpretation of the period of conflict in which we live, it provides a helpful frame of reference for evaluating—with justified optimism—the contemporary crisis in Western civilization.

Not only did the publisher thus endorse the book, but according to the letter, there had been

> scores of enthusiastic letters from clergymen of many denominations throughout the country who see in this deeply spiritual and scholarly work a source of inspiration . . .

Niebuhr's reaction to this "deeply spiritual and scholarly work," with its "justified optimism," appeared just after Pearl Harbor in a review for *The Nation,* December 20, 1941, which concluded:

> All this, in other words, comes very close to being unmitigated bosh. The uninitiated ought to know that the author is Chairman of the Department of Sociology at Harvard University, which proves that the decline of a sensate culture manifests itself by "Signs and Wonders."

Bishop Scarlett, meanwhile, had enjoyed the book and sent a copy of it to the Niebuhrs as a Christmas present. Four days before Christmas he sent them the following urgent telegram:

> Have just read your review in current Nation. SOS. Ignore Christmas gift in current mail. You will feel happier if you return it unopened. Please buy cigarettes and yellow roses. They're non-controversial. Charge to our account. Much love.

The Niebuhrs refused to return the package. According to Scarlett, they kept it unopened on the living room table as "a symbol that friendship transcends differences of opinion."

Reinhold Niebuhr's thank you letter was written early in the New Year:

> I am sorry that about the only time that I allowed myself to be really nasty in a review should have run across, by this curious coincidence, your great kindness to us and your thoughtfulness at Christmas-time. This will teach me a lesson never again to be uncharitable in a review and to remember "by the bowels of Christ," as Cromwell said, that I may be wrong.
>
> Anyway we haven't disagreed for so long that it is probably a good thing to have had this disagreement. The only person I

know of who agrees with me is X.[5] But there may be others. I won't try to marshal them however on my side.
We had a nice Christmas and I am sure you had. Funny how private bliss shuts out public woe, though even the public woe is not what some of the Christians think it is, since at least we can have an easier conscience than we had a year ago. I am finding isolationists who can barely conceal a sense of relief. But evidently we will have a lot of bad news before it will be better.

Ursula Niebuhr also wrote a thank you letter, which dealt with the Sorokin matter as diplomatically as possible:

> We had the best Christmas present from you. We laughed ("laffed and laffed") over your wire, and your nicely wrapped book stands on our table as a "cheer-inspirer." We do have—or had—a couple of copies, and both got rid of them on the theory that it was not an immortal tome to keep!! And it happened to be quite the "nastiest" review Reinhold has ever written—too—to make it worse. But some people seem most enthusiastic about it—I only dipped in it, to be frank.

Scarlett's answer to Niebuhr is dated January 8, 1942. Also a diplomat, he managed to maintain his own point of view while laughing with them about theirs.

> If X agrees with you, it must have been before he read your review . . .
> So glad you had a happy Christmas. I suppose the private bliss at millions of firesides is what helps to keep the world sane. But like you, I have felt almost light in conscience since Pearl Harbor. We had been so badly divided . . .

After Pearl Harbor, UDA made a great effort to expand. Frank Kingdon became its president, while Niebuhr remained as chairman, and some of the liberals from the William Allen White Committee joined its ranks. So deeply did Niebuhr feel the need for its expansion that he was once prevailed upon to make the pitch at a fund raising dinner. Visibly in an acute state of embarrassment, he grew so ruddy, so moist, so distressed at the job of begging people for money that his success was enormous.

[5] X is a distinguished academic who refused, even twenty years later, to be identified as critical of Sorokin.

"People gave," Loeb recalls, "in order to let him sit down." But despite the excellence of his results, Niebuhr vowed never to do it again.

The growth of UDA in numbers, however, was never as great as its founders had hoped, though its influence was considerable. And by the time the election of 1944 came around, UDA was still too small to take any independent part. "We were the pre-egghead-eggheads," says Loeb. "But we couldn't operate all by ourselves. So many UDA members joined up, at least for the campaign, with the National Citizens' Political Action Committee." This organization, headed by Sidney Hillman, had, like the American Labor Party, allowed Communists to join, and a few of them had worked their way to the top. "So there some of us were," said Loeb wryly, "in the United Front after all."

One of the separate but allied organizations developed by the National Citizens' PAC was called the "Religious Associates." When the Republican candidate for President, Thomas E. Dewey, made a speech in Boston that raised religious issues, the Religious Associates prepared a round-robin letter objecting to the speech and saying, in effect, that because of it they were going to support Dewey's opponent, Franklin D. Roosevelt.

Niebuhr refused to sign this letter. "I was for Roosevelt before Dewey's speech. I was for him because of his foreign and domestic policy. Damned if I'll sign a hypocritical letter."

Politically, for the duration of the war, the United States was relatively united. The young men in uniform, the older men and women of all parts of society, had the identical aim: to win the war as fast as possible and bring the boys home. What few people suspected was that a new fissure was soon to open up, not within the nation, but within the victorious alliance. The Western Alliance, in effect, was an international form of the United Front. And after the worst of the fighting was over, Roosevelt, like many less wise than he, assumed he could make agreements with the Communists and not be betrayed. The Communist who later betrayed him, and Churchill too, by breaking the agreements made at Yalta about free elections in Eastern Europe was the hardest-core Communist of all, Joseph Stalin.

But during the war and for the first several years of the Truman administration, it was considered in many quarters to be almost un-American to be anti-Russian.[6] When the UDA metamorphosed into the ADA in 1947, James Wechsler recalled in *Age of Suspicion:*

> It is a clue to the American atmosphere in those months that there was great disagreement as to whether the founding conference of what became known as Americans for Democratic Action should be held in public or in private, and that the most serious opposition to its creation was communist, not conservative. There were some active liberal politicians who were reluctant to identify themselves with the movement lest it offend those of their constituents who were enrolled in the communist fronts . . . There were intimations that the tone of the new group, descended as it was from the UDA, was too "anti-Soviet" and too permeated with "red-baiting." There were murmurs of doubt as to whether any truly progressive group should identify itself with the foreign policy . . . committed to the Truman doctrine in Greece and Turkey; it was still considered . . . little short of war-mongering to support active opposition to Soviet expansion.[7]

Nevertheless the first conference took place in Washington, D.C., with Niebuhr and Elmer Davis presiding. Co-chairmen of the organizing committee were Wilson Wyatt and Leon Henderson, with James Loeb as Secretary-Treasurer. Other people active from the beginning were Mrs. Franklin D. Roosevelt, Franklin D. Roosevelt, Jr., Paul Porter, Joseph Rauh, Jr., and Arthur Schlesinger, Sr. and Jr. So many of the leaders had been part of the government under President Roosevelt that the group was nicknamed by Elmer Davis, "The U. S. Government in Exile."

Barry Bingham, publisher of the *Louisville Courier-Journal* was head of

[6] The kind of internal Communist infiltration still going on in the United States after the war was exemplified by the Committee for the Arts and Sciences and Professions headed by Harold Ickes, former Secretary of the Interior: when Ickes prepared a speech in Chicago in September, 1946, there was one paragraph containing mild criticism of the Soviet Union; when the "Old Curmudgeon" colorfully refused to remove it, all the mimeograph machines mysteriously broke down: there was not a copy of the speech for the press. Other Americans, too young to have experienced United Front tactics in the thirties, had their baptism by fire in the American Veterans Committee, and won out by staying up all night in order to prevent the communists from controlling a rump session.

[7] In 1946, Niebuhr had travelled abroad and come home warning of Soviet expansion.

a press committee which achieved wide publicity for the first general statement, drafted by Robert Bendiner. This statement included a provision for screening new members so as to prevent Communist infiltration. It also defined liberalism as

> a demanding faith which rests neither on a set of dogmas nor on a blueprint, but is rather a spirit which each generation of liberals must learn to apply to the needs of its own time. The spirit itself is unchanging—a deep belief in the dignity of man and an awareness of human frailty, a faith in human reason . . .

It is not difficult to picture Niebuhr, big square hand on round bald brow, studying these words late at night, his glasses down at the end of his nose. Should he subscribe to the phrase "dignity of man" without making it clear that man's dignity comes from his freedom rather than from his virtue? And should he allow that small bark, "human frailty," to sail off, loaded to the gunwhales and tipping, with the terrible weight of human sin? Should he append his name to a document based on faith in reason?

The theologian must have hesitated, but the pragmatist signed.

Later he told friends that he had enjoyed the meeting and felt that it had accomplished a good deal, but that he had felt "partly inside and partly outside—just as I do in conventional church."

To be partly outside both religious and secular groups is the role of the prophet, not as a deliberate measure but as a result of his vision which is always somewhat different from theirs.

In many ways Niebuhr's vision has been very different indeed. Parts of it, moreover, he continues to amend. This ability of his to change his mind when the facts so warrant has caused his adverse critics to condemn his "inconsistency" and his sympathetic ones to applaud his "capacity for self-correction" as one of "his most intriguing virtues." But parts of his vision he has changed not at all, and their validity is being recognized today in a way quite different from any that he, even at his most "prophetic," was able to anticipate.

20

The Concepts of the Prophet

FOR Niebuhr's contemporaries—indeed for modern man since the Enlightenment—an important and rarely questioned assumption was that science, in time, would solve the basic mysteries of nature and man and history.

Niebuhr has long and strenuously denied this possibility in regard to man and history and has been called a pessimist and obscurantist for his pains. Today, with stunning impact, the possibility emerges that science may not even solve the basic mysteries of nature. Dr. Warren Weaver, vice president of the Rockefeller Foundation in charge of medical and natural sciences, compares man's knowledge to a clearing being extended within a limitless forest: the greater the circumference of the clearing, the greater the contact with the unknown and perhaps unknowable. And Joseph Wood Krutch writes in *Measure of Man:*

> Newton told us that the mysterious heavens were as knowable to common sense as our own back yard; Einstein tells us that our own back yard is as mysterious as the heavens were ever supposed to be.

Some religious people have greeted these admissions on the part of science with ill-concealed smugness. Their assumption seems to be that now religion can rush back in where science fears to tread. Niebuhr is not among their number. His enthusiasm for new learning goes back to include even science's original challenge, in the seventeenth century, to the prestige of religion. As he wrote in *Children of Light:*

> Modern culture represents the revolt of new thought, informed by modern science, against a culture in which religious authority

> had fixed premature and too narrow limits for the expansion of science and had sought to restrain the curiosity of the human mind . . .

This modern culture, however, according to Niebuhr, then proceeded also to fix premature and too narrow limits on its picture of man and history. Its attitude was to "venerate science in place of religion [and] worship natural causation in place of God." Thus it excluded from its calculations man's salient characteristic, his freedom which not only distinguishes him from every other creature but also distinguishes history from nature.

The modern tendency to equate history with nature is a form of confusion Niebuhr has deplored ever since his first attacks on John Dewey. And as he summed up at the Kent School in 1955:

> There are of course, many sequences and causal coherencies in human history and therefore scientific elements in historiography. But it is significant that the meaning of historical events has frequently been obscured not by the real historian but by social scientists who sought abortively to bring history into the realm of nature and thus deny the characteristically historical aspects of the human scene. In short, our culture has been intent upon equating history with nature at the precise moment when history revealed the dangerous possibilities of human freedom which were not at all like nature.

One contributory cause—and perhaps also result—of this confusion was America's reluctance to award to history the prestige she was awarding to science.

For many Americans, in effect, history began with their own birth; they had little interest in what had preceded it and they could not understand why Niebuhr cared so much about it. From the time of the first settlers, had not America's eyes been on the future whence cometh our salvation? More than a hundred years ago, that eagle-eyed observer, Alexis de Tocqueville, had noted in *Democracy in America:*

> In the midst of the continual movement which agitates a democratic community, the tie which unites one generation to an-

> other is relaxed or broken. Every man readily loses trace of the ideas of his forefathers or takes no care about them.[1]

The rejection of history by modern Americans, however, has been partly ambivalent. As was noted by that eagle-eyed contemporary observer, Charles Frankel in *The Case for Modern Man,* Henry Ford said, "History is bunk," and also established a museum in Dearborn so that future generations could absorb the history of Henry Ford. Said Frankel:

> At one extreme, Americans have been very interested in history, trying to recapture between the covers of novels or the walls of museums images of the past which they have been just as busily erasing in their daily lives. At the other extreme, Americans have been convinced that they are bound by no inherited precedents.

America's rejection of inherited precedents, however, is as nothing compared to that of the Soviet Union. For the Russian Communist, who by definition, is on "the other side of the revolution," everything is going to be different, and also in accordance with the logic of history as defined by Marxist-Leninist Science. Niebuhr's view of how scientific this is would agree with that of Dr. Zhivago:

> Marxism a science? . . . Marxism is too little in control of itself to be considered a science. The sciences are better equilibrated. Marxism and objectivity? I don't know of any movement more shut in upon itself and remoter from the facts than Marxism.

Among the facts from which the Marxist scientists are remote, according to Niebuhr, is the same fact from which many western social scientists are remote, namely the indeterminate freedom of the human agent who eludes the most comprehensive historical theories. In *Pious and Secular America* Niebuhr uses the Marxists' own key leader as one example with which to refute their historical determinism.[2]

[1] This readiness to lose trace, Will Herberg said in his contemporary sociological study, *Catholic, Protestant, Jew,* is sometimes deliberate, particularly on the part of second generation Americans. Their desire is to cut the ties with parents who by accent or custom are still identifiable with the land of origin: to be the Indistinguishable American is their apparent aim, and this is facilitated by the nation's unique opportunities for physical and social mobility.

[2] This "determinism" of the modern Marxists is so rigid as to be compared to the "predestination" of the old Presbyterians. At the same time, Niebuhr points to

> Lenin is one of those figures in history whose "contingent" emergence in the historical scheme makes nonsense of any philosophy of history which relies upon the alleged discernment of "patterns" and "objective forces" as the clues to historical development. Trotsky, in his *History of the Russian Revolution,* has difficulty in placing Lenin in the framework of his deterministic creed. He finally settles for the idea that "great men" can hasten the fulfillment of the "logic" of historical development. As a matter of fact, Lenin did more than hasten the fulfillment. Without his unique gifts the revolution in Russia would not have been possible.

Another modern view of objective forces and patterns in history is that of Arnold Toynbee with whom Niebuhr has disagreed both on the central point of Toynbee's historical cycles and also on peripheral points such as Toynbee's definition of Judaism as "a fossilized remnant of a Syriac civilization." In subsequent editions of his monumental study, Toynbee removed such slurs and also re-emphasized the difference between his own cyclical view of history and that of the ancient Greeks: whereas they thought there was little that man could do to change history, Toynbee thinks there is much that our "post-Christian civilization" can do to avoid following its predecessors into oblivion. He and Niebuhr therefore are not so far apart as once they were, and when Niebuhr's *Structure of Nations and Empires* was published in 1959, Toynbee reviewed it with enthusiasm in the *New York Times.*

Since Niebuhr denies that clear-cut patterns and predictable objective forces exist in history, what kind of meaning can he find? If history cannot be equated with nature, perhaps there is no use studying it at all: perhaps it is, as stated in *Macbeth,* but "a tale told by an idiot, full of sound and fury, signifying nothing."

Niebuhr does not deny that there are "patches of meaninglessness" in history. But there are also, he says, "patches of meaning." This meaning he describes in St. Paul's phrase as "the light that shineth in darkness," with the darkness as important to remember as the light. The darkness Niebuhr refers to as mystery, but so thoroughly is it connected in his

---

Marxism's "extravagant voluntarism" which includes "pretensions of omniscience" on the part of the Communist elite.

mind with meaning that *Mystery and Meaning* was the title he gave unwittingly both to a sermon published in *Discerning The Signs of the Times* in the early forties and to an essay published in *Pious and Secular America* in the late fifties.

When Niebuhr first started using the word mystery, it was a dirty word: its implication was that of Dostoyevski's Grand Inquisitor who stated insultingly that all man needs to be happy is "miracle, mystery and authority." It would be hard to choose, in fact, which of these three words was more of an anathema to the American democratic descendants of the French and American Revolutions.

Concurrent with Niebuhr's use of the word, however, there has been a growing revolution in the world of science based upon twentieth century discoveries that there may be, even within the world of nature, impenetrable barriers to man's knowledge: that some things, because of their own characteristics or those of man, will presumably forever remain a mystery.

The first of these discoveries was Albert Einstein's theory of relativity, in 1905, which, in effect, denied the possibility of man's knowing absolute motion, if indeed such a thing could be said to exist in a universe where everything, observer as well as observed, is perpetually in motion.

A second was Werner Heisenberg's Principle of Indeterminacy which did for the microcosm what relativity did for the macrocosm: in effect, Heisenberg denied the possibility of man's discovering the velocity and position of an electron at the same time.[3]

A third was Nils Bohr's Principle of Complementarity, in 1957, according to which man cannot think of light as acting either like particles or like waves since paradoxically it appears to act like both.

The students of science, moreover, were being joined in their new uncertainties by the students of the tools of science, namely the philosophic

[3] Said Lincoln Barnett in his lucid popularization, *The Universe and Dr. Einstein:* "To prove that this indeterminacy is a symptom not of man's immature science but an ultimate barrier of nature, Heisenberg presupposed that [an] imaginary microscope . . . is capable of magnifying by a hundred billion diameters—i.e., enough to bring an object the size of an electron within range of human visibility. . . . Inasmuch as an electron is smaller than a light wave, the physicist can "illuminate" his subject only by using radiation of a shorter wave length. . . . But the photoelectric effect . . . showed that photons of ordinary light exert a violent force on electrons; and x-rays knock them about even more roughly."

mathematicians. Early in the twentieth century Bertrand Russell began calling mathematics "the subject in which we do not know what we are talking about, nor whether what we are saying is true." And in 1931, Kurt Gödel published his now famous proof which assailed not only mathematical certainty but some of the most sacred assumptions of logic itself.

Actually, *in*ductive logic, for some time, had been suspect: when man had observed that each snowflake is different from its fellows, he had "induced" that all snowflakes would always be different from each other. Today this view would be held as a probability rather than a certainty since there is no guarantee in nature or in logic that some day a snow storm may not occur in which two or all of its flakes are identical.[4]

But until Gödel, *de*ductive logic had been considered wholly reliable. What Gödel did, according to Ernest Nagel and James R. Newman in their book, *Gödel's Proof*, 1958, was to show

> that it is impossible to establish the internal consistency of a very large class of deductive systems—elementary arithmetic, for example—unless one adopts principles of reasoning so complex that their internal consistency is as open to doubt as that of the systems themselves.

Niebuhr, perhaps because he has deplored the equating of nature and history, rarely makes use of discoveries in the field of natural science or mathematics to reinforce his own point of view.[5] And there exist, admittedly, serious hazards in bringing from the world of inanimate matter analogies for the world of man. Still, perhaps the following loose parallels might be suggested:

[4] The laws of probability, as Heisenberg showed, apply only to large numbers: with two test-tubes connected at the top by a horizontal tube, one can predict that many gas molecules will divide themselves evenly between the tubes, but with only three molecules there is no telling where they will be.

[5] Niebuhr spent a year at the Princeton Institute for Advanced Studies in 1958 without even trying to meet Gödel who has worked there for some time. This may, of course, be just as well, since one Princeton trustee who asked a mathematician high on the faculty there to introduce him to Gödel was told he would first have to tutor in higher math for a year. The trustee dutifully took the tutoring and at the end of the year asked for the introduction. The mathematician sadly shook his head. "I'm afraid you'll need another year." "The hell with it," said the trustee, and he too has never yet met Gödel.

¶ Einstein says it is impossible for man to take ultimate measurements of speed because he himself is in motion; Niebuhr says it is impossible for man to make ultimate judgments in history because man himself is moving within time and history;

¶ Heisenberg says an object is changed by the process of being viewed; Niebuhr says that the acting self is changed by the process of being viewed by the self-transcendent self;

¶ Bohr denies either-or in regard to light; Niebuhr denies either-or in regard to religion;

¶ Gödel shows that man's reason operates within a sphere which logic cannot make wholly logical; Niebuhr points to the limits of logic in the sphere of the self and its existential encounters.

Among the fields of modern learning of which Niebuhr does make use to reinforce his own point of view is one that he only recently credits with having matured. This is the field of analytic philosophy which in its youth was known as logical positivism. Negatively its contribution has been to raise question about all statements that are not either self-evident, logical, or scientifically provable. Positively its contribution has been to force greater precision in the use of language which in turn has shown up the unanswerability of some philosophic questions as lying more in their phrasing than their substance. Niebuhr, who has long differentiated between "faith as speculation" and "faith as a quality of life," expresses gratitude to analytic philosophy for having "freed us from engaging in rational but spiritually irrelevant 'proofs' " of the existence of God, for example. As he wrote in *The Christian Century*, May, 1960,

> I believe that the emergence of philosophical analysis . . . has made our apologetic task simpler by emphasizing that in the Christian drama we are dealing with a system of meaning for which no irrefutable rational proof can be given but to which we must bear witness by the quality of our lives.[6]

Another field of modern learning from which Niebuhr has progressively gleaned more insights is that of the psychological sciences. When a phy-

[6] Niebuhr's own imprecision of language however sits none too well with the analytic philosophers. Said one in regard to Niebuhr's theory of history, it exists "at *such* a metaphorical level that it can't be used—or, rather, it can be used too easily, just because it's so vague."

sician friend sent him the following quotation from the *Saturday Review* April 2, 1955, Niebuhr's letter of thanks said he wished it had arrived in time for inclusion in *The Self and the Dramas of History.* The quotation deals with the conclusions drawn at Washingtion University in St. Louis by a group of natural, social and psychological scientists including four Nobel Prize winners:

> When science first turned—in psychology—to the study of man's total personality, so much emphasis was placed on the conditioned reflex that man came to be regarded simply as a complicated machine; this conclusion was largely determined in advance by the method of study. The approach has yielded a great deal of important information, but it has also tended to eclipse the subjective side of selfhood, its ineradicable awareness. The self is not merely the sum of its roles, as William James contended in his most fruitful mistake; it is preeminently that which is aware of itself as having roles. There is always an element of mystery in this self-awareness—mystery being defined as a problem the data of which encroach on the subject itself.

To question whether a conclusion has been partially determined in advance by the method of study is itself a relatively new phenomenon; another is to question whether a method of study valid in one sphere can necessarily be carried over to other spheres. In the psychologist's laboratory, for example, determinism has been a necessary hypothesis; but this is not generally recognized as proving that man does not have free will in life and history. Similarly, in the philosopher's study, the impossibility of irresolvable paradox has been a necessary hypothesis, but this is not generally recognized as proving that irresolvable paradox does not exist in life and history. All along Niebuhr had insisted, not that the methods of science were wrong for the study of nature, but that they could not automatically, and trailing clouds of prestige, be carried over to the study of life and history.

For history, to Niebuhr, includes not merely the indeterminacies of nature but the far more complex and interrelated indeterminacies of man the viewer and the actor in history:

> Man's freedom to transcend the natural flux gives him the possibility of grasping a span of time in his consciousness and thereby

> knowing history. It also enables him to change, reorder and transmute the causal sequences of nature and thereby to make history.

History thus includes not just recorded events but events not recorded, events still going on, events that were prevented from occurring, events that may occur. It is made up partly of natural vitalities (like geography) and partly of man-created artifacts (like constitutions). As William Lee Miller has well expressed it, for Niebuhr, "history is culture moving through time."

The importance of time to the understanding of man and history is, as Niebuhr says, an Hebraic rather than a Hellenic concept. To the ancient Greeks what mattered was the eternal, the unchanging. They had little interest in the realm of time and history and assumed that it moved in predetermined cycles. Their view of the unimportance of what happened in this world was then adopted by sections of early and medieval Christianity which stressed the importance of preparing oneself for the *next* world.

The ancient Hebrews, on the other hand, were extremely interested in the here and now, what preceded it and what in time might follow it. This world, to them, was the arena where man, in his freedom, exercises his individual and collective responsibilities. At the same time, they made it clear, through their eschatological hopes and fears, that all meaning is not exhausted by what happens in the here and now.

Niebuhr considers himself Hebraic in his view of history. For him, as for them, as he says in *Faith and History,* there are "tangents of moral meaning in history; but there are no clear and exact patterns." Part of this moral meaning, in fact, includes the human tendency to distort history in the very process of viewing it:

> Insofar as the human mind in both its structure and in its capacities of observation has a vantage point over the flux of historical events, it is possible to achieve valid historical knowledge, though this knowledge will never have the exactness of knowledge in the field of natural science. But insofar as men, individually or collectively, are involved in the temporal flux they must view the stream of events from some particular locus. A high degree of imagination, insight, or detachment may heighten or enlarge the

> locus; but no human power can make it fully adequate. That fact is one of the most vivid examples of the ambiguity of the human situation. The pretension that this is not the case is an aspect of the "original sin" which infects all human culture.

Not only does man, of necessity, view history through his own preconceptions but history itself is open to varied interpretations for a number of reasons. One, says Niebuhr, is that "the freedom of the human agent introduces complex and incalculable factors into the flow of cause and effect." Another is that "there are events in history which could be fully understood [only] if the secret motives of [the] human agent could be fully known." Still another is that "historical events do not follow each other in a 'necessary' manner;" and not even the best of social scientists can repeat an historic experiment sufficiently often, or under sufficiently controlled conditions, to be able to predict with accuracy its outcome. "History repeats," Niebuhr sums up, "but never exactly."

As for the preconceptions of the person viewing history, these run the gamut of human opinion, and are based in many instances on some form of revelation. In regard to this word (also a highly suspect one in the twentieth century), Niebuhr tells his classes he prefers his brother Richard's definition to any of his own. Richard Niebuhr has written in *The Meaning of Revelation:*

> By revelation in our history, then, we mean that special occasion which provides us with an image by means of which all the occasions of personal and common life become intelligible.

Revelation, in this sense, need not be the exclusive possession of religious people. Albert Camus, the brilliant French secularist, wrote shortly before his untimely death in an automobile accident: "The great revelations a man receives in his life are few, usually one or two. But they transfigure him, like his luck." And for the secular Existentialists, according to William Barrett's *Irrational Man,* revelation means the form of immediacy exemplified by the difference between noting that "men are dying" and "I am dying."

Even so passionate and lifelong an atheist as Bertrand Russell reported an experience, in 1901, that for him was revelation. It was, he said,

> not unlike what religious people call a "conversion" . . . I became suddenly and vividly aware of the loneliness in which most

> people live, and passionately desirous of finding ways of diminishing this tragic isolation.

On the basis of this experience he went on to build a philosophy, as he said in *A Free Man's Worship*, on "the firm foundation of unyielding despair." Yet here too there was a form of mystery combined with meaning:

> a strange mystery it is that nature, omnipotent but blind . . . has brought forth at last a child subject still to her power, but gifted with sight, with knowledge of good and evil.

Since, in Russell's view, there is nothing outside of man to which man can turn for help (man himself being the product "of forces which had no prevision of the end they were achieving"), man must rely all the more on himself and on his fellows. Such human self-reliance and mutual aid, for Russell, have their own dynamic:

> Even if the windows of science first make us shiver after the cosy indoor warmth of traditional . . . myths, in the end the fresh air brings vigor and the great spaces have a splendor of their own.

And the duties implied by this philosophy end up, in the personal sphere at least, being not very different from the biblical precept of love for the neighbor. Says Russell in a passage sometimes quoted by Niebuhr:

> The life of Man is a long march through the night, surrounded by invisible foes, tortured by weariness and pain . . . One by one as they march, our comrades vanish from our sight . . . Very brief is the time in which we can help them . . . Be it ours to shed sunshine on their path . . . to strengthen failing courage, to instill faith in hours of despair.

The tragic isolation of man was a form of revelation for Bertrand Russell which enhanced rather than negated the importance of human history. But to many Hindus and Buddhists and those western thinkers like Aldous Huxley whom Niebuhr calls the "modern mystics," the very meaninglessness of history is itself a form of revelation. For them the importance of life lies in escaping the round of recurrence and particularity and blending oneself in the universal and immutable. For Niebuhr this point of view is far more of an anathema than that of Bertrand Russell, since it denies not only the importance of the here and now, but by implication also man's responsibility in history. And Niebuhr deplores the fact that, in the twentieth century,

> it is evidently more respectable philosophically to delve into a realm of pure mystery (about which nothing can be said but that it is at the same time a fullness of being and the absence of being) than to accept the Christian affirmation that the mystery of the divine has been disclosed and transmuted into meaning by historical revelation.

To the religious Jews as well as the Christians this historical revelation took the form of an event. To the Jews the event was the Covenant of God with Abraham, later elucidated to Moses in the Law. To the Christians the event was the Second Covenant through Jesus Christ whereby, as Niebuhr says in *Faith and History,* the New Israel or "the Israel of God . . . ceases to be a particular people or nation [and is] gathered together upon the basis of its acceptance of the revelation by faith."

This acceptance of revelation by faith does not come by human willing alone (according to Graham Greene the avoidance of this faith also does not come by human willing alone). As Niebuhr said in the second volume of the Gifford Lectures:

> The disclosure of God's sovereignty over life and history, the clarification of the meaning of life and history, is not completed until man is able, by faith, to apprehend the truth which is beyond his apprehension without faith. The truth is not completely beyond his apprehension; otherwise Christ could not have been expected. It is nevertheless beyond his apprehension, or Christ would not have been rejected. It is a truth capable of apprehension by faith; but when so apprehended there is a consciousness in the heart of the believer that he has been helped to this apprehension. This consciousness is summed up in the confession, "No man can say that Jesus is the Lord, but by the Holy Spirit."

This acceptance of Jesus as the Lord stems back in history, as Will Herberg points out, to the action of a few Jews two thousand years ago. If, says Herberg, *all* Jews then had accepted Jesus as the Messiah, there would be no

Christianity today, since the life, death and teachings of Jesus would have been incorporated into Judaism. Similarly, if *no* Jews had accepted Jesus as the Messiah, there would be no Christianity today, since all the early followers were Jews. Therefore, Herberg concludes, the history of the western world was radically altered by the fact that some Jews accepted, and some Jews rejected, the revelation of God in Christ.

Niebuhr, when asked about this in class, said:

> I think I agree with Herberg. I don't know whether the acceptance and rejection of Christianity by Jews had quite the effect that Herberg says, but it was certainly inevitable that some Jews should have accepted and some rejected, because Jesus was in one sense so Jewish and in another sense so offensive to Jewish spirituality.

For two thousand years there has been another linkage between Jews and Christians, Niebuhr points out, in that both derive "their whole sense of the moral from the righteousness of God rather than from 'objective' patterns of history." In *Pious and Secular America* he wrote:

> The prophets of Israel did not define justice as neatly as Aristotle did. But they defined it more relevantly. For according to the prophets . . . the judgment of God was critical of the elders, and judges, and princes, because they "turned aside the needy at the gates." . . . Justice was not an equal justice but a bias in favor of the poor . . . The prophetic sense of justice was in short relevant to the perennial problems of the human community where power is needed to establish order but always exacts too high a price for its services.

Jesus' teaching that the judgment of God was critical of "the elders, and judges, and princes," was one reason they put him to death. The crucifixion, Niebuhr said in *Beyond Tragedy*, was not the kind of "substitutionary atonement which outrages the moral sense," the blood offering of one man to make up for the sins of all. Instead it was an act pointing toward God's reconciliation with man and demonstrating the irresolvable paradox that God's "mercy is partly the fulfillment and partly the contradiction of his justice." This is a meaning in history that if appropriated must be done so existentially, by the self rather than by the mind alone. As Niebuhr wrote in *The Self and The Dramas of History:*

> If the individual rises above the courts and judgments of the community to appeal to a more ultimate judgment . . . he faces a judgment more, rather than less, severe than the judgments of the community. He is judged by the norm of love for the neighbor . . . The ultimate judgments which are interpreted by the key of the Christ revelation can, in short, never be socially irrelevant. They can not prompt the individual to defy the community for the sake of his own "pursuit of happiness"; nor do they prompt him to flee the collective enterprises . . . of men to escape into some realm of "eternal bliss." The believer is indeed promised the "peace of God which passeth understanding." It passes understanding, however, because it is a peace which contains the pains and sorrows of suffering love.

For Niebuhr the revelation in Christ is, therefore, "what man is and should be and what God is in relations with man." It is central to his thinking, but its centrality needs no reinforcement from any kind of magic. As with the Grand Inquisitor's mystery, Niebuhr also redefines the word miracle. As he says in *Christian Realism and Political Problems:*

> We do not believe . . . that revelatory events validate themselves by a divine breakthrough in the natural order. There is a great spiritual gain in this position which is in accord with Christ's own rejection of signs and wonders as validations of his messianic mission ("This wicked generation seeketh a sign.") It leads to an apprehension of the points of revelation by repentance and faith, that is to say, it insists that the truth of revelation must be apprehended by the whole person and cannot merely be accepted as a historical fact, validated by the miraculous character of the fact.

Spiritually valid as this view may be, Niebuhr is well aware that it is heretical in the eyes of many Christians. So great is his own "nonchalance of faith" however that he appears neither distressed by their accusations nor determined to challenge their views. For him the mystery of human freedom is so great and the meaning in history so imprecise that there is room both for literal and symbolic belief in the miracles of the Bible. Believing as he does in the hidden as well as the revealed Christ, he seems to feel that, unless clearly wrong, the explicit content of other people's faith—or unfaith—is more God's business than his own.

As for the miracles in the Bible, he divides these into three groups: those in which he can believe, those in which he cannot, and a third group in which belief has been essential but need not be literal. As to the first, he says in *Christian Realism and Political Problems:*

> The healing miracles of Jesus, for instance, are credible because we recognize the depth and height of spirit in the dimension of each personality and the consequent spiritual dimension of bodily ill. Psychosomatic medicine corroborates such a conception.

As to the second, he himself does "not believe in the virgin birth," for example. In this regard his attitude might be comparable to that of the minister who said, "My attitude toward the virgin birth is that of St. Paul. And what did St. Paul say? He never mentioned it."

As to the third, Niebuhr writes in *Faith and History*, "the belief in the resurrection is itself a miracle of a different order, and a miracle without which the church could not have come into existence." What was essential was "the recognition of the true Christ in the resurrection." For here was "not merely the culmination of the whole series of revelations but the pattern of all subsequent confrontations between God and man. They must contain the crucifixion of self-abandonment and the resurrection of self-recovery. Men must die to sin with Christ and arise with him to newness of life." On the other hand, Niebuhr's "impression," in the Living Library Volume, "was that historical scholarship seemed to indicate that the story of the empty tomb was an afterthought and that the really attested fact was the experience of the risen Christ among his various disciples."

Where, in fact, has the line ever been unequivocally drawn between the miraculous and the ordinary, the supernatural and the natural? Did man evolve by plan or accident? What on earth is extrasensory perception? Who is right, the new parent who views the arrival of his or her own alive and secret-faced infant as an unbelievable and miraculous event, or the obstetrician who views it as a normal and run-of-the-mill event? To the Psalmist the starry heavens revealed the wonder of God; to the modern British poet, R. P. Lister, quite the opposite:

> Above me, far above my upturned face,
> Farther than thought can reach or voice can utter
> Brood the immensities of outer space

> Which is, I think, a quite revolting place.
> Hard though it is, I much prefer the gutter.[7]

Yet the greatest scientist of the twentieth century, a man who took no part in religious observance, looked on outer space with a feeling close to that of the Psalmist and found in this feeling (without which, he said, a man "is as good as dead") the creative hypothesis for his own and other scientific discoveries. Said Albert Einstein, "The most beautiful and most profound emotion we can experience is the sensation of the mystical. It is the dower of all true science." Yet too great a sense of the mystical can apparently also be a detriment to science. Niebuhr credits, not the Ancient Hebrews who preferred to marvel at the universe, but the Ancient Greeks who preferred to investigate it, with being "the first to thrust impious hands into nature," and thus give science its start. And in modern times the mystical Orient has yet to make a significant contribution to science.

It matters, therefore, in science, as Einstein says, whether we "wonder and stand rapt in awe" and what it is that we wonder at. Similarly it matters in history whether we find meaning and what kind of meaning this is. To some contemporary Americans, for example, the key event in history (though the Britons view it as of little importance) was the landing of the Pilgrims and the founding of the New Israel on these shores. For other Americans the new world was epitomized less by an event than by a myth, a myth they retell to each generation even though Parson Weems admitted having made it up. If, in fact, proof were discovered that the Father of His Country had lied about the cherry tree, his patriotic followers would brush this off with an "oh well, boys will be boys." For as Niebuhr points out, our preconceptions are themselves revealed by what we think of as the rule (or "the exception that proves the rule") and what we think of as the exception that is simply an exception:

> One of the greatest hazards of right judgment is the fact that an individual in [our] group is merely an individual to us, while an individual in another group wrongfully becomes "typical" in our imagination. Thus a white criminal is merely a criminal to a white man, but a Negro criminal seems immediately to be typical rather than unique.

[7] *The New Yorker*, December 5, 1953, quoted with permission of author.

What is true of races in relation to each other is also true of religions and nations; and the fanatic believers and patriots who see the meaning of history centered in their own group can cause great damage in history through their misreading of history. So great was such damage during the lifetime of Paul Valéry, the French poet who lived through two terrible Franco-German conflicts, that he turned against the study of history altogether:

> History is the most dangerous product that the chemistry of the intellect has invented. Its properties are well known. It engenders dreams, it intoxicates the people, it begets false memories, it exaggerates their reactions, keeps old wounds open, disturbs their sleep, leads them to delusions of grandeur or of persecution, and makes nations bitter, arrogant, insufferable and vain.

Niebuhr, on the other hand, thinks that history properly studied is perhaps the most important subject of all, particularly today and particularly for Americans who have so suddenly been propelled into a position of world leadership. As he wrote in *Daedalus*, Winter, 1959:

> Nothing in history is predictable, and analogies from the past are too inexact to become the basis of confident predictions. Nevertheless, education for a youthful nation, lacking experience, must rely on the study of history so that premature conclusions and hazardous predictions will be discouraged. . . . No particular set of academic courses can furnish the new or the old generation with the wisdom sufficient for performing our tasks and solving our problems adequately. But every form of education that brings the experience of the past to bear upon present problems, and that enlarges the realm of insight beyond that gained in concrete and immediate experience, will help the new generation to face the unprecedented dilemmas of our day.

In his attempt to understand and face these unprecedented dilemmas Niebuhr has travelled arduously, not only mentally through time but also physically through space.

21

Transatlantic Salesman

LIKE a giant bumblebee, Niebuhr flew back and forth across the Atlantic, cross-pollinating American and European ideas, churchly and secular ideas, theological and political ideas.

This process, extending over more than a decade, started officially, in 1936, when the leaders of the Ecumenical Movement sent Niebuhr to England to help prepare for the world conference on Church, Community and State, to be held in Oxford the following year.[1] Some of Niebuhr's warmest transatlantic friendships have dated from that period.

One was with Sir Stafford Cripps, later Chancellor of the Exchequer when the Labour Party came to power. This tall, ascetic intellectual was later lampooned by Winston Churchill who said, "There, but for the grace of God, goes God." But Cripps and the ebulliant American nonetheless saw many mundane matters in the same light. Says Niebuhr in retrospect, "Cripps was baffled by my theology, but we agreed on politics because I was a simple-minded Socialist in those days." Niebuhr, in fact, credits—or debits—Cripps with the fact that Niebuhr remained a simple-minded Socialist as long as he did: for Cripps so persuasively demonstrated the creative relevance of socialism to the British political scene that Niebuhr assumed a comparable relevance to the American one. (In 1959, the difference between the two nations was suggested in the British revue, *Drop*

[1] The U.S. Federal Council of Churches, of which Niebuhr was an active member, was related to the World Council of Churches. Later, in 1950, the Federal Council, the Church World Service, the United Council of Church Women, and other missionary and interdenominational groups, consolidated to form the National Council of Churches of Christ. In 1960, this organization reported a membership of 33 communions representing some 32 million people, with another 40 communions participating in at least one of its 70 program units.

of a Hat: "The British have two Parties, the Labour Party which Americans consider Socialist, and the Conservative Party which Americans consider Socialist.")

Since Niebuhr's work for the World Council of Churches centered on the two fields of "International Justice and Goodwill" and "Industrial Relations," he was as interested in Labour's view of foreign policy as its view of domestic policy. The Italian invasion of Ethiopia had proved to Sir Stafford Cripps and a small group around him—as it did to the Conservative Sir Winston Churchill and a small ground around *him*—that pacifism was futile and the only hope for the democracies lay in some form of collective security. But such a view was very unpopular in Britain—as it was in America. This was the period when young Britons signed the "Oxford Oath," pledging never to bear arms, even in defense of their country. Yet, within a few years, many of the signatories were piloting R.A.F. planes with such courage during the Battle of Britain that Churchill, by then Prime Minister, spoke on behalf of his countrymen the immortal, "Never have so many owed so much to so few."

Another of Niebuhr's transatlantic friendships was with the beloved Archbishop of Canterbury, William Temple, whose original greeting of Niebuhr became, in church circles at least, as famous as Stanley's greeting of Livingstone. "At last," said Temple, "I have met the disturber of my peace." (Temple, whose sense of humor was as evident as Cripps' was not, then proceeded to trouble Niebuhr's peace by inventing the limerick about sin and Niebuhr at Swanwyck. See Chapter 12).

Niebuhr was also troubling other Britons' peace, partly because he felt so at home in his wife's native land that he sounded off as freely as on his own side of the Atlantic and partly because the British were paying more attention to him at that time than were his own compatriots. A secular British journal devoted an editorial to Niebuhr's denunciation of "the hypocritical pretensions of the bourgeois humanism of the Anglo-Saxon nations," and a religious one admitted that "in the military establishment which Christianity must never cease to be, Dr. Niebuhr . . . is attached to the *artillery*."

Niebuhr's effect on Britons was potent not only when he visited their shores, but when they visited his. John Baillie, Principal of New College in Edinburgh, returned from teaching at Union Seminary (1929-34) with the word that "intellectually, Niebuhr is head and shoulders, he is legs and ankles, above any other American." And Baillie, more than any one person, is given credit for Niebuhr's being invited to deliver the Gifford Lectures.

A vignette of Niebuhr's British friends, Baillie and Temple, appears in a letter Niebuhr wrote to American friend, Scarlett, in 1946. Under discussion was whether Scarlett, then Bishop of Missouri, should attend the first and most controversial meeting of ADA. Niebuhr, after noting Scarlett's ever-present political courage, said that in this instance he would not presume to give advice even though Scarlett had requested it.[2] It is always difficult, Niebuhr said, to know "how much business the church, and the leaders of the church, have in purely political matters, particularly when specific action leads to disruption in the church." And he went on to give an example based on the British experience:

> John Baillie tells the story of Queen Elizabeth [the Queen Mother] asking him, "Do you agree, Dr. Baillie, with Archbishop Temple's views in politics?"
> "I do, Madam," said Baillie.
> "Do you think," said the Queen, "that they are necessarily related to his Christian convictions?"
> "Most of them are I should think," said Baillie. "Most of them, yes. But all of them? There is a line somewhere where political questions do not follow necessarily from religious convictions. I do not know where that line is. But I have an idea that when Dr. Temple insists upon the nationalization of banking he is speaking too specifically and can not speak thus as the head of the Church of England."

There is no record of an answer to Niebuhr's letter, but Bishop Scarlett did attend the ADA meeting and took active part in its work for a considerable time.

When the invitation for the 1939-40 Gifford Lectures came to Niebuhr, he had just reached the stage, according to the Living Library Volume, of being able for the first time to face his students without feeling himself to be an academic fake. But facing the sophisticated audience in Edin-

[2] So outspoken was Scarlett on issues of social—and racial—justice, that in many circles he was known as the "Conscience of Missouri."

burgh would be quite another matter, since there would be not only students but experts, not only theoretical experts but those who had put their theories to the test of experience. What was Niebuhr to talk to them about? He had no theological specialty, like Christology or Ecclesiology; he did not even have a Ph. D. Finally, as he said in the Living Library Volume, "I chose the only subject I could have chosen because the other fields of Christian thought were beyond my competence. I lectured on 'The Nature and Destiny of Man.' "

To the layman, this "only" subject looks suspiciously like *the* only subject: what else, in effect, matters beside human nature and destiny? In retrospect, therefore, Niebuhr's modest disclaimer sounds rather less than modest—yet, at the time, the lectures, which ranged the fields of theology, philosophy, history, economics, political science, and psychology, managed to convey Niebuhr's true vein of modesty: "I dinna understand a word ye said," a wee Scots lady was reported by *Time* as telling Niebuhr, "but somehow I ken ye were making God great." And unprecedentedly large crowds came back to listen and applaud. To the Gifford Lectures, above all Niebuhr's books, the oft-quoted statement applies: "You may not always understand *Niebuhr*, but you can't hear or read Niebuhr without reaching a better understanding of *yourself*."

Niebuhr does not think of the Gifford Lectures as his magnum opus, but other people do.[3] Certainly they are to the body of his work what *Faust* is to Goethe's or *The Niebelungen Lied* to Wagner's. For the layman the second volume is more difficult than the first: said the late Paul Hutchinson, "The second volume of the Gifford Lectures can not readily be made comprehensible to the middle brow." And a Britisher recalled, in this regard, Byron's comment on Coleridge: "Explaining metaphysics to the nation/I wish he would explain his explanation." For the student of theology, on the other hand, the second volume is not only essential but readily comprehensible. Said a recent graduate of Virginia Theological Seminary, "During the first year, when the first volume is assigned, it's almost too difficult, but by third year, when the second volume is assigned, it's a breeze."

Breeze or no, the second volume, like the first, makes provocative reading. One distinction, for example, is between the periods of history when "a Christ is *not* expected" and those when "a Christ *is* expected," with

[3] For Niebuhr his magnum opus is usually the book he is in the process of writing.

the modern era, to some readers' surprise, turning out to be one of the latter, with "history itself the Christ, which is to say that historical development is redemptive."

In demolishing the idea that history is redemptive, Niebuhr did not mean that history is not creative. There are, he says, frequent renewals and rebirths in history, but there is always the likelihood that destructiveness will link itself to creativity at each new level of achievement. The discovery of atomic energy, that paradoxical fact and parable of our times, followed the Gifford Lectures by five years. And even as the lectures were being delivered, history was moving in on the lecturer. German bombs began dropping on Britain, and American wives and children were ordered stateside. "The King of England," small Christopher Niebuhr reported to his grandmother on arrival, "told all little American boys they had to go home."

For Niebuhr, to have children was the fulfillment of an early dream. The Gifford Lectures are dedicated

To my wife
Ursula
Who helped, and
to my children
Christopher and Elisabeth
who frequently interrupted me
in the writing of these pages.

Yet from these interruptions the theologian was able to draw new conclusions. As he wrote, for example, in the *Nation,* between the delivery of the first and second Gifford series,

> Nothing revealed in the life of races and nations is unknown in individual life. The sins of pride and of lust for power and the consequent tyranny and injustice are all present, at least in an inchoate form, in individual life. Even as I write, my little five-year-old boy comes to me with the tale of an attack made upon him by his year-old sister. The tale is concocted to escape paternal judgment for being too rough in playing with his sister. One is reminded of Germany's claim that Poland was the aggressor and the similar Russian charge against Finland.

Niebuhr's ability to learn from unlikely sources is balanced—to the dismay of his more academic colleagues—by an ability to forget even the most likely sources from which he has learned. "A scissors-and-paste historian" was one negative comment by a scholar on the author of the Gifford Lectures; "He is never loyal to his sources," said another. And fifteen years after the lectures were printed, Emil Brunner, the distinguished Swiss theologian, registered a scholarly complaint in the Living Library Volume:

> With us European scholars it is customary to give our readers some information as to the sources of our thought. Not infrequently we are somewhat pedantic—perhaps even somewhat fussy—with our references and our footnotes, but on the whole this European tradition seems to me to be praiseworthy. On this point Reinhold Niebuhr leaves much to be desired. . . . To give just one example, which happens to be close to me personally. In reading the first volume of his most significant work, the Gifford Lectures . . . I was somewhat astonished to find no mention of the fact that in this work Reinhold Niebuhr had been strongly preoccupied with certain ideas which I had put forward in my book, *Man in Revolt*. . . . This was all the more surprising inasmuch as Niebuhr had informed me personally by word of mouth in the year 1938, just as he was beginning to prepare those lectures, that my book was claiming a great deal of his attention. Nor am I the only one who wondered about Niebuhr's silence on this point. It may seem petty to bring such a criticism to bear on so monumental a work, in addition to which it may look like an author's wounded vanity. Nonetheless I venture it . . .

Niebuhr's answer in the Living Library Volume was characteristically contrite:

> Emil Brunner's generous essay with its one complaint . . . gives me the opportunity to make some amends for a grievous omission in my *The Nature and Destiny of Man*. I read Brunner's book some time before giving my lectures, and profited greatly from his analysis of the doctrine of sin. . . . Subsequently I became involved in tracing the doctrine through as much of history as I could encompass. In the process I lost sight of Brunner and did not refer to his work, though, as he confesses, I had written appreciatively to him about the book. It was a grievous error not

> to acknowledge my debt to him, though my omission was occasioned by finding no specific agreement or disagreement with him which would require a footnote. I may say that Brunner's whole theological position is close to mine and that it is one to which I am more indebted than any other.

When called to account for a mistake in one of his old books, Niebuhr tries to make amends if someone has thereby suffered an injustice. But otherwise he has no more interest in his literary off-spring than the proverbial raven-mother who deserts her young as soon as they are out of the shell.

In answering a criticism by Paul Ramsey of *An Interpretation of Christian Ethics,* for example, Niebuhr said:

> It is of course perfectly legitimate to hold an author accountable for his various works. But I was only dimly feeling my way in this book toward a realistic and valid Christian ethic. I disavowed some of my ideas and amended others in later works, which roughly represent my present position. I am not therefore able to defend, or interested in defending, any position I took in *An Interpretation of Christian Ethics.*[4]

This statement, in turn, jarred several of his former students who have continued to find valuable insights, particularly in regard to grace and myth, in Niebuhr's *An Interpretation of Christian Ethics.*

Nor is Niebuhr today one bit more interested than he ever was in tracing the ideas he uses back to their source. His mind is not a sorting-machine but a great meat grinder into which chunks of fact and idea are constantly being fed, and the result is his own inimitable mixture. One of his friends jokingly says he would not dream of divulging an original idea to Niebuhr lest it appear, elaborated and improved, in Niebuhr's next article, with its author totally oblivious of having appropriated it.

[4] At the time this book was published (1935), John Haynes Holmes compared it to sailing along the Maine Coast: In addition to "the clouds of fog," there were "bursts of sunshine which radiantly reveal wonders of sky and sea." Among the clouds of fog, Niebuhr subsequently agreed with Holmes and other critics, was the phrase "impossible possibility" to describe the pinnacle of Christian love. This pinnacle Niebuhr now defines as "the perfect good which is not beyond our possibilities, as the history of Martyrdom proves, but which is certainly not within the conventional possibilities of our existence." (Speech in 1957 to graduating class of Union Seminary.)

Niebuhr's obliviousness of the source of his ideas is so thoroughgoing that he once forgot that an idea he wished to use was his own. In the fall of 1953 he told a small group of students that he was writing a new book with the tentative title, "The Mystery of Self and the Dramas of History." Some months later one of the students asked how the book was coming along. "Fine," said Niebuhr, "except I can't find a title." He mentioned several possibilities having to do with politics and world affairs.

"But what's the matter with 'The Mystery of Self and the Dramas of History?' "

"Why, it's wonderful!" said Niebuhr. "How did you ever come to think of it?"

When the student explained, Niebuhr was dumbfounded, not at the lapse in his own memory but at the retentiveness of the student's. "Imagine," he said wonderingly, "your keeping that in your mind all this time."

When Niebuhr returned from delivering the Gifford Lectures, Union Seminary was at his feet. Across the street at Columbia too, Niebuhr was Big Man on Campus. His Alma Mater, Yale, also took note of his importance by granting him an honorary Doctor of Divinity in 1942. (His previous D.D.'s had come from Eden, in 1930; Grinnell, in 1936; Wesleyan, in 1937; University of Pennsylvania, in 1938; and Amherst in 1941.) Said Professor Frederick A. Pottle at the Yale Commencement:

> Dr. Niebuhr, a graduate of the Yale Divinity School, first attracted the uneasy attention of the world as the socialist pastor of a working-class church.[5] It has been his business ever since to keep his hearers uneasy and fascinated. At Union Theological Seminary he immediately rose to a position of commanding influence as a theologian, a position guaranteed by the invitation to deliver . . . the Gifford Lectures. . . . In his magazine *Christianity and Crisis* he has led the fight of anti-pacifist churchmen against isolationism. He draws larger crowds of college students than any other preacher. . . . It is not because he is soothing, for his words are about as comfortable as the utterances of Jeremiah. . . . It is his belief that the modern world has rejected the

[5] Niebuhr's Bethel Church in Detroit was middle, not working, class. As *Advance* recollected in May, 1945, "The backbone of the congregation continued to be a group of prosperous families of German antecedents."

> Christian Gospel not so much because it is incredible as because it seems irrelevant. That great numbers of men in these days are finding it to be relevant is due in no small measure to the profundity and eloquence of Reinhold Niebuhr.

That same year of 1942, Niebuhr flew back to England, on behalf of the USO, in one of those bucket seats with which our servicemen became so intimately acquainted. And, in 1943, he was back there again, under the auspices of the English Committee on War Aims. On both occasions he visited the installations where Allied servicemen were on guard against the enemy, and on his return to the United States, in 1943, he reported to General Frederick Osborn of Special Services that our troops urgently needed more education in regard to our war aims. Hatred of the enemy, he felt, was not enough: there should be comprehension of the positive values of freedom and justice, which were not only worth dying for but also worth living and working for. In *The Nation*, August, 1943, he wrote:

> Compared with [the] British program, the U.S. Army is culturally and educationally poverty-stricken . . . The American soldier . . . lacks help in finding the spiritual and moral significance of the titanic struggle in which he is engaged. [What he needs is] serious discussion about the meaning of the war and the best means of using the fruits of victory creatively.

In Britain, by the summer of 1943, Niebuhr's influence had grown to a point where, on the occasion of Oxford University's awarding him a Doctorate, he was compared by the students to their own revered theologian, C.H. Dodd; epidemic on campus, according to the *Anglican Church Times* was the Commandment:

> Thou shalt love the Lord thy Dodd with all thy heart, and all thy soul . . . and thy Niebuhr as thyself.

Back in the United States, Niebuhr's influence continued to expand to new areas. From Sir Stafford Cripps and other British friends, Niebuhr had acquired, earlier than most Americans, the sentiment in favor of an eventual homeland for the Jews. (This sentiment was then reinforced by American friends such as Rabbi Stephen Wise.) In 1941, Niebuhr came out publicly in favor of this Zionist aspiration in a speech before the national convention of the B'nai B'rith, and again, in 1942, before the Union of Hebrew Congregations. By 1944, he had, with Bishop Francis McConnell, Daniel A. Poling, Henry Atkinson and William Foxwell Albright, helped to found the American Christian Palestine Committee and, as its first treasurer, was taking part in their seminars all over the United States (Philadelphia in October, Chicago in November, and Princeton the following summer).

At no time, however, was Niebuhr an uncritical Zionist. He believed, as he wrote in the *Nation*, January, 1942, that the displaced Jews of Europe must have a national homeland and that this, because of its 3500 years of organic and historic association, should be Palestine. (At the same time he also wished to encourage the immigration of refugee Jews to America.) Still he was never unmindful of the rights of the Arabs—he pronounced the word, "Ay-rabs." He told the Anglo-American Commission of Inquiry in Washington, D. C., in January, 1946, that the Arabs must be helped to find a measure of justice and security to make up for what they would have to relinquish in Palestine.[6] And throughout the forties and fifties he urged that somewhere in the "vast hinterland of the Middle East," perhaps in Iraq where the population is much smaller today than in Biblical times, there be established a haven for the Arabs displaced by Jewish immigration. And the United States, he insisted, should take the diplomatic lead in urging other nations to join with it in spurring economic development for the whole region.

There were times, therefore, when Niebuhr disagreed with the American Christian Palestine Committee on which he remained for many years as a member of the Executive Council. But he worked with them nonetheless on a pragmatic basis. Carl Hermann Voss recalls a crossing of the paths he was able to arrange between Niebuhr and the peripatetic Zionist emissary, Abba Eban, then Israel's articulate representative at the United Nations: place, the Hotel DeWitt Clinton in Albany, N.Y.; time, a hot July afternoon in 1949. Introductions were brushed aside as the two rapid-speaking, rapid-walking men approached one another. "I imagine

[6] Niebuhr sympathized with the suggestions of Judah Magnes, Ernst Simon, and Martin Buber for a binational state, but he felt that their specific proposals were unrealistic, since a parity of population of exactly one-half Jews and one-half Arabs could never be maintained.

you fellows are going to need a lot of money," Niebuhr said. "Are you going to get some loans?" And for two hours there was detailed and knowledgeable discussion of Israel's financial problems. The board member of the defunct Delta Cooperative was thus able to help another small idealistic enclave surrounded by hostile neighbors.

Niebuhr's views about the importance of money in his own life had been challenged, in 1944, when Harvard University, in addition to awarding him a D.D., offered him the post of University Professor which would have approximately doubled his salary, not to mention his prestige. Niebuhr was strongly tempted to accept it. There were dialogues with Mrs. Niebuhr and President Conant of Harvard, with Justice Felix Frankfurter and Bishop Scarlett. Niebuhr finally turned down the offer on the ground that as University Professor he would be a member of four or five departments and therefore have a decisive voice in none. At Union Seminary there was jubilation though not a thorough understanding of his motives. Mrs. Nola Meade, his secretary, said, for example, "Dr. Niebuhr knew the boys here needed him more than the boys at Harvard. That's why he stayed."

The boys' need was real enough although not always couched in the most theological terms. In the *Student Cabinet* the following song was immortalized:

When it's eight o'clock on Thursday night
    And books become a bore;
Then we'll leave our desks and climb the golden stair,
We will gather at the master's feet
    A-sitting on the floor,
When the beer is served at Reiny's
    We'll be there . . .

Oh how wonderful it is to listen
    To the master's voice,
As he 'lucidates the issues of the day;
Oh how marvelous, how sanctified
    Our souls they do rejoice
When Reiny's clearcut vision points the way . . .

Every eye is resting on him
    Every ear is straining hard

Just to catch the pearls of wisdom as they fall;
Oh production is prolific
And the "Saints" have their reward,
Thursday nights when Reiny's really on the ball.

Niebuhr's impact on students and faculty was not only spreading through the country but was reaching a new dimension in depth. From one of the many universities Niebuhr visited during the war came this letter from the Dean:

> It would be difficult for me to put into words the appreciation which exists on the campus for what you did in your three addresses. Not in all my fourteen years here have I seen anything like it. The interesting thing is that you got hold of the most thoughtful and intelligent crowd on campus, including a good many men on the faculty. . . . We are hearing from every quarter about the real change in attitude which you produced in men who were floundering about . . . in the face of the present confusion. . . . I hope you were not too tired by the process.

He *was* tired; but how could he rest when his younger countrymen were risking life, limb, sanity, and future for aims about which they, and many of their fellow citizens, were "floundering"? Niebuhr therefore intensified not only his personal efforts but also his organizational ones.

During the whole of the war period (1939 to 1945), Niebuhr worked with the World Council of Churches' Commission on a Just and Durable Peace.[7] Which was the primary value, peace or justice? Was vengeance or mercy to be the Allies' attitude toward a defeated Germany? In 1945, the so-called Morgenthau Plan had been put forward: its provisions would have reduced Germany to the level of an agricultural nation. In Niebuhr's view—as in that of most Americans—this plan would lead neither to peace nor justice. Yet how else was Germany to be kept from rearming and catapulting the world into a fourth war in a hundred years? How could she be helped to become a functioning democracy rather than a cradle for dictatorship?

[7] One of Niebuhr's fellow Commission members was John Foster Dulles, later Secretary of State. The two men did not see eye to eye on many issues, Dulles appearing too moralistic to Niebuhr, and Niebuhr appearing too impious to Dulles. Niebuhr did, however, appreciate Dulles' pre-Pearl Harbor efforts to mobilize American public opinion on the side of internationalism though he later ferociously attacked Dulles' policies of brinkmanship.

Shortly after the end of the war, Niebuhr was sent, together with a small group of experts, by the United States Department of State to study the intellectual scene in Germany and report back on how best democratization could be encouraged.

Such an impact did this visit have upon Theodor Heuss, later President of the Federal Republic of Germany, that a decade later he started out his article on Germany in *The Atlantic*, April, 1957, by recalling it:

> In the fall of 1946 an American commission consisting of government officials, educators, and scientists, toured Germany. (I have a particularly vivid memory of Reinhold Niebuhr, the theologian, who was a member of the group.) . . . I took part in the candid conversations between the Americans and their German opposite numbers, and thought that the talks . . . served a useful purpose. For the oversimplifications of political propaganda had created on both sides misunderstandings which could be at least partly cleared up by personal meetings . . .

Niebuhr returned from this trip more perturbed about the world than when he had started. The German problem, he warned, was rapidly becoming the Russian problem. Again, in his realistic view of events, he was ahead of many, if not most, of his countrymen. This was two years before the Russian-instigated Communist coup in Czechoslovakia which was as shocking to the West in the forties as the Russian crushing of the rebellion in Hungary was to the neutralist countries in the fifties.

In his warnings to his countrymen, Niebuhr recommended the same kind of firmness in regard to our erstwhile ally, Russia, as he had recommended a decade before in regard to our erstwhile enemy, Germany:

> Russia's truculence cannot be mitigated by further concessions. Russia hopes to conquer the whole of Europe strategically and ideologically.

We must also, he said, learn from the past and not again allow a defeated Germany to sink into apathy and inflation and thus become a power-vacuum. The despair Niebuhr had seen among Germans in the Ruhr after World War I must not again be whetted by starvation: "A little more justice now would obviate the necessity of charity later." Nor should a comparable economic collapse be permitted in Germany, lest Communist propaganda blame this on Western capitalism and thus enable the German Communists to "save" the country, as the Nazis had once claimed to be doing. Regardless, therefore, of American loathing for the Nazis' crimes—the Nuremberg Trials were just getting under way—we must not keep punishing Germany to the point where she could no longer stand as a bulwark against Russia.

To clarify this point, Niebuhr quoted a German whom he described as "an heroic anti-Nazi" who said about himself and his countrymen:

> The rigor of our fight against Communism must be our penance for having allowed the Nazi tyranny to arise. But I hope we get some support from the West. Or do the democracies believe that a proper punishment for permitting one tyranny to arise is to subject us to another?[8]

These were among the points Niebuhr had in mind when Henry Luce, trustee of Union Seminary and publisher of *Life, Time* and *Fortune,* asked Niebuhr to write an article on Germany for *Life* in 1946. "But you won't print what I want to write," Niebuhr said. Luce promised that they would —and they did.

Reaction to the article (October 21, 1946) was stormy. Some anti-Germans took one look at the by-line, Reinhold Niebuhr, and wrote in suggesting he be sent back to the Germany he so obviously came from. Some Jews were appalled to find Niebuhr willing to forgive the Germans to the point of helping them. Other people who did not consider themselves anti-German still thought Niebuhr soft on Germany; others who had not yet had their eyes opened to the full perils of Stalinism thought Niebuhr was red-baiting; others thought Niebuhr was un-American when he reminded his fellow countrymen that the whole of western culture was implicated, at least indirectly, in the sins of Nazism. As he had written in *Fortune,* July, 1942:

> It is wrong to worship force and to make power self-justifying. But such an error could not have arisen in a civilization that had not made the opposite mistake and assumed that men were in the process of becoming purely rational. It is perverse to make the

[8] Niebuhr had two sources of contact with these heroic anti-Nazis: one was through Paul Hagen's "Neue Beginnen"; the other was through the World Council of Churches. As John Bennett has pointed out, "even among the Junkers . . . and the conservative old Lutherans . . . there was a strain of dignity and decency. Many of the generals who finally rose against Hitler were from that background."

> interests of our nation the final end of life. But this error could not have achieved such monstrous proportions if our culture had not foolishly dreamed and hoped for the development of "universal" men, who were bereft of all loyalties to family, race, and nation. It is monstrous to glorify war as the final good. But that error could not have brought us so close to disaster if a comfortable civilization had not meanwhile regarded peace as a final good and had not expected perfect peace to be an attainable goal of history.

After the war, moreover, Niebuhr did not want to see his countrymen bask either in a false innocence or a false security: "We thought that victory over a particular group of nations which threatened our peace would guarantee our security. Since then we have discovered that the roots of discord are never merely in our foes but in ourselves."

Luce not only printed Niebuhr's article as written but he kept requesting other articles for *Life* and *Fortune. Time,* too, meanwhile, was frequent in its quotation of Niebuhr and climaxed its interest in a Cover Story. This enthusiasm of Luce's for Niebuhr was viewed with a witty and wicked eye by William Lee Miller in *The Reporter,* January 13, 1955:

> TIME seems to like Niebuhr, and also to like the theological "fashion" for which he is the chief spokesman. But this Lucenthusiasm may demonstrate what Mr. Niebuhr himself might call the hazards and perils—possibly even the ambiguities and paradoxes—of success. For Mr. Niebuhr may find himself the victim of his own greatness, admired but misunderstood, praised but not followed. . . . TIME and LIFE themselves provide excellent examples of much that Mr. Niebuhr criticizes. Niebuhr warns against the cocky assurance that America is an innocent nation, and says we should remember the limits and perils of our great power; LIFE speaks glowingly of "The American Century." Niebuhr indicts the comfortable who look on their prosperity as evidence of their virtue . . . : LIFE lyrically extols the achievements of American capitalism with four-color pictures. Niebuhr counsels against extravagant estimates of man's ability to control history; TIME and LIFE denounce the Democrats for losing China. . . . Niebuhr says that history does not have its final meaning . . . within itself; TIME marches on.

Niebuhr too, meanwhile, was marching on to further honors. Princeton awarded him a D.D. in 1946; Glasgow University in Scotland awarded him one in 1947, as did New York University. He lectured in San Francisco and in Upsala, Sweden, and preached, it seemed, almost everywhere in between. On a preaching-visit to St. Louis, his schedule grew so tight that Bishop Scarlett arranged for a police escort to get him to his train. Niebuhr's bread-and-butter letter was reminiscent of the long-ago entry in *Leaves* that described his enjoyment of "stepping on the gas:"

> The police escort was wonderful. Took just 4 minutes to get to the station. The taxi driver enjoyed it as much as I. Sense of power!!

Other times he was weary beyond description, but he flogged himself forward. One thing prophets rarely seem to know how to do is rest or relax.

Prophet or no, Niebuhr lived his life during those years as if a time-bomb were ticking away inside him. Not a minute was wasted and no activity pursued that did not have some purpose. His reading was geared to whatever book or lecture or sermon he was preparing and, according to one visitor, when Mrs. Niebuhr tried to have him take a brief respite by suggesting he go for a walk, his surprised answer was, "Where to?"

In the post war period, in addition to all his old commitments, he also took on new ones, helping to establish The American Association for a Democratic Germany, The Committee for Cultural Freedom, The Resettlement Campaign for Exiled Professionals and the ADA. Rarely, according to Nola Meade, was a call made by a worthy group or individual upon his limited time or financial resources without receiving some kind of help. He sent books and packages abroad, he helped new arrivals find jobs, and he fired barrages of words against all forms of individual and group indifference. This was the time when the pressure to bring the boys home was causing a military as well as an emotional disarmament. As in the years after the First World War, the thought of another armed clash was so abhorrent that many Americans put their heads in the sand. Said one European critic, "If the U. S. insists on turning her back and acting like an ostrich, she might at least think of how she appears to us."

In the course of Niebuhr's vocal and written barrages, some of his shots went wild, but others hit home with deadly accuracy. Nor was their emphasis always on the negative side. When, for example, the Marshall Plan for United States aid to war-torn Europe was formulated, he supported it with enthusiasm. And at the World Council of Churches in Amsterdam the following year, 1948, he recommended that Christians speak out whenever "there is a clear relation between the love commandment and some obvious answer to even a complex political issue."

This ecumenical conference was the direct—if postponed—outgrowth of the Oxford meeting, in 1937, at which Niebuhr had played a minor role. Now he was one of the major figures, together with Barth, Tillich, and Brunner. No one agrees which one was Everest, but all agree that Niebuhr was at least Himalayan. He, on the other hand, was alarmed by the lofty heights to which the hopes of many delegates seemed to be soaring. Soon after his arrival he wired home, via The Religious News Service:

> I am frankly a little frightened by the extravagant expectations which some of the delegates and many of the friendly observers have for the General Assembly . . .
> It is, to be sure, an historic occasion—the first truly legislative and authoritative assembly of the non-Roman churches of the world. It may well become a turning point in the history of Protestantism, for it may arrest the tendency toward endless division and move in the opposite direction toward unity and order.
> The Assembly cannot, however accomplish what some devout souls expect of it . . . It cannot achieve a complete unity of Protestantism . . . The processes of history are slower than that . . .

And even more frightening to Niebuhr was the expectation of some devout souls that the Assembly could "speak a simple or grand word which will solve the problems between Russia and the West." . . . Against them Niebuhr insisted that "there is nothing in the Christian faith which gives us a sudden freedom over these tragic ambiguities of world politics." This was the period when the United States and Canada were about to join NATO; Niebuhr wrote on September 4, 1948:

> The risks of war in the present situation are . . . great. But we can make no decisions which do not contain some risks of war If we are too afraid of those risks, we will do what the nations did in Hitler's day. We will increase the risks of war in our effort

to avoid war. It would be nice if we could vault over all these ambiguous and risky decisions and make one big decision for peace. But life is not like that . . .

Niebuhr's realistic attitude toward the world and the church was like ice water dashed in the faces of the uncritically hopeful. As a result, they and others questioned the depth of Niebuhr's basic ecumenicity. William John Wolf, in the Living Library Volume, for example, wrote that the Church is "a critical omission in Niebuhr's social picture of redemption." And John Bennett, Niebuhr's old friend and colleague, had long been suggesting that Niebuhr put more emphasis on "the creative possibilities of a Christian group that has been brought to repentence."

On the other hand, Charles Kegley wrote in the Living Library Volume, that "one is especially aware of [Niebuhr's] role in ecumenical thought and life;" and D. B. Robertson, in his introduction to *Applied Christianity*, says about the ecumenical philosophy and purposes, "none was more influential than Niebuhr in [their] development and formulation."[9] In Niebuhr's view this involved a dual form of action: "the effectiveness of the World Council of Churches rests . . . [upon] the policy of speaking boldly to the churches even on controversial issues while refraining from speaking for the churches to the world on issues upon which it is impossible to assume or to achieve a common mind."

Christian Faith and Social Action contains reference to the stimulating contact Niebuhr and others of the Fellowship of Socialist Christians "had with the growing ecumenical movement . . . beginning with the World Conference in Oxford in 1937." And in the Living Library Volume, twenty years later, Niebuhr referred to his own "growing appreciation of the Church." At the same time, Niebuhr continues to warn that the Church stands in constant danger of itself becoming the Anti-Christ, since it is tempted, like the Pharisee, to say in prayer, "I thank thee Lord that I am not like other institutions."

Thus the Church, he claims, "stands under divine judgment and must continually repent." It also stands to learn from the various disciplines of secular culture. As Niebuhr wrote in *Christian Century* the year after the Amsterdam Conference:

[9] Niebuhr's interdenominationalism had started during his first pastorate when he joined the Detroit Council of Churches.

> We are the heirs of a spiritual history which includes a secular revolt against religion . . . It is not the first or the last time that a facet of the full truth has been clarified and restored by heresy after being obscured by orthodoxy. There are certain insights which come to us in the same way from modern secularism.[10]

The secular world, in Niebuhr's opinion, also stands in need of judgment. He becomes extremely impatient with those American secularists who would rather die than see one penny of federal funds go toward transporting children to parochial school (he nods wryly at the dictum that "anti-Catholicism is the anti-Semitism of the liberal"). After all, Niebuhr argues, these extremists do not object to the federal government paying the salary of chaplains of the major faiths. As to the absolutist secularism of Russia and China, it is as great an evil, he believes, as is an absolutist clericalism. Sometimes Niebuhr's impatience with both forms of absolutism explodes, and he quotes the statement of the medieval cleric: "The Church is like Noah's Ark; one could not stand the stench within, were it not for the storm without."

That such an attitude on his part shocks people Niebuhr is well aware. But he has never thought it a bad idea to shock people. From Amsterdam, for example, he reported on September 25, 1948, that the consensus of

> the churches from the most divergent . . . backgrounds . . . on the place of the Church in modern life . . . was, politically speaking, so far left of center (at least the American center) that it will shock many Americans. It may also do them good.

Just as Niebuhr does not mind shocking his churchly colleagues, so he does not mind shocking the secular world. When the U.S. State Department sent him to Paris as one of the delegates to the UNESCO conference, in 1949, he found himself in conflict, not with Barth, but with Bertrand Russell, making use, not of secular insights to jar religious complacency, but of religious insights to jar secular complacency. As he told the UNESCO delegates (his remarks were published in *International Organization*, 1950):

[10] One of these was the granting to women of "fuller recognition as persons . . . even now the religious communities lag behind the civil . . . on this standard of ethics."

> Our culture has been so accustomed to ask every tomorrow to justify the actions of today, that it does not know how to gain support for responsibilities which are intrinsically right, though they may remain immediately unrewarded. Perhaps we have to learn the meaning of the words, "Seek ye first the Kingdom of God and its righteousness and all these things shall be added unto you." Sometimes the immediate utility of an action is the more certainly achieved if it is not sought too directly. . . . It is indeed a fact that thousands of people are engaged in UNESCO activities . . . who are prompted . . . by illusions. No one can deny that some important results have been accomplished in history under the spur of illusions. But illusions are always finally dispelled by the hard facts of history. The work in which UNESCO is engaged requires a "long pull" and not a short one. One could wish therefore that it would be carried on in such fashion as not to be subject to the enervation of disillusionment.

Enervation had been a cause of concern to Niebuhr since the time of *Leaves*. He knew it to be a common reaction to having one's illusions blasted—and yet by profession he was an illusion-blaster. Enervation was, moreover, particularly dangerous to the western world, for the Communist nations were spurred by a whole complex of illusions and were consequently, at least temporarily, bursting with dynamism—a dynamism that was reinforced by the real and visible strides they were making toward industrialization. The West, on the other hand, already industrialized, had been shaken by the emergence of two kinds of dictatorship in thirty-five years. The redemptive history on which the West had pinned its hopes had itself turned out to be an illusion—or in the memorable phrase of Arthur Schlesinger, Jr., "history had betrayed her votaries."

In 1949, still another shock occurred: the Russians exploded their own atomic bomb. Not only the values of the West but its physical survival were in jeopardy. Said the American prophet whose assumption is that to state a problem realistically is to move one step toward its solution:

> We are delicately poised on the razor edge of history . . . we were the generation which was promised all the good things which a technical civilization could produce, but were left unprepared for either the perils of atomic destruction or the evils of communism.

22

Selling Democracy

UNPRECEDENTED were the hazards of the postwar world, but unprecedented too were the resources for meeting these hazards. "*Hazards and Resources*" was significantly the title of a key article Niebuhr wrote in April, 1949, in *The Virginia Quarterly Review*. Not only could atomic energy be turned toward peaceful solution of man's oldest physical problems but his oldest social problems too might the better be solved now that some of the brushwood of modern illusions had been burned away.

Left visible were the basic truths that for Niebuhr have never been static, but dynamic. He has, in fact, compared them to a magnetic field. Here the lines of tension are perennial, between the acting and viewing self, between the self and its society, and between one society and another.

Niebuhr, who had spent the first two decades of his teaching-and-writing career probing back to the causes of evil in history, shifted gears in the latter forties and probed ahead to the possible forms its remedies might take. To the optimists he had said that destructiveness may accompany man's creativity; now, to the pessimists he said that creativity may accompany man's destructiveness. "Truth often rides into history on the back of error," and it is important, first, for the self to be sufficiently open for such truth to be recognized, and secondly for society to be sufficiently open for such truth to be acted upon. For, said Niebuhr in *Faith and History* in that same year of 1949, "history is . . . a realm of endless possibilities for renewal and rebirth." The future will continue to hold hope as long as there is sufficient opportunity for truth to keep emerging and for error to keep being corrected.

Already during the war, as Niebuhr flew the Atlantic in his bucket seat, he had conjectured that the self-corrective system of democracy was the primary aim for which the Allied forces were fighting. Through their heroic efforts, backed by the industrial might of the home front, this system was being saved from its enemies. But how was it to be saved from its friends?

His answer appeared in 1944, as *The Children of Light and the Children of Darkness*, a book whose revealing sub-title was "a vindication of democracy and a critique of its traditional defense."[1] Said the Preface:

> The excessively optimistic estimates of human nature and of human history with which the democratic credo has been historically associated are a source of peril to democratic society; for contemporary experience is refuting this optimism and there is danger that it will seem to refute the democratic ideal as well.

These "excessively optimistic estimates" are maintained by the Children of Light whom Niebuhr has divided into the soft utopians, or liberals, and the hard utopians, or Communists. There is danger to democracy also, however, from the Children of Darkness "who know no law beyond their will and interest." Theirs is a moral cynicism first delineated by Machiavelli's *Prince* and brought to final fruit by Hitler's atrocities. Yet there is guile, Niebuhr says, even a form of wisdom, in these Children of Darkness: for they at least recognize the power and pervasiveness of human self-interest. In contrast, the Children of Light are foolish; for in their belief "that self-interest should be brought under the discipline of a higher law," they forget that this higher law may itself become the vehicle for human self-interest. As a result, Niebuhr says in *Children of Light*, "some of the greatest perils to democracy arise from the fanaticism of moral idealists who are not conscious of the corruptions of self-interest in their professed ideals."

Other perils to democracy arise from excessively *pessimistic* estimates of human nature and history. Such pessimism was epitomized for Niebuhr in the secular thought of Thomas Hobbes and in the religious thought of Martin Luther. These thinkers' denial of the average man's capacity to govern himself led straight to the argument for an unchallengeable ruler.

[1] The biblical text upon which the title is based is Luke (16:8): "The children of this world are in their generation wiser than the children of light."

As Niebuhr points out, this argument is both wrong in substance and inconsistent in application. He therefore sets his epigram, "man's capacity for justice makes democracy possible; but man's capacity for injustice makes democracy necessary," immediately ahead of the statement that

> in all non-democratic political theories the state or the ruler is invested with uncontrolled power for the sake of achieving order and unity in the community. But the pessimism which prompts and justifies this policy is not consistent; for it is not applied, as it should be, to the ruler. If men are inclined to deal unjustly with their fellows, the possession of power aggravates this inclination. That is why irresponsible and uncontrolled power is the greatest source of unjustice.

It is the source of injustice when wielded by the Children of Darkness; Niebuhr castigates Martin Luther for having misread the scriptural passage about strong rulers being necessary because of man's sin and as a result having advised the princes of his day ruthlessly to crush the uprising of the desperate peasants, advice which the princes proceeded with enthusiasm to obey.

But uncontrolled power is also the source of injustice when wielded by the Children of Light; Niebuhr therefore also castigates the idealistic leaders of the French Revolution for the bloodbaths and the Terror that occurred during their terms of leadership.

In thus criticizing the French Revolution, Niebuhr was treading on American as well as French toes. To many Americans the French Revolution was not merely contemporaneous with the American Revolution; it was equally understandable and glorious. Sidney Carton's famous last words on the guillotine have re-echoed in the hearts of idealists everywhere: "It is a far far better thing that I do, than I have ever done . . ."

What these idealists failed to recognize, said Niebuhr, was the connection that existed between the Enlightenment ideals that preceded, and the Napoleonic dictatorship that followed, the overthrow of the King. Said Niebuhr on the Mike Wallace Show in 1958, "In the light of history Stalin will probably have the same relation to the early dreamers of the Marxist dreams which Napoleon has to the liberal dreamers of the eighteenth century."

These liberal dreamers of the eighteenth century were the optimists par excellence.[2] Their optimism was derived, said Niebuhr, from "the assumption that increasing freedom meant increasing rationality," that once the average man was released from the shackles of the Nobility and Church on the one hand, and ignorance on the other, his actions would follow the dictates of reason and justice. This naïve rationalism, as Niebuhr calls it, left out of account several crucial factors. One was the inevitable "tension and conflict between self-interest and the general interest." Another was the inordinacy of human self-interest: "they were wrong about man because they equated the survival impulse with self-interest and thought that what they called self-love would be harmless if only it were not frustrated." Instead of being harmless, the self-love of the revolutionary leaders themselves, operating under the aegis of their highest ideals, became lethal. Their form of rationalism which, as Niebuhr said, had been of such value "when it diluted the religious dogmatism of the medieval period," itself became a rigid dogmatism which left no room for anyone, in all sincerity and idealism, to disagree.

Dictatorship, Niebuhr therefore concludes, is often the consequence "of the discord between competitive utopian schemes"; it was no accident that "the Terror began by guillotining Royalists and ended killing every revolutionist who was in disagreement with the faction that controlled the guillotine." In Russia too there was bloody suppression of the moderate revolutionary group by the extremist one. Nor is this parallel between the two revolutions fortuitous, since both relied on the thought of the Enlightenment. This thought, Niebuhr says, although

> revered by many liberals who abhor communism, was basically totalitarian . . .[3] Its totalitarianism did not stem so much from its materialism as from its naive rationalism and its consequent determination to "redeem" society by forcing men to accept rationally approved standards of justice.

[2] Intellectually, says Niebuhr, this optimism harked back to Adam Smith who believed "in the harmlessness of egoistic man"; to Rousseau who believed "in the goodness of natural man"; and to Locke who saw "self-interest in conflict with the general interest only on the low level where 'self-preservation' stands in contrast to the needs of others."

[3] Niebuhr quotes J. L. Talmon's *Totalitarian Democracy* in this connection.

The rationally approved standards of justice, moreover, were almost as full of hidden contradictions as the men who tried to enforce them. Said Niebuhr in the aforementioned "Hazards and Resources":

> The French Revolution proclaimed "liberty, equality and fraternity" a little too blithely. For liberty and equality are just as much in contradiction as they are complementary to each other. A society can destroy liberty in its search for equality; it can annul the spirit of equal justice by a too consistent devotion to liberty.

And it can destroy the fabric of society in the attempt rigidly to enforce what the ruling group considers to be self-evident truths. It was the fragmentation of France by her own rival idealists that laid the groundwork for the emergence of a strong man, i.e., Napoleon. Meanwhile the naïve rationalism reached a frenzied climax with the statue of Reason placed at the altar of Notre Dame Cathedral. Niebuhr pays less attention to this idolatrous incident than to the current lesson he feels it has to teach: that "fanaticism can speak in the name of 'reason' or 'Marxist-Leninist Science' as easily as in the name of God." And in 1958, on the Mike Wallace Show, Niebuhr warned his fellow citizens that "there are frightening similarities between what Khrushchev says and what Robespierre said. The Russians may be modern in a technological sense but they are still ruled by dogmas that are not true to the facts."

These dogmas are not true to the facts because, like those of the eighteenth century from which, in part, they derive, they place the major source of evil outside of man: in the French Revolution the institution of royalty was seen as the source of evil; in the Russian Revolution, the institution of property was seen as the source of evil. In both instances the idealists' expectation, as Niebuhr says, was not "redemption from some evils but redemption from all evil." And even today there is a carry-over of this utopianism in the democratic West as well as in Russia:

> The conclusion most abhorrent to the modern mind is that the possibilities of evil grow with the possibilities of good, and that human history is therefore not so much a chronicle of the progressive victory of good over evil, of cosmos over chaos, as the story of an ever increasing cosmos, creating ever increasing possibilities of chaos.

For Niebuhr, as for the prophets before him, the source of evil lies not outside but inside man.

The sin of the Children of Darkness is relatively easy to see, but the sin of the Children of Light is often masked from others and especially from themselves. One name Niebuhr gives it is "interested reason." This is a combination of three allied concepts. One is Freud's theory of rationalization: man's unconscious tendency to give socially palatable reasons for doing what he wants to do anyway. The second is Marx' theory of the ideological taint: man's unconscious tendency to have his class in society determine his basic values. And the third is Niebuhr's own theory of the spectacles of man's time and place in history through which he must view history.

Evidence of interested reason at work often comes less from what the person asserts than from what he never thinks to question. In *Beyond Tragedy* Niebuhr gave examples of such nonquestioning on the part of two of the most brilliant minds of all time:

> Aristotle was not wise enough to see that his justification of slavery was incompatible with the facts of human nature and the experience of history. Plato was not wise enough to see the weaknesses of the Spartan system, which he used as model for his utopia.

Today part of man's interested reason is his assumption, based partly on prideful hope and partly on scientific method, that everything can be explained by its specific causes. Said Niebuhr in the Gifford Lectures:

> A scientific age will seek and also find specific reasons for the jealousy of children, or the power lusts of mature individuals, or the naive egotism of even the saintly individual, or the envies and hatreds which infect all human relations. The discovery of specific causes of these evils has obscured and will continue to obscure the profounder truth, that all men, saints and sinners . . . are inclined to use the freedom to transcend time, history, and themselves in such a way as to make themselves the false center of existence.

One corollary to the assumption of specific cause (besides its denial of original sin) is the insistence that man can control man, society, and history through manipulation of these specific causes. Here is another potentially totalitarian offshoot of eighteenth century thought. As Niebuhr says in *Christian Realism and Political Problems:*

> A scientific humanism frequently offends the dignity of man, which it ostensibly extols, by regarding human beings as subject to manipulation and as mere instruments of some "socially approved" ends. It is this tendency of a scientific age which establishes its affinity with totalitarianism, and justifies the charge that a scientific humanism is harmless only because there is not a political program to give the elite, which its theories invariably presuppose, a monopoly of power.[4]

Thus a modern age, in effect, denies not only that indeterminate freedom of the individual which makes him, to some extent, unmanageable, but it also denies what Niebuhr calls the "organic forces" in society and history which themselves, to some extent, are unmanageable.

These organic forces were originally stressed by the Irish-born political philosopher Edmund Burke and are described by Niebuhr as "the sense of kinship . . . common language . . . geographic unity and continuity, a common historical experience . . . and sometimes, the fear of a common foe."[5] These are the givens with which each generation must work; its economic and political developments are only "later forces of communal cohesion."

No single generation, therefore, and no dictator no matter how potent, can manipulate people into social cohesiveness. As Niebuhr said (long before the Congo confusion) in *Christian Realism and Political Problems,* "the fact is that even the wisest statecraft cannot create social tissue. [All it can do is to] cut, sew and redesign social fabric to a limited degree."

The form this cutting, sewing, or redesigning takes is nonetheless of vast importance. For if the society is formed in too narrow a pattern, the result may be a strait-jacketing of its own growth; there are, says

[4] One of the science-grounded thinkers who was honest enough to spell out the need for this elite was H. G. Wells.

[5] Niebuhr both admits his debt to Burke who lived at the time of the French Revolution, and also points to the interested reason that prejudiced the highly placed Burke in favor of the French aristocracy.

Niebuhr, "many forms of initiative in society which even the wisest plan may destroy." Or if the pattern calls for too much starch, there may be either an unbending stiffness or a severe crumpling. Niebuhr adds, "In a traditional or tyrannical form of social organization, new forces are either suppressed or they establish themselves at the price of social upheaval." The ideal garment, therefore, with which democracy might be compared, is the maternity dress: it can stretch to a variety of shapes and still maintain its basic function.

The function of democracy is a dialectic one, not only as to aim (the maintenance of order together with justice and liberty) but also as to method. As Niebuhr writes, "It is the highest achievement of democratic societies that they embody the principle of resistance to government within the principle of government itself."

This resistance, in order to be creative, must be freely expounded and tolerantly accepted. The concept of "Her Majesty's Loyal Opposition" includes the assumption that to be opposed is not to be disloyal. This assumption stands in contrast to the practice of some pseudo-democracies where the defeated candidate for office is forced to flee the land rather than safely remain and act as spokesman for the minority which might, in due time, legally become the majority.

The tolerance with which opposing views are heard is, however, a far cry from the indifference which Lord Chesterfield thought to be its synonym. Religiously speaking, Niebuhr says, tolerance is based on the attitude expressed by John Saltmarsh in the seventeenth century:

> Let us not assume any power of infallibility toward each other . . . for another's evidence is as dark to me as mine to him— until the Lord enlighten us both for discerning alike.

And practically speaking, tolerance follows the advice of Lord Acton, "when you perceive a truth, look for a balancing truth." Niebuhr combines both in his statement:

> Democracy cannot exist if there is no recognition of the fragmentary character of all systems of value which are allowed to exist within its frame.

And because of this fragmentariness, he says, it is healthy to have many such systems of value vying constantly with one another:

> The triumph of common sense is . . . primarily the wisdom of democracy itself, which prevents [any one] strategy from being carried through to its logical conclusion. There is an element of truth in each position which becomes falsehood precisely when it is carried through too consistently.

Democracy must, therefore, also include elasticity. The Americans have a written constitution, the British an unwritten one, both of which have proved to be equally flexible when necessary. One ironic example Niebuhr appears to relish is that

> The American constitution was designed to prevent the emergence of the very political parties without which it has become impossible to maintain our democratic processes.

The founding fathers, in other words, were not wise enough to foresee the need for these parties but they were wise enough to devise a constitution which was not shattered by the emergence of what they wished to prevent.

Niebuhr, be it said, was also not wise enough to foresee the need to keep these national parties two in number—having been a member of a third party, the Socialist, he did his best to form a fourth one, a Labor Party. Today he admits the providential aspect of the failure of these plans and points to the flexible, tentlike quality of the two existing parties, both of which include every shade of political opinion, although in differing proportions, thus discouraging the splintering of parties that contributed to the demise of the Weimar democracy in Germany and still, at times, paralyzes democracy in France. In regard to the American system, he said at the Kent School in 1956, "I may be opening myself up to the charge of patriotism, but I *like* this mess."

A similar attitude was broadcast by Adlai Stevenson over the Yale radio station during his week as Chubb Fellow in 1959: "There is a wonderful healthy confusion in the American system—better than logic could work out."[6]

[6] When asked whether he has been much influenced by Niebuhr, Stevenson's answer was, "I don't know, but I hope so." And a Newsweek account of America's Ambassador to the UN, in March, 1961, mentioned that Stevenson finished his hectic diplomatic day by reading a Niebuhr book at night. "Probably puts him to sleep," was the comment by one of Niebuhr and Stevenson's irreverent younger friends.

Although logic could not have worked out our system ahead of time, we can apply logic in restrospect and note the number of forces-in-tension through which it came into being: democracy, says Niebuhr in *The Structure of Nations and Empires,* developed in the West through

> a long and tortuous process. It required both a religiously motivated defiance of political authority and an independent middle class which had sources of power in the economic life and not in the state machine.

Our treasured ideals of liberty and equality, therefore, did not spring full-blown from the brows of the founding fathers or even from the French and English eighteenth century philosophers on whom the Americans drew for insights. Liberty, an ideal unknown in the previous democracy of ancient Greece, by its slaves, and equality, an ideal unknown by its women, were both, according to Niebuhr, "weapons of the commercial classes who engaged in stubborn conflict with the ecclesiastical and aristocratic rulers of the feudal-medieval world." These classes needed liberty because they were growing economically, and their economic growth, in turn, enabled them to achieve the political power which they used to fight for equality. This equality, the characteristic ideal of the underdog, was something they wished for themselves but achieved also, as a by-product, for the classes below them.[7]

The success of the middle classes continued for centuries by dint partly of their own efforts and partly of such providential developments as the voyages of the explorers which opened up new continents, the invention of the printing-press which facilitated the spread of new ideas, and the scientific and technical discoveries that improved manufacturing and distribution. Their success, the middle classes assumed, would continue indefinitely, and in this assumption, Niebuhr says, lay one aspect of their interested reason:

> The social and historical optimism of democratic life . . . represents the typical illusion of an advancing class which mistook its own progress for the progress of the world.

[7] "Equality," Niebuhr believes, was "derived partly from Christian and partly from Stoic sources." The Christian sources were the Bible and the Sectarians. Of the latter, Gerard Winstanley, leader of the Diggers, is the one Niebuhr most frequently quotes.

This progress of the world, they also believed, would continue into the future and would result in a new human being and a new society whose perfection would be the justification for the ruthless efforts made on their behalf by their progenitors. Niebuhr points to "the highly emotional and essentially religious response" by the Enlightenment to the idea of posterity and quotes, as an example, Diderot's prayer:

> Oh posterity, holy and sacred! Supporter of the oppressed and unhappy, thou who art just, thou who art uncorruptible, thou who wilt reveal the good man and unmask the hypocrite, consoling and certain idea, do not abandon me. Posterity is for the philosopher what the other world is for the religious.

Man's view of posterity is often a clue to his interested reason. Today, for example, there is the extreme attitude of the Communist Chinese, like that of the Russians under Stalin, that no sacrifice is too great to ask of the present generation for the sake of the future ones. In contrast there is the extreme attitude of some Americans, that no self-indulgence by the present generation is too great to ask future generations to pay for: as a result, our natural resources have been used up at a prodigal rate, and the public sector of the economy, particularly its schools, has been starved in favor of the private one. This problem, however, is not simple to solve, since now to starve the private sector without expanding the public one would cause serious new problems. As Niebuhr says, "A return to medieval asceticism in an economy of abundance is ridiculous." At the same time he worries that "the other alternative of more goods and services may lead to a tremendous pressure upon the consumer to adopt more and more luxurious living standards for the sake of keeping the economy healthy." The proper solution, as he sees it, lies both in providing more schools and hospitals at home and offering more aid to needy nations abroad.

The Enlightenment believed not only in the perfectibility of the individual but also viewed society as no more than an aggregation of improving individuals: society's harmony would automatically evolve out of individual improvement. In Niebuhr's view this was a gross overestimation not only of moral man but of immoral society. For him communal harmony stems primarily, not from individual benignness, but from the healthy interraction of all the individuals and groups that coexist within the democratic field. As he said in *Children of Light,* "an ideal democratic order seeks unity within the conditions of freedom; and maintains freedom within the framework of order." This maintenance of order, he had first pointed out in *Moral Man,* rests ultimately upon power, both the power that is balanced by countervailing power, and the power that overarches the many forms of economic, political and social power that compete, visibly and invisibly, with one another.[8]

This need for power to be exercised in the interest of justice has been hidden at times from the idealistic Children of Light who underestimated man's self-interest and consequent tendency toward injustice. It was rarely, if ever, hidden, however, from the average citizen whose common sense and experience of life led him to view the political scene with realism. As Niebuhr often says today, it is the customer rather than the shoemaker who knows whether the shoe fits. And increasingly Niebuhr has voiced faith in the pragmatic wisdom of the man on the street, the average reader, and once, in a moment of hyperbole, in *The Self and the Dramas of History,* "the peasant mother." There is, he says, "a wholeness of view among the simple which grasps . . . truths not seen by the sophisticated."

Scripturally his point of view is grounded in the text, "I thank thee, Father, that Thou has withheld these things from the wise and prudent and revealed them unto babes." Personally it is grounded in his experience of people, starting in Detroit. Already then he noted that some of the most creative of his parishioners were the business men—and twenty years later he admitted in *Christianity and Society,* Fall, 1950 that

> business men . . . have a more precise sense of justice in feeling their way through the endless relativities of human relations than professional teachers of morals. Practical experience has made them sensitive to the complex web of values and interests in which human decisions are reached, while the professional teachers of religion and morals deal with the simple counters of black and white. This certainly is one of the reasons why the pulpit frequently seems so boring and irrelevant to the pew.

[8] As he noted in *Irony of American History,* "one of the most prolific causes of delusion about power in a commercial society is that economic power is more covert than political power."

In his support of common sense and the average person, however, Niebuhr does not sink into what he calls a sentimental egalitarianism. Some questions of national defense, he says, are too complex and necessarily secret for the average person to judge them intelligently. For this reason, Niebuhr calls foreign affairs "the Achilles heel of democracy," since they too must be handled by knowledgeable persons rather than by the man on the street. But these knowledgeable persons must be responsible ultimately to the man on the street who elects either them or whoever appointed them. This makes them answerable to public opinion, but not for each decision. Niebuhr would disapprove frequent referendums, for example: there can be, he says, a tyranny by the majority as well as by a minority; and in regard to the minorities that exist within a democracy, he recommends a more honest admitting than is our wont of the hierarchy in which these place themselves—until they are, themselves, displaced.

Near the top of this hierarchy, he believes, are the opinion leaders, whether diplomats or government officials, journalists or academics, economists, lawyers, business men, or labor leaders, who by native endowment plus extensive training, and not by race, sex, wealth, or creed, have equipped themselves to make the judgments on the fundamental issues that a modern state must face. The power and responsibility of these people cannot—and should not—be handed down to their descendants: each generation must have all its members educated so that a new hierarchy can equip itself. To *Walter Lippmann and his Times* Niebuhr contributed a chapter wherein he describes this group by the historically hated words "aristocracy" and "elite." But he broadens the boundaries of this group so generously that any old-time aristocrat would throw up his manicured hands in dismay. Niebuhr refers, for example, to the two disparate classes

> [who] were members of the elite in foreign affairs . . . in the great debate before World War II . . . the taxi drivers and the 'international bankers.' Both classes were free of the liberalistic and moralistic illusions that infected the clerical and academic elite . . . and gave a pacifist taint to the political judgments of the nation. The taxi drivers . . . had their insights by virtue of a native common sense and earthy wisdom . . . The

> international bankers . . . had an understanding derived from their world-wide connections. Their understanding of America's role in world affairs was not significantly blurred by the admixture of economic interest which entered into their calculations. At any rate, we must not expect absolutely untainted or disinterested wisdom in public affairs . . . An open society winnows truth from error partly by allowing a free competition of interests and partly by establishing a free market of competing ideas."

This free market of ideas must, Niebuhr believes, be maintained except for minimal limits placed upon libel, slander, and pornography. As he wrote from Amsterdam on August 14, 1948, "Sometimes when one sees a case of flagrant unfairness in the news, one is tempted to work for a tightening of the standards. But it would be well to check, rather than obey, that impulse. The fact is that almost every restriction upon freedom of speech contains more perils than the dangers which arise from its misuse."

Thus Niebuhr agrees with Herbert Butterfield that "democracy is limited warfare." And he points out that it was not Jefferson, the child of the Enlightenment, but Madison, the child of Calvinism, who had the wisdom to insist that limited warfare be maintained between the three branches of the U.S. Government. (There is a form of creative tension also between the two great documents of American history, Jefferson's Declaration of Independence which has inspired Children of Light all over the world, and the U.S. Constitution which recognizes the guile of the Children of Darkness, thus providing safeguards also against the power of masked self-interest in the Children of Light.)

The limited warfare of democracy must, however, remain sufficiently limited so that the social fabric is not destroyed. This danger of tearing apart society is ever-present, and the American statesman most aware of it was Abraham Lincoln.[9] Said Niebuhr in *The New Leader*, February 23, 1959:

[9] Niebuhr wrote in the Gifford Lectures, "These twin evils, tyranny and anarchy, represent the Scylla and Charybdis between which the frail bark of social justice must sail. It is almost certain to founder upon one rock if it makes the mistake of regarding the other as the only peril."

> It is significant that in his scale of values [Lincoln] placed first the preservation of the unity of the nation. "My primary purpose," he declared, "is to save the Union." Thereby he offended all or most of the abolitionists, who thought that the primary purpose of any decent statesman should be the abolition of slavery. The fact that Lincoln proved that the union could not be saved without emancipating the slaves, which incidentally he did by proclamation and as a war measure, made him "the Great Emancipator" and constitutes the second reason for his hold on the imagination of the nation. Perhaps the fact that his scale of values was not that of a pure idealist but of a practical statesman, gave him an added appeal to the imagination of the "common man" who is a little uneasy with pure idealists.
> I have a vivid memory of a debate I had years ago with a pure idealist, who had accused me of "moral bankruptcy" because of my belief in a pragmatic approach to the tangled issues of the political order. I finally said to him, "We could express the difference between our viewpoints if I confessed that my national hero is Lincoln, while yours is William Lloyd Garrison who was, in my opinion, a self-righteous prig." "Lincoln," exclaimed my idealistic friend and enemy, "that cheap politician, that vulgar compromiser."

In addition to being Niebuhr's national hero Lincoln was also, Niebuhr claims, "America's greatest theologian." This estimate is based in part on Lincoln's type of religious humility, a quality which Niebuhr believes is essential to the functioning of democracy even though it is also "no simple moral or political achievement." It was this humility which enabled Lincoln to fight for what he considered right without feeling the need to portray the other side as wholly wrong. "It seems strange," Lincoln had said about the South, "that any men should dare to ask a just God's assistance in wringing their bread from the sweat of other men's faces. But," he immediately added, "let us not judge that we be not judged." Niebuhr wrote in *Discerning the Signs of the Times* (1946):

> The condemnation of even a wicked foe is made in "fear and trembling" because we know that even that judgment stands under a more ultimate one. And by that fear and trembling our righteous wrath is saved from degenerating into self-righteous vindictiveness.

Another reason for Niebuhr's admiration for Lincoln was Lincoln's self-knowledge and awareness of how interested reason worked within himself and other men. Said Lincoln:

> The shepherd drives the wolf from the sheep's throat, for which the sheep thanks the shepherd as his liberator, while the wolf denounces him for the same act as the destroyer of liberty.

Wryness was only one aspect of Lincoln's humor which ranged from the subtle to what Niebuhr calls "frontier humor." Lincoln's face was itself a map of limited warfare, with the laughing wrinkles around the eyes matched by the deep-etched lines of sorrow around the mouth. In Niebuhr's view these two qualities are connected not only in Lincoln, but potentially in everyone. In one of his most seminal sermons, Humour and Faith, in *Discerning the Signs of the Times,* Niebuhr says,

> insofar as the sense of humour is a recognition of incongruity, it is more profound than any philosophy which seeks to devour incongruity in reason.

This incongruity of the human situation starts at the profoundest level and cannot ever be wholly resolved:

> The real situation is that man as a part of the natural brings his years to an end like a tale that is told; and that man as a free spirit finds the brevity of his years incongruous and death an irrationality.

Either man ignores this incongruity or he faces up to it; and if he faces up to it, he either moves toward despair, in which case laughter is "an expression of [the] sense of the meaninglessness of life," or he moves toward faith, in which case, "laughter is the beginning of prayer. . . . The intimate relation between humour and faith is derived from the fact that both . . . are expressions of the freedom of the human spirit."

Man, in his freedom, can rise above himself and above his society and thus recognize not only human foibles but the ludicrous aspects of human pretension, the very kind of pretension whose "absurdity increases with our lack of awareness of it." Laughter, in this instance,

> contains a nice mixture of mercy and judgment, of censure and forbearance. We would not laugh if we regarded these foibles as altogether fitting and proper. There is judgment, therefore, in

> our laughter. But we also prove by the laughter that we do not take the annoyance too seriously.

As for human pretension, it is important that we be able to recognize it in ourselves, our fellows, and our nation. The deflation by humour is one of the secret—or not so secret—weapons of democracy.[10] For if some of the people, some of the time, can see their nation's posture as prideful, they may be able to reduce this pridefulness before the nation's allies are alienated or its enemies enraged. Being able to laugh at our own faults may thus be the first step toward correcting them, and far preferable to having the faults so rigorously condemned by others that we ourselves become defensively enraged and thus accentuate the faults:

> This alternative between contrition on the one hand and fury and hatred on the other faces nations as well as individuals. It is, in fact, the primary spiritual alternative of human existence.

Humour therefore is indispensable, Niebuhr believes, in national leaders "who have the duty of organizing their fellow-men in common endeavors." They, with the help of their fellow citizens, must act as "observers of an ironic situation in which they are collectively involved," and as a result guide the nation toward an abatement of the irony.

In *Irony of American History,* Niebuhr showed how to distinguish irony from the other forms of drama in which nations as well as individuals become involved, namely comedy, pathos and tragedy:

> Irony consists of apparently fortuitous incongruities in life which are discovered, upon closer examination, to be not merely fortuitous . . . A comic situation is proved to be an ironic one if a hidden relation is discovered in the incongruity. If virtue becomes vice through some hidden defect in the virtue; if strength becomes weakness because of the vanity to which strength may prompt the mighty man or nation; . . . if wisdom becomes folly because it does not know its own limits—in all such cases the situation is ironic. The ironic situation is distinguished from a pathetic one by the fact that the person involved . . . bears some responsibility for it. It is differentiated from

[10] In dictatorship a similar humour exists but is vitiated by the citizens' awareness of their own helplessness.

> tragedy by the fact that the responsibility is related to an unconscious weakness rather than a conscious resolution.

The ironic situation also differs from the pathetic and the tragic in that it is capable of being dissolved if the person or nation becomes conscious of his or her involvement in it. Such awareness leads, as with laughter, to "a no-man's land between faith and despair." If despair is the final destination, there may be "a desperate accentuation of the vanities to the point where irony turns into pure evil." As an example Niebuhr points to the efforts of Soviet communism "to cover the ironic contrast between its original dreams of justice and virtue and its present realities by more and more desperate efforts to prove its tyranny to be 'democracy.'"

If faith, however, is the final destination, there may come an abatement of the pretension, in the form of contrition; "contrition," Niebuhr writes, "is the socially relevant dimension of love." We must note, for example, that the American way of life, of which we are so proud, is not necessarily for everyone the best way of life. And although our democracy is a contingent value of enormous importance, it is not an ultimate value. "It deserves our conditioned loyalty as the best form of human society we know," Niebuhr says, but it does not "deserve the unconditioned loyalty which is the mark of true religion." In this respect, therefore, he agrees with Father Gustave Weigel who said:

> My religion's faith impels me to affirm and support democracy, but democracy is not my religious faith.

Niebuhr further points out that a too uncritical, or idolatrous, attitude toward our own form of government is not only wrong but dangerous. It is wrong, he wrote in the *Religious News Service*, July 12, 1947, because "the meaning of man's existence is only partly comprehended in his social relations . . . If democracy makes itself the end of existence it is only a little better than communism which equates the meaning of life with the life of the community." And it is dangerous because

> the more we indulge in an uncritical reverence for the supposed wisdom of our American way of life, the more odious we make it in the eyes of the world, and the more we destroy our moral authority, without which our economic and military power will

> become impotent. Thus we are undermining the reality of our power by our uncritical pride in it.

The uncritical pride, or self-righteousness, of Americans had historic roots. The Puritans and their followers assumed that American prosperity was God's reward for American virtue; the Enlightenment thinkers, like Jefferson, assumed that American virtue would continue to follow on the heels of American prosperity.[11] Although in one sense both were correct, in that without American diligence the country would not have grown so fast or so well, in another sense both were wrong, since they ignored the providential or fortuitous factors that also contributed to this growth. The development of scientific technics, for example, Niebuhr says, came just at the right moment for the opening up of the new continent.

Through taking credit where credit was not due, and priding themselves that they deserved their good fortune, Americans, Niebuhr said, were involving themselves in the very kind of irony that in history has often turned into tragedy. It was in this connection that he reminded them of Isaiah's warning to Babylon (47:7,8,9):

> Thou saidst, "I shall be a lady forever" . . . therefore . . . these two things shall come to thee in a moment in one day, the loss of children, and widowhood.

The rulers of Babylon were too arrogant to heed warnings and the city was destroyed. Even today it stands as a ravaged pile of sunbaked brick, suggesting that man can heed the handwriting on the wall or ignore it and perish as the wall crumbles. But America still has the ramparts she watches and within them the freedom and opportunity to build afresh. If, says Niebuhr, a "sense of an ultimate judgment upon our individual and collective actions should create an awareness of our own pretensions . . . the irony would tend to dissolve into contrition . . ." from which might arise a new life of creativity. One international form this might take would be a reduction of our moralistic preachments to

[11] In *Irony of American History* Niebuhr wrote: "Two facts about America impressed the Jeffersonians. The one was that we had broken with tyranny. The other was that the wide economic opportunities of the new continent would prevent the emergence of those social vices which characterized the . . . overcrowded continent of Europe. Jefferson regarded the distinction between American democracy and European tyranny . . . as absolute."

allies and neighbors. Another might be a United States attitude of empathy rather than resentment when some of the uncommitted nations give vent to anti-Americanism. Why would not an ally fear our power and hate its own dependence upon it? Why would not a new nation envy our wealth and hate our self-congratulations in regard to it?

To recognize the pretensions of one's own nation is an important job for the individual and the small group. And to sense the irony in which these pretensions place the nation takes the kind of perspective of which humor is one facet. Niebuhr therefore deplores the fact that so many Americans are "morally complacent, self-righteous and lacking in a sense of humor," and that they compound the "humorless idealism of our culture" by making "simple moral distinctions between good and bad nations, the good nations being those which are devoted to liberty." These Americans need to remember that justice is as important as liberty, especially in a world where the rich nations like their own are daily growing richer while the poor nations, comparatively, grow poorer. Nor must Americans rise to heights of self-righteous indignation when in some of the poorest and least developed nations the Communist claim of painlessly providing economic plenty is believed, at least for a time.[12]

Niebuhr also points out that our Communist enemies—as were the Nazis —are so humorless that there is little chance that the irony of their position will be abated from within: "No laughter from heaven could possibly penetrate through the liturgy of moral self-appreciation in which the religion of communism abounds."

In trying to arouse his countrymen to the need for perspective and humor, Niebuhr wore himself out to the point of losing some of his own. In late October, 1948, for example, after the Amsterdam Conference, Charles Taft, a prominent lay leader in the World Council of Churches

[12] "Time," in this respect, "is on our side," Niebuhr wrote in *The New Republic*, February 13, 1957. "However much the battle may run against us for decades . . . the contest between a free society and a tyranny is one in which the tyranny has all the immediate advantages in the colored continents, while we have all the ultimate ones." These ultimate ones he later defined as "providing a form of community that does not exact the price of despotism for the boon of order" and that allows history to "flow through the alternations of government . . . taking courses that not the most prescient leaders . . . could have foreseen. This is its ultimate virtue because this characteristic of an open society conforms to the nature of man as both creature and creator of history" (*Christianity and Crisis*, July 24, 1961).

invited Niebuhr to speak at a Council meeting in Cincinnati. This city had long been carried for the Republicans by Charles Taft's brother, Senator Robert Taft. Niebuhr, in national politics a Democrat, had regretfully predicted in a *Christianity and Crisis* editorial that the imminent presidential election would go to the Republican Thomas E. Dewey rather than to the Democratic incumbent Harry S. Truman. This editorial had been sent by C. C. Burlingham to the *New York Herald Tribune* which had reprinted it under the misleading headline, "Theologian Supports Dewey."

After thanking Charles Taft for his introduction, Niebuhr started his address jovially enough: "I am embarrassed to be here in Cincinnati, for I'm not a Republican."

There was a ripple of laughter, whereupon Charles Taft reached over for the microphone and said, "Even though you predict like one."

The crowd roared with laughter—but Niebuhr for the first time in memory could think of no riposte. Solemnly he cleared his throat: "I am here to discuss the relevance of Christian faith to social conditions . . ."

As Niebuhr's fatigue increased, some irascibility accompanied it. Said one of his devoted admirers wistfully, "If Reinie had not been a theologian, he would have made a good field marshal." And, in 1948, when another book by Pitirim Sorokin was published, Niebuhr forgot his promise to Scarlett and wrote in *Christianity and Society* that "every futility in the moralism of our age is distilled into this book."

Finally a group of his more thoughtful students came to him. "Look, Reinie," said John Dillenberger, their spokesman. "You're running like mad. It's no good. On the public platform you've become merciless; you lambaste everyone. Only in class do you take time to be fair. We want you to slow down a bit and make like a theologian."

But Niebuhr shook his head. "The crisis of the time is too great for me to be a theologian."

The crisis of the time he had judged correctly: within a short period world tensions would explode into the Korean War. But he had not judged the crisis within himself correctly, until it too exploded.

23

With One Hand Tied . . .

THERE had been warnings. For fifteen years Niebuhr had disregarded them: his was not the talent to be buried in the ground, nor were the years of his maturity a period in which the sensitive spirit could retire from the problems of society.

Then in February, 1952, he suffered several small attacks which resulted in headaches, partial paralysis, and a temporary inability to speak with fluency. Rumors about the severity of the attacks augmented as they flew. These, in many instances, were like the rumors of his own death that Mark Twain termed highly exaggerated. One theologian wrote to a minister he had seen the day before:

> I still find myself deeply moved, and indeed shocked, by what you reported yesterday of Reinhold Niebuhr. This is a dreadful tragedy, for he should rightly be at the full climax of his powers at this period in his life . . . I judge from your statement that these successive shocks are wrecking him, and his work is thus definitely at an end.

The true situation, meanwhile, was relayed by Mrs. Niebuhr to a close friend with accuracy, starting at the very beginning:

> This note is just to let you know that Reinhold is at the hospital undergoing treatment and observation. He has been overdoing terrifically the last weeks and months, and also had a perfectly ghastly few months ahead, so this forced halt may be all for the good.
>
> A couple of days ago he had two or three little "attacks." I don't know how else to describe them, which the doctor calls vaso spasms, which might indicate a disturbance of the circula-

> tory system. These spasms may or may not indicate some other condition, but in any case the element of fatigue and exhaustion is emphasized. He will be at the hospital for a couple of weeks and will be out of circulation for the rest of the semester, all of which again may be a good thing, and in the future he will have to live a much more sensible life. Yesterday he confessed to looking forward to more time for writing and even got slightly snobbish about people who go about yapping.

But the spasms did not cease—and the doctors became concerned, since among the other conditions was always the possibility of a tumor. But Mrs. Niebuhr's deep concern continued to be understated, as she kept the family friend informed:

> Just a word to say R. is going through a bad time. . . . The brain surgeon and the neurologists are in consultation now. The past ten days have shown symptoms of something, so there will probably be an operation to see what that something is. Today he is more cheerful . . .

The operation was a standard procedure called pneumoencephalogram. It involves drilling two holes into the top of the skull so that air can be injected, thereby facilitating more accurate X-rays. The drilling takes several hours during which the patient must remain conscious, his face covered with a sheet. Occasionally, as this patient later told friends, a nurse would lift the sheet and smile at him. The brief and wordless communication with another human being, he admitted, was inordinately comforting.

As soon as he was wheeled back to his room, he asked for pencil and paper. He scrawled a note to his mother who remembered that the sight of those few words in his handwriting was more reassuring than a tome from anyone else would have been. Said his sister, "One advantage of having an illegible handwriting when you're healthy is that when you're sick there is so little change." He also jotted down a few notes on the mystery of the human self which he hoped to include in a new book whose basic ideas he evolved while under the sheet: *The Self and the Dramas of History.*

The air encephalogram showed that no further operation was necessary. Ursula Niebuhr's relief sings in her note to the old friend. Reinhold, she said, had strenuously objected to "all that carpentering they did to his poor head" but was now "in good shape."

Home they went from the hospital, but the convalescence dragged on. Ursula Niebuhr's companionship during this difficult period was of a constant and unsentimental helpfulness that turned some of those who had been neutral observers into ardent fans. She managed to be on hand when needed—and not on hand when not needed. She continued her own work, often late into the night after the patient had gone to sleep —but when he was awake and depressed, she would pop in with a snack for the body or the soul—a spot of fruit juice or a snippet of gossip—or both. Her worries she kept to herself, although on rare occasion they spilled out to the old friend:

> R. is very limited in strength, but is up and about and very philosophic and good in face of it all—but the prospect is not cheerful. This we have to realize. I do not know how much he realizes.

The good and philosophic patient, meanwhile, was filled with annoyance at his own apparent inability to be sufficiently good and philosophic. As he wrote to the spouse of a fellow-sufferer:

> I am sure X is a more virtuous patient than I am. I find this period of convalescence extremely difficult. I am not strong enough to do real work and yet getting more normal every day, so that I am overcome with a sense of futility.

The model hospital patient was turning into the convalescent grizzly bear. And the feeling of futility was extending itself back into the past, ex post facto, as well as forward into the future:

> I am ashamed that my convalescence proves to be spiritually so hard because it reveals a certain lack in me, a reliance upon jobs and pressures rather than on inner calm. I think therefore with all the inner pain connected with it, it can be a means of grace. . . . One faces the ultimate question about the significance of one's work and realizes that everything one does remains so fragmentary and incomplete except as God completes it.

If the proof of a pudding is in the eating, the proof of a theology must at least be partly in the living. Niebuhr had spent the first sixty years of his life exerting "the courage to change what can be changed." Now he was being forced to learn "the serenity to accept what cannot be changed." The experience of illness and pain, the threat of momentary extinction, and the even worse threat of degeneration through brain damage, had given him a new perspective in depth. As he later told the graduating class at Union Seminary in June, 1957,

> If I have any regret about my early ministry, it was that I was so busy being what I thought to be a prophet of righteousness, that I was not sufficiently aware of the importance of the pastoral ministry to the maimed, the halt and the blind, in short to all people who had to resign themselves to the infirmities of the flesh and who must finally face the threat of extinction.

This resignation could take the form of despair or of deeper wisdom. Here is one of the great mysteries of human personality: why do some people grow with suffering and others shrink? Again and again Niebuhr turned back to the two old ladies in Detroit, the one who died resentful that anyone as virtuous as she should have to give up life; the other who died in physical agony but with praise on her lips for the two glorious gifts she had received during her lifetime, her daughters.

Niebuhr's attitude toward the shiftless husband of the latter woman has itself evolved over the years. In *Leaves,* as a young minister, he exploded against "that drunkard of a husband." Some thirty years later, in the Living Library Volume he described the man as subject to fits of insanity. One year later, in a sermon, the form of insanity was defined as the disease of alcoholism, and finally, in a sermon in 1959, the man was described simply as an invalid.

To be an invalid gave Niebuhr a better understanding not only of himself but of the Bible: in a letter he said, "I have become convinced that altogether healthy people must have a good deal of difficulty in understanding the final mysteries of grace." (One can almost hear a soft British voice saying, "Reinhold has become slightly snobbish about people who go about exuding health.") And at the Kent School, 1956, he pointed out that the meaning of life and history were "revealed in a man who uttered a cry of despair before his ultimate triumph and thus gave an indication of how close meaninglessness and chaos are to the triumph of faith."

Niebuhr had previously noted the Bible's preference for the halt and the lame. In *Irony of American History* which was on the presses when illness struck its author, he had written:

> Superficially the Biblical preference for "sinners," for the poor, the foolish, the maimed, the sick and the weak seems to be just as perverse a "transvaluation of values" as Nietzsche charged. Its justification lies in the fact that as certainly as failure may ironically issue from pride and pretension, so also may success of a high order be derived from seeming failure.

But existentially he had perhaps not known, in the days of his exuberant health, the full worth of what he came to call "the uncovenanted mercies of life"—the fact of friendship, for example, and of prayer. As he wrote during his illness to Scarlett, "I think I can say without sentimentality that prayer is more real and necessary, as is the communion of prayer with real friends like you." And to a friend whose illness was graver than his own:

> One feels so helpless to do or say anything . . . but just to express one's love and sympathy. I hope it will not be too long before you can get home. That will be something to look forward to. My experience has been that one is grateful for all the little and big things that one can look forward to. It eases the trial of patience of the total situation.

After Niebuhr's illness, some of his colleagues sensed a difference in him. Said Paul Scherer of Union Seminary:

> I'm something of a convert. The reason I was wary was I thought Niebuhr's emphasis on futility and frustration did not carry any aspect of grace. . . . Now he speaks with a new mellow note—a diapason—I think now he is a truly creative theologian.

And Niebuhr's summer neighbor, Bishop Angus Dun of Washington, D.C., wrote after Niebuhr's illness:

> Certainly those of us who have had an opportunity to know him well have realized that he is much more besides a really brilliant intellect. While reticent in a personal way, he is clearly sensitive to the needs of and problems of those around him and gives

> himself very generously when he can be of help. The quiet courage and faith he has shown in meeting his very burdensome illness is evidence of the reality of his own religious life.

As for this "reality of his own religious life," Niebuhr once answered a student's question:

> When I was sick and in despair I sometimes felt that God was close and I was at peace. But it didn't last. Between times I could not feel him.

Among such times were the months of what a doctor writing in the *New York State Health News* described as the "natural depression which follows . . . hemiplegia."[1] Niebuhr's own description while in the throes of it shows a remarkable objectivity:

> One of the troubles with this disease is that it leads to pretty serious depressions. My anxiety seems to become unsurmountable.

His anxiety, moreover, was enhanced by the brief but repeated relapses that also sometimes follow the onset of this form of illness. To a fellow sufferer he wrote:

> I know that these disappointments are worse than the first shock of the disease.

It was only, therefore, after the first half year of the illness that Niebuhr was able to write to a friend:

> I am gradually coming out of the "dark night of the soul" and the future looks brighter. . . . I won't be able to teach this fall. but I will be able to do some work.

Niebuhr's objectivity or self-transcendence was noted at the time by one of his doctors who waxed remarkably subjective about it:

> It was a rare privilege to work with Dr. Niebuhr last summer and it is gratifying that things went so well. I really believe that Dr. Niebuhr's success was due to his very rare qualities and very rare strength. It is his own greatness that made him a success in this undertaking as it has in others. He has an extraordinary

[1] N.Y. *State Health News,* December 1957: Dr. Donald A. Covalt.

> ability to face his own self objectively, with humility and lack of fear. He would not like my saying this, but I believe it to be true.

In corresponding with those worse off than himself Niebuhr's usual reticence was sometimes abrogated. To Herbert Elliston, for example, the brilliant editor of *The Washington Post*, who like Niebuhr had been stricken at the height of his powers, Niebuhr wrote:

> Perhaps X has forwarded my letter to her to you, but I thought so much about you that I want to write you additionally just to share some experiences of mine with you in the hope that they may be of some help. I don't think you ought to worry too much about having a depression because of your experiences. I am not an expert but I know that I was worried about this and found out subsequently that the bad circulation affects the "hypothalamus" in the brain which controls the emotions. I was, for instance, subject to crying after I dealt with even a minor emotional thing, such as expressing gratitude, and I found to my relief that this had a purely physiological cause.
>
> I know that the problems you face are very great. It is not a simple thing to be cut down from creativity to inactivity so suddenly. I found that I had to live partly on the hope that I would gain strength, and partly on the realization that this was quite out of my hands whether I would or not, and therefore that I'd better not hope too desperately for a convalescence which might not materialize. I have since found that if one gets even a moderate strength back one can be very happy with doing a moderate amount of work. I sincerely hope your experiences will be something like mine in that respect.

Elliston's experiences did come to be something like Niebuhr's in that respect: he returned to writing a weekly column and occasional editorials. But his original attack had been much worse than Niebuhr's—and when the relapse came, he died in his sleep.

Another form of activity Niebuhr continued to engage in was politics. All through the summer and fall of 1952 he was passionately concerned with the presidential election. Toward the end, he told James Loeb that he hoped that Stevenson, if elected, would choose Thomas K. Finletter as his Secretary of State. "But Reinie," Loeb said, "you're supposed to be the great Pessimist—and here you are already staffing Stevenson's Cabinet."

The television set given to Niebuhr by his friends in ADA was not only a source of political stimulation but by summer it had caused the theologian again to become what he had been in his boyhood: a baseball fan.

Another valued gift was presented by the Faculty and Directors of Union Seminary: an electric typewriter with a foot pedal so that Niebuhr could type despite the residual paralysis in his left arm and hand. On this machine Niebuhr pecked out letters full of typographical errors and warm feelings. To one:

> I feel like an old traveller who warns of pitfalls and tells of the end of the road. The one consolation is that these mild attacks are insurance against severe attacks which might be injurious to life. . . . But what a problem of spiritual patience it is. . . . At least I find it so.

The effect of this letter on its recipient was revealed in a note dictated to a mutual friend:

> To think that Niebuhr should show weakness, that is itself a comfort. I have felt somewhat weak myself . . . and have tried hard to think of Job and how he shouldered his burdens.

Niebuhr too had been thinking about Job, but from the theological more than the personal viewpoint. The Book of Job, he concluded in *Humanism and the Christian Faith,* is "a profoundly and wonderfully impious book" whose poetic section—as against the prose introduction and epilogue—raises two ultimate questions: the first, how shall we understand the contrast between man's grandeur and misery, and the second, why does meaningless suffering occur. (The two prose parts, on which Archibald MacLeish's *JB* is primarily based, Niebuhr feels are "a distinct let-down from the lofty poetic treatment of the eternal mysteries.")

Job's sufferings were both physical and spiritual and also the result of interaction between these two forms of suffering.

The interaction between body and mind had long interested Niebuhr on an intellectual level. Now he was unintentionally finding out even more about it, and the result was a heartfelt agreement with Paul Tillich's statement in *The Courage To Be,* that "in man nothing is 'merely biological' " nor is anything " 'merely spiritual' "; "every cell of his body participates in his freedom," and "every act of his spiritual creativity is nourished by his vital dynamics."

The Self and the Dramas of History was the book written during Niebuhr's illness, or as he said in the Preface, during "two years of enforced leisure." In it he tried to express the complexity of the mind-body interaction, but was forced to fall back on terms which he admitted were unthinkable. One was the resurrection of the body. This was a concept that Niebuhr had balked at during his Yale years. Now it appeared to him as "the stone rejected by the builders" that could form the foundation of the temple:

> the unthinkable idea of the resurrection of the body guards and supports the unthinkable but directly experienced . . . unity of the self as animal organism and as free spirit.

The human self, moreover, cannot fulfil itself within itself, but must move outward toward other persons and society:

> Therefore the death and resurrection of Christ is felt to be symbolic of the dying of self to its narrow self, that it may truly live.

The society, however, to which the individual devotes himself cannot provide all the means through which the self can truly live. As Niebuhr had said in the *Gifford Lectures*:

> The individual faces the eternal in every moment and in every action of his life; and he confronts the end of history with his own death. The dimension of his freedom transcends all social realities. His spirit is not fulfilled in even the highest achievements of history; his conscience is not eased by even the most unequivocal approbation of historical courts of justice; or need it be finally intimidated by historical condemnations. On the other hand, the individual life is meaningful only in its organic relation to historical communities, tasks and obligations. [It is therefore organically that] the individual self is grounded in a collective history as surely as it is based in a physical organism. Its ful-

fillment is not possible without the fulfillment of the whole drama, yet the fulfillment of the total drama offers no adequate completion of meaning for the unique individual.

In *The Self and the Dramas of History*, Niebuhr explicitly joined to the unthinkable concept of the resurrection of the body the further, and equally unthinkable, concept of the general resurrection:

> The resurrection of the individual is incredibly related to a "general resurrection which completes the whole human story, and which is associated with the "coming again" of the suffering Savior in triumph. . . . This hope implies that the antinomies of history will express themselves to the end but are not able finally to overcome the meaning of human existence. They are therefore not overcome by man's gradual triumph over nature. They grow with that triumph so that the most explicit evil, the "anti-Christ," appears just at the end of history. One need hardly analyze our current . . . perils of tyranny and atomic destruction to prove that this incredible hope for the end of history is more in accord with actual experience than the alternative hopes which have beguiled, and then disappointed, past generations.

Niebuhr's view of history has never been dependent on any firm conviction about whether or not life on this planet may some day cease because of a cooling or heating of the sun. As he said in a letter, April 25, 1957, "the world may or may not come to an end according to the speculation of the scientists." But whether it does or not, Niebuhr says it is important to continue thinking of "an eternity at the end of time" in addition to the "eternity over time." This dual symbol means that,

> if history is significant there must be not only intimations of its meaning within the flux of time [which would be eternity over time] but there must be a summary of its total meaning which presumably is only in God's mind and about which we speculate [which would be eternity at the end of time].

When a student wrote to Niebuhr asking him please to explicate his thoughts on eternity. Niebuhr answered:

> There is no simple answer to this as to other similiar questions, because Christianity has compounded Hebraic and Hellenic sym-

> bols. In Greek thought eternity is a simple proposition. It rests in the eternal structures through which time flows. Therefore the Hellenic-Johannine Gospel speaks of "eternal life." But the Hebraic thought is more wedded to time and therefore speaks of "everlasting life," which in literal terms would simply mean an infinite term of life. You can see that neither symbol is quite thinkable, though I think both are relevant in describing the eschatological overtones in all religious thought. I hope this doesn't make the opaque more obscure.

These eschatological overtones are necessary, Niebuhr thinks, for a valid perspective upon history, but he does not interpret them literally. For one thing, he says, no man can know for certain what happens after death or what is the ultimate purpose of human history. Indeed as early as the *Gifford Lectures* he had rocked the conventionally religious by insisting that it was

> unwise for Christians to claim any knowledge of either the furniture of heaven or the temperature of hell; or to be too certain about any details of the Kingdom of God in which history is consummated.

And his own admitted scepticism about these details extends today to all human "affirmations about ultimate judgment." As he wrote in a letter, in 1955,

> Karl Barth has recently turned universalist and believes that all people will ultimately be saved. I don't know upon what basis one can make these judgments, but I do know that the Biblical approach to the matter has emphasis on the decisions we make here and now. With that I will content myself and leave the rest to the literalists.

This here and now, he believes, has a dimension beyond what is immediately discernible. And it is in this connection that he interprets St. Paul's controversial statement that "if in this life only we had hoped in Christ we are of all men most miserable." For Niebuhr this means that "there is a religious, but not moral, answer to our moral dilemma. . . . The dilemma belongs to the permanent condition of sinful humanity, that 'our reach exceeds our grasp,' that Christ gives us a clue to the meaning which overarches all our meanings and refutes them; that we are bidden to undertake responsibilities the end and consequences we can not see and must bear burdens involving guilt and frustration which are particularly vexatious to citizens of a fortunate nation which had never before known real frustrations."

In addition to disputing the people who are certain they understand survival after death, Niebuhr also disputes those who are certain there is none. In regard to the former, he wrote in the *London Sunday Times* early in 1958, in an article entitled "Survival After Death,"

> the first question is . . . "survival of what?" Men have believed in the "soul's" survival after death in all civilizations and cultures. Indeed the belief is shared by both civilized and primitive man. But in all the millennia of human history there has been no evidence of such survival. The evidence allegedly supplied by the "spiritualists" is so tawdry and petty that, as one of our American religious philosophers put it: "This kind of evidence prompts the dismal conclusion that if men survive after death, their intellectual faculties are subject to rapid degeneration."[2]

On the other hand, Niebuhr continues, there is unquestionably "a dimension of value and meaning in the lives of our loved ones which death challenges but cannot annul." And in regard to the people who deny this because they are certain that death is the end of everything, bad as well as good, he recalls an episode of his Detroit days that the shy young minister did not record in *Leaves*:

> I was called to the bedside of an old reprobate woman who had been the madam of a bawdy house. When I asked her why she, who had never darkened the doors of a church, desired the ministries of religion, she replied, "I hope that if one dies one is really dead, but one can't be sure." She wanted some kind of insurance against a possible ultimate judgment, which proves that as far as we are concerned, the meaning of life which transcends our immediate life appears not so much as a comfort as a sense of judgment.

Niebuhr's own feeling about death was perhaps best expressed in the funeral prayer he delivered after his illness for a close friend:

[2] In his scepticism toward spiritualists, Niebuhr was more realistic than was the scientist, Freud, who, according to his biographer, Ernest Jones, was repeatedly taken in by them for a time.

> Our Father, before whom a thousand years are but as yesterday when it is past and as a watch in the night, we, who bring our years to an end like a tale that is told, worship thee . . . Thou redeemest our life from destruction and crowneth us with loving kindness . . . We thank thee that though our years are brief, thou savest our life from vanity by making us coworkers together with thee . . .
> We give thee thanks this day particularly for thy servant X who has been taken from our company to be with thee. In our sorrow and grief, we remember with gratitude all thy grace which was mediated through him. We thank thee for the quiet dignity of his spirit and for the unpretentious goodness which rebuked our vanities and brought us to our true selves. We remember the uncomplaining patience with which he bore his physical infirmities and out of weakness was made strong. We thank thee for his love; and his learning which made his love rich in all knowledge and discernment. . . .
> O God, the Lord over life and death, . . . we pray particularly for those who shared his life intimately and are so grievously stricken by this great loss: for his children and for her who was the partner of his life. Visit her with thy grace and in her lonely hours sustain her by the blessed memories of shared joys and sorrows of their life together, and by the blessed hopes which we have as disciples of the risen Lord . . .

The coming of death can be a tragedy but the facing of the inevitability of death can bring a new dimension to living. It can also bring a new dimension to religion. Said Niebuhr in a letter to a young couple who could not decide whether or not to offer religious instruction to their children:

> I don't think that children can be expected to have a full appreciation of the Christian faith until they confront the ultimate problem of both sin and death, and they confront the problem of sin in its ultimate form only when they know that there is a problem of forgiveness beyond the forgiveness of mother and father. I think this does not necessarily come at a conscious moment but grows implicitly in the deepening experiences of life. I think that the religion of children consists of gratitude and aspiration and so forth primarily, and I would not think it

> advisable to hasten the process of understanding . . . [On the other hand] my brother used to call attention to the danger of sentimentalizing religion for children to such a degree that we only talked about God as "kind to birdies and little children." . . . I am impressed by the fact that an adequate parental faith creates an environment which children gradually appropriate according to their experience.

But what about parents who have no religious faith, adequate or otherwise? If they are convinced atheists, Niebuhr believes, they "shouldn't teach a religion which they do not themselves share to their children." On the other hand,

> if parents are not convinced atheists, if they have what most modern parents have, a kind of vague faith and a vague willingness to have more faith, they ought to expose their children to religion.

Niebuhr had learned, through painful and honest observation of himself and the wider scene, why man needs the grace of forgiveness. But grace, according to the Bible, is power as well as forgiveness, and in his debility Niebuhr learned why man stands in need of that as well. For debility brings with it its own temptations. One is to use it as a shield against risk and possible failure: if one stops trying one can never fail. And failure, for the first time in his life, was dogging his attempts at creativity. When he first started writing again, after his illness, some of the articles came home dragging rejection slips behind them. Niebuhr did not question the editors' judgment; he simply kept on trying.

When he then started teaching again failure seemed to be dogging him there too. His voice was weak—and fatigue made him reel. But the worst aspect of all, he confessed to his wife, was that "the students don't ask questions the way they used to. They don't challenge me. It must be that I'm not challenging them." It did not take Mrs. Niebuhr long to discover that the students were simply, and temporarily, trying to spare their weary professor by stifling their questions until such time as his vigor returned. When it did return the questions did too, not only in the classroom but in the halls and in his office. Eventually Niebuhr went back on full schedule, though no longer a superhuman one. In retrospect he told a young colleague:

> What a foolish thing it is, when your job is to educate, not to leave enough time for students to come see you. I realize now that I didn't give them enough time before I took sick. The warning signal should have been when they started apologizing for bothering me. They shouldn't apologize. But I was progressively drawn into doing more and more, travelling more and more. Some good friend would say, "oh come on out and talk to us." It was so hard to refuse.

It was hard to refuse, he also admitted, because the invitations were enhancements to the original sin of pride. "I am not as brash as I used to be," he now says, "but neither am I as creative." For decades he had been teaching that pride cometh before a fall; now, paradoxically, he was emphasizing that pride cometh also before a rise: that if there is not a minimum of egocentricity, there will be no ambition, and if there is no ambition, there will be no accomplishment. Niebuhr had come thus to agree with Alexander Pope that "ambition is the glorious fault of angels and of gods." Fault though it often is, it is also often the prerequisite for courageous action. In *Discerning the Signs of the Times,* right after World War II, Niebuhr had asked:

> How shall we judge the great statesman who gives a nation its victorious courage by articulating its only partly conscious and implicit resources of fortitude; and who mixes the most obvious forms of personal and collective pride and arrogance with this heroic fortitude? If [Churchill] had been a timid man, a more cautious soul, he would not have sinned so greatly, but neither would he have wrought so nobly.

Niebuhr's growing tolerance toward certain forms of pride has led some of his colleagues to insist that Niebuhr now believes in a form of innocent pride.[3] Niebuhr disputes the term. Pride is rarely innocent, he says, though

[3] In the Gifford Lectures Niebuhr had castigated the vanity of beautiful women as a form of pride; today he notes the need for a minimal amount of vanity as a form of feminine mental health (in mental hospitals a sign of returning normality has often been the unkempt apathetic female's first request for a mirror.) Thus ambition —and even aggressiveness—seems to join anxiety as being a source of both creativity and destructiveness. As Niebuhr wrote in *The New Republic,* February 27, 1961, "The dynamics of selfhood are always in tension between the push of ambition and

without it man may not dare sufficiently. As he wrote in his chapter in *The Search for America*, 1959, "aggressiveness . . . cannot be eradicated from [man's] will without destroying his creative potentialities in the process."

As for Niebuhr's own creative potential, after his illness, opinions differ. One teaching colleague, watching students respond to Niebuhr, says that he is constantly reminded of Oliver Wendell Holmes' remark that "all education is moral." And a hard-bitten politician says, "Somehow when Reinie is preaching, I want to cry; but when he is through, I want to get out there and fight." Yet some of the more idealistic students complain about Niebuhr's insistence that people not allow themselves to be carried away by illusion: "How can we ever tell where the limits of the possible are, unless we try to do the seemingly impossible?" And they particularly resent being advised by a Christian theologian to follow a prudential middle way. These students and others, nonetheless, overflowed the Seminary's largest hall, in May of 1960, when Niebuhr gave the noonday lecture, and their standing ovation was so prolonged that Niebuhr was forced to return from his front row seat to the podium to take a curtain call. At the sight of the moisture beading his brow, the applause increased rather than waned, and Niebuhr finally was able to end it only by charging, head down, from the room.

As for the writing, his facility has returned to the financially measurable point where he is paid as much as $2500 for a single short article. And qualitatively speaking, his four new books have been received by the experts and the public with as much excitement—pro and con—as were his previous books. One doctor who heard that a small-stroke victim was writing a book could not believe that the author was covering new material. Another doctor, who knows Niebuhr personally, was willing to believe it, but still marvelled.[4] Perhaps Niebuhr's decision to keep writing was like that of Samuel Johnson who also recovered from a series of small strokes. Johnson, to test his remaining powers, set himself the

---

the pull of creative responsibilities. Without the latter, ambition may become purely self-regarding and self-defeating. But without ambition the creative pull of responsibility cannot take hold."

[4] Said a stranger who met Niebuhr socially: "His attitude toward his illness is so wonderfully honest. He is neither defensive nor self-pitying. It is simply a fact, together with other facts he clearly considers to be of greater importance."

task of composing a sonnet in Greek. On its completion, he decided that it was a dreadful sonnet; but then he concluded that if he had sufficient judgment to see that it was dreadful, then surely he was well enough to keep on writing.

Niebuhr is not only writing books that are given enthusiastic reviews, but he is writing enthusiastic reviews of other people's books. In the *New York Post,* Niebuhr said, for example, about Elmer Davis' last volume:

> I was glad . . . to discover something in the book which did not win my hearty assent. Otherwise the concurrence would have been embarrassing and Davis would have seemed much too wise for a mortal man.

And in letters to writers who have sent him their books, his praise is unstinted. "A superb job," he wrote to one; and to another who had sent merely an outline, "I trust you to do anything you set out to do." To James Wechsler who had sent him a prepublication copy of *The Age of Suspicion,* 1953:

> I spent the entire day yesterday reading your autobiography, putting everything else aside as I became more and more entranced. . . . You have given us about the best description of the political and spiritual situation in our country in the last decades. I think your book is invaluable as history as well as good autobiography, and I hope it will have a very wide sale.

To students his generous comments on their written assignments are even more precious than the high marks he tends to give. A typical example: "A-minus: Very good, though I naturally do not agree with much of this." The same mark of A-minus appeared on a paper with whose contents Niebuhr did agree: "You speak with wisdom on many issues. But a little lacking in organization. I like your general approach." The lowest mark in the class was a B-minus; the comment: "I find the conjunction, 'loyalty to God and loyalty to neighbor' of no help when we have to choose between two conflicting loyalties . . . and between two evils."

Niebuhr was not only speaking words of approval; he was also resisting the temptation to speak words of disapproval. Professor Robert E.

Fitch, Dean of the Pacific School of Religion in Berkeley, California, reports one such occasion:

> During the second semester of 1952-53 I was teaching at Union until Niebuhr should get well. However he did show up occasionally at a thesis seminar conducted by John Bennett. One day . . . a student was making a report of Niebuhr's handling of certain book reviews. Then he came to a review by Niebuhr of one of Brunner's books. The student remarked that this book contained a "fallacy" which Niebuhr had severely castigated elsewhere, but that he said nothing about it in [this] review. . . . Niebuhr owned up with a grin that he had kept silent on the offending item, and that he had preferred this time to speak a word of encouragement.

Niebuhr's mitigation of his own disapproval extends sometimes, ex post facto, into the past. As he told the Columbia interviewer:

> Perhaps I ought to confess . . . that I'm not as sure as I was in my Detroit days that Henry Ford was quite as bad as I thought him to be. . . . [Nonetheless] contrasting Ford's idealism without self-knowledge and Fred Butzell's idealism and shrewd self-knowledge awakened me from my moralistic slumber.

Niebuhr's desire "to speak a word of encouragement" in regard to other people is so strong as to be sometimes predictable. One university dean no longer writes to Niebuhr for references regarding former students because he knows from experience that these will be laudatory. On the other hand, when Niebuhr wishes to be negative, in person or in writing, he can still do it with the old forcefulness. A student recently asked him what the point of moral striving was if man's best efforts would always be tainted by sin. Niebuhr's eyes flashed blue lightning: "It's our duty to act responsibly in history." And Niebuhr still rises to prophetic wrath when confronted by indifference or irresponsibility on the part of the young or anyone else. "The greatest illusion of all is to think that life consists in getting as much for yourself as possible."

By and large, however, he likes the new generation. He likes the way they marry young and take on early the responsibility for a family. He also likes the way some of them challenge the values of the status quo. What distresses him in fact is not the rebellion of some of the Beat but the apathy of some of the well-behaved. This apathy stems in part, he told Peter Loeb, the Harvard son of his old friends, from the fact that "our domestic problems appear to be tolerably solved and our foreign problems appear to be insoluble."[5]

Niebuhr, himself an ex-tamed cynic, is aware that young people today do not so much need to have their idealism tempered as to have it aroused. To them he says, "There must be a passion for justice." But some students nonetheless continue to look upon Niebuhr's passionate writings of the past and present with the scorn that only the very young can feel. To them the words of T. S. Eliot might well apply: "Writers are remote from us because we *know* so much more than they did. Precisely, and *they* are that which we know."

Certainly Niebuhr's basic precepts have permeated the secular as well as the religious world. The historian, James McGregor Burns, wrote in the *New York Times Magazine,* August 31, 1957 that

> the modern thinker . . . has learned, partly from the teachings of men like Reinhold Niebuhr and partly from his own researches, that man is a complicated mixture of motives and attitudes, a mixture of compassion and egotism, of nobility and malice . . .

And the Princeton professor of religion, Paul Ramsey, wrote in the *New York Times Book Review* three years later that "the convictions that [Niebuhr] voiced have now become common coin."

Niebuhr's views about man have not changed since the time of the Gifford Lectures but today he voices them with more humor. "The self" he quotes a great mystic as saying, "is like an onion which it is possible to peel off layer upon layer". . . Niebuhr then adds that "the self is indeed like an onion in another way; for the more layers you peel off by conscious contrivance, the more pungent the vegetable becomes."

This added dimension of humor appears in almost every lecture and every sermon, and is often directed against himself. In James Chapel in 1959, for example, he said:

[5] "Holy Smoke," said Peter Loeb afterwards. "I knew Reinie could *write* epigrams but I didn't know he could just up and *say* them." Often Niebuhr does up and say them; but like smooth pebbles on the beach, they have usually been rolled around in his mind for some time. Another near-epigram he came out with in conversation concerned an old friend whose two children had suffered mental breakdowns. "It wasn't anything he *did,*" Niebuhr said sadly, "it was what he *was,* that was damaging to the children."

> When one is young it is natural to be polemical. As one grows older one wonders whether one is less polemical because one has grown in wisdom or because one has diminished in energy.[6]

And in class he tells, as an example of the subtlety of the power drive, about the day he wanted to go for a walk with his then-small daughter who did not wish to stir. After he had explained the values of fresh air and exercise, she finally accompanied him and they had what he thought was a fine time. On the way home he said, "Now aren't you glad you decided to come along?" She turned a pair of blue eyes, much like his own, upon him. "I didn't 'decide,'" she said balefully. "You were just bigger."

His humor extends also to the foibles of other people. Of Sir Isaiah Berlin whose malicious wit is famous, Niebuhr says, "I always tell him I want to be the *last* to leave a tea party at which he is a fellow-guest." And like Berlin, Niebuhr knows the value of deft exaggeration. When Bishop Scarlett mentioned, of a mutual acquaintance, that "no one has gone farther on the brains he has," Niebuhr quoted him as having said, "No one has gone so far on so few brains." When Scarlett expostulated, Niebuhr answered, "I know it isn't what you said, but my way makes a much better story."

What Niebuhr himself says still has the power to arouse expostulation on the part of others. In 1959, one subscriber to *Christianity and Crisis* wrote in to complain about Niebuhr's "peculiarly nasty and supercilious chortling over Senator Knowland's defeat . . . We have more than enough political cowardice. It really doesn't need the encouragement it might receive from people who write nonsense draped in a mantle of Christian authority."

Niebuhr did not reply. "I have learned," he says cheerfully, "not to expect fairness in any polemical exchange."

This is just as well, for several of the debates in which Niebuhr engaged after his illness, like those before it, concerned matters about which feelings ran high and debate often made the two sides even less reconcilable than they were before.

[6] In the mid-thirties, humor did not characteristically appear in a Niebuhr sermon. According to Charles Burton Marshall, "The structure . . . was rigorous—permitting no moments of diversion from the line of reasoning, and employing no flourishes of wit . . ."

24

But Still Fighting

The three kinds of controversy in which Niebuhr continues to be engaged are those in which he criticizes someone else's ideas and is not answered, those in which his ideas are criticized and he does not answer, and those in which there is a lively exchange.

One of the liveliest exchanges has been with the dean of European theologians, Karl Barth. Extending over thirty years, it started by pen in the late twenties, continued face to face at the World Council of Churches Amsterdam meeting in the forties, and was climaxed, by pen, in the early sixties. Its poignancy was increased by the fact that Niebuhr has been outspokenly grateful to Barth for many insights of the latter's "Neo-Orthodoxy," and by the fact that Barth, according to the Swiss theologian, Oscar Cullmann, has "considered Niebuhr a worthy opponent."[1] (When Barth does not consider a theologian a worthy opponent, this can be made painfully evident: "verbal sadism," was the description by an American theologian of Barth's treatment of a European colleague during the pre-Amsterdam discussion meetings.)

Niebuhr's appreciation for Barth started ahead of that of most Americans because of Niebuhr's fluency in German, and in 1928, Niebuhr, still partly in the liberal camp, favorably reviewed the first of Barth's books to be translated into English:

> Barth continues to look upon the brutalities of history with a wholesome contrition . . . In so far as Barth reintroduces the note of tragedy in religion (as it condemns all achievements of history by bringing them into juxtaposition to the "holiness of

[1] The Reverend Imre Bertalan quotes Cullmann in this regard.

> God") it is a wholesome antidote to the superficial optimism of most current theology.

For Barth the "holiness of God" meant that "one can *not* speak of God simply by speaking of man in a loud voice." And during this period, in successive editions of his famous *Commentary on Romans,* Barth was urging that God be "distinguished qualitatively from men and from everything human and . . . never identified with anything which we can name, or experience, or conceive, or worship."

In the twenties and thirties, however, the American religious liberals were busily identifying God with numerous things they could name: with Love, with Reason, with Democracy, or even in some cases with the League of Nations. Basic to their point of view was what Barth, in a later heated exchange with Niebuhr in *Christian Century,* 1948-9, termed "this dreadful, godless, ridiculous opinion that man is the Atlas who is destined to bear the dome of heaven upon his shoulders."[2] According to Barth, it is God, not man, who created and sustains the world, and the Bible is "the record not of *man*'s correct thoughts about God, but of *God's* correct thoughts about *man*" (how man is in a position to know this is one question Niebuhr raises). Said Barth in *The Christian Century:*

> The word of God, the Holy Spirit, God's free choice, God's grace and judgment, the Creation, the Reconciliation, the Kingdom, the Sanctification, the Congregation . . . [are] the indication of *events,* of concrete, once-for-all, unique divine *actions,* of the majestic mysteries of God that cannot be resolved into any pragmatism.

The pragmatism of the religious liberals was to interpret the Bible in such a way that man's reason could make sense of it, and man's ethics could make use of it: mystery, in short, was banished in favor of meaning, not the symbolic meaning of myth but the specific meaning of a working blueprint. Niebuhr too, in the late twenties and early thirties, was critical of the religious liberals, especially their teaching that Jesus was "the good man of Galilee" whose example was a blueprint that if only followed by everyone would lead to perfection of the individual and peace for society.

[2] Niebuhr's side of the debate has been reprinted in *Applied Christianity* edited by D. B. Robertson.

Niebuhr's vantage point of criticism at that time was his qualified Marxism. But Barth's insistence that *all* man-made schemes of society stood under God's judgment helped Niebuhr in turn to criticize this same Marxism. "I awakened from my Socialist slumber," he recalls, partly as a result of reading Barth, together with Augustine and Pascal, and partly as a result of national and international events. As he wrote in the Living Library Volume:

> It is difficult to know whether the criticism of both liberal and Marxist views of human nature and history was prompted by a profounder understanding of the Biblical faith; or whether this understanding was prompted by the refutation of the liberal and Marxist faith by the two world wars and the encounter of a liberal culture with two idolatrous tyrannies, first Nazism and then Communism.

Barth's personal attitude toward Nazism was to resign his Chair at Bonn University one year after Hitler came to power and to settle instead in Switzerland whence he continued to attack fascism in its various forms. These criticisms, combined with Barth's emphasis upon every moment of history being a moment of judgment, encouraged many a German Protestant heroically to resist Nazism. Niebuhr, in the *Christian Century* debate, gives Barth credit for the crisis theology which made "great contributions . . . to the struggle against tyranny in recent decades. Its interpretation of the Christian faith helped to create a heroic heedlessness, a disposition to follow the scriptural injunction, 'Be careful in nothing.' "

At the same time, however, Barth's strictures against liberalism and Marxism were being adopted by the reactionary forces within Germany, including the Nazis, to strengthen their own position. Their claim was that Hitler was Germany's savior from all these Reds—Reds being defined not only as Marxists and liberals but anyone to the left of themselves, including the Social Democrats who were both as anti-Communist as they and far more effective in persuading other people to be anti-Communist. Said Niebuhr ruefully in 1934:

> As one who bears a few wounds from doing battle against complacent liberalism, I must confess that this appropriation of

> Barthian thought by reaction almost persuades me to return to the liberal camp as a repentant prodigal.

But not yet.

Instead he included Barth's neo-Orthodoxy, together with liberalism and Marxism, as idea-systems from which he had gleaned important insights but whose basic presuppositions he rejected. He therefore has resisted attempts to bracket his thought with Barth's, calling his own view "Pauline realism."[3]

Another of the major differences between Niebuhr and Barth has been their attitude toward the secular world, both in terms of learning from it and of the Church's relation to it. Barth, says Niebuhr, "has sought to dispense with all non-Biblical sources of judgment," while Niebuhr wishes the Church to pay serious attention to "any norms which come to us out of the broad sweep of a classical, European or modern cultural history." And Barth emphasizes not, as Niebuhr does, what man can do in history, but what God has already done. According to Barth, God through Christ has already "robbed sin, death, the devil and hell of their power and has already vindicated divine and human justice in His person."

Characteristically, therefore, Barth's address at Amsterdam was reprinted under the title, "No Christian Marshall Plan," and in it he insisted that the Church has no "systems of economic and political principles to offer the world." Niebuhr's answer, which initiated the *Christian Century* debate (October 27, 1948), was pointedly entitled "We Are Men And Not God." Of Barth's theology he said that although it contains "a wholesome warning against the pat schemes of Christian moralists . . . and [has] resulted in a very powerful witness to Christ in the hour of crisis . . . perhaps [it] is constructed too much for the great crises of history. It seems to have no guidance for a Christian statesman of our day . . . It can fight the devil if he shows both horns and both cloven feet. But it refuses to make discriminating judgments about good and evil if the devil shows only one horn or half of a cloven foot . . . Yesterday . . . many of the Christian leaders of Germany . . . discovered that the church may be an ark in which to survive a flood. Today they seem so enamored of this

[3] James Bissett Pratt, for example, in *The Religious Liberals Reply*, lumped Niebuhr's thought together with Barth's in what Pratt called "the new SuperNaturalism."

special function of the church that they have decided to turn the ark into a home on Mount Ararat and live in it perpetually."

Barth did not think this attack by Niebuhr was fair. His rebuttal, however, was not without friendliness or humor:

> It is obvious that, so far as Niebuhr is concerned, I did not express myself clearly. I clearly did not succeed in expressing my quite simple thought and quite simple purpose in such a way that my meaning as it travelled from my brain and manuscript through the ether to the ear and thought-world of Niebuhr, conveyed what I intended. When I read his exposition, I cannot help recalling the concave mirror in which I recently saw my reflection in the Musée Crévin in Paris, and did not know whether to laugh or cry.

Niebuhr's apparent lack of understanding indicated to Barth the depth of the problem of communication between persons and groups who held such differing views of the Bible. In Barth's view the Anglo-Saxons, including Niebuhr, were entirely wrong in their presumption that they can "theologize on their own account . . . and quote the Bible according to choice." In contrast, Niebuhr's view of how the Bible should be treated appeared in a defense he made of some aspects of theological liberalism in *The Christian Century*, May 24, 1956:

> We are in danger of sacrificing one of the great achievements of 'liberal' theology. That was the absolute honesty with which it encouraged the church to examine the scriptural foundations of its faith. This honesty involved not only loyalty to the truth but also fidelity to the standards of the whole of modern culture, which rightly insisted that no facts of history could be exempted from historical scrutiny in the name of faith. Christianity was a historical religion. It rested upon facts of history as interpreted by faith. But the faith would have to be profound enough to remain secure even though peripheral myths with which former ages surrounded the truth of faith [were exploded]. In short, this honesty toward the scriptural foundations of the faith was not only an act of loyalty toward the whole enterprise of modern culture but it was also a method of purifying the Christian faith. For this honesty made it imperative for the

> believer to accept Jesus as the Christ because the revelation of God validated itself to him existentially . . .

This was by no means the first time Niebuhr had insisted that "no facts of history could be exempted from historical scrutiny" whether these reinforced what appeared in the Bible, or contradicted it. In the Gifford Lectures, for example, he had written that "Barth's belief that the moral life of man would possess no valid principle of guidance if the Ten Commandments had not introduced such principles by revelation is as absurd as it is unscriptural."

In addition to being exposed to historical scrutiny, the Bible, Niebuhr insisted, should also be exposed to the test of individual and group experience, or in other words, that "the revelation of God validate itself . . . existentially." In regard to the ecumenical movement, for example, he had denied "that the Church as Church can establish the authority of the Gospel. That must be self-authenticating in our experience." But it was not until 1960, in an article of the second *Christian Century* series on *How My Mind Has Changed In The Last Ten Years*, that the self-styled "repentant prodigal" admittedly returned, in large part, to the liberal fold:

> When I find neo-orthodoxy turning into sterile orthodoxy or a new Scholasticism, I find that I am a liberal at heart, and that many of my broadsides at liberalism were indiscriminate.

The debate with Barth, meanwhile, had continued. In Niebuhr's view Barth had moved the pole of God and the Bible so far from the pole of man and history that the dialectic between them was snapped. Worthy as Barth's view had been in the peaks of crisis, it offered insufficient guidance for "the foothills where most of life is lived." Particularly disastrous, Niebuhr felt, was the neutralism it encouraged in the long range struggle between the free world and the Communists. Said Niebuhr in the last, and unanswered, section of the 1949 *Christian Century* debate:

> One cannot deny that much of what passes for Christianity in the Western world is no more than a simple confidence that God is our ally in our fight with communism as he was in our fight with Nazism. And isn't it nice that God is always on our side! Let us not forget to pay tribute to Barth's influence . . . in extricating Christian faith from the idolatries of our day.

But let us also, he said, not follow Barth's inclination "to regard the difference between communism and the so-called democratic world as insignificant." For "we are men and not God, and the destiny of civilizations depends upon our decisions in the 'nicely calculated less and more' of good and evil in political institutions." Sometimes these decisions lie between two evils; in politics, Niebuhr said, we must be prepared to "use evil in every moment . . . to hold worse evil in check." Indeed this choice between evils may be the most crucial choice we make, since a choice between goods is less hazardous and a choice between a good and an evil is less lonely.

When the Russians bloodily repressed the brave Hungarian rebellion in October, 1956, there was no word of reproach from Karl Barth who, before then, had written rather glowingly of the situation in Hungary. Niebuhr wrote a provocative article entitled, "Why is Karl Barth Silent About Hungary?" But Barth remained silent until 1958 when he published his "Letter to a Pastor in the German Democratic Republic," i.e., East Germany.[4] In it he referred to "a well known American theologian" who had asked "Why is Karl Barth Silent About Hungary?" In Barth's opinion this theologian was

> a hard boiled politician safe in his castle [who] as is customary with politicians who lead an opponent onto slippery ice, wished either to force me to profess his own brand of primitive anti-communism or to expose me as a secret pro-communist, and thus in one way or another to discredit me as a theologian.

Niebuhr, needless to say, was not silent in return. In *The Christian Century*, February 11, 1959 he wrote:

> Barth . . . is certainly neither a "primitive anti-communist" nor a "secret pro-communist." He is merely a very eminent theologian, trying desperately to be impartial in his judgments. The price of this desperation is of course moral irrelevance.

In Barth's Letter to the East German Pastor there is criticism of communism, but it is balanced, and perhaps over-balanced, by his criticism of the American way of life which he equates with self-indulgence and

[4] This Letter is now available in book form, with a valuable introduction by Robert McAfee Brown, as "How to serve God in a Marxist land."

complacency. Whereas the Communists have open totalitarianism, he says, the West has creeping totalitarianism.

Barth therefore warns the East Germans against praying to be relieved from the various forms of Communist oppression under which they are suffering lest these "useful scourges" be replaced by the "fleshpots of Egypt" and lest their church's purification through suffering be replaced by "liberation in accordance with the ideas of Adenauer."

"There," said Niebuhr, "is the old dilemma of the pure prophet again . . . the dilemma is so deep that I would prefer to let the eminent theologian stew in it for a while, at least until he realizes that he is not the only prophet of the Lord. Barth is a man of talent to the point of genius. But even a genius cannot escape the dilemma that the price of absolute purity is irrelevance and that the price of relevance is the possible betrayal of capricious human loves and hates even in the heart of a man of God."

And in the May, 1960, *Christian Century* article Niebuhr cut the final tie between himself and Barth:

> I record these developments without too much animus because Barth has long since ceased to have any effect on my thought. . . . What seventeenth century Lutheran orthodoxy did to Luther in a century, Barth managed to do to his own thought in a few decades.

If this latter comment stems from lack of animus, the reader can scarcely avoid wondering what comment might have stemmed from animus.

Niebuhr's debate on the subject of the Bible has continued, not with Barth, but with the American Fundamentalists.[5]

Answer to Niebuhr from the Fundamentalists has come from many sources. The most searching and inclusive was that of Professor Edward J. Carnell whose book, *The Theology of Reinhold Niebuhr,* was published in 1951. In it, like Father Weigel, Professor Carnell deplored Niebuhr's questioning of "authority," and, like Barth, he deplored Niebuhr's questioning that the whole of the theological task centers on the

[5] Billy Graham is one of these (see Chapter 25). Niebuhr said in *Life,* "Graham's appeal to the scripture [is] in terms which negate all the achievements of Christian historical scholarship. Graham admits that success eluded him until he could say merely, 'The Bible says.' "

Scripture. Said Carnell, "An undercurrent of scepticism runs through the entire theology of Niebuhr," and Niebuhr's "view of the person of Jesus is sheer blasphemy." Carnell therefore brackets Niebuhr not, as some religious liberals still do, with neo-Orthodoxy, but with unqualified liberalism:

> For both liberal and Niebuhr . . . the Bible is authoritative only at those points where there shines through a clarification of an experience gained earlier.

That this experience, or its interpretation, can be a faulty guide, Niebuhr admits. There is in his approach to the Bible a recognition of the ever-present possibility of sin and error. There is in it also, however, the hope of an ever-present means of correcting sin and error which does not exist when people simply open their minds like baby birds and swallow down whatever Biblical text some religious authority chooses to feed them. In the Living Library Volume, Niebuhr therefore writes:

> Professor Carnell is concerned to know upon what basis one can maintain the absoluteness of the Christian faith while recognizing the relativity of any formulation of the meaning of the faith and the corruption of the experience to which it may be subject. My answer is that the faith proves its absoluteness precisely where its insights make it possible to detect the relativity of the interpretations and to question the validity of any claim, including our own, that we have been redeemed. At those points it is proved that faith has discerned and is in contact with the "true" God and not with some idol of our imagination.

On the other hand, Carnell credits Niebuhr with "intellectual honesty and . . . personal integrity," noting that "most theologians who agree with Niebuhr . . . are too timid to come right out and say so. Niebuhr at least is not."

Nor is Carnell timid about coming right out and accusing Niebuhr not merely of blasphemy but of condoning what Carnell calls "self-controlled sensualism." Niebuhr, he says, by seeking "to explain sin *psychologically* rather than *theologically*" ends up in the position of sympathizing with "the psychology of the one indulging." This does not mean that Niebuhr is a libertine—but that he is too tolerant of sexual peccadillos because he does not see that all sins, even the mildest, are *"a transgression of the objective law of God."*[6] Says Carnell:

> While it cannot easily be gainsaid that Niebuhr has succeeded in making a profound contribution toward explaining the elements involved in the decisions of sensualism . . . there are yet reasons to believe that his final conclusions are extremely deficient in Christian content . . . Existentialism seems able to process only the profligate . . . while the Bible indicts all who transgress the law, however selective their sins may be. It is conceivable on Niebuhr's conclusions, therefore, that one could decide for fornication with moderation and respectability, indulging in non-marital intercourse with the same restraint and imperturbability that he would if eating or drinking.

Niebuhr, in turn, has been anything but imperturbable about sensuality. He defines it as one of the serious corruptions of man's freedom. This freedom, furthermore, Niebuhr conjectures, may have stemmed biologically from man's sexuality which is unique in nature. For of all the animals, man is the only one with the freedom to decide when, where, and with whom to make love, or whether not to make love at all. The sex impulse, therefore, may become an expression of man's freedom at its loftiest or its lowest.

At its loftiest, Niebuhr said in *Christian Realism and Political Problems,* the sex impulse can be an expression not only of love but of agape:

> The commandment to love the neighbor as the self must finally culminate in the individual experience in which one self seeks to penetrate deeply into the mystery of the other self and yet stand in reverence before a mystery which he has no right to penetrate. This kind of love is a matter of law in the sense that the essential nature of man, with his indeterminate freedom, requires that human relations should finally achieve such an intimacy. But it is also a matter of grace because no sense of obligation can provide the imagination and forebearance with which this is accomplished. Such intimacy is of course closely related to sacrificial love, for the intermingling of life with life predisposes to sacrificial abandonment of the claims of the self for the needs of the other.

[6] Compared to other theologians, Niebuhr is very sparing in his use of italics.

> If the intimacy of personal friendship, in which life is interwoven with life, is one of the pinnacles of *Agape* it must follow that a sexual partnership has a natural basis for such *Agape* far beyond other partnerships. The sexual union as a parable, symbol, and basis for *Agape* has been little appreciated in Christian thought.

At its lowest, the sexual impulse may not only be an attempt to escape from human freedom by submerging the self in one of the self's vitalities, but it may also be an expression of inordinate self-centeredness or sin. Niebuhr's disapproval of casual intimacies rests in part upon the tendency for the partner to be treated as a thing or *it* rather than as a person or *thou*. Niebuhr who has done his share of pastoral counseling says that the male of the species is more deadly than the female in this regard, more likely to avow affection or promise fidelity in order to achieve his own fulfillment, and then emotionally or literally absconding from concomitant responsibility.

It is, therefore, within the framework of marriage, Niebuhr believes, that the sexual impulse can best become the foundation of a "covenant." This solemn agreement between two persons not only tends to change one or both of them but also to set in motion new events, like the arrival of children, which are not reversible. As with the covenants of the Bible, marriage is an agreement which rests upon the honesty and integrity of each partner and upon the loyalty that exists between them.

For Niebuhr honesty, integrity and loyalty are key and related words. Honesty and integrity might even be defined as a form of loyalty—loyalty to the self's highest aspects—while loyalty to another person over the years involves not only honesty and integrity but that highest aspect of the self which is the grace of forgiveness. In all events, Niebuhr distinguishes sharply between a one time peripheral lapse which may be forgiven, and the "perpetual or habitual defiances of the basic loyalties."

Niebuhr also occasionally jokes about monogamy in theory, blaming the missionary influence in Africa for the fact that some native chiefs have now divorced all but one of their wives, thus leaving the others to starve. But when confronted with news of trouble in the marriage of friends, Niebuhr is visibly distressed. He is well aware of the hazards to marriage in the modern world and he recognizes that its dissolution is sometimes necessary: "A relation rooted in love is maintained by grace and can become intolerable when love is lacking." At the same time he points out that if a marriage can, by grace or effort or both, survive in the modern world, "it is likely to be a more ideal marriage than the 'traditional' one."

Critical as Niebuhr is of modern promiscuity, he is equally critical of some of the religious critics of this promiscuity. "In the field of sex, particularly, the morbid rigor of the law-enforcer has a secret affiinity with some of the same forces which actuated the law violator." There must, he says, both be

> strictness in the maintenance of a standard and sympathy for the offender. It will be remembered that Jesus rebuked the persons who were punishing the woman taken in adultery with the telling remark, "Let him who is without sin cast the first stone." That remark was particularly appropriate in restraining the law-upholders in a case involving a violation of the sexual code. It calls attention both to the universality of guilt, though in various shades, and to the possible relation of the zeal of the law-upholder to the hidden or suppressed violation of the standard in his own life.

This standard, in modern times, ranges all the way from the condemnation of even mental lusting, in what Niebuhr calls "the perfectionist love-ethic of the New Testament," to the attitude of the Kinsey Report which Niebuhr calls a "consistent naturalism and its logical fruit, a crude hedonism, in terms of which the achievement of orgasm becomes the *summum bonum* of his value scheme." This attitude toward orgasm, which Lionel Trilling has paraphrased as "the more the merrier," is based not only upon a tacit value scheme but upon other presuppositions of which Kinsey, according to Niebuhr and Trilling, was not sufficiently aware.[7] As Niebuhr wrote in *Christianity and Crisis*, January 11, 1954:

> I objected not to the nature of the inquiry but to the ridiculous and ignorant presuppositions which informed it and determined its conclusions. Kinsey is so naive in his approach to human and historical problems that he seems unaware of the fact that the

[7] Trilling's classic essay on Kinsey appears in a volume of his essays, *The Liberal Imagination*, and also in *An Analysis of the Kinsey Reports* edited by Donald Porter Geddes. Both books are available in paperback, the former published by Anchor and the latter by Mentor.

> presuppositions of an inquiry, in any historical study, do determine the results even more than the data . . . The whole performance is informed by such an ignorance of the complexity of every human problem . . . that one must come to the conclusion that an apprenticeship in investigating gall wasps is not a sufficient preparation for guiding mankind in a very complex problem of relating the strong and biologically based sexual impulse to the whole range of creative human aspirations.

Some of Kinsey's fellow scientists, however, approved the inquiry and its presuppositions. Said Dr. Clyde Kluckhohn in his *New York Times* book review on September 13, 1953, "This is science, serious science, and science in the grand style." Yet other fellow scientists did not approve. Dr. Karl Menninger, for example, wrote in *The Saturday Review*, September 26, 1953:

> As for an orgasm being the chief criterion of sexuality, everyone knows that one orgasm can differ from another as widely as do kisses. A kiss by Judas is one thing, a kiss by Venus is another, and a kiss by a loving mother still a third. The orgasm of a terrified soldier in battle, that of a loving husband in the arms of his wife, that of a desperate homosexual trying to prove his masculinity, and that of a violent . . . brute raping a child are not the same phenomena. . . . They may add up to the same numbers on an adding machine, but they don't add up to significant totals in human life.

Niebuhr's attacks on Kinsey—he was the only theologian asked to contribute to the *Analysis of the Kinsey Reports*—were never answered directly by Kinsey. Such ignoring by a scientist of a theologian's criticism seems quite typical in the twentieth century. Erich Fromm, the psychoanalyst, for example, has never answered any of Niebuhr's frequent published criticisms, and in a letter said, "I have never answered Niebuhr, nor have I read him thoroughly enough to give a responsible reaction to his thought."

One answer by a scientifically oriented writer did come to Niebuhr—from beyond the grave. H. G. Wells, whom Niebuhr had met in London in 1923 during the first Sherwood Eddy travelling seminar, was subsequently attacked by Niebuhr, first for what Niebuhr called Wells' evolutionary idealism, and then for what Niebuhr called Wells' desperation.[8] In *Faith and History*, 1949, Niebuhr wrote, "shortly before his death, Mr. Wells' desperate optimism had finally degenerated to complete despair."

While *The New Yorker* had given *Faith and History* a favorable, short, unsigned review, it gave the book's successor, *The Irony of American History*, in 1952, an unfavorable, long, and signed review. The reviewer, Anthony West, attacked Niebuhr for defeatism and for providing people with "moral justification for taking the easy and timid way out." What West did not say, and what the reader had no way of suspecting, was that West was the son of H. G. Wells. West, who had taken his mother's name, was, therefore, like Kinsey in that he did not admit his own presuppositions nor make allowance for their effect on his conclusions. One of these conclusions was stated by West in his answer to a letter questioning the basis of his review:

> Niebuhr's religious dogma is that man cannot by the use of reason control or plan his future; his destiny is arranged for him by God, and it is sin for him to do it.

To see that this is, at least in part, a misreading of Niebuhr, one need only turn to *Irony of American History*, the book West must have read in order to review it so carefully. In it Niebuhr contrasted the ancient Greek myth of Prometheus with the ancient Hebrew myth of the Fall of Man, pointing out that while to the ancient Greeks man was guilty of "hubris" whenever he attempted to conquer nature or develop culture, in the Bible man was freely given "dominion over the fish of the sea, and over the fowl of the air, and over the cattle, and over all the earth," or in short, as Niebuhr said, both over nature and the arts of civilization. In the Biblical view, therefore,

> the destructiveness of human life [is] primarily the consequence of exceeding, not the bounds of nature, but much more ultimate limits. The God of the Bible is, like Zeus, "jealous." But his jealousy is aroused not by the achievements of culture and civilization. Man's dominion over nature is declared to be a

[8] Evidence of this desperation was Wells' reliance upon a scientific elite who, as Niebuhr said, "would establish a world authority, sufficiently powerful to dictate the standards of universal truth which would inform an educational program for the whole of mankind."

> rightful one. Divine jealousy is aroused by man's refusal to observe the limits of his freedom. There are such limits because man is a creature as well as a creator. The limits cannot be sharply defined. Therefore distinctions between good and evil cannot be made with absolute precision. But it is clear that the great evils of history are caused by human pretensions that are not inherent in the gift of freedom. They are a corruption of that gift. . . . Man is not involved in guilt by asserting his creative capacities [which include reason]. . . . According to the Biblical view destructiveness is not an inevitable consequence of human creativity. It is not invariably necessary to do evil in order that we may do good.

When West was reminded of this passage, his answer was that

> I cannot believe that God would give man the imaginative and rational powers to know as much of the universe as he has discovered with the one hand, and would impose the limitations upon him that Niebuhr describes with the other. I despise Niebuhr's obscurantism, and I despise his concept of a jealous God.

When the West review was published, Niebuhr was in the first difficult period of his convalescence. Around that time a novel by West was published. It was greeted with reviews even less favorable than West's review of Niebuhr. A copy of the novel was sent to Niebuhr as a get-well present. After the long discouraging summer, Niebuhr dictated a letter of thanks:

> I have been slow in acknowledging your kind gift which came to me in the country, because I waited until I came back to the city and could dictate a letter. I appreciate your thoughtfulness in sending me West's book. . . . I read the book with great interest and with an increased understanding of the kind of world view which made West's review possible. I still think it is a little peculiar that as able a magazine as *The New Yorker* should pick a critic of novels for a work in political thought and life, but those are the hazards of exposing one's work to criticism.

A lifelong friend and colleague of H. G. Wells was Bertrand Russell. He too has frequently been criticized by Niebuhr and has never publicly answered. To a letter requesting his views, he replied:

> I am sorry to say that I have no opinion about Niebuhr, either favourable or unfavourable, as I have read very little of his writings.

Their areas of disagreement, however, are many and basic. One is religion. Said Russell,

> the knowledge exists by which universal happiness can be secured; the chief obstacle to its utilization . . . is the teaching of religion. Religion prevents children from having a rational education; religion prevents us from removing the fundamental causes of war; religion prevents us from teaching the ethic of scientific cooperation.

Another area of disagreement is human sin. Said Russell:

> Those who have a scientific outlook on human behavior . . . find it impossible to label any action as "sin;" they realize that what we do has its origin in our heredity, our education, and our environment, and that it is by control of these causes, rather than by denunciation, that conduct injurious to society is to be prevented.

Yet despite these fundamental disagreements between Russell and Niebuhr, there have been—such is the mystery of human personality—remarkable parallels in their lives. Both followed in the career-footsteps of their respective fathers; both once, and unsuccessfully, ran for public office; both are devastating polemicists; both have been active members of intellectual and political groups of the left; both wrote for their respective country's *New Leader*, and both even wrote articles entitled "Why I Am Not A Christian"; both started out as pacifists and then publicly renounced pacifism, although Niebuhr's renunciation preceded that of Russell who seems in recent years to be returning to an atomic variation of it (see Chapter 26); and both saw through the false promises of Communism far earlier than most of their cohorts on the left; both, as writers, turn out clean copy at tremendous speed; both have devoted a lifetime to attempting to build justice in society; and both were delegates to the UNESCO conference in Paris in 1949.

One American scientist who agrees with Russell on the subjects both of religion and sin is Dr. Lawrence Kubie, psychoanalyst and human cyclotron who throws off more radioactive ideas per day than most people do in a lifetime. With him Niebuhr has had prolonged arguments which Kubie occasionally has had mimeographed and sent to mutual friends. To Kubie's point that the teaching of religion does all the damage Russell claims plus causing neurosis, Niebuhr answers that the wrong teaching of religion can indeed do great damage to children, but that neurosis is not the only danger to guard against: there is also the danger of inner monologue or complacency which is heightened when children are taught to blame whatever they do wrong on their heredity, education or environment. "It is the business of religion," says Niebuhr, "to create a sensitive conscience," or, in other words, "to make man conscious of the fact that his inadequacies are more than excusable limitations—that they are treason against his better self."

This Kubie denies. What is necessary in his view is "to find out how to avoid entering the neurotic prison in which everyman now lives his life," and for this purpose we need "the light which psychiatry sheds on the earliest steps of human development." One of these steps, Kubie agrees with Freud, is the infantile dependence on the seemingly omnipotent parent, to which religion is but an unconscious later harking back. Such an explaining-away of religious awe does not distress Niebuhr; according to that argument, he points out, the *rejection* of God can be explained away as an unconscious harking back to adolescent rebellion. What does distress him is the fact that the belief in a purposeless universe may invite irresponsibility. He further deplores the fact that a man as intelligent and well-informed as Kubie can say that religious faith leaves "no room for proof or evidence; indeed the mere demand for proof or evidence is a denial of belief." As Niebuhr wrote in a letter to one of the mutual friends:

> I was rather put out by the ignorance of Kubie's approach and I told him so. . . . I told him that he complained of the neurotic satisfaction which religious people gained in their sense of superiority over the irreligious, yet he defined religion in

> such a way that it must give him a tremendous sense of superiority over religious people. For faith, to him, is pure arbitrariness . . . and the idea that religious people simply wait for some magical intervention on their behalf borders on the ridiculous. I don't think he has ever read any exposition of religion, not only in the 20th, but in the 19th century.

The demand for proof or evidence—and the corollary refusal to believe what cannot be proved or quantitatively measured—has certainly been a creative hypothesis. Like the denial of sin and of irresolvable paradox, it has borne wondrous fruits. But the question remains, does it apply in every field? For the scientist like Kinsey or Kubie, or the philosopher like Bertrand Russell or Sidney Hook, scientific method is the ultimate authority.[9] For Niebuhr, on the other hand, this form of authority is like the Catholic view of the Church, or Barth's view of the Scriptures: he feels impelled to test it against experience, his own and that of other men and societies throughout history. Although the net of science has caught many fish, the freedom of man swims through it, and so, presumably, does God's. Man's love, moreover (as distinguished from his sexual outlets), also swims through it, and so, presumably, does God's. In a letter to a friend, in 1960, Niebuhr said that the coherencies of reason, like the methods of science, can be used as "the preliminary test of truth," but "the final arbiter . . . is the experience of incongruities in life and history which cannot be digested in logically coherent systems."

As for those like Kubie or Hook who insist that only what is caught by the net of science can be believed, Niebuhr says:

> All atheists have a God. And it is quite clear that for Kubie the meaning of life consists in the promise of history that scientific intelligence will gradually master everything. I think that that faith is naive and he thinks my faith is incredible.

[9] According to Sidney Hook who admits he "wholeheartedly accepts scientific method as the only reliable method of reaching truths about man, society and nature," every conception of God must "be sufficiently determinate to make possible specific inferences of the *how, when* and *where* of his operation," and every experience of God must be of "sufficiently determinate character to permit of definite tests." Such a setting up of science's methods above even God impresses the religious person the way the Fundamentalist insistence that the world was created in exactly seven days impresses the scientist.

> I think we have the debate between historic faith and the Enlightenment in a nutshell there.

It is a debate that continues and Niebuhr believes that it should. There must be, he said in May, 1960, "a dialogue between biblical faith and all the disciplines of modern culture in hopes that some day a creative synthesis may be reached."

He thus ends up disagreeing both with the dogmatic Christians like Barth who, he says, refuse "to enter into dialogue with secular culture," and also with the dogmatic secularists like Kubie who so misrepresent religion that they cannot enter into dialogue with it. Instead, Niebuhr suggests, there should be a component of agnosticism in both faith and atheism. At the same time he notes that the completely agnostic position of, "I cannot know; therefore I will not concern myself," cannot very well be maintained in the atomic age when man's responsibilities call for heart-searching decisions based upon some ultimate frame of meaning.

For himself, Niebuhr, in the agnosticism of his faith, hopes to continue the dialogue with the agnosticism of the secularists. As he wrote in a letter in 1956:

> I do think that the Christian faith must finally give a more relevant answer to modern skepticism about what the affirmation means, "God was in Christ reconciling the world unto himself." If I have some years left to work I think I'll try to analyze that problem more fully.

PART III

The Unfinished Reel

"After reading all that has been written, and after thinking all that has been thought, on the topics of God and the soul, the man who has a right to say that he thinks at all, will find himself face to face with the conclusion that, on these topics, the most profound thought is that which can be the least easily distinguished from the most superficial sentiment."

EDGAR ALLEN POE

25

The Growing Edge

FOLLOWING Niebuhr's illness, if Hollywood had decided to film his life, the movie would presumably have been entitled "The Niebuhr Story," and not, as the irrepressible Robert Bendiner once suggested, "Die Wacht am Reinie."

Yul Brunner, made up to look like John Barrymore, would have played opposite Grace Kelly, only slightly aged.

"The lives of many intellectuals," Niebuhr has said, "are boring," since the drama, such as it is, resides in their thought rather than in their lives. But with the onset of his illness there came to be a dramatic structure in Niebuhr's own life, with the climax provided by the question of whether or not the faith he had spent a lifetime promulgating would be capable of lifting him from the black pit of powerlessness and despair.

Many people have visited this pit, but the most characteristic age for the visit, according to psychiatric writers such as Erik H. Erikson (in *Young Man Luther*), is in the late teens and early twenties. Niebuhr went into it forty years after that age, without either the natural resource of the young body or the psychological resource of feeling the future to contain numberless years ahead.

The fact that he came out of the pit with a new dimension of creativity was attributable of course not only to his faith; people without faith, after all, have also recovered from strokes, and Niebuhr was aided by a devoted family and the most up-to-date medical techniques. But there was, nonetheless, drama in the test to which his faith was put and not found wanting. As for his subsequent influence, it is no more measurable than it ever was, but it is still undeniably potent. Said Arthur Schlesinger, Jr., for example, in 1956:

> No man has had as much influence as a preacher in this generation; no preacher has had as much influence in the secular world.

And when Niebuhr gave his annual sermon in the Harvard Chapel in 1960, an unprecedented five hundred people had to be turned away.

Because Niebuhr can no longer travel much, his presence is missed in many of his favorite haunts. In Washington, for example, a State Department official has said about an advisory committee, "Now that Niebuhr is absent, our discussion has been incredibly unrealistic." And at Harvard, several members of the faculty have organized themselves into an informal "Atheists for Niebuhr," so that their repugnance at the current religious revival[1] should not be interpreted as including him.

Niebuhr, in point of fact, shares the repugnance at much of this revival which includes what he calls religiosity, or faith in faith, rather than religion, or faith in God. In this connection he agrees with Paul Tillich's dictum: "Christ came on earth to destroy all idolatry, including the idolatry of himself." And one of Niebuhr's first controversies after regaining his health was with the National Council of Churches over its sponsorship of Norman Vincent Peale, and with the New York Protestant Council over its sponsorship of Billy Graham. In *Christianity and Crisis,* January 24, 1955, Niebuhr gave some of his reasons:

> Our modern religiosity . . . expresses various forms of self-worship. . . . The most disquieting aspect of such religiosity is that it is frequently advanced by popular leaders of the Christian Church, and is not regarded as a substitute but as an interpretation of that faith. The gospel admonition, "Repent ye, for the kingdom of heaven is at hand" . . . would seem to have little affinity with the "power of positive thinking."
>
> It is significant that while this modern religiosity makes for self-esteem . . . the nation is helped to find . . . its rightful place . . . in the alliance of free nations by many shrewd and critical "secular" thinkers who help us to weigh our responsibilities and judge the hazards of the task in which we are engaged. One

[1] By 1958, the ratio of church membership to the total population of the United States had grown to 63 per cent. This was more than three times higher than church membership had been at the peak of the religious revival of the 1880's. It was also increasing at three times the rate of the population increase (5 *vs.* 1.7 per cent).

> must come to the conclusion that religion per se and faith per se are not virtuous, or a cause of virtue. The question is always what the object of worship is, and whether the worship tends to break the pride of self so that a truer self may arise, either individually or collectively. . . . We can therefore take no satisfaction in the pervading religiosity of our nation. Much of it . . . aggravates, rather than mitigates, the problems of a very successful people.

So complex and paradoxical were these "problems of a very successful people," Niebuhr felt, that it was essential for Americans to stop believing in the Santa Claus of simple solutions, in the secular as well as in the religious sphere.

In the religious sphere one of the most popular of these simple solutions was that of Billy Graham whose type of Christianity, Niebuhr said in *Christianity and Society*, Summer, 1955, was "almost completely irrelevant" to the collective problems of the nuclear age. Niebuhr liked Graham personally—referring to him as "a reasonably modest and wholly personable young man." Niebuhr also approved Graham's insistence that segregation is un-Christian. But Niebuhr disapproved Graham's "wholly individualistic conceptions of sin and his perfectionist ideas of grace." Billy Graham, said Niebuhr,

> told reporters that he was going to Europe because Europe was "strategic" . . . which is to assume that the conversion about which he speaks will or may affect our collective destiny. How this is to be done is made apparent by the assertion that the "hydrogen bomb was made by man which proves that there is something wrong with man" which religious conversion can cure. The hydrogen bomb does indeed reveal the ambiguity in which the whole human enterprise is involved. But it is not a "wickedness" which the good man can simply renounce while the unredeemed man continues to make bombs.

Contrasted with this simple view of Billy Graham was the complex and realistic one of Winston Churchill who, as Niebuhr said,

> gave a better exposition of the situation in which we stand than has been given by any religious analysis . . . [Churchill's was] the first clear statement of the fact that the increasing

> security of the last few years is derived from the increasing awareness of the awfulness of atomic warfare . . . "security is the sturdy child of terror and survival the twin brother of annihilation." Churchill did not try to declare this ironic, not to say tragic, situation good . . . he did not offer some simple alternative to this situation. Neither conversion in Billy Graham's version of Christianity nor the world government of which our more rationalistic idealists dream can solve the predicament of modern man. There are, however, resources in Biblical faith for understanding the predicament which will prevent vain resort to false solutions.

Billy Graham's type of conversion, Niebuhr said in *Life*, July 1, 1957, offers hope to individual sufferers from particular problems, such as alcoholism or adultery, but even this hope, Niebuhr felt, is oversimplified: at the Graham rallies, people are offered "a new life, not through painful religious experience but merely by signing a decision card. Thus, a miracle of regeneration is promised at a painless price by an obviously sincere evangelist. It is a bargain."

Nor, according to Niebuhr, is the kind of conversion preached by Graham the only or even the best way to become a Christian: "some . . . who are most clearly saints have probably never been 'converted' in Graham's sense." And Graham's assumption that those who are converted are also saved, Niebuhr says, adds to "the moral and spiritual perplexities of our age":

> Actually there are no "saved" people in the whole world good enough to save the world. The catastrophic drama in which we are involved proves that nations, as well as individuals, must repent if they would be saved; but that nations do not repent and that the source of their self-righteousness is frequently precisely the Pharisaism of these same saved individuals who do not understand the depth of their involvement in collective sin.

For people to understand the depth of their involvement in collective sin, Niebuhr says, ministers must appeal not only to the emotions of the congregation "but to the mind; that is, it is necessary rationally to analyze the social situation, conformity to which means the violation of the love commandment."

Niebuhr's attempt rationally to analyze Graham caused an emotional storm. So many letters streamed in following the *Life* article that Niebuhr jokingly told a friend that anyone daring to criticize Graham in print should be paid double the usual stipend because of the added secretarial costs of coping with the ensuing correspondence. Niebuhr then turned and made this experience the basis of a *Christian Century* article, September 4, 1957 which he whimsically entitled "After Comment, The Deluge."

Some of the people who wrote in defending Graham were those who, Niebuhr assumed, had had genuine religious experiences. In his view, however, these people pointed up, "by their charitable spirit, that there can be a real difference in types of conversion; for the most vituperative letters also came from 'converted' Christians, who made their experience the basis of a fierce self-righteousness." Said one Protestant to Niebuhr, "I am ashamed to find you among the Jewish rabbis and Catholic priests who criticize Billy Graham. Would that we were as loyal to our cause as the Catholics are."

But the outcry against Niebuhr on Graham was as nothing to the outcry against Niebuhr on his statement that there is no need for Christians to try to convert the Jews. Niebuhr's original article was printed in the *Journal of the Central Conference of American Rabbis*, but his views were summarized in *The New York Times* of April 15, 1958.[2] His main point was that the two forms of biblical religion are essentially so close that there is no need for Jews to move from their own ancestral faith, especially since Christianity has been associated with such prolonged and fanatical persecution of this faith that a modern Jew can hardly avoid feeling guilt if he associates himself with it. The problem of irreligion among the Jews, "no worse than among the Gentiles, [is] a serious problem," Niebuhr believes, but it is one for the rabbi more than the minister, unless the irreligious Jew, himself, chooses otherwise.

Disagreement with this point of view was widespread among Christians. Said George Sweazey, Chairman of the National Council of Churches'

[2] Niebuhr not only writes for Jewish periodicals but is often quoted or referred to in their pages. Today, said Judd L. Teller in *Commentary*, March, 1959, "nearly all American rabbinical periodicals in English manifest some kind of preoccupation with Niebuhr." Niebuhr's own view of Judaism follows that of Franz Rosenzweig who defined the relationship of Christianity and Judaism as being that of two religions with one center, with Christianity serving the purpose of carrying the prophetic message to the Gentile world.

department on the Christian Approach to the Jews, in *The Christian Century*, April 29, 1959,

> If a person in spiritual need is of Hebrew ancestry, shall we pass by on the other side, hoping that a rabbi will chance to come along and care for him? . . . Religiously we are all Jews. It is intolerable that we should abandon those to whom we owe so much just at the border of our Promised Land.

Many Jews, however, seemed quite willing thus to be abandoned. According to *Time*, September 28, 1959,

> Rabbi [Arthur] Hertzberg realizes that peaceful theological coexistence with the Jews—advocated by leading Christian theologians, including Reinhold Niebuhr and Paul Tillich—would be something of a revolution for traditionally proselytizing Christianity, but he thinks that practice in coexistence might be valuable . . .

Niebuhr's own feeling about the differences that exist between Christianity and Judaism echoes that of Martin Buber whom he quotes in *Pious and Secular America*, 1957:

> To the Christian, the Jew is the stubborn fellow who is still waiting for the Messiah; to the Jew, the Christian is the heedless fellow who in an unredeemed world declares that redemption has somehow or other taken place.

In the same book Niebuhr also recommends that the dialogue between Christians and Jews continue and that both engage in further dialogue with the secular disciplines. On behalf of religious Christians and Jews he says, we must be willing to

> acknowledge that modern psychiatry and social sciences have validated the efficacy of "common" grace more explicitly than any saving grace which we may claim as religious people.

Niebuhr had grouped Christianity's overly simple panaceas with those of the rationalistic idealists. Before World War II such idealists or "utopians" had been epitomized for him by the Pacifists.[3] After the war

[3] A postwar estimate of Niebuhr's influence in this regard was given by Paul Ramsey in *The New York Times*, June 19, 1960: Before the war, "Reinhold Niebuhr suc-

they were epitomized for him by the World Federalists. Both fitted in to his generalization that

> men always transcend any given social situation enough to imagine a more perfect one, even to a degree which exceeds the possibilities of history. Utopianism misinterprets this transcendent vision as a simple historical possibility.

Niebuhr did not quarrel with the World Federalists' transcendent vision; as he says, "To build a world community must and will engage the conscience of mankind for ages to come." But he did quarrel with their assumption that a world government in the near future is a simple historical possibility. They think, he said, that "we lack an international government because no one has conceived a proper blueprint for it." But the fact is that we lack, not a blueprint, but the degree of social cohesion that must precede it:

> Politically minded people easily suffer from the illusion that . . . organization creates society. Societies are not created by political mechanism but by attitudes of mutual respect and trust. Where these exist, social relations are established and traditions formed. These in turn are gradually codified and given definition and precision by legal enactments.

Such mutual respect and trust grow partly through the experience of living together and partly through the exercise of power—implicit or explicit. To date, the major sources of international power reside not in a central overarching authority, comparable to the United States federal government, but in the nation-states themselves. As Niebuhr had said in a letter to *The Nation* on January 24, 1942, "The international community is as different from the national community as the nation is from the family."

At the same time he also warned against assuming that the nation-states in their relations with one another are so completely "immoral" as

---

ceeded, almost single-handedly, in driving to the wall the isolationism which then was wide-spread in the Protestant Churches. This took overt form in the pacifism that had spread between the wars to denominations not traditionally 'peace churches.' "

to be determined by considerations of selfishness alone.[4] He thus ended up being as much in conflict with the cynical promoters of Real-Politik as with the rationalistic idealists. As he wrote, in 1942,

> The finest task of achieving . . . justice . . . will be done neither by the Utopians who dream dreams of perfect brotherhood nor yet by the cynics who believe that the self-interest of nations cannot be overcome. It must be done by the realists who understand that nations are selfish and will be so till the end of history . . . but that none of us, no matter how selfish we may be, can be *only* selfish.

One aspect of this realism is to recognize the United Nations for what it is, and not destroy it by prematurely overloading it. The UN, Niebuhr writes, is invaluable as "a forum of world opinion," as "a clearing-house for diplomacy," and as "the scaffolding of . . . minimal forms of community." But it is not a world government with power to enforce its will except in localized conflicts. Indeed its effectiveness is predicated upon relative agreement between the major powers; when this is absent, the Security Council is paralyzed by the veto or by abstentions. As for the Assembly, with the many new small nations having the same vote as the old major powers, its structure does not sufficiently correspond to the realities of power for it to be as effective as most of its member-nations would like to see it be.

The U.S. Senate also gives the same vote to a small state like Nevada as to a large state like California. But this historically evolved regional arrangement is balanced both by the greater influence of the large states in the House of Representatives and by the existence of federal officials who are elected by the citizens of all the states. Organizationally the UN has nothing comparable to the U.S. House of Representatives nor to the direct election of federal officials. And factually it does not have the kind of police force to enforce its decisions if any of the major powers decide to defy it (viz., Russia's actions in Hungary in 1956). The United States, therefore, says Niebuhr, must not abdicate responsibility to the UN for her own major decisions, for if we do, then

[4] As early as *Moral Man and Immoral Society* Niebuhr noted that "human society is partly an artful contrivance which enables men to serve one another indirectly, even though their primary motives may be to serve themselves."

> our devout expressions of loyalty to it . . . become but a screen for our irresponsibility; for the United Nations can do nothing without the leadership of the western powers.

The United States, at the same time, like the other "strong nations . . . must have her policies within the framework of the UN Charter." Such policies, of which Niebuhr approves, include NATO, Euratom, The European Coal and Steel Community, The Organization of American States, the World Bank, and others he hopes will be devised. As he said in *Faith and History*, 1949:

> To establish community in global terms requires the exercise of the ingenuity of freedom far beyond the responsibilities of men of other epochs . . . The expansion of the perennial task of achieving tolerable harmony of life with life under ever higher conditions of freedom in ever wider frames of harmony represents the residual truth in modern interpretations of history. But this truth is transmuted into error very quickly if it is assumed that increasing freedom assures the achievement of the wider task.

This "wider task" will require all the resources of human reason and morality in order for nations not to pursue a too-narrow self-interest. For a too-selfish nation will alienate its friends, inflame its enemies and thus weaken itself. In the Marshall Plan, said Niebuhr, "prudent self-interest was united with concern for others in a fashion which represents the most attainable virtue of nations."[5]

The wider task will also require, on the part of some people if not all, the kind of religious humility that remembers that the God of the Bible is the God before whom the nations are both "as a drop in the bucket" and also less virtuous than they pretend to be. As Niebuhr says, "No nation ever supports values which transcend its life if they are diametrically opposed to the preservation of its life." (One example might be the high-sounding U.S. policy of liberation for the satellite countries which

[5] And he further noted in *Christianity and Crisis*, May 13, 1957, that nations need citizens who "have loyalties and responsibilities to a wider system of values than that of the national interest—to a civilization for instance, to a system of justice, and to a community of free nations. These moral concerns will serve to leaven the mind of a nation and prevent a national community from defining its interests too narrowly."

was proudly announced by Secretary of State Dulles, but from which the United States was forced to back down at the time of the Hungarian Rebellion because it conflicted with our own national survival.)

Finally the wider task will require the kind of realism which recognizes the facts of power but knows that force which is only force is less powerful than force combined with the prestige that comes from a devotion to justice and a reputation for living up to agreements.

Niebuhr's "liberal realism" as Kenneth W. Thompson calls it in his *Political Realism and the Crisis of World Politics,* stems partly from Niebuhr's view of man and history and partly from his continuing dialogue with some of the people who have been—and still are—making foreign policy.[6] For example, Thompson writes:

> In tracing the evolution of American thinking on foreign policy no one can afford to overlook the role played by that remarkable body of men who made up the Policy Planning Staff during its earlier more active years. Created in 1947 by General Marshall as the first regular office of the Department of State to be charged with considering problems from the standpoint of the totality of American national interest, it has bequeathed a corpus of thought that both reinforces the main stream of scholarly thinking . . . and adds a new dimension. . . . The writings of George F. Kennan, Paul H. Nitze, Louis J. Halle, C. B. Marshall, and Dorothy Fosdick carry the prestige and authority of the practitioner . . . who [has] been on the firing line . . .

And in regard to this corpus of thought, George Kennan, now the U. S. Ambassador to Yugoslavia, said, "Niebuhr is the father of us all."

Other of these liberal realists, according to Thompson, are Professor Hans J. Morgenthau, whose first book "bears the imprint of Niebuhr's influence more than that of any other American scholar," and journalists-extraordinary, Walter Lippmann and James Reston. Lippmann's estimate of Niebuhr's importance appeared in Chapter 3; as for Reston, he writes, "I suppose the thing Niebuhr has done for me more than anybody else is to articulate the irony of our condition as a country in the

[6] "Balanced realism was the term coined by Harry Rex Davis in his illuminating Ph.D. Thesis (1951 University of Chicago), "The Political Philosophy of Reinhold Niebuhr."

world today." Reston therefore singles out Niebuhr's *Irony of American History* as having been of "profound personal effect on my thinking, particularly the chapter in it on 'prosperity and virtue.' "[7] This same book was also singled out by Professor Arnold Wolfers, Director of the Washington Center of Foreign Policy Research, who as Professor of International Relations at Yale assigned it to his students.[8] Wolfers, an old friend who approves Niebuhr's realism, says that "perhaps our discussions have encouraged him on occasion to take a hard look at the realities of international politics. I am afraid we are both considered hard-boiled realists; but we are both very much concerned with the moral aspects . . ."

Niebuhr's dual emphasis on hard-boiled realism and the moral aspects led him to attack the "grand simplifiers" of United States foreign policy, namely the militarists and the moralists. Theirs, Kenneth Thompson recalls, was "an all-or-nothing approach. Either we renounce totally the exercise of force, say, in the Middle East . . . and couch foreign policy in unqualified moral terms, or we send increasing numbers of arms . . . and intervene overtly in every local dispute. Such an approach has no room for more limited and proximate moral and political actions."

Partly because Niebuhr stresses precisely such limited and proximate actions, his direct influence is impossible to trace. But as Wolfers said in a letter, Niebuhr's *in*direct influence has been considerable:

> None of us working in international relations on the outside can ever hope to be able to prove that a decision-maker would have acted differently if he had not heard or read what one of us brought to his attention. But at least in the case of Niebuhr, many prominent men agree that they have been deeply influenced by his thought and, therefore, probably influenced in their actions.

[7] "I have not seen as much of Niebuhr as I would like to," continued Reston, "for he had already had his stroke before I came upon him . . . There is, however, in the country today a kind of political and religious Chautauqua financed by foundations . . . where I have had the opportunity to hear him talk."

[8] The phrase, "ironies of American history," appeared in a book-jacket recommendation of Robert Lowell by his fellow-poet, Elizabeth Bishop. Said she in a letter, "I don't know whether the phrase was original with Niebuhr or not; perhaps it was. I did read that book and felt I learned a great deal from it. (In fact I read all his books.) By the time I wrote that blurb, in 1959 or 1958, the phrase seemed to be so familiar . . . that I felt free to change it to the plural and still put it in quotes."

One of the decision-makers reported, in his characteristically witty and double-edged way, a small instance of Niebuhr's direct influence. Dean Acheson wrote that "one of my assistants, Marshall Shulman, was much addicted to Niebuhr, and I know that at least one quotation from Niebuhr appeared in a speech which I delivered and in the authorship of which I played a minor part."

Another quotation from Niebuhr, via another source, popped, like one of Grimm's frogs, out of Secretary of State Acheson's mouth. As Charles Burton Marshall wrote in a letter to Robert Good in 1952:

> On one occasion Secretary Acheson made a speech on short notice to a group of publishers. There was not time to produce a text. He spoke from notes which I hurriedly prepared for him. The speech was a success and in response to a number of requests . . . it was then made public. *The New York Times* published it as an article in its magazine section . . . It clearly reflects, through two vicarious stages, the gist of Dr. Niebuhr's approach to the problems of our national policy. In the course of his remarks the Secretary used the phrase, "the pattern of responsibility," as a key concept to the United States role in world affairs. This phrase was seized upon by the publisher as the title for the book, edited by McGeorge Bundy, presenting Mr. Acheson's main ideas on foreign policy. Mr. Acheson got the phrase from my notes. I in turn had picked it up from Dr. Niebuhr's discourse to the Policy Planning Staff on the occasion of a visit [to Washington] as I recall, in November . . . of 1950.

For Niebuhr the dual outline of this pattern of responsibility had been formulating since *Reflections On the End of an Era* in 1934. That was the book in which he first dealt with the need to avoid "an alternating of fanatic illusions and fretful disillusions"; and a decade later, in *Children of Light,* he warned lest we be "driven to alternate moods of sentimentality and despair" when faced with the inevitable frustrations arising out of a responsible attention to our national and international duties. For Niebuhr a nation's maturity, like that of an individual, means resisting the temptation to indulge in violent mood swings. It was the overoptimists, he noted, who toppled into overpessimism; the despairing who clutched after false gods; and in neither case could friend or enemy set his course by such a wildly fluctuating compass.

Niebuhr, needless to say, was not alone in recommending that the nation steer a straight and dependable course. The Truman-Acheson emphasis was also upon the need for firmness and patience particularly in relation to the Russians. Said Marshall Shulman (the Niebuhr "addict") in this connection:

> I think this is a case not so much of a direct influence, but of a more indirect charging of the atmosphere . . . I think you will find in many of Dean Acheson's speeches a similar spirit of emphasis upon a steady public opinion which continues hopefully to do what needs to be done, without undue expectations. It may be that the lesson we were all learning in diplomacy, of the limitations on what could be done, was fortified by Niebuhr's philosophical development of the limitations of the human situation. He was, in any case, an important bridge between the idealists and the liberals outside the government, who tended to think in terms of ideal moral solutions, and the people in the government who found themselves wrestling with the actual available alternatives, none of them ideal.[9]

In pointing to the dangers of violent mood-oscillation, Niebuhr varied the names of the two extremes. Sometimes he called them "sentimentality" and "cynicism;" sometimes "optimism" and "pessimism;" sometimes "the fury of self-righteousness" and "the apathy of despair;" sometimes "hysteria" and "complacency." And today he also warns against combining, as well as alternating between, these two extremes: "We are curiously hysterical about communism but complacent about the possibilities of an atomic war."[10]

At the Kent School, in 1955, Niebuhr delivered an address on "The Christian Idea of Education" which stressed the scriptural background for these warnings:

[9] Marshall Shulman, now at Harvard, together with Henry L. Roberts and Alexander Dallin of Columbia, recently prepared a report for the Senate Foreign Relations Committee which recommended among other things that the United States avoid "wild alternations between optimism and pessimism."

[10] President Eisenhower in his report to the nation, after the collapse of the 1960 Summit Conference in Paris, also warned against "complacency" and "hysteria," while President Kennedy, on July 25, 1961, in regard to Berlin, repeatedly appealed for "perseverance . . . and steady nerves . . . during the long days ahead."

> According to St. Paul, those who do not have [the] key to the mystery of life and of God are tempted either to sleep or be drunken, to be either complacent or hysterical when confronted with the evils of history. But those who have the key are enabled to watch and be sober.[11]

To watch and be sober is "to be prepared for new corruptions on the level of world community which drive simple idealists to despair." Niebuhr had devoted a sermon to the subject of maturity in *Beyond Tragedy,* 1937. In it he showed, on the individual level, how maturity is an outgrowing of child*ish*ness without a loss of child*like*ness, the latter being defined as "the honesty of knowing that we are not honest." In recent years he has expanded the concept of maturity to the collective level. Speaking of the United States, he said with a touch of autobiographical poignancy, we "are like some adolescent suddenly called upon to assume a father's responsibility for a numerous family." This mature role was not, moreover, of our choice; it was forced upon us by history: "We shivered on the brink of world responsibility," said Niebuhr, in 1960, "until history pushed us in."

Now we are faced not only with this responsibility but also with the atomic irony of finding ourselves "more impotent to master our destiny in the day of our seeming omnipotence than we were in the day of our weakness." To bear these tensions maturely and into the foreseeable future is the greatest challenge the nation has ever faced. As Niebuhr wrote in the aforementioned "Hazards and Resources":

> We are constantly tempted to weaken the virtue of our cause by too unqualified claims for it, and to suffer from periodic fits of disillusionment when the moral ambiguity of our position becomes apparent. We must resist this temptation the more resolutely because we not only have great power but are called upon to exercise its responsibilities in a world situation in which there are no possibilities of pure and unequivocal justice. Yet there are tremendously important moral decisions to be made. Above

[11] On return from Kent, Niebuhr said in a letter, "I don't think my address was too successful." Yet according to Kent trustee and CBS executive, the late Louis T. Stone, response to this address was "ecstatic." Since Stone was versed in ratings, and since Niebuhr often practices as well as preaches modesty, the Stone verdict is likely to have been the more accurate one.

> all, it is important that we fulfill our responsibilities with steadiness and resolution, without the distractions of the alternate moods of cynicism and sentimentality.

During the McCarthy period "hysteria" had mounted in the United States to the point where many innocent people were falsely accused of communism. One young man who has since left the employ of a U. S. Intelligence organization was appalled to hear in a briefing on Communist tactics in the United States that Reinhold Niebuhr was the prime example of communism infiltrating the Protestant churches and that Niebuhr was probably a party member.

For Niebuhr to extricate himself from false accusations of communism was relatively easy: his public record of Communist-battling stretched back into the thirties. But many others of the falsely accused lost their jobs, their peace of mind, and on occasion their future usefulness to society. Niebuhr did what he could to help them and he attacked not only McCarthy but also the House Un-American Activities Committee whose methods of action based on guilt by association, Niebuhr felt, were both a travesty of justice and an example of totalitarian techniques arising within the ranks of those ostensibly fighting totalitarianism.

So strongly did Niebuhr object to the assumption of guilt-by-association that on February 22, 1959, he was one of the signers, together with Professor Edmond Cahn of the New York University Law School and other distinguished members of the Bar, of an appeal published in *The New York Times* to commute the sentence of Morton Sobell. Sobell had been sentenced two years previously (April 1, 1957) to thirty years in prison. His trial had been linked with that of Julius and Ethel Rosenberg who were subsequently executed for treason. Niebuhr had no doubt that the Rosenbergs were Communists or that they had given atomic secrets to our then-ally, the Russians. They, therefore, he felt, deserved life imprisonment (his reasons for wanting to see the death sentence commuted were "political as well as moral," and in fact the reputation of the United States abroad did take a bad dip when the Rosenbergs were executed).

Niebuhr also assumed that Sobell was a Communist, but not one who had necessarily been connected with the Rosenbergs. As he said in a letter, May 18, 1959, "There was no evidence that Sobell gave any atomic secrets to Rosenberg and only one witness related him to Rosenberg at all," this witness being Max Elitcher whose statements were shown to be of doubtful veracity and who claimed as facts events which were never corroborated. Therefore, Niebuhr continued, "I signed the appeal for commutation of Sobell's sentence . . . because Sobell was tried together with the Rosenbergs at a time of undoubted public hysteria. . . . The absence of a separate trial was an injustice to Sobell. In the public mind he is still involved in the guilt of the Rosenbergs."

For holding this point of view Niebuhr was attacked both from the far left for his assumption that Sobell was a Communist, and from the far right for being, himself, too close to the Communists. A Hearst columnist, Jack Lotto, wrote a syndicated column on April 11, 1959, which was bruited by the Albany, N.Y., *Times Union* as "an authoritative weekly roundup of Communist and pro-Communist Activities." Said Lotto about the Sobell clemency appeal:

> This was by no means the first participation in Red-instigated or pro-Communist activities by the best known of the self-described "anti-Communists," Dr. Reinhold Niebuhr.
>
> A professor at the Union Theological Seminary . . . Dr. Niebuhr recently joined a drive to kill the House Un-American Activities Committee.

Three local Protestant clergymen immediately wrote in to the *Times Union* to protest the Lotto implication that Niebuhr was pro-Communist. And the paper's religion editor, Dr. Carlyle Adams, devoted his weekly column on May 9, 1959, to an impassioned defense of Niebuhr which linked him, in a form of *innocence*-by-association with Albert Schweitzer, Archbishop Temple, and Paul Tillich. Mr. Adams was also specific and articulate on the subject of Niebuhr's anti-communism:

> Dr. Niebuhr has dared what many other critics of Communism have feared to do—he has made a thorough study of Marxism and all aspects of Communism. This is a task which should occupy far more people than it does in our day. Believers in democracy have an obligation to know what Communism is—and what is wrong with it.
>
> In a generation where it still is possible for a man to be stolen from a jail and lynched without . . . trial, we need minds like that of Reinhold Niebuhr which insist on objective judgment

> and search for truth—even in a case such as the Sobell case to which Mr. Lotto referred.

The publisher of the *Times Union*, Gene Robb, was also the recipient of letters on the subject of the Lotto column. He wrote in answer to one:

> I would personally agree with you completely that the seeking of clemency for a convicted spy or a convicted revolutionary Communist is something that a minister or any other individual can do without being a Communist himself. The difficulty arises when the non-Communist who seeks such clemency finds that the Communist apparatus itself has made the seeking of clemency a part of its immediate program. I am sure there are many better ways to explain this than Mr. Lotto pursued but it is not always easy and I can only hope that the response of Carlyle Adams is adequate. It is a demonstration of our good faith.

When the Adams column and Robb's letter were sent to Niebuhr, his answer was quiet rather than wrathful:

> I think it was rather nice of the Editor to put his religious editor on the task of refuting Mr. Lotto.
> At the same time I find it rather disturbing that long after the McCarthy period one cannot ask for clemency for a Communist without being accused of communism.

Certainly it was true in the late fifties, as it had been earlier, that society needed criticism by individuals sufficiently courageous to take an unpopular stand even though, or especially because, the issues of justice were not clear-cut. As Niebuhr told the students graduating from Union Seminary in 1957,

> To speak the word of truth and faith in a nation and generation involved in such . . . predicaments . . . is certainly a hazardous undertaking.

For him, moreover, it was hazardous physically; although his recovery from his illness was extraordinary, it was not complete. Fatigue could still cause the muscles of the left arm to go into spasm, which kept him from sleeping, thus adding to the fatigue. This vicious cycle could not only cast him into the depths of exhaustion and depression but might also lead to a recurrence of the original attacks.

To speak the word of truth in the form of a new book was hazardous for Niebuhr professionally too. He had regained the pre-illness heights of prestige and in ways even surpassed them. In addition to more honorary degrees (Columbia presented a S.T.D. in 1954) and promotion to Vice President of Union Seminary, he was elected to the 250-member National Institute of Arts and Letters and then to its fifty-member Academy. He was made an active advisor to the Fund for the Republic and was asked for more articles and speeches than he had time and strength to handle. When the invitation came in 1958 to spend a year at the Institute for Advanced Studies at Princeton (taking the place of George Kennan) in order to write a full-length book on the current crisis in the light of all history Niebuhr hesitated. "I've had a joyful life. Why not call it a day? It's surely hazardous to go out now and attempt a big new job at which I might fail."

On the other hand, there was the challenge of new learning and new people, and the possibility of bringing a new perspective to a confused and floundering world. "It would be wonderful to do one more thing well."

This one more thing would of necessity involve what Arthur Koestler, himself a political expert and literary man invading the field of science in *The Sleepwalkers*, called "creative trespassing." In order to achieve perspective on all of history, Niebuhr would be poaching on realms of learning that were not within his already broad field of competence. Having lived in an academic community for thirty years, he knew how jealously the interdisciplinary fences are guarded and with what persistence the guards can shoot.[12] Yet his conviction was that, in addition to the valuable analyses of the specialists, the modern world also needed the attempted—and less easily proved—syntheses of the generalists.

There was still another complication in regard to the Princeton assignment. Mrs. Niebuhr was Chairman of the Religion Department at Barnard and could not readily break off her work in the middle of the academic year in order to accompany him. Yet he could not go alone.

But somehow or other, they went.

And somehow or other, they ended up having so stimulating and

[12] Catherine Drinker Bowen, in *Adventures of a Biographer*, reported what happens to a biographer who roams even into the adjacent field of history. Not only was she shot at during the period of research but also, by academic reviewers, after the book was published.

productive a time that they had mixed feelings about returning to New York. Jeremy Bernstein, one of the brilliant young physicists at the Princeton Institute for Advanced Studies, wrote afterward about Niebuhr:

> There was a wonderful interaction with him on general subjects —contemporary politics, the meaning of history, the relation between science and society, etc. We had a regular lunch group and he frequently came and ate with us. . . . The average age was about thirty. We enjoyed his humour, wisdom and wide experience. I was, myself, always very fascinated by the way in which he would extract the general from the particular, using a language which was deceptively simple, but really enormously subtle and abstract.
>
> He had never met any of the younger generation of physicists before and he found it interesting that they are quite normal and human. It was a kind of mutual friendship toward which we all look back with great pleasure.[13]

As for the book, it was written within the year, and it covered, as its title suggests, *The Structure of Nations and Empires: A Study of the Recurring Patterns and Problems of the Political Order in Relation to the Unique Problems of the Nuclear Age.*

Checked and rechecked as the book was, stylistically by Mrs. Niebuhr (said Dr. Niebuhr in the Preface: "If this volume should be more lucid, as I hope it will be, than my previous books, the credit will belong to her"), and factually by many of Niebuhr's professorial friends, the manuscript remained a source of deep anxiety to its author. While it was being checked, according to James Loeb who visited in Princeton, Niebuhr was distressed by one of the comments which ignored the sweep of the author's daring generalizations and concentrated instead on nit-picking tiny mistakes of time and place. And when advance copies of the book were sent to a variety of professionals, the intervening summer vacation prevented some of them from sending word to its author. "I've never worried so much about a book before," Niebuhr told Loeb. Part of this worry probably stemmed from the exhaustion concurrent with the effort of writing it, and part from the boldness of his generalizations. Were

[13] On the Mike Wallace Show Niebuhr warmly referred to these young physicists, some of whom he had found wiser than many social scientists.

they correct and therefore useful, or wildly wrong and therefore dangerous? Only the experts with competence in the fields he invaded could say, and then only tentatively, since events would have the final word. Diffidently the Preface admits:

> I am well aware that only an amateur would be sufficiently ignorant of the complexities of history and of the varied interpretations of historical events to have the temerity to undertake so ambitious a project. I therefore crave the indulgence of the specialists in the various fields of thought and of action, which I have traversed, if I have not done justice either to the obvious facts or to the important differences in the interpretations of those facts in their several fields.

When the reviews came out, they ranged in general from the enthusiastic to the adulatory. Among the enthusiasts were Toynbee and other well known historians.[14] Many an author, receiving such reviews, would have lost not only his worries but his entire supply of humility. Not so, Niebuhr. Harry R. Davis and Robert C. Good, whose comprehensive *Reinhold Niebuhr on Politics* appeared in 1960, after *Structure of Nations* had been reviewed, noted in their preface Niebuhr's "quality of authentic humility which was revealed to us in his . . . total lack of prideful self-consciousness about his written work."

This lack of prideful self-consciousness appears when Niebuhr speaks as well as when he writes. In 1958, he was presented, at a huge Waldorf Astoria Dinner in honor of Roosevelt Day, with an award for ten years of service to the liberal cause at home and abroad. Presenting the award was Thomas K. Finletter; speakers scheduled to follow Niebuhr were Averell Harriman and Adlai Stevenson. Niebuhr straightened his tie, ran a big-knuckled hand over his pate, pulled his long nose further downward, and spoke out rapidly in a deep voice. By the end of one sentence he had every person's full attention; by the end of two sentences he had every person laughing. "In academic circles," he said, "they don't think I'm a liberal at all. They think a liberal must have mild illusions about

[14] Also among the enthusiasts was Perry Miller, Professor of American Literature at Harvard, an outspoken secularist, who reviewed the book for *America*, the Catholic magazine. "I'm so much of a heretic in their eyes," said Niebuhr jokingly, "that I guess they thought it suitable to ask an even greater heretic to review my book."

human nature. I don't have mild, or any kind of, illusions about human nature—except of course my own: that is what you might call a *residual* illusion."

After the laughter subsided, he put across his main point which, uniquely for the political arena, ended up being as brief as previously bruited. "Liberalism," he said, "means openness—openness both to the promise and the perils of the future. It doesn't stay with the present and the past. Even our idea of liberalism must be open."

A no-longer-young couple joined in the standing ovation. When it finally died down, a tablemate who had been a distinguished public servant abroad and at home, leaned forward. "I've known several men who, you might say, have had great *careers,* or have led great *lives.* But this is something different: this is a great man."

"I don't agree," said a provocative writer. "I've interviewed great men, from Churchill to Frank Lloyd Wright. And they all had a touch of the charlatan: a sort of mask between their face and the rest of the world."

"And this one doesn't?"

"That's right."

"Deliberately, do you suppose?"

"It couldn't be. You'd sense the strain. No, there's a transparency here —a genuine clarity. I think what you have is something even more unusual than a great man: I think you have a good man."

Good and great are adjectives about which people are bound to disagree. But no one, even Niebuhr's severest critics, seems to disagree that he is a man ready to take the risk of saying what he thinks.

As William Kirkland wrote in *The Christian Century,* May 13, 1959,

> One of the pre-eminent characteristics of Reinhold Niebuhr is his courage in tackling the thorniest, most dilemma-ridden issues that confront us . . . and getting on record with some concrete word about what we must do.

And this is still precisely what Niebuhr is doing.

26

The Open End

History in the mid-twentieth century has come to roost, like the storks of Holland, upon the rooftops of ordinary people. What must we do, separately and together, to prevent the stork from giving way to the vulture?

For the last several decades Niebuhr's basic ideas have been pointing the way toward a number of answers. But until recently few people had felt the need to ask the question. And as Niebuhr himself noted in the Gifford Lectures, in regard to the coming of Christ, few things appear so absurd as the answer to an unasked question.

The coming of Christ, "the light that shineth in darkness," for Niebuhr still provides illumination for the darkest problems of the hour. This is not to claim, he says, that the Christian faith can provide specific answers to the technical problems of the nuclear age, but that it can provide a framework in which valid answers can be sought and false ones discarded.

As he had written in *Irony of American History:*

> The real question is whether a religion or a culture is capable of interpreting life in a dimension sufficiently profound to understand and anticipate the sorrows and pains which may result from a virtuous regard for our responsibilities; and to achieve a serenity with sorrow and pain which is something less but also something more than "happiness." Our difficulty as a nation is that we must now learn that prosperity is not simply co-ordinated to virtue, that virtue is not simply coordinated to historic destiny and that happiness is no simple possibility of human existence.

In the personal sphere there is still the possibility of the kind of happiness Niebuhr calls private bliss, but in the collective sphere happiness, which for him means Aristotle's harmony, is not a simple possibility. For America is now the hegemonous nation of the free world, and while an individual—or small powerless nation—may hide in what Niebuhr calls some "storm cellar of security," a great nation cannot. In that sense, he says, "there is no escape from guilt in history." The nation which attempts to escape guilt by fleeing responsibility will find guilt, like death for the individual, waiting at Samarra: the guilt for not having been responsible. As for the individual, Niebuhr says, "the real problem for the Christian is not how anyone as good as he can participate in unethical political activity, but how anyone as sinful as he can dare to set himself up as judge of his fellow man."

This awareness of our own sin, collective as well as individual, is important, he wrote in *The Christian Century* May 11, 1960, because "we must know ourselves one with our enemies . . . in the bonds of a common guilt by which [our common] humanity is corrupted." This in no way means that we should "connive with their injustice [or] renounce our responsibility to our own civilization;" what it means is that America should "dispel all its vainglorious illusions about itself as a 'Christian civilization,' and work to set the frame of meaning in which [some] accommodations can take place." For the Communist enemy, unlike the Nazi enemy, is one which is "not purely evil and with which we must come to terms or perish." Thus are the two giants locked in a common fate "not anticipated in the evolutionary hopes of the one giant or the revolutionary illusions of the other. But actual history curiously refutes the vain pictures which men in their pride make of history."

Among the vain pictures which men make of history are some in contemporary America, "a young nation whose apprenticeship for . . . leadership has been brief [and whose] thought has been informed by the political ideals of the past two centuries rather than by the experience of past ages."[1]

One factor that the past ages knew and the past two centuries forgot was the perennial aspect of human insecurity. The cave man had been insecure because of weather and wild animals; the Romans had been insecure because of the arbitrary whims of their rulers; the medieval citizen had been insecure because of the political chaos; the Renaissance

[1] The true end of the nineteenth century, Niebuhr now estimates, came in Europe after World War I and in the United States after the Depression.

citizen had been insecure because of the religious chaos; and everyone had been insecure because of the plague and other diseases whose cure was unknown. As these specific insecurities were overcome, the basic insecurity of man was obscured. As Niebuhr said about the present, in Union Seminary *Tower* at the time of his partial retirement in May, 1960,

> The insecurities of the age are but the enlargements of the insecurities of life itself, about which a mature faith has always known and which have always provided an ultimate test of the vitality and honesty of such faith.

The atomic proportion of our insecurity is, however, new. As Niebuhr noted in *Virginia Quarterly*, Autumn, 1950, "we have not been accustomed to calculated risks; we have thrived for a long time on 'safe investments' . . . Now we sow with no certain guarantee of a harvest." And indeed we must continue to refuse "prematurely" to resolve the tension involved in this uncertainty lest in trying to reap too early we destroy the possibility of a harvest at all. Even before the Russians had developed their own atom bomb, Niebuhr reminded his countrymen in *Christianity and Society*, Summer, 1948:

> The kind of patience required for living in an insecure world and for meeting truculent adversaries with forebearance as well as firmness, is a religious rather than moral achievement. It accepts the moral ambiguities of our situation as our fate and does not try to achieve goodness, either by fighting Russia in the name of justice, or capitulating to Russia in the name of peace.

Capitulation, moreover, tempting as it may seem to those who want peace above everything else, would paradoxically not achieve the peace for which they yearn. "The consequence would be the unification of the world under despotic conditions which would hardly guarantee peace. Resistance to such despotism is almost inevitable; revolts would ensue which would make the Hungarian revolt seem like a picnic."

Our predicament therefore is a paradoxical as well as a dual one. Because of the nuclear dimension,

> We have come into the tragic position of developing a form of destruction which, if used by our enemies against us, would mean

> our physical annihilation; and if used by us against our enemies would mean our moral annihilation. What shall we do?

Typically, Niebuhr starts out by demolishing alternative answers which he considers to be illusions. One such answer is the neutralism of Karl Barth. In contrast, Niebuhr likes to quote the distinction made by Archibald MacLeish, that "the world is divided into two kinds of people: the pure and the responsible." And for the responsible person, Niebuhr claims, Barth's viewpoint is so stratospheric as to be irrelevant.

Niebuhr also attacks the proponents of a holy war against communism. Because the Communists are atheist materialists is no reason for us to forget that we are godly materialists. A holy war, he says, is always wrong because it denies to the opposite side the opportunity to evolve in its own way "toward a greater measure of freedom and justice." As for those American Catholic Bishops whose pronouncements have been interpreted as an encouragement to such a holy war, Niebuhr says with a twinkle, "Sometimes I wish the Pope had *more* power than he does over the American Hierarchy."

A third answer Niebuhr considers to be an illusion is that of the atomic pacifists:

> The pacifists have a simple answer. Let us simply renounce the use of such a weapon, together with our enemies if possible, but alone if necessary. This answer assumes that it is possible to summon the human will to defy historical development with a resounding no. But where is this "human will" which could rise to such omnipotence? Unfortunately we do not have moral access to the Russian will . . . Could we possibly, as a nation, risk annihilation or subjugation for the sake of saying no to this new development of destruction? Could we risk letting the Russians have the bomb while we are without it? The answer is that no responsible statesman will risk putting his nation in that position of defenselessness. Individuals may, but nations do not, thus risk their very existence.

Just as Niebuhr's experience with pacificism enabled him to see that such a gesture on our part would be dangerous, so did his experience with Marxism enable him to see that it would be futile: "granted the Russian hope and belief that it has the possibility of bringing its peculiar redemption to the whole world, it is not likely to be impressed by any 'moral' gesture from what it believes to be a decadent world."

One of the proponents of atomic pacifism has been Bertrand Russell. Before Russia had nuclear bombs of her own, Russell had favored preventive war; but after she had them, he favored the West's announcing that survival is more important to us than freedom and disarming unilaterally if necessary. Russell's long-time friend, Sidney Hook, took issue with him in a debate in *The New Leader* starting in April, 1958, and continuing into April, 1960. And Niebuhr, Hook's former antagonist, took his side in *Daedalus*, 1959:

> Bertrand Russell is a great philosopher; but this irrelevant advice proves, as Sidney Hook observed, that mathematical logic is not a substitute for common sense.

Hook and Niebuhr still start from opposite poles, but more and more they agree on contingent matters. For Niebuhr, furthermore, faith in God includes the awareness that the self's view must always stand under divine judgment, while for Hook "faith in intelligence" includes the continuing possibility of self-correction. Thus in practice as well as in theory, Niebuhr demonstrates the charitableness that stems from biblical faith while Hook demonstrates the reasonableness that stems from a wide-lensed rationalism. In his reasonableness, in fact, Hook made a public admission that must have hurt to make since it goes in part against his reliance on human intellect. In *The New Leader*, he said,

> One of the most surprising events in my intellectual life has been the discovery that men like Winston Churchill have had much more common sense in political affairs than individuals immeasurably more gifted in powers of abstract reasoning. The explanation, I suppose, is that politics is essentially an historical and psychological discipline, not like a chess game.

For Niebuhr nothing in history or politics has ever been like a chess game.[2] In chess a skillful player can rely on either-or logic and to some extent on the predictability of his opponent. In history or politics, on the other hand, there is both-and instead of either-or, there are un-

[2] Niebuhr has no interest in chess, bridge or other games of skill in which he would presumably excel were he to be interested.

expected by-products instead of semipredictability, and the "men" may suddenly decide to move on their own. The very fact that a thinker as sophisticated as Sidney Hook should be surprised to find history and politics different from a chess game appears to indicate another point which Niebuhr believes that the past two centuries have forgotten, namely the existence of paradox.

In bargaining, for example, nationally as well as individually, if one side has the power and firmness to walk away from the bargaining table empty-handed, the other side is likely to come around, whereas if the first side is desperate for an agreement, this may not materialize. Why? Human freedom perhaps. Whatever its cause, and whether or not it fits into the canons of logic, its operation is a fact that diplomats, politicians and lawyers must take into account.[3]

Niebuhr specifically takes it into account in his answer to the problem of peace. If, as Russell suggests, we were to announce that survival is our primary aim, with freedom only secondary, we would be less likely to survive than if we continue to insist that freedom to evolve in our own way is our primary aim, with survival only secondary. For inasmuch as we show weakness, we encourage their intransigence; nature is by no means the only force to abhor a vacuum, and the feeding of small bites to dictators enhances rather than spoils their appetites. Instead we should be certain that the Communists know, as Hitler did not know for sure when he invaded Poland, and as the North Koreans did not know for sure when they invaded South Korea, that the United States stands ready to use force in defense not only of her own, her allies' and the neutralist nations' territorial integrity but also of their political integrity. Such firmness on our part—plus the atomic dimension of our armaments—has already, for years, Niebuhr conjectures, kept the peace over Berlin.

To make and hold such bargains takes the ability to live with tension without swinging wild between pessimism and optimism. For if the atomic

[3] With small children and dogs the same perverse phenomenon occurs. "All right, don't come," is one way to bring them on the run. Some irreverent thinkers have suggested that God so set up the world that he could say to man, "all right, *don't* believe"; and that Christ's humiliating death was a signal of "all right, *don't* follow me." Niebuhr, according to Yale's Chaplain, William Sloane Coffin, persuaded some young men uncertain about the ministry to enter it by saying to them sincerely, "if you can stay out, stay out."

bargain fails, the results are too horrible to contemplate. So appalled is Niebuhr when he tries to picture these that he sometimes says he hopes he would be among the first to be killed. But then he catches himself up and points to the very unthinkableness of war's devastation as the paradoxical dimension that may, for the first time in history, save the world from war's devastation.

There are, furthermore, historical parallels for the existence of two great rival groups forced to live in tension for centuries. After the Crusades, Niebuhr noted in *Structure of Nations,* Islam and Christianity gave up trying to eliminate each other, as did Catholicism and Protestantism after the Religious Wars. Today, Niebuhr says, "the magnitude of the tools of war is the parallel to the victoryless war." It is as if we and the Russians had already fought each other to a standstill. Niebuhr, in fact, hopes that the magnitude of the tools plus the reluctance of both sides to suffer atomic retaliation, may lead, in order to prevent accidental war, to an eventual closing down of the atomic club, a stopping of large-scale nuclear testing, and some day, although not in the foreseeable future, an enforceable disarmament agreement. For disarmament, he says "is not the cause, but the fruit, of relaxed tensions," and the tensions between East and West may in time relax because "the more you coexist, the more trust may be built."

Meanwhile, he said, during discussions held by the Fund for the Republic, later published as *Foreign Policy and a Free Society,*

> Could I suggest that we would perform more effectively . . . by analyzing the predicament in which we and the Russians are. How similar it is! . . . We are in a common predicament in regard to the burden of the arms race. We are in a common predicament in regard to preserving our strategic security. We are in a common predicament in relation to the political and economic realities in Asia and Africa . . .

When two groups take note of their common predicament, they may also note that despite their deep antagonism, they have a common goal: "Take the orthodox and secular Jews in Israel. They don't trust each other at all. They have a common interest in Israel which holds them together."

This common interest, however, between Russia and the West, like that between the orthodox and secular Israelis, has not yet had time to grow organically to the point of bearing explicit formulation. As Niebuhr said at the Fund for the Republic:

> A covenant between Russia and ourselves is impossible because you have to spell out in what way you will protect yourself against the other guy. The Israelites could not establish a constitution.[4] Why? Because some wise people said this thing has to settle down. If we try to write a constitution now, we will try to protect ourselves against you in such a way that we will just get into a fight . . . But we have to live together.

Paradoxically, therefore, the best way for the West to protect itself may be to eschew an explicit agreement about protecting itself, and rely instead on implicit understandings based upon the goal common to both sides. In *The New Leader*, August 1-8, 1960, Niebuhr concluded:

> It may be that the only hope of escaping a nuclear catastrophe is by the implicit, rather than explicit, agreement of both sides not to use the dread instruments. The impulse of survival dictates such a course. It is already in effect; for even the most violent quarrels have not yet prompted either side to grasp or use the ultimate weapons. There is, of course, no guarantee against catastrophe through miscalculation. Perhaps this narrow margin of our safety is the hard fact which no politician dares to acknowledge.

To rely only on implicit agreement, in one light, appears perilous and novel—yet, in another light, it appears as dependable and ancient as courtship itself. For what young lover has not passed through the period when to demand that the partner spell out the meaning of the relationship may doom the whole relationship.

In addition to the ancient problem of timing, Niebuhr says, there is also the ancient problem of recognizing that proximate solutions can best be found when "we have the humility to recognize that the ultimate solution is beyond the competence of mortal man." Part of the proximate solution to the problem of international coexistence, he believes, is to correct the beam in our own eye, racially, economically and politically, while maintaining as much contact as possible with the Communists in

[4] Niebuhr's use of the ancient term "Israelites" rather than the modern "Israelis" may be a slip indicating the biblical source of many of his political judgments.

the hope that the mote in their eye will become so evident to them that they take measures to correct it. Already, Niebuhr noted in *Structure of Nations,*

> there is a measure of democracy in the Soviet oligarchic system through the power of the central committee as the final court of appeals. It is significant that Khrushchev . . . found it necessary and possible to appeal from the apex of the pyramid of power, the "presidium," to the central committee . . .
> The fact that . . . Gomulka came to power in Poland against Russian pressure because the Polish central committee gave him victory over the Stalinists proves that the central committees of Communist parties may be in the category analogous to the Whig aristocracy in the House of Commons and Lords in the 18th century.
> The Soviet . . . tyranny contains one other aspect of an "open society." First, the system allows a certain opportunity in education . . . The other is . . . related to the educational process . . . It is the reliance of the regime upon the expert in general and upon the physical scientist in particular . . . This "New Class" . . . may ultimately provide the leaven . . . [although] intelligence per se is not as politically subversive as the past centuries assumed.

This concept of the leaven has always been part of Niebuhr's thinking. And today he extends it from the prophet to every citizen.

> The only possibility of creating real moral integrity and spiritual vitality . . . is to stand *outside* of this world, to stand outside of it psychologically, to be emancipated of its culture, to feel in a different way than this world feels . . . I believe we must stand outside because we must create a new world, and the only way to create a new world is to establish ourselves outside the old one as far as we can in order to get a fulcrum upon it.

This challenge to stand outside, yet not above, the battle has traditionally been accepted not only by the prophet but by the creative artist. Even on the Russian side of the iron curtain this is still to some extent possible as Boris Pasternak showed. As for the American side, James Baldwin, the gifted novelist, said in the *New York Times,* January 25, 1959:

> Every society is really governed by hidden laws, by unspoken but profound assumptions on the part of the people, and ours is no exception. It is up to the American writer to find out what these laws and assumptions are. In a society much given to smashing taboos without thereby managing to be liberated from them, it will be no easy matter.

Nor will it be an easy matter in the current period of mass culture with everyone seeing and hearing the same material, and subjected to the same depersonalizing influences. As early as *Reflections at the End of an Era* Niebuhr had sadly pointed to the

> unpolitical desocialized creature who lives in a modern urban apartment house, in a dwelling full of people but without any neighbors, subsisting upon the proceeds of the labor of others with whom he has not the slightest human contacts.

And today he agrees with the statement by Daniel Day Williams that "the anxiety of 'non-belonging' is perhaps the deepest of all anxieties." Nonetheless Niebuhr insists that the individual try to summon the grit and the self-understanding to bear it. For self-understanding, he says, is essential not only as the direct root of charity but as the indirect root of courage. "Courage is the fruit of integrity which comes from self-knowledge." And the self-knowledge which is essential today should also include the wider self, namely the community. We must, in other words, learn to

> do justice both to the general values which our cause embodies beyond our own interest and to our tendency to value these too highly because our cause embodies them. It would mean, in short, that insights into the mixture of motives in the espousal of ideals which can only be learned, as it were, in the final wrestling of the soul with God, should be incorporated into institutions which can know nothing of such wrestling. In that sense the Christian faith must be a "leaven" . . . it must derive as the prophets did, insights for collective action which are drawn only from individual . . . experience.

If the prophet, the artist and the citizen with integrity are the individual leaven, is there also a collective one? Niebuhr at one time thought there was. In the late twenties, at the height of his Marxism, he briefly hoped that the proletariat might serve as this collective leaven since it was already in so many ways outside bourgeois democratic society. In the early thirties, at the height of his neo-Orthodoxy, he briefly hoped that the Church might serve as this collective leaven since its loyalty to the Kingdom of God set it outside all kingdoms of this world. But this hope too turned out to be illusory and he is now grateful for the providential developments that caused

> the present "post Christian" Western civilization [to be] really a nice compromise between secular and religious faiths in which we are saved from . . . the cruelty of consistent this-worldliness . . . and the irresponsibility of consistent other-worldliness.

Today Niebuhr sees the collective leaven as the small group within a democracy that can both reinforce the courageous individual and spur him to higher efforts. As Niebuhr said in his introduction to Wilber L. Schramm's *Responsibility in Mass Communications*, the small group, through its "esprit de corps . . . the standards set by tradition, and the mutual loyalty of a unit of responsibility gives power to the individual to do what is right."

For the individual—aided or not aided by the small group—to do what is right, there must be many dimensions of openness. Within the individual himself there must be the open mind, ready to receive new facts; the open heart ready to receive spoken and unspoken responses from other people; a personality open to new encounter not only with persons but with ideas; and a spirit open to judgment and forgiveness. For society there must also be a form of openness—internally to dialogue between its own constituent groups—and externally to the needs and judgments of other cultures. For Americans this means an awareness not only of the way our own democracy evolved but also the reason it cannot be exported as a packaged product to the undeveloped nations. "Free elections," for example, Niebuhr says, "are not the simple boon of community which we assumed them to be." As a result, he insisted on the Mike Wallace show that even our definition of democracy should remain open:[5]

[5] In *Children of Light* Niebuhr had defined democracy as "a method of finding proximate solutions for insoluble problems." His next book, as yet untitled, will deal with these proximate democratic solutions and contrast them with the dogmatic ones of communism.

> On the one hand, democracy is an absolute necessity of justice, and on the other hand, democracy is a luxury which is attainable only by a highly technical and very balanced society. These two things do not quite fit. You have to spell them out if you are talking about them.

In spelling them out, there are several factors to bear in mind. One is that these new nations may be, as we were in our youth, prone to utopianism: "Utopia seems a plausible goal to the peoples who have never experienced the tortuous processes of history except in terms of expectation." Because of this utopianism, the new nations may also be more naïve in regard to communism than we now are: "This despotism which we regard with abhorrence is rather too plausible to decaying feudal, agrarian and pastoral societies." And we must not, like a petulant adolescent, withdraw our support when the new nations cannot, or do not, follow our example in organizing their society. In fact, Niebuhr says, we might be more appreciative than we have been of "the one-party democracies," such as that of Tunisia, for example, "which do not suppress parliamentary and civil liberties but which likewise do not engage in the hazardous alternation of political authority which characterizes the mature democracies."

We must also try to be understanding when emerging nations demand independence even when this seems to us to be premature and when we recognize, as they may not, that "the independence of a nation is no guarantee of justice within the nation." And we must try to see ourselves through their eyes, as predominantly white, like their former masters, and as predominantly so wealthy that our barest necessities appear to them as the wildest luxuries.

Lastly, we must be less prone than we have been, until recently, to identify democracy with free enterprise. As Niebuhr wrote after World War II, "We defined democracy in such a way as to make it suitable for our luxurious circumstances" but not for the poverty of either war-torn Europe or the new nations emerging from the crumbling of the erstwhile European empires. And in doing so we not only forgot that "a minimum of social health is a presupposition of democratic life," but we "assumed that if only [people] guard freedom, community will take care of itself." In regard particularly to the new nations, therefore, Niebuhr said to

Mike Wallace, "we must expect to have many a defeat before we . . . have ultimate victory."

At this point Mike Wallace probed, characteristically, to the heart of the matter: "But do you believe in an ultimate victory? Why are you so sure of an ultimate victory?"

"I'm not sure," Niebuhr answered, "I hope for an ultimate victory, but I think there's a serious ambiguousness about it. On the one hand you say, because it is right, it must be victorious. On the other hand you say, it's right whether it's victorious or not. That is what I believe about a free society—that it's right, victorious or not."

In the evolvement of our own free society, we should recognize, Niebuhr had said in *Irony of American History,* "the fortuitous and providential element in our good fortune . . . We have variously attributed American prosperity to our superior diligence, our greater skill or (more recently) to our more fervent devotion to the ideals of freedom." Now the time has come for us to admit that "we are not a sanctified nation" and that it was more our luck than our motivation that was better than that of other people. For if we continue to "assume that all our actions are dictated by considerations of disinterested justice . . . the natural resentments against our power . . . will be compounded with resentments against our pretensions to a superior virtue," and we will thereby be the ones to be weakened.

For it is not only individuals but great nations that "face the alternative of dying because they strive too desperately to live or of achieving new life by dying to self." This painful paradox appears whenever the nation finds its power, prestige or pride challenged by the "emergence of new social forces in history."

Today these new social forces are emerging explosively both without and within the United States. In addition to the dynamism of Communism there is the dynamism of nationalism working in areas such as Africa which until recently had been somnolent. And within the United States the long-established power of the WASPS (White Anglo-Saxon Protestants) has been challenged on the one hand by minority religious groups and on the other by minority racial groups. Niebuhr therefore concludes his adaptation of this paradox by saying that if the challenge by new groups, or by old groups with new power, causes the established groups to "make even more extravagant claims for the absolute validity of their power and justice than they have previously made, and to regard the competitor . . . as a foe of all order and justice," they may be destroyed. But if "the old forms and structures . . . are renewed rather than destroyed by the vicissitudes of history," they will move forward to new creativity.

One of the old structures that has been renewed rather than destroyed by history has been Western capitalism. As Niebuhr said in James Chapel, 1959,

> We all have mixed economies today. History's inadvertence—or Providence—dissolved the conflicting dogmas of the right and left into a creative synthesis.

This synthesis continues, however, to be a tension-filled one: "The debate between 'freedom' and 'planning' is . . . inconclusive because only the most grievous extremes of the two warring creeds have been refuted by experience, while the wisest communities have mixed the two creeds in varying proportions."

Within the United States Niebuhr approves the combination of private enterprise with public welfare; he also approves the "countervailing" forces of big labor and big business, sometimes referring to these as the "great fiefs of modern feudalism." He also approves many aspects of British Socialism, but points to the mitigation of its dogmas by practical experience: drugs, for example, beyond a basic minimum supply, must now be paid for by the individual in order to prevent free-loading by the insatiable (shades of the Delta Cooperative).

Because of his approval of the mixed economy, together with his appreciation of Burke and his praise for Winston Churchill as "the best exemplar of conservatism in our day [who in himself provides] a living and vivid display of the way personality and tradition interact in a healthy free society," Niebuhr has been denounced by people on the left as having become too conservative.[6] Said one secular academic, "Niebuhr is

[6] The most knowledgeable estimate of Niebuhr's "conservatism" appears in John Bennett's Living Library Chapter. Said Niebuhr in his Living Library answer: "I don't want to challenge his very fair conclusions at all, but merely underline his judgment that any conservatism which is merely interested in the preservation of some *status quo* would be anathema for anyone who had drawn inspiration from the Old Testament prophets. American conservatism, which is nothing more than a decadent liberalism, would be doubly unacceptable."

again reflecting the mood of his times. In the effervescent twenties, he was an optimist, in the Marxist thirties he was a radical, and now in the fat fifties he's just another middle of the roader." And one religious academic went so far as to demand that Niebuhr relinquish the mantle of prophet:

> Tragic, it seems to me, is that Niebuhr's Christian prophetism at the moment is only a note of anxiety. It has lost its Marxist expression and has not found another positive one. Pragmatism is always limited and instrumental.

Niebuhr's response to such comments is that he "would not want to be against something just for the sake of maintaining a reputation as a prophet." He furthermore freely admits that pragmatism is "limited and instrumental," going on to point out that it stands "on the abyss of cynicism," this being one reason why those who believe in it must remain open to criticism by friend, foe, and God. On the other hand, since "the human situation is partly subject to remedy and partly not," he sees pragmatism as essential to responsible political decision.

Such responsible decision, he believes, should take into account the fact that paradox operates in a positive as well as negative manner. For if the nuclear paradox of arming lethally to avoid use of lethal arms is a negative one by which we live, a positive one is the new assumption of responsibility by the United States in international affairs:

> The burdens of world leadership which we assumed reluctantly, after the second World War . . . have really been the means of our economic and moral wellbeing . . . We have also embarked on a continued technical assistance program to the technically backward nations. The conscious political motive was to save both Europe and Asia from falling into the clutches of communism. But the wholesome by-product was that we exported enough wealth to keep a tolerable fiscal equilibrium in a dollar-hungry world and to drain enough surplus from our economy to keep it healthy.
>
> Nothing in history has better revealed the "providential" necessity of nations being forced by factors, not of their own contriving, into doing what is necessary for their own well-being, though it runs counter to their unspoiled "nature." Without

> these unwanted burdens we would have become morally intolerable to the world and our economy would have been incapable of preserving its relative health.
>
> But we can not count on providence alone to save us. There must be some foresight in all human activity, even though faulty foresight is frequently mercifully corrected by unwanted but helpful historical patterns.

Whether or not Niebuhr still deserves to wear the mantle of prophet, he still rises in prophetic wrath against racial injustice. "Racial hatred," he said in *The New Leader*, April 11, 1960, "is the most vicious of human vices." And he rejoices in the growth of racial justice for the Negro. Indeed, one of the historical patterns he discerns is the similarity of the Negro revolt in the twentieth century to the Cromwellian revolt in the seventeenth century, with the Negro churches playing the creative role today that the Puritan sects did in Cromwellian England.[7]

In regard to the Christian Church as a whole, however, Niebuhr's recommendation is that it "make fewer ideal demands upon the community for a while and center upon this problem in its own life."[8] Part of this internal problem, Niebuhr told the Union graduates in 1957 is that

> our churches are friendly, even to the point of being chummy. They have mixed the natural community of race and class too much with the community of grace. Hence the grievous entanglement of our churches with racial pride in a day when the state leads the church in establishing racial brotherhood.

Not only the state but the secular organizations have led the church; Niebuhr frequently lauds the music and theatre worlds for breaking the color line with Marian Anderson, and the sports world with Jackie Robinson. Although the white churches, Niebuhr says, have "not played a very impressive role in solving the issue of justice," there have been instances where Catholic priests have been heroic, aided by the hierarchical church structure which partially frees them from local pressures, and there have

[7] In the seventeenth century, he continues, the Peasants' Revolt was successful because they were able to get support from the middle class. Today the Negro "peasants" have their own middle class: "That is one significance of the students leading the sit-ins."

[8] A cogent discussion of Niebuhr's views on this problem appears in Gordon Harland's recent *The Thought of Reinhold Niebuhr*, Oxford, 1960.

been, "thank God," Niebuhr says, "some heroic Protestant pastors too."

But the problem with which they deal is both more profound and more terrible than many well-meaning people realize. As Niebuhr wrote in *Christianity and Society*, Summer, 1942,

> if we imagine that race pride is only a vestigial remnant of barbarism, which civilization is in the process of sloughing off . . . we are bound to follow wrong policies in dealing with specific aspects of the problem.

One reason for the potency of racial pride is that like other vices it is a corruption of a good. The love felt by an individual for his group is a good in that it draws him out of himself into a wider concern and area of responsibility. But this good turns to evil when the individual considers his own community so superior to others that he looks down on all people who noticeably differ from it. "The predisposition to think ill of a divergent group is a dark and terrible . . . evil in the soul of man." It is conducive both to unjust actions and to a blindness on the part of the perpetrator to the damage he thus inflicts.

On the other hand, racial pride, Niebuhr says, can be "curiously compounded with other more honorable motives." The southern white mother who resists integrated schools may understandably "be worried about the adequacy of her child's education in a class consisting of children with very different cultural backgrounds."

Like all complex human problems, those of race relations, Niebuhr says, are not wholly amenable to solution by law; there must also be grace—"only the infinite mercy of God can match the infinite pathos of man"—and there must also be an organic working out of new patterns. As Niebuhr wrote at the time of the Supreme Court decision outlawing segregated schools:

> The Court decision had the effect of making the good people better and the bad people worse. That may be a too simple judgment. It is better to be content with the judgment that the enforcement of the constitutional insistence on equality before the law prompted those who were already eager to establish racial equality to become more zealous in their labors . . . On the other hand the confirmed racists were driven to hysteria . . . They are

> engaged in trying by every kind of terror to prevent the establishment of integrated schools. Their activities have confronted the nation with an even more basic problem than racial justice, namely the preservation of law and order . . . [thus proving] that even an essentially healthy democratic society is nearer to the abyss of anarchy and lawlessness than we would like to think.

All in all, Niebuhr is less optimistic about the racial problem than the nuclear one. "I doubt," he said in a 1959 sermon, "whether the white and Negro races have enough agape and wisdom to live together soon in tolerable amity and equality." And among the by-products of America's failure is the fact that "in the underdeveloped countries there are many who fear and hate White America because of its mishandling of the color problem." It may therefore be the role of the American individual at this time in history to take self-sacrificial action in the racial field rather than the battlefield, and Niebuhr sees the courage necessary for both forms of action as comparable.

Such courageous individuals may or may not be religious. As Niebuhr said at Union Seminary on May 10, 1960:

> It took me a long time—longer than it should have—to realize that no religion can guarantee personal integrity. Religion is a good thing for honest people but a bad thing for dishonest people . . .[9] and the church has not been impressive because many of its leaders rationalize.

The kind of rationalization Niebuhr condemns is typified by the apartheid of the nationalist party in South Africa whose inspiration and support has historically been a Christian church:

> In the Nazi days we Christians could complacently assume that the inhumanities were the fruit of "paganism." But we have been reminded by the South African tragedy that the Christian faith can be . . . the instrument of inhumanity.

This same kind of religious rationalization was revealed in the political sphere at the time of the 1956 Rebellion when two Hungarian bishops,

[9] This phrase he says is an adaptation of Mary McCarthy's statement in *Memoirs of a Catholic Girlhood* that "religion is a good thing for good people but a bad thing for bad people."

"oozing with biblical piety . . . came to terms with malignant tyranny." In condemning these actions, however, Niebuhr admits, "of course there is always an element of self-righteousness when one views these problems from the outside."

To view such problems honestly—from the inside or the outside—demands historical perspective. And this perspective was precisely what Niebuhr feared that many Americans lacked. In the Introduction to *The Structure of Nations*, he said:

> I was prompted by the conviction that our generation . . . might be tempted to forget the lessons which the past history of man offers every new generation. I thought the temptation to overestimate the novelty of the present situation was particularly great in a young nation, suddenly flung to a position of world responsibility by its great power.

Niebuhr's implication that the nuclear dilemma can be lived with, even if it cannot, in the foreseeable future, be solved, caused him to be accused of optimism. Said Professor Robert Strausz-Hupé in the *Saturday Review*, August 26, 1959:

> I am quite sure that Dr. Niebuhr takes all too sunny a view when he opines that the peril of war will be lessened by "mutualities of trade and culture which will increase as the revolutionary animus abates in Russia in the second and third generation of post-revolutionary leaders."

Sunny, however, is too strong a word for Niebuhr's view of the desperateness of the current problem. At the same time, he points to the vastness of its dimensions—"what a tr-remendous dr-rama it is, wr-restling on the abyss of nuclear-r destr-ruction"—as providing a paradoxical impetus toward its being responsibly handled.[10]

Certainly the Russians have indicated their awareness of the suicidal dangers of atomic conflict. "Only a fool," said Khrushchev, "would want

[10] "In the nuclear age," said an American physician, Dr. Frank Fremont-Smith, former president of The World Federation for Mental Health, to the members of the Soviet Academy of Medicine in Moscow, 1960, "you cannot safeguard the future of your children and we cannot safeguard ours; therefore *you* must safeguard *our* children, and *we* must safeguard *yours*." To this, many Soviet doctors nodded agreement.

war today." The end of us or them or both, even the end of history itself, could occur at any moment. Nor does Niebuhr picture God as striking down the hand that pushes the button to start such final war. That is not the way God works in history: God has never been an Indian-giver about man's freedom. Man has had, and will have, the power to decide whether to sink or swim with his fellows. This decision will be made partly on an individual basis and partly on a collective one. The salvation of the individual and of the group are, as the Bible claims, inextricably linked.

Yet God does work in history, in ways unpredictable by man as to time and place, but visible sometimes in retrospect to the eyes of faith. Though the wicked do flourish like the green bay tree, the proud are in time cast down from their seats; though the suffering of individuals and nations does seem unjustly apportioned, there are those with true humility who are exalted. It is therefore especially important in the atomic age, Niebuhr says, to ponder the ways of God with man. For "the truth expressed in religious symbols is created not by a particular faith but by the human situation. It is validated therefore not by a dogma but by historical experience."

Historical experience, moreover, also reveals a dimension of empirical reality that goes beyond the consistencies of logic. As Niebuhr wrote in 1944, "There are crimes too terrible to be punished by the hand of man; and there are punishments in history more terrible than any crime deserves, so that the God of history is more terrible and more merciful than any of our nicely calculated schemes of justice."

Thus Niebuhr stands like a grizzled prospector at the foot of the Biblical mountain. "Don't give up," he shouts to his contemporaries streaming in discouragement toward him. "There's gold in them thar hills."

The gold furthermore can be mined by the non-religious person as well as the religious one. This is true of the Bible and also of Niebuhr's books which are based, ultimately, upon it.[11] As Arthur Schlesinger, Jr., wrote in his review of *Faith and History*, Niebuhr's most biblical book:

[11] Persons of many forms of religious belief and unbelief joined with those from many nations and walks of life as sponsors of the Professorship of Social Ethics named for Reinhold Niebuhr which was presented to Union Seminary at the time of Niebuhr's partial retirement in 1960: Frank Altschul, W.H. Auden, John Baillie, Adolph A.

> Reinhold Niebuhr succeeds in restating Christian insights with such irresistible relevance to contemporary experience that even those who have no decisive faith in the supernatural find their own reading of experience and history given new and significant dimensions. . . . The Christian account of human motivation is massive, subtle, and intricate . . .

And the call to action in history is unequivocal. "Life has no meaning," says Niebuhr, "except in terms of responsibility." He thus stands diametrically opposed to the ancient Chinese philosophers quoted by Dr. Leo Szilard. This atomic physicist, who has refused to have an operation for cancer lest it prevent him from finishing his last important work, told a *New York Herald Tribune* reporter on April 6, 1960:

> Soon after Hiroshima I went to see Einstein. As I walked into his study, Einstein looked at me sadly and said, "You see. The ancient Chinese were right. One must not ever do anything." Einstein meant by this statement that if you take action that has important consequences you assume responsibilities that you cannot foresee. For you can never really know the more remote consequences of your action.

That unforeseen by-products are certain to appear in history is one of history's meanings. Some of these by-products will be new. Niebuhr does not agree with Ecclesiastes, that "there is nothing new under the sun." Instead he speaks often of the "emergence of novelty" and firmly believes,

---

Berle, Jr., Jonathan B. Bingham, Chester Bowles, Heinrich Brüning, Emil Brunner, Ralph J. Bunche, Samuel McCrae Cavert, Grenville Clark, Charles W. Cole, Dame Isobel Cripps, John S. Dickey, C.H. Dodd, Truman Douglass, David Dubinsky, Angus Dun, Sherwood Eddy, T.S. Eliot, Louis Finkelstein, George B. Ford, Harry Emerson Fosdick, Will Herberg, Sir Hector Hetherington, William E. Hocking, Paul G. Hoffman, Douglas Horton, Hubert H. Humphrey, Jr., Robert M. Hutchins, Stanley M. Isaacs, Barbara Ward Jackson, George F. Kennan, Clark Kerr, Grayson L. Kirk, Herbert Lehman, Johannes Ernst Lilje, Walter Lippmann, Henry R. Luce, Charles Malik, Jacques Maritain, Sir John Maud, Millicent C. McIntosh, J. Irwin Miller, Sir Walter H. Moberley, Robert Oppenheimer, G. Bromley Oxnam, Alan Paton, Andre Philip, Sir Sarvepalli Radhakrishnan, Joseph L. Rauh, Walter Reuther, Eleanor Roosevelt, Beardsley Ruml, William Scarlett, Arthur M. Schlesinger, Jr., Charles Scribner, Jr., George N. Shuster, Hans Simons, Lord Stansgate, Adlai E. Stevenson, Benjamin Strong, Charles P. Taft, Sir Thomas Murray Taylor, Norman Thomas, Paul Tillich, Channing H. Tobias, Arnold Toynbee, W.A. Visser't Hooft, Arnold Wolfers and Henry M. Wriston.

as he said in *Children of Light,* that "the community must constantly re-examine the presuppositions upon which it orders its life, because no age can fully anticipate or predict the legitimate and creative vitalities which may arise in subsequent ages." On the other hand, Niebuhr does not neglect the old. Again and again he calls attention to what St. Paul called "the abiding things," which Niebuhr thus paraphrased in *Irony of American History*:

> Nothing worth doing is completed in our lifetime; therefore, we must be saved by hope. Nothing true or beautiful or good makes complete sense in any immediate context of history; therefore, we must be saved by faith. Nothing we do, however virtuous, can be accomplished alone; therefore, we are saved by love. No virtuous act is quite as virtuous from the standpoint of our friend or foe as from our standpoint. Therefore, we must be saved by the final form of love which is forgiveness.

But there is nothing soft or easy about Niebuhr's biblical view of forgiveness. In an age of standardization, he warns that society's values can never be the substitute for those which the self evolves through shattering encounter with other persons and with God; in a time of depersonalization, he stresses the unique and irreplaceable individual; and in a century of unprecedented danger, he stresses the need for unprecedented personal and collective responsibility: "We are never the prisoners of historical destiny even though all pretensions of being its master have crumbled."

Having, in sum, always had the courage to shoulder, when necessary, the grinding burden of widespread disapproval, he today has the courage to ask others to do the same.

POSTSCRIPT

After Reinhold Niebuhr retired from Union Seminary in 1960, he spent an academic year as a fellow of the Institute of War and Peace Studies at Columbia. The following academic year, he went to Harvard, where he taught a course in the Divinity School and lectured in the Department of Government. His Harvard lectures were later published as *The Democratic Experience*, with Paul Sigmund, his colleague in the government course, as co-author. In the autumn of 1962 the Niebuhrs went for a half-year to Princeton, where Dr. Niebuhr lectured in the Department of Politics. The following year he was Virginia Gildersleeve Visiting Professor at Barnard.

In January, 1963, the Niebuhrs moved to a new apartment at 404 Riverside Drive, close to Columbia and Union Seminary. Old and new friends would walk with Niebuhr daily along the Hudson, his most frequent companions being W. D. Davies, the young Franklin Delano Roosevelt III, a close friend and neighbor, and Rabbi Abraham Heschel of the Jewish Theological Seminary. Until 1967 Niebuhr continued to conduct a graduate seminar for scholars from Columbia, Union Seminary and Fordham.

Nineteen sixty-three saw the publication of *A Nation So Conceived*, a book done in collaboration with Professor Alan Heimert. In 1968, Professor Ronald Stone's collection of Niebuhr's essays, *Faith and Politics*, was published. Two great national problems engaged Niebuhr in these years: racial equality and the Vietnam War. In 1965 Niebuhr wrote the Introduction for *Mississippi Black Paper*, a report of the civil rights struggle edited by Hodding Carter III. From the beginning of the voter registration drive in the South, Niebuhr had received first-hand reports from young leaders who were involved in the work. During 1964-65 Niebuhr became more and more convinced that the irony of American involvement in Southeast Asia was turning into tragedy. He remained as Honorary Chairman of Americans for Democratic Action partly because of his opposition to the war. He also defended the antiwar activities of William Sloane Coffin, the Yale Chaplain.

By 1967 the Niebuhrs were spending more than half the year in their Stockbridge home. And in 1969 they moved there from New York. Niebuhr continued, however, to write editorials for *Christianity and Crisis* and *The New*

Leader, many of which were devoted to questioning American involvement in Vietnam; and he continued to keep up his varied and voluminous correspondence.

Two signal honors came to Niebuhr in these years. In 1964 the president awarded him the Medal of Freedom. In 1967 Hebrew University in Jerusalem conferred an honorary doctorate on him, and President Avraham Harman of the University travelled from Jerusalem to Stockbridge in 1970 to present him with the degree. In January, 1971, Niebuhr published on the "Op Ed" page of *The New York Times* a tough denunciation of American policy in Vietnam. And in May of that year, his last essay, *Mission and Opportunity: Religion in a Pluralistic Culture* appeared in *Social Responsibility in An Age of Revolution*, edited by Rabbi Louis Finkelstein.

In late May, 1971, a month before his 79th birthday, his health which had been precarious for so long began to fail. Because of the devoted attention of Mrs. Niebuhr and several nurses, he did not have to go to the hospital. To the very last day he brightened at the sight of his loved ones, and the end was a peaceful one.

BIBLIOGRAPHY

Books by Reinhold Niebuhr

DIARY

Leaves from the Notebook of a Tamed Cynic, New York, Willett, Clark & Colby, 1929.

SERMONIC ESSAYS

Beyond Tragedy, Essays on the Christian Interpretation of History, New York, Scribners, 1937.

Discerning the Signs of the Times, Sermons for Today and Tomorrow, New York, Scribners, 1946.

BOOKS BASED ON LECTURES

The Contribution of Religion to Social Work, New York, Columbia University Press, 1932.

An Interpretation of Christian Ethics, New York, Harper & Brothers, 1935.

The Nature and Destiny of Man, A Christian Interpretation

Vol. I, Human Nature, New York, New York, Scribners, 1941.

Vol. II, Human Destiny, New York, Scribners, 1943. (Since 1949 Scribners has been printing a one-volume edition of these Gifford Lectures.)

The Children of Light and the Children of Darkness, A Vindication of Democracy and a Critique of Its Traditional Defence, New York, Scribners, 1944.

Faith and History, A Comparison of Christian and Modern Views of History, New York, Scribners, 1949.

BOOKS DEALING WITH SOCIETY (not based on lectures)

Does Civilization Need Religion? A Study in the Social Resources and Limitations of Religion in Modern Life, New York, Macmillan Co., 1927.

Moral Man and Immoral Society, A Study in Ethics and Politics, New York, Scribners, 1932.

Reflections on the End of an Era, New York, Scribners, 1934.

BOOKS DEALING WITH HISTORY (not based on lectures)

The Irony of American History, New York, Scribners, 1952.

The Self and the Dramas of History, New York, Scribners, 1955.

The Structure of Nations and Empires, **A Study of the Recurring Patterns and Problems of the Political Order in Relation to the Unique Problems of the Nuclear Age, New York, Scribners, 1959.**

BOOKS OF ESSAYS

Christianity and Power Politics, New York, Scribners, 1940.
Christian Realism and Political Problems, New York, Scribners, 1953.
Pious and Secular America, New York, Scribners, 1958.
Man's Nature and His Communities, New York, Scribners, 1965.

COLLECTIONS OF NIEBUHR WRITINGS

Love and Justice, edited by D. B. Robertson, The Westminster Press, 1957.
Essays in Applied Christianity, edited by D. B. Robertson, Meridian, 1959.
Reinhold Niebuhr on Politics, edited by Harry R. Davis and Robert C. Good, Scribners, 1960.
The World Crisis and American Responsibility, edited by Ernest W. Lefever, Association Press.

RECORDINGS OF REINHOLD NIEBUHR

(obtainable through the Audio-Visual Center, Union Theological Seminary, Broadway at 120th Street, New York 27, New York.)
The Niebuhr Memoir in The Oral History Collection, Columbia University.

LECTURES

Humanism and the Christian Faith
Communism as a Rival to the Christian Faith

SERMONS

Judgment and Fulfillment in and beyond History
Our Lord's Conception of the Providence of God

INDEX

Index